Principles of Transaction Processing

The Morgan Kaufmann Series in Data Management Systems

Series Editor, Jim Gray

Principles of Transaction Processing
Philip A. Bernstein and Eric Newcomer

Using the New DB2: IBM's Object-Relational Database System
Don Chamberlin

Distributed Algorithms
Nancy Lynch

Object-Relational DBMSs: The Next Great Wave
Michael Stonebraker

The Object Database Standard: ODMG-93, Release 1.2
Edited by R.G.G. Cattell

Active Database Systems: Triggers and Rules For Advanced Database Processing
Edited by Jennifer Widom and Stefano Ceri

Joe Celko's SQL for Smarties: Advanced SQL Programming
Joe Celko

Migrating Legacy Systems: Gateways, Interfaces, and the Incremental Approach
Michael Brodie and Michael Stonebraker

Database: Principles, Programming, Performance
Patrick O'Neil

Database Modeling and Design: The Fundamental Principles, Second Edition
Toby Teorey

Readings in Database Systems, Second Edition
Edited by Michael Stonebraker

Atomic Transactions
Nancy Lynch, Michael Merritt, William Weihl, and Alan Fekete

Query Processing for Advanced Database Systems
Edited by Johann Christoph Freytag, David Maier, and Gottfried Vossen

Transaction Processing: Concepts and Techniques
Jim Gray and Andreas Reuter

Understanding the New SQL: A Complete Guide
Jim Melton and Alan R. Simon

Building an Object-Oriented Database System: The Story of O_2
Edited by François Bancilhon, Claude Delobel, and Paris Kanellakis

Database Transaction Models for Advanced Applications
Edited by Ahmed K. Elmagarmid

A Guide to Developing Client/Server SQL Applications
Setrag Khoshafian, Arvola Chan, Anna Wong, and Harry K.T. Wong

The Benchmark Handbook for Database and Transaction Processing Systems, Second Edition
Edited by Jim Gray

Camelot and Avalon: a Distributed Transaction Facility
Edited by Jeffrey L. Eppinger, Lily B. Mummert, and Alfred Z. Spector

Readings in Object-Oriented Database Systems
Edited by Stanley B. Zdonik and David Maier

Principles of Transaction Processing

Philip A. Bernstein

Eric Newcomer

Morgan Kaufmann Publishers, Inc.
San Francisco, California

Senior Editor Diane D. Cerra
Production Manager Yonie Overton
Production Editor Elisabeth Beller
Text Design Rebecca Evans & Associates
Cover Design Ross Carron Design
Cover Photo Tony Stone Images, Tom Paiva Photography
Copyeditor Ken DellaPenta
Proofreaders Jennifer McClain, Erin Milnes
Composition Fog Press
Illustration Cherie Plumlee
Indexer Steve Rath
Printer Courier Corporation

Morgan Kaufmann Publishers, Inc.
Editorial and Sales Office
340 Pine Street, Sixth Floor
San Francisco, CA 94104-3205
USA

Telephone 415/392-2665
Facsimile 415/982-2665
E-mail mkp@mkp.com
WWW http://www.mkp.com

Order toll free 800/745-7323

01 00 99 98 97 5 4 3 2 1

Library of Congress Cataloging-in-Publication Data is available for this book.

ISBN 1-55860-415-4

For Luisa and
Jane, Erica, and Alex

Foreword

Jim Gray, Microsoft Research

This book is the most readable explanation yet of the transaction concept. It also explains the basic techniques used to implement transactions. It is an excellent guide through the terminology and ideas in traditional business processing, in distributed object-oriented systems, and in webs. It describes how these systems work and gives excellent advice on how to design for them.

The transaction concept is emerging as the equivalent of contract law for distributed systems. It is a general way of structuring the interactions between autonomous agents in a distributed system. We are searching for principles to structure the explosive growth of computers and distributed systems. How should we structure interactions between people and computers? How about interactions among objects in a distributed object-oriented system? Traditionally, these interactions have had vague *maybe-once* semantics–where a request may be processed zero or one times. It is hard to understand the behavior of systems with maybe-once semantics.

The best model of such interactions is that each interaction is a transaction with some *exactly-once* simple guarantees, similar to the guarantees found in contract law. Each transaction is a state transformation with four key properties–the ACID properties: *Atomic* (all or nothing), *Consistent* (legal), *Isolated* (independent of concurrent transactions), and *Durable* (once it happens, it cannot be abrogated). These transaction concepts first appeared in traditional business record-keeping systems, but they are now becoming the standard way to structure client/server and distributed systems.

Over the years, we have developed simple and elegant techniques that implement the ACID properties. This book gives a very readable and compact tour of those techniques (transactional RPC, two-phase commit, logging, and locking). It covers the basic concepts quickly and clearly, avoiding the obscure details.

Transactions are a way to structure the interactions, but how should we structure the systems themselves? Transaction processing systems have a particular request-response style. Each request is processed as a workflow that may in turn invoke other flows. Bernstein and Newcomer do an excellent job of explaining the design alternatives and the issues of structuring these flows as direct or queued transactions and as two- or three-tier client/server systems. In addition, they connect these concepts to specific systems ranging from mainframe CICS systems, to Object Request Brokers like CORBA, to the recent web servers from Netscape and Microsoft.

Object-oriented systems are also embracing these concepts. Both CORBA/OpenDoc from the Object Management Group and COM/Microsoft Transaction Server[1] from Microsoft offer transactional invocation. All these systems employ a few common concepts and techniques: exporting interfaces to a request broker, transaction granularity authorization, server classes, queuing, and load balancing.

Phil Bernstein has been a leader in the transaction processing field for almost 20 years. He invented many of the technologies presented in this book. The book is the evolution of a class that Phil Bernstein has been teaching for over a decade.

Like Phil, Eric Newcomer has been active in the TP industry for nearly 20 years. He has worked on application design, product documentation, and TP standards. Eric coauthored the STDL TP language standard adopted by X/Open.

The book's style is clear and very accessible. Each chapter is fairly self-contained so that it can be used as either a text or a reference. It is an excellent place to learn about this important topic.

1 At press time, the Microsoft Transaction Server product name was not yet final.

Contents

Preface

Why Read This Book?

Transaction processing is the software technology that makes distributed computing reliable. Large enterprises in transportation, finance, telecommunications, manufacturing, government, and the military are utterly dependent on transaction processing applications for electronic reservations, funds transfer, telephone switching, inventory control, social services, and command and control. Many large hardware vendors, such as Digital, HP, IBM, Stratus, Tandem, and Unisys, receive much of their revenue from selling transaction processing systems. The market for transaction processing products and services is many tens of billions of dollars per year. The rapid expansion of electronic commerce on the Internet and World Wide Web will expand the high-end transaction processing market even further, requiring systems that can process millions of transactions per day. But despite the importance of transaction processing, there is little written for a systems professional to get a quick and broad introduction to this technology. This book is designed to fill this gap.

The software environment of most large-scale transaction processing (TP) systems is based on a TP monitor product, such as ACMS, CICS, Encina, IMS, Pathway/TS, TOP END, or TUXEDO. These products help create, execute, and manage TP applications and are essential for scalability to high transaction loads. For most software engineers, this is obscure technology—some kind of software glue that seems to be needed beyond operating systems, database systems, communications systems, and application programming languages. This book demystifies TP monitors by explaining how they contribute to the performance, security, scalability, availability, manageability, and ease of use of TP systems. We explain them outside and in—the features they offer to application programmers and how they're constructed to offer these features.

This book is an introduction to TP, intended to meet the needs of a broad audience, including

- application programmers with an interest in building TP applications
- application analysts who design applications for deployment on TP systems
- product developers in related areas, such as database systems, operating systems, and communications
- marketing and technical support engineers for both systems and application products

- computer science undergraduates and graduates looking for an introduction to this topic

The focus is on the principles of TP, not on a prescription for how to build a TP application—"how come?" not "how to." We present the technology as it exists in today's products and pay only modest attention to good ideas that are still beyond current practice. We include examples from many products, although we do not dwell heavily on any one of them.

We do not assume any special prerequisites, other than "system sophistication." We expect most readers will have some familiarity with SQL and database systems, but this background isn't necessary.

After finishing the book, you will understand how TP monitors work and when to use one, and how a TP monitor and database system work together to support reliable distributed TP applications. You will be able to learn quickly how to use any TP monitor product or server-oriented database system.

Summary of Topics

The enterprise that pays for a TP system wants it to give fast service and be inexpensive to buy and operate. This requires that the system be shared by many users and usually that it runs many applications. Application programmers want to be insulated from this complexity. An application programmer's job is to understand what the business wants the transaction to do and write a program that does it. The system software should make it possible to run that program on the shared TP system. This is what TP monitors do, and it is the main subject of the first half of this book, Chapters 1–5.

Users of a TP system want to think of it as a sequential processor of transactions, one that's infinitely reliable, gives them its full and undivided attention while it executes their transaction, executes the whole transaction (not just part of it), and saves the result of their transaction forever. This is a tall order and doesn't at all describe what's really going on inside the system: the system executes many transactions concurrently and fails from time to time because of software and hardware errors, often at just the wrong moment (when it's running *your* transaction), and has limited storage capacity. Yet, through a combination of software techniques, the system can approximate the behavior that the user wants. Those techniques are the main subject of the second half of the book, Chapters 6–10.

As computing technology evolves, TP technology will evolve to support it. We discuss some major trends in Chapter 11: server commoditization, object-oriented programming, nested transactions, and the Internet and World Wide Web.

Here is a summary of what you'll find in each chapter:

1. Introduction—Gives a broad-brush overview of TP application and system structure. Describes basic TP monitor capabilities, the ACID properties of transactions, the two-phase commit protocol, the industry-standard TPC performance benchmarks, how TP differs from time-sharing, batch processing, and decision support, and examples of two TP applications.
2. Transaction Processing Monitors—Explains the three-layer architecture of a TP monitor: the presentation server, which manages the display device; the workflow controller, which routes transaction requests between servers; and transaction servers, which run the application. We discuss how this architecture differs from two-tier database servers and drill down into the mechanisms that support each layer:
   - Presentation server—front-end forms and menu management, interfaces for 4GL client tools, authentication
   - Workflow controller—routing requests, directory services, session management, transaction bracketing, workflow logic, transaction exceptions, savepoints
   - Transaction server—mapping servers to threads and processes

   We close by showing how TP monitors can be used to support transactions on the World Wide Web.
3. Transaction Processing Communications—Explains remote procedure call and peer-to-peer (e.g., IBM SNA LU6.2) conversations, the two most popular paradigms for transactional communications in a distributed TP system. We explain how interfaces are defined, how directory services are used, and how clients and servers bind to each other. We give detailed walkthroughs of message sequences, showing how the two paradigms differ, and cover performance, management, and fault tolerance issues.
4. Queued Transaction Processing—Shows how persistent message queues can increase reliability. We give detailed walkthroughs of recovery scenarios. We explain the internals of queue managers, with IBM's MQSeries as an example. And we describe how persistent queues can support multitransaction requests in workflow applications.
5. Transaction Processing Monitor Examples—Explains most of the popular TP monitor products' capabilities using the model of Chapters 2–4. We describe IBM's CICS and IMS, BEA Systems' TUXEDO, Digital's ACMS, AT&T/NCR's TOP END, Transarc's Encina, Tandem's Pathway/TS, and the Microsoft Transaction Server.[1] We also describe Microsoft's Internet Information Server, and Netscape's HTTP Server, as well as give

1 At press time, the product name was not yet final.

a summary of the X/Open Distributed TP model and the Object Management Group's Object Transaction Service.

6. Locking—Explains how locking works in most commercial database systems and what application programmers can do to affect its correctness and performance. We explain how lock managers implement locks and handle deadlocks. We explain how performance is affected and controlled by lock granularity, optimistic methods, batching, avoiding hot spots, avoiding phantoms, and supporting query-update workloads using lower degrees of isolation and multiversion methods.
7. High Availability—Identifies what causes failures and how transactions help minimize their effects. We discuss checkpoint-based application recovery, using stateless servers to simplify recovery, and warm and hot standby systems that use process pairs to reduce recovery time, as in IBM's IMS/XRF and Tandem's Non-Stop SQL.
8. Database System Recovery—Explains how database systems use logging to recover from transaction failures, system failures, and media failures. We describe the undo and redo paradigm, how and why logging algorithms work, log checkpointing, recovery algorithms, some fancy but popular logging optimizations, and archive recovery.
9. Two-Phase Commit—Explains the two-phase commit protocol in detail. We carefully walk through recovery situations and show where and why the user must get involved. We describe popular optimizations such as presumed abort and transfer of coordination. And we explain how database systems and transaction managers interoperate, such as the X/Open transaction management architecture and the Microsoft Distributed Transaction Coordinator.
10. Replication—Describes the most popular approaches to replication: primary-copy replication, used by most SQL database systems, where updates to a primary are propagated to secondaries, and multimaster replication, used by Lotus Notes and Microsoft Access (described here in detail), where updates are applied to any copy and propagate to other copies. Also covers algorithms for electing a primary, quorum consensus, and replica recovery.
11. Conclusion—Discusses major directions where TP technology is headed: low-priced servers leading to commoditization of TP products, object-oriented programming for better component reuse, nested transactions for modeling the program-subprogram structure of applications in transactions, and the Internet and World Wide Web as a platform for access to high-volume transaction services.

Acknowledgments

Many years before we embarked on this writing project, this material began as a set of course notes, presented to nearly one thousand people over 10 years at Digital Equipment Corporation and at the Wang Institute of Graduate Studies (gone but not forgotten). Countless improvements to the course notes suggested by "students," most of them practicing engineers, helped the first author develop these notes into what became the outline for this book. We thank them all. Without the rich detail they provided, we would never have attempted to write this book.

We were lucky to have five reviewers take the time to read and comment on the entire manuscript. Joe Twomey provided the most thorough review we have ever seen of a manuscript this long. His huge number of suggestions added enormously to the breadth and clarity of the result. Jim Gray applied his prodigious intellect and breadth of knowledge in transaction processing to challenge us in every chapter to be more complete, up-to-date, and clear-headed. We also received many good ideas for improvements of every chapter from Roger King, M. Tamer Özsu, and Karen Watterson. We're very grateful to them all for investing so much time to help us.

Many other people gave generously of their time to carefully review selected chapters—to correct our blunders, point out holes, and, often, to fill them in. We really appreciate the help we received from Dexter Bradshaw, Ian Carrie, Gagan Chopra, Per Gyllstrom, Vassos Hadzilacos, Dave Lomet, and Alex Thomasian.

It was a major challenge to include many examples of products, applications, and benchmarks, and to get them right. We could never have done it without the substantial assistance of the engineers who work on those artifacts. In some cases, they drafted entire sections for us. In all cases, they reviewed several iterations to think through every detail. While we take full responsibility for any errors that slipped through, we are pleased to share the credit with Mario Bocca (Chapter 1 examples), Ed Cobb (IMS), Dick Dievendorff (MQSeries), Wayne Duquaine (LU6.2), Terry Dwyer (TUXEDO), Keith Evans (Pathway/TS), Ko Fujimura (STDL), Brad Hammond (Wingman), Pat Helland (Microsoft Transaction Server), Greg Hope (Microsoft Transaction Server), Larry Jacobs (Encina), Barbara Klein (IMS), Walt Kohler (TPC-C), Susan Malaika (CICS), Michael C. Morrison (IMS), Wes Saeger (Pathway/TS), David Schorow (Pathway/TS), Randy Smerik (TOP END), and Tom Wimberg (ACMS).

We thank Addison-Wesley Publishing Company for permission to republish excerpts (primarily in Chapter 8) from *Concurrency Control and Recovery in Database Systems,* by P. Bernstein, V. Hadzilacos, and N. Goodman.

We thank our editor, Diane Cerra, for her encouragement, flexibility, and good advice, as well as Elisabeth Beller and the staff at Morgan Kaufmann for their efficiency and careful attention in the production of the book.

Finally, we thank our families and friends for indulging our moaning, keeping us happy, and accepting our limited companionship without complaint while all our discretionary time was consumed by this writing. It's over…for awhile ☺.

Trademarks

Designations used by companies to distinguish their products are often claimed as trademarks. In all instances where Morgan Kaufmann Publishers is aware of a claim, the product names appear in initial capital or all capital letters. Readers, however, should contact the appropriate companies for more complete information regarding trademarks and registration.

The following trademarks or registered trademarks are the property of the following organizations:

TOP END is a trademark or registered trademark of AT&T/NCR Corporation.

BEA Jolt is a trademark or registered trademark of BEA Systems, Inc.

Ingres is a trademark or registered trademark of Computer Associates International, Inc.

ACMS, ACMS Desktop, ALPHA, DATATRIEVE, DECforms, DECmessageQ, Digital, MicroVAX, OpenVMS, Reliable Transaction Router, VAX are trademarks or registered trademarks of Digital Equipment Corporation.

HP-UX is a trademark or registered trademark of Hewlett-Packard Computer Company.

AIX, AS/400, CICS, CICS/ESA, CICS/MVS, CICS/VSE, CICS/400, DB2, DRDA, IMS, MQSeries, MVS, MVS/ESA, OS/2, OS/400, POWER PC, SOM, VSE/ESA are trademarks or registered trademarks of IBM Corporation.

Informix is a trademark or registered trademark of Informix Corporation.

i86 is a trademark or registered trademark of Intel Corporation.

Kerberos is a trademark or registered trademark of Massachusetts Institute of Technology.

Microsoft Access, Microsoft Back Office, Microsoft Internet Information Server, Microsoft Visual Basic, Microsoft Visual C++, Microsoft Visual J++, Microsoft SQL Server, Microsoft RPC, Windows, Windows NT are trademarks or registered trademarks of Microsoft Corporation.

Netscape is a trademark or registered trademark of Netscape Communications Corporation.

TUXEDO is a trademark or registered trademark of Novell, Inc.

CHAPTER 1

Introduction

1.1 The Basics

The Problem

A *business transaction* is an interaction in the real world, usually between an enterprise and a person, where something is exchanged. It could involve exchanging money, products, information, requests for service, and so on. Usually some bookkeeping is required to record what happened. Often this bookkeeping is done by a computer, for better scalability, reliability, and cost. There are many requirements for such computer-based transaction processing, such as the following:

- A business transaction requires the execution of multiple operations. For example, consider the purchase of an item in a department store. One operation records the payment, and another operation records the removal of the item from inventory. It is easy to imagine a simple program that would do this work. However, when scalability, reliability, and cost enter the picture, things can quickly get very complicated.
- Volume adds complexity and undermines efficiency. Customers don't like being delayed because a salesperson is waiting for a cash register terminal to respond. Enterprises want to minimize the expense of executing transactions.
- To scale up a system for high performance, transactions must execute concurrently. Uncontrolled concurrent transactions can generate wrong answers. At a rock concert, when dozens of operations are competing to reserve the same remaining seats, it's important that only one customer is assigned to each seat.
- If a transaction runs, it must run in its entirety. In a department store sale, the item should either be exchanged for money or not sold at all. When failures occur, as they inevitably do, it's important to avoid partially completed work, which would make the customer or the store very unhappy.
- When a business grows, it must increase its capacity for running transactions, preferably by making an incremental purchase (and not throwing out the current implementation and starting over).
- When the cash registers stop working, the department store might as well be closed. Systems that run transactions are often "mission critical" to the business activity they support. They should hardly ever be down.
- Records of transactions, once completed, must be permanent and authoritative. This is often a legal requirement, as in financial transactions. Transactions must never be lost.
- The system must be able to operate well in a geographically distributed enterprise. Often, this implies that the system itself is distributed, with processors at multiple locations. Sometimes, distributed processing is used to meet other requirements, such as efficiency, incremental scalability, and resistance to failures (using backup systems).

In summary, transaction processing (TP) systems have to efficiently handle high volume, avoid errors due to concurrent operation, avoid producing partial results, grow incrementally, avoid downtime, and never lose results. It's a tall order. This book describes how it's done.

What's a Transaction?

An *on-line transaction* is the execution of a program that performs an administrative function by accessing a shared database, usually on behalf of an on-line user. Like many system definitions, this one is impressionistic and not meant to be exact in all of its details. One detail is important: A transaction is always the *execution* of a program. The program contains the steps involved in the business transaction—for example, recording the sale of a book and debiting the inventory.

We'll use the words "transaction program" to mean the program whose execution is the transaction. Sometimes the word "transaction" is used to describe the message sent to a computer system to request the execution of a transaction, but we'll use different words for that: a *request message.* So a transaction always means the execution of a program.

We say that a transaction performs an administrative function, though that isn't always the case. For example, it could be a real-time function, such as making a call in a telephone switching system or controlling a machine tool in a factory process-control system. But usually it's an administrative function, such as selling a ticket or transferring money from one account to another.

Most transaction programs access shared data, but not all of them do. Some perform a pure communications function, such as forwarding a message from one system to another. An application in which no programs access shared data is not considered true transaction processing because such an application does not require many of the special mechanisms that a transaction processing system offers.

There is usually an on-line user, such as a department store clerk or ticket agent. But some systems have no user involved, such as a system recording messages from a satellite. Some transaction programs operate *off-line,* or in batch mode, which means that the multiple steps involved may take longer than a user is able to wait for the program's results to be returned—more than, say, 10 seconds.

Transaction Processing Applications

A *transaction processing application* is a collection of transaction programs designed to do the functions necessary to automate a given business activity. The first on-line transaction processing application to receive widespread use was an airline reservations system: the SABRE system, developed in the early 1960s as a joint venture between IBM and American Airlines. SABRE was one of the biggest computer system efforts undertaken by anyone at that time, and

Application	Example Transaction
Banking	Deposit or withdraw money from an account
Securities trading	Purchase 100 shares of stock
Insurance	Pay an insurance premium
Inventory control	Record the arrival of a shipment
Manufacturing	Log a step of an assembly process
Retail	Record a sale
Government	Register an automobile
Internet	Place an order using an on-line catalog
Telecommunications	Connect a telephone call
Military command and control	Fire a missile
Media	Download a video clip

Figure 1.1 Transaction Processing Applications Transaction processing covers most sectors of the economy.

still is one of the largest TP systems in the world. It connects more than 300,000 devices worldwide and has a peak load of nearly 4200 messages per second. Like other TP applications for large enterprises, SABRE helps American Airlines be more competitive. They can handle a large number of flights, allow passengers to reserve seats and order special meals months in advance, and offer mileage-based bonuses. It also generates revenue, since the airline charges a transaction fee for travel agents that use it.

Today, there are many other types of TP applications, and new ones are emerging all the time. We summarize some of them in Figure 1.1. As the cost of running transactions and of managing large databases decreases, more types of administrative functions will be worth automating as TP applications, both to reduce the cost of administration and to generate revenue as a service to customers.

In its early years, the TP application market was driven primarily by large companies needing to support administrative functions for large numbers of customers. Such systems often involve thousands of terminals, dozens of disk drives, and many large processors and can run hundreds of thousands of transactions per day. Large TP systems will become even more important as online services become popular on the Internet. However, with the downsizing of systems has come the need for small TP applications, too, ones with just a few displays connected to a small server, to handle orders for a small catalog business, course registrations for a school, or patient visits to a dental office. All of these applications—large and small—rely on the same underlying system structure and software abstractions.

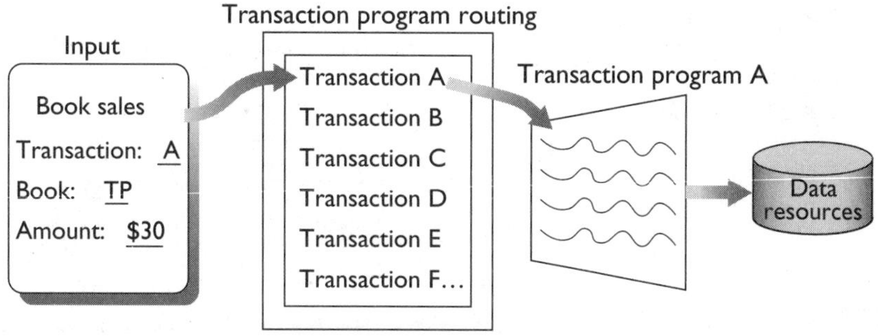

Figure 1.2 Transaction Application Parts A transaction application gathers input, routes the input to a program that can execute the request, and then executes the appropriate transaction program.

A Transaction Program's Main Functions

A transaction program generally does three things:

1. Gets input from a display or other kind of device, such as a bar code reader or robot sensor
2. Does the real work being requested
3. Produces a response and, possibly, sends it back to the device that provided the input

Each invocation of the transaction program results in an independent unit of work that executes exactly once and produces permanent results. We'll have more to say about these properties of a transaction program shortly.

Most transaction processing applications include some code that does not execute as transactions. This other code executes as an ordinary program, not necessarily as an independent unit of work, executing exactly once and producing permanent results. We use the term *transaction processing application* in this larger sense. It includes transaction programs, programs that gather input for transactions, and maintenance functions, such as deleting obsolete inventory records and updating validation tables used for error checking.

As shown in Figure 1.2, a transaction application generally consists of three parts:

1. The first part gathers input to provide to the transaction program. For example, it displays forms for the user to provide input and displays menus where the user can select the kind of transaction program to run. This part usually includes some input validation to ensure that the data being provided by the user is correct. It collects the input provided by the user (e.g., from an input form and menu selection) and turns it into a communications message.

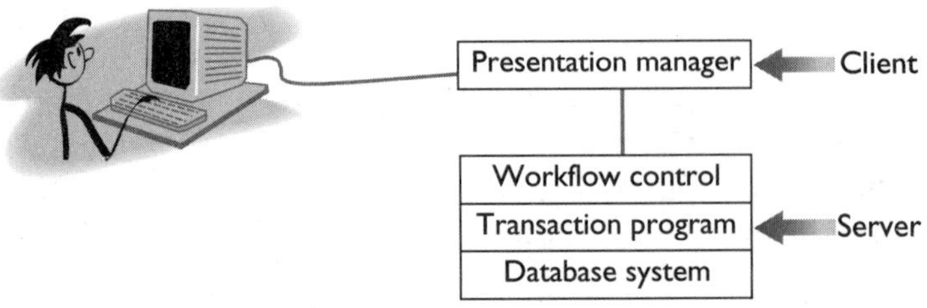

Figure 1.3 Software Structure of a TP System The client part manages I/O with the input device. The server sends the request to an appropriate transaction program to execute it.

2. The second part of the application takes a communications message (from the first part) and turns it into a call to the proper transaction program. In a centralized system, this is simply a matter of calling a local program. In a distributed TP system, it requires sending the message to a system where the program exists and can execute. This is a significant piece of work; it usually requires some application programming and/or updating system tables.
3. The third part of the application is the transaction program, which executes the request to perform the work that the user expects to be done, typically by reading and writing a shared database, possibly calling other programs, and possibly returning a reply that is routed back to the device that provided the input for the request.

1.2 The TP System

A *TP system* is the computer system—both hardware and software—that processes the transaction programs. The software parts of a TP system are usually structured as shown in Figure 1.3. The TP system has two main elements:

1. Client—The display device talks to a presentation manager program, which manages graphical input/output (I/O), such as the forms and menu management that we mentioned previously. That program generally runs as a separate operating system process, talking directly to the display. Its job is to produce a request message that is sent to another part of the system whose job is to actually execute the transaction.
2. Server—The second part is the transaction program. It includes a workflow control function that moves the request message from the presentation manager to the appropriate application program. If more than one application is needed, this workflow control function tracks the state of the request as it moves between applications. Each application typically accesses a database system that manages shared data. In turn, all these functions use the operating system underneath.

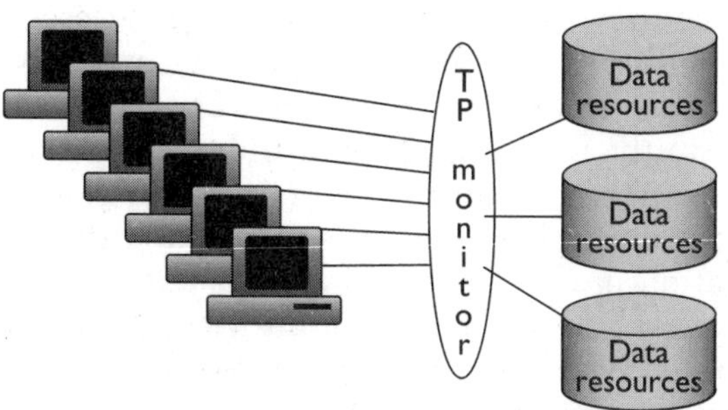

Figure 1.4 **Basic TP Monitor Function** A TP monitor connects multiple clients to multiple servers to access multiple databases, while making efficient use of network and operating system resources.

For example, in an order processing application, the client would manage the forms and menus through which a user can place an order. The server would have the transaction program that actually processes the order, and the database that keeps track of orders, catalog information, and warehouse inventory.

The transaction programs that run in the server are of a limited number of types, predefined to match operational business procedures such as shipping an order or transferring funds. Typically, there are a few dozen, but usually no more than a few hundred; when applications become larger than this, they are usually partitioned into independent applications of smaller size. Each one of these programs generally does a small amount of work. There's no standard concept of an average size of a transaction program because they all differ based on the application. But a typical transaction might have 0–30 disk accesses, a few thousand up to a few million instructions, and at least two messages, but often many more depending on how distributed it is. The program is generally expected to execute within a second or two, so that the user sitting at a display device can get a quick response. Later on we'll see another, more fundamental reason for keeping transactions short, involving locking conflicts.

Databases play a big role in supporting transaction programs, often a bigger role than the application programs themselves. Although the database can be small enough to fit in main memory, it is usually much larger than that. Some databases for TP require a large number of disk drives, pushing both disk and database system software technology to the limit.

In addition to database systems, TP monitors are another kind of software product that plays a major role in TP system implementation. A TP monitor acts as a kind of funnel or concentrator for transaction programs, connecting multiple clients to multiple server programs, which potentially access multiple databases (see Figure 1.4). The TP monitor maximizes the efficient use of operating system resources. In a distributed system, where clients and servers execute on different processors, the TP monitor also optimizes the use of the network.

A TP monitor structures the operating system's processes and processes communication mechanisms as an environment that's more hospitable for TP applications. For example, it provides functions that client applications can use to route requests to the right server applications, that server applications can use to run distributed transactions, and that system managers can use to balance the load across multiple servers in a distributed system. Using these functions, an application programmer can write a program that processes a single transaction request and use the TP monitor's facilities to scale it up to run on a large distributed system with many active users.

The computers that run these programs have a range of processing power. A display device could be a dumb terminal, a low-end personal computer, or a powerful workstation. Depending on the power of the device, presentation services may execute on a server that communicates with the display (for a dumb terminal) or on the display device itself. Similarly, the transaction program and database system could run on a low-end PC server or a high-end mainframe. Both the client and server could be a distributed system, consisting of many computers that collaborate to perform the function.

Some of these systems are quite small; they may only have a few display devices connected to a small server, say, in a PC LAN environment. Big TP systems tend to be enterprisewide, such as airline and financial systems. The big airline systems have on the order of 300,000 display devices (terminals and ticket and boarding-pass printers) and a few thousand disk drives, and may execute several thousand transactions per second at their peak load.

We're going to talk a lot more about the software structure of this type of TP architecture in the next chapter.

1.3 Atomicity, Consistency, Isolation, and Durability

Transactions have four critical properties that we need to understand at the outset. Transactions must be

- Atomic—The transaction executes completely or not at all.
- Consistent—The transaction preserves the internal consistency of the database.
- Isolated—The transaction executes as if it were running alone, with no other transactions.
- Durable—The transaction's results will not be lost in a failure.

This leads to an entertaining acronym, ACID. People often say that a TP system executes ACID transactions, in which case the TP system has "passed the ACID test."

Let's look at each of these properties in turn and examine how they relate to each other.

Atomicity

First, a transaction needs to be *atomic* (or *all-or-nothing*), meaning that it executes completely or not at all. There must not be any possibility that only part of a transaction program is executed.

For example, suppose we have a transaction program that moves $100 from account A to account B. It takes $100 out of account A and adds it to account B. When this runs as a transaction, it has to be atomic—either both or neither of the updates execute. It must not be possible for it to execute one of the updates and not the other.

The TP system guarantees atomicity through database mechanisms that track the execution of the transaction. If the transaction program should fail for some reason before it completes its work, the TP system will undo the effects of any updates that the transaction program has already done. Only if it gets to the very end and performs all of its updates will the TP system allow the updates to become a permanent part of the database.

By using the atomicity property, we can write a transaction program that emulates an atomic business transaction, such as a bank account withdrawal, a flight reservation, or a sale of stock shares. Each of these business actions requires updating multiple data items. By implementing the business action by a transaction, we ensure that either all of the updates are performed or none are. Furthermore, atomicity ensures the database is returned to a known state following a failure, reducing the requirement for manual intervention during restart.

The successful completion of a transaction is called *commit.* The failure of a transaction is called *abort.*

Handling Real-World Operations

During its execution, a transaction may produce output that is displayed back to the user. However, since the transaction program is all-or-nothing, until the transaction actually commits, any results that the transaction might display to the user should not be taken seriously because it's still possible that the transaction will abort. Anything displayed on the display device could be wiped out in the database on abort.

Thus, any value that the transaction displays may be used by the end user only if the transaction commits, and not if the transaction aborts. This requires some care on the part of users (see Figure 1.5). If the system displays some of the results of a transaction before the transaction commits, and if the user inputs the information to another transaction, then we have a problem. If the first transaction aborts and the second transaction commits, then the user has broken the all-or-nothing property. That is, the user has used as input some, but not all, of the results of the first transaction, which will be reflected in the second transaction.

Some systems solve this problem simply by not displaying the result of a transaction until after the transaction commits, so the user can't inadvertently make use of the transaction's output and then have it subsequently abort. But

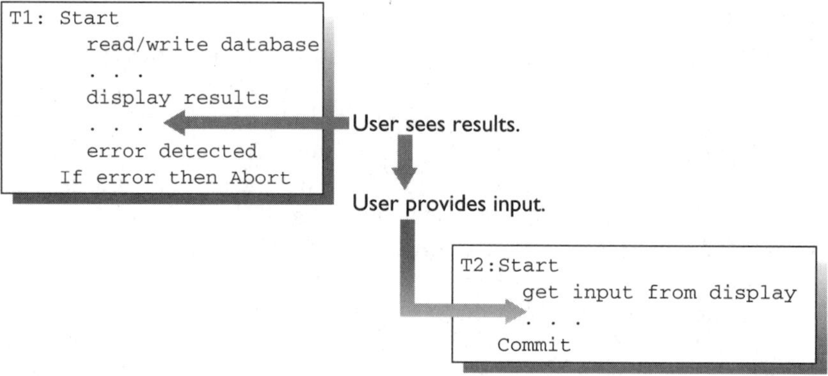

Figure 1.5 Reading Uncommitted Results The user reads the uncommitted results of transaction T1 and feeds them as input to transaction T2. Since T1 aborts, the input to T2 is incorrect.

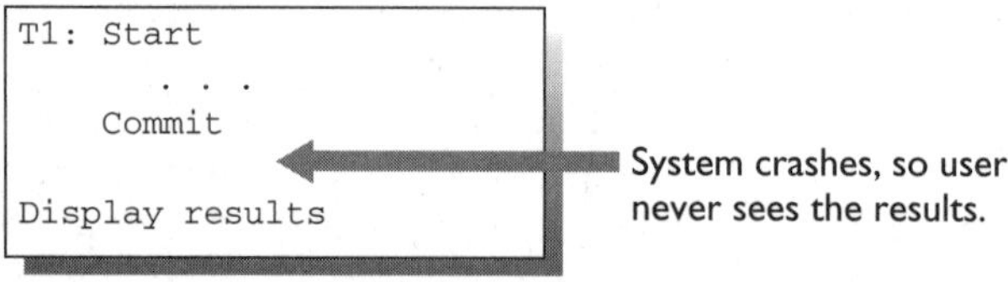

Figure 1.6 Displaying Results after Commit This solves the problem of Figure 1.5, but if the transaction crashes before displaying the results, the results are lost forever.

this too has its problems (see Figure 1.6): if the transaction commits before displaying any of its results, and the computer crashes before the transaction actually displays any of the results, then the user won't get a chance to see the output. Again, the transaction is not all-or-nothing; it executed all of its database updates before it committed but did not get a chance to display its output.

We can make the problem more concrete by looking at it in the context of an automated teller machine (see Figure 1.7). The output may, for example, be dispensing $100 from the machine. If the system dispenses the $100 before the transaction commits, and the transaction ends up aborting, then the bank gives up the money but does not record that fact in the database. If the transaction commits and the system fails before it dispenses the $100, then you still do not get the full result—the database says the $100 was given to the customer, but in fact the customer never got the money.

The problem with these real-world operations is that they are not *recoverable,* that is, they cannot be undone if their transaction aborts. Although nonrecoverable operations seem to produce an unsolvable problem, the problem can actually be solved using persistent queues, which we'll describe in some detail in Chapter 4.

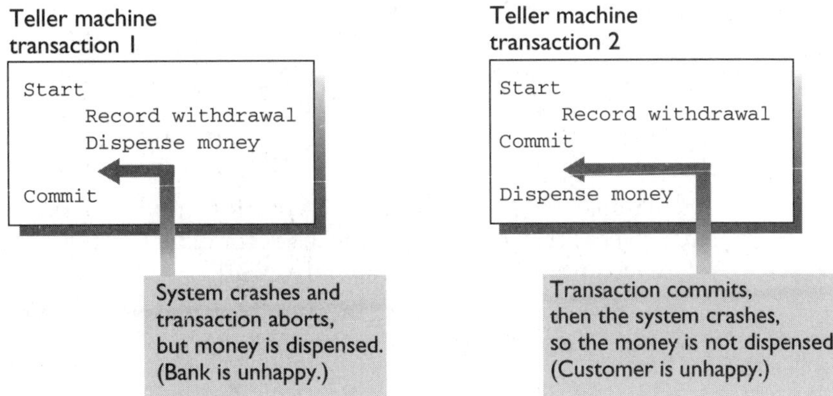

Figure 1.7 **The Problem of Getting All-or-Nothing Behavior with Real-World Operations** Whether the program dispenses money before or after it commits, it's possible that only one of the operations executes: dispense the money or record the withdrawal.

Compensating Transactions

Commitment is an irrevocable action. Once a transaction is committed, it can no longer be aborted. People do make mistakes, of course. So it may turn out later that it was a mistake to have executed a transaction that committed. At this point, the only course of action is to run another transaction that reverses the effect of the one that committed. This is called a *compensating transaction*. For example, if a deposit was in error, then one can later run a "withdrawal" transaction that reverses its effect.

Sometimes, a perfect compensation is impossible because the transaction performed some irreversible act. For example, it may have caused a paint gun to spray-paint a part the wrong color, and the part is long gone from the paint gun's work area when the error is detected. In this case, the compensating transaction may be to record the error in a database and send an e-mail message to someone who can take appropriate action.

Virtually any transaction can be executed incorrectly, so a well-designed TP application should include a compensating transaction type for every type of transaction.

Consistency

A second property of transactions is *consistency*—a transaction program should maintain the consistency of the database. That is, if you execute the transaction all by itself on a database that's initially consistent, then when the transaction finishes executing the database is again consistent.

By consistent, we mean "internally consistent." In database terms, this means that the database satisfies all of its integrity constraints. There are many possible kinds of integrity constraints, such as the following:

- All primary key values are unique (e.g., no two employee records have the same employee number).
- The database has referential integrity, meaning that records only reference objects that exist (e.g., the Part record and Customer record that are referenced by an Order record really exist).
- Certain predicates hold (e.g., the sum of expenses in each department is less than or equal to the department's budget).

Ensuring that transactions maintain the consistency of the database is good programming practice. However, unlike atomicity, isolation, and durability, consistency is a responsibility shared between transaction programs and the TP system that executes those programs. That is, a TP system ensures that a set of transactions is atomic, isolated, and durable, whether or not they are programmed to preserve consistency. Thus, strictly speaking, the ACID test for transaction systems is a bit too strong, because the TP system does its part for C only by guaranteeing AID. It's the application programmer's responsibility to ensure the transaction program preserves consistency.

Isolation

The third property of a transaction is *isolation.* We say that a set of transactions is isolated if the effect of the system running them is the same as if it ran them one at a time. The technical definition of isolation is *serializability.* An execution is *serializable* (meaning isolated) if its effect is the same as running the transactions serially, one after the next, in sequence, with no overlap in executing any two of them. This has the same effect as running the transactions one at a time.

A classic example of a nonisolated execution is a banking system, where two transactions each try to withdraw the last $100 in an account. If both transactions read the account balance before either of them updates it, then both transactions will determine there's enough money to satisfy their requests, and both will withdraw the last $100. Clearly, this is the wrong result. Moreover, it isn't a serializable result. In a serial execution, only the first transaction to execute would be able to withdraw the last $100. The second one would find an empty account.

Notice that isolation is different from atomicity. In the example, both transactions executed completely, so they were atomic. However, they were not isolated and therefore produced undesirable behavior.

If the execution is serializable, then from the point of view of an end user who submits a request to run a transaction, the system looks like a standalone system that's running that transaction all by itself. Between the time he or she runs two transactions, other transactions from other users may run. But during the period that the system is processing that one user's transaction, it appears to the user that the system is doing no other work. But this is only an illusion. It's too inefficient for the system to actually run transactions serially because there is lots of internal parallelism in the system that must be exploited by running transactions concurrently.

If each transaction preserves consistency, then any serial execution (i.e., sequence) of such transactions preserves consistency. Since each serializable execution is equivalent to a serial execution, a serializable execution of the transactions will preserve database consistency, too. It is the combination of transaction consistency and isolation that ensures that executions of sets of transactions preserve database consistency.

The database typically places locks on data accessed by each transaction. The effect of placing the locks is to make the execution appear to be serial. In fact, internally, the system is running transactions in parallel, but through this locking mechanism the system gives the illusion that the transactions are running serially, one after the next. In Chapter 6 on locking, we will describe those mechanisms in more detail and present the rather subtle argument why locking actually produces serializable executions.

Durability

The fourth property of a transaction is *durability.* Durability means that when a transaction completes executing, all of its updates are stored on a type of storage, typically disk storage, that will survive the failure of the TP system. So even if the transaction program or operating system fails, once the transaction has committed, its results are durably stored on a disk and can be found there after the system recovers from the failure.

Durability is important because each transaction is usually providing a service that amounts to a contract between its users and the enterprise that is providing the service. For example, if you're moving money from one account to another, once you get a reply from the transaction saying that it executed, you really expect that the result is permanent. It's a legal agreement between the user and the system that the money has been moved between these two accounts. So it's essential that the transaction actually makes sure that the updates are stored on some nonvolatile device, typically disk storage in today's technology, to ensure that the updates cannot possibly be lost after the transaction finishes executing. Moreover, the durability of the result often must be maintained for a long period. For example, some tax regulations allow audits that can take place years after the transactions were completed.

The durability property is usually obtained via a mechanism that starts by having the TP system write a copy of all the transaction's updates to a log file while the transaction program is running. When the transaction program issues the commit operation, the system first ensures that all the records written to the log file are out on disk, and *then* returns to the transaction program, indicating that the transaction has indeed committed and that the results are durable. The updates may be written to the database right away, or they may be written a little later. However, if the system fails after the transaction commits and before the updates go to the database, then after the system recovers from the failure it must repair the database. To do this, it rereads the log and checks that each update by a committed transaction actually made it to the database. If not, it reapplies the update to the database. When this recovery activity is complete, the system resumes normal operation. Thus, any new transaction will read a database state that includes all committed updates. We describe log-based recovery algorithms in Chapter 8.

1.4 Two-Phase Commit

When a transaction updates data on two or more systems in a distributed environment, we still have to ensure the atomicity property, namely, that either both systems durably install the updates or neither does. This is challenging because the systems can independently fail and recover. The solution is a special protocol called *two-phase commit* (2PC), which is executed by a special module called the *transaction manager.*

The crux of the problem is that a transaction can commit its updates on one system, but a second system can fail before the transaction commits there, too. In this case, when the failed system recovers, it must be able to commit the transaction. To commit the transaction, it must have a copy of the transaction's updates. Since a system can lose the contents of main memory when it fails, it must store a durable copy of the transaction's updates before it fails, so it will have them after it recovers. This line of reasoning leads to the essence of two-phase commit: Each system accessed by a transaction must durably store its portion of the transaction's updates before the transaction commits anywhere. That way, if it fails before the transaction commits, it can commit the transaction after it recovers (see Figure 1.8).

To understand two-phase commit, it helps to visualize the overall architecture in which the transaction manager operates. The standard model of a TP monitor with integrated transaction manager was introduced by IBM's CICS (Customer Information and Control System) and is now promoted by X/Open (see Figure 1.9). In this model, the transaction manager talks to applications, resource managers, and other transaction managers. The concept "resource" includes databases, queues, files, messages, and other shared objects that can be accessed within a transaction. Each resource's resource manager offers operations that must execute only if the transaction that called the operations commits.

The transaction manager processes the basic transaction operations for applications—Start, Commit, and Abort. An application calls Start to begin executing a new transaction. It calls Commit to ask the transaction manager to commit the transaction. It calls Abort to tell the transaction manager to abort the transaction.

The transaction manager is primarily a bookkeeper that keeps track of transactions in order to ensure atomicity when more than one resource is involved. Typically, there's one transaction manager on each node of a distrib-

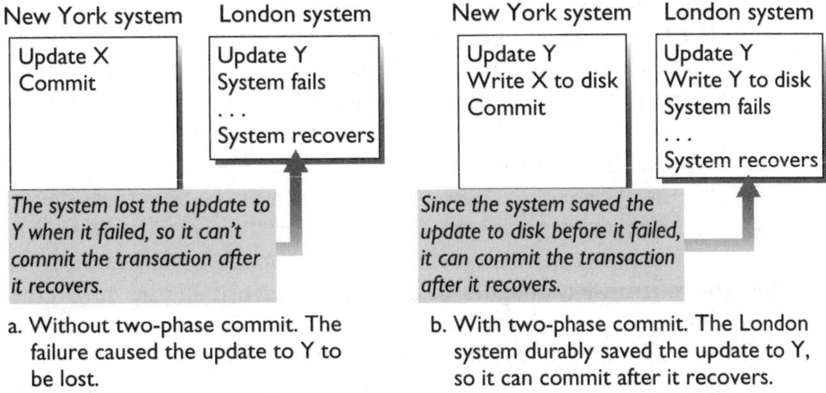

Figure 1.8 How Two-Phase Commit Ensures Atomicity With two-phase commit, each system durably stores its updates before the transaction commits.

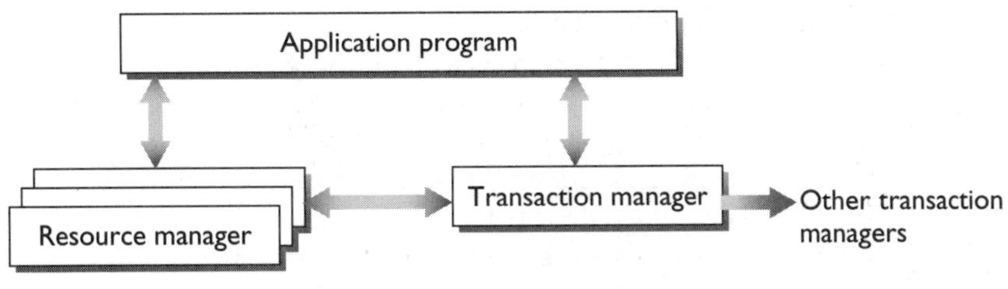

Figure 1.9 X/Open Transaction Model The transaction manager processes Start, Commit, and Abort. It talks to resource managers and other transaction managers to run two-phase commit.

uted computer system. When an application issues a Start operation, the transaction manager dispenses a unique ID for the transaction called a *transaction identifier*. During the execution of the transaction, it keeps track of all of the resource managers that the transaction accesses. This requires some cooperation with the application, the resource managers, and the communication system. Whenever the transaction accesses a new resource manager, somebody has to tell the transaction manager. This is important because when it comes time to commit the transaction, the transaction manager has to know all the resource managers to talk to in order to execute the two-phase commit protocol.

When a transaction program finishes execution and issues the commit operation, that commit operation goes to the transaction manager, which processes the operation by executing the two-phase commit protocol. Similarly, if the transaction manager gets a message to issue the abort operation, it tells the database systems to undo all the transaction's updates, that is, to abort the transaction at each database system.

When running two-phase commit, the transaction manager sends out two rounds of messages—one for each phase of the commitment activity. In the first round of messages it tells all the resource managers to prepare to commit by writing the results of the transaction to disk, but not actually to commit the transaction. At this point, the resource managers are "prepared to commit." When the transaction manager gets acknowledgments back from all the resource managers, it knows that the whole transaction has been prepared. (All resource managers have durably stored the transaction's updates before the transaction commits anywhere.) So it sends a second round of messages to tell the resource managers to actually commit. Figure 1.10 gives an example execution of two-phase commit with two resource managers.

Two-phase commit avoids the problem in Figure 1.8a because all resource managers have a durable copy of the transaction's updates before any of them commit. Therefore, even if a system fails during the commitment activity, as the London system did in the figure, it can commit after it recovers. However, to make this all work, the protocol must handle each possible failure and recovery scenario. For example, in Figure 1.8b, it must tell the London system to commit the transaction. The details of how two-phase commit handles these scenarios is described in Chapter 9.

Two-phase commit is required whenever a transaction accesses two or more resource managers. Thus, one key question designers of TP applications must answer is whether or not to distribute their transaction programs among multiple resources. Using two-phase commit adds overhead (due to two-phase commit messages), but the option to distribute can provide better scalability (adding more systems to increase capacity) and availability (since one system can fail while others remain operational).

1.5 Transaction Processing Performance

Performance is a critical aspect of TP systems. No one likes waiting more than a few seconds for an automated teller machine to dispense cash or for an airline agent to say whether a flight has seats available. So response time to end users is one important measure of TP system performance. Companies that rely on TP systems, such as banks and airlines, also want to get the most transaction throughput for the money they pay for a TP system. They also care about system scalability, that is, how much they can grow their system as their business grows.

It's very challenging to configure a TP system to meet response time and throughput requirements at minimum cost. It requires choosing the number of systems, how much storage capacity they'll have, which processing and database functions are assigned to each system, and how the systems are connected by communications links to the network of displays and to each other. Even if you know the performance of the component products being assembled, it's hard to predict how the overall system will perform. Therefore, vendors need to advertise the performance of preconfigured systems, so customers can make rational comparisons between competing products.

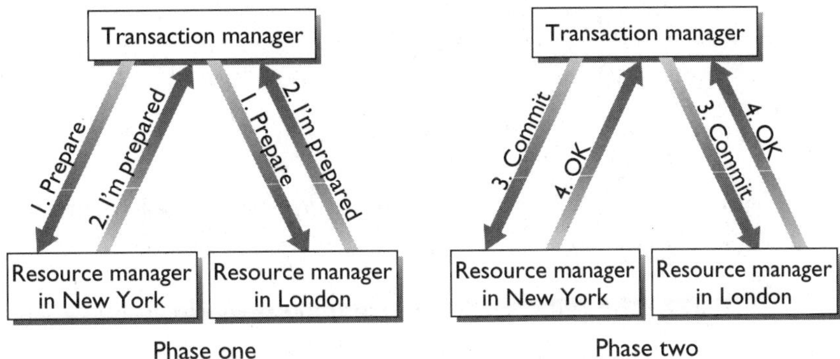

Figure 1.10 The Two-Phase Commit Protocol In phase one, each resource manager durably saves the transaction's updates before replying "I'm prepared." Thus, both resource managers have durably stored the transaction's updates before either of them commits in phase two.

To respond to this need, vendors formed an independent consortium called the Transaction Processing Performance Council (TPC), which defined the first TP system benchmarks that could be used to provide apples-to-apples comparisons of different vendors' products. Each TPC benchmark defines standard transaction programs and characterizes a system's performance by the throughput that the system can process under certain workload conditions, database size, response time guarantees, and so on. There are two main measures of a system's performance: the maximum throughput it can attain, originally measured in transactions per second (tps) and now measured in transactions per minute (tpm), and the cost of the transaction rate, measured in dollars per tps or tpm. The cost is calculated as the list purchase price of the hardware and software, plus five years' vendor-supplied maintenance on that hardware and software (called the *cost of ownership*).

The TPC-A and TPC-B Benchmarks

The first two benchmarks promoted by TPC, called TPC-A and TPC-B, model an automated teller machine application, which debits or credits a checking account. When TPC-A/B were introduced, around 1989, they were carefully crafted to exercise the main bottlenecks customers were experiencing in TP systems. The benchmarks were very successful in encouraging vendors to eliminate these bottlenecks—so successful, in fact, that by 1994 nearly all database systems performed very well on TPC-A/B. Therefore, the benchmarks have now been retired and replaced by TPC-C. Still, it's instructive to look at the bottlenecks the benchmarks were designed to exercise, since one can still run into them today on a poorly designed system or application.

Both benchmarks run the same transaction program, but TPC-A includes terminals and a network in the overall system, while TPC-B does not. TPC-B stresses the database only, similar to a batch processing environment, while

TPC-A includes human "think time" at a display device. In either case, the transaction program performs the sequence of operations shown in Figure 1.11 (with the exception that TPC-B does not perform the read/write terminal operations).

In TPC-A/B, the database consists of

- account records, one record for each customer's account (total of 100,000 accounts)
- a teller record for each teller, which keeps track of how much money is at the bank teller or automated teller machine (total of 10 tellers)
- one record for each bank branch (one branch minimum), which contains the sum of all the accounts at that branch
- a history file, which records a description of each transaction that actually executes

The transaction reads a 100-byte input message from a terminal, including the account number and the amount of money to be withdrawn or deposited. The transaction uses that information to find the account record and update it appropriately. It updates the history file to indicate that this transaction has executed. It updates the teller record to indicate that a certain amount of money has been deposited to or withdrawn from that teller. And it updates the amount of money at the bank branch in the same way. Finally, for TPC-A, it sends a message back to the display device to confirm the completion of the transaction.

The benchmark exercises several potential bottlenecks in a TP system:

- There's a large number of account records. The system must have 100,000 account records for each transaction per second it can perform. To randomly access so many records, the database must be indexed.
- The end of the history file can be a bottleneck, because every transaction has to write to it, and therefore to lock and synchronize against it. This synchronization can delay transactions.
- Similarly, the branch record can be a bottleneck because all of the tellers at each branch are reading and writing it, which also can cause performance problems. However, TPC-A/B minimize the effect of this potential bottleneck by requiring a teller to execute a transaction only every 10 seconds.

Given a fixed configuration, the price/performance of the TPC-A/B application depends on the amount of computer resources needed to execute it: the number of processor instructions, disk I/Os, and interactions with the display. For each transaction, a high-performance implementation uses around 100,000 instructions, two to three disk I/Os, and two interactions with the display. Most successful TP system vendors can produce a benchmark implementation in this range.

```
Start
  Read message from terminal  (100 bytes)
  Read and write account record  (random access)
  Write history record  (sequential access)
  Read and write teller record  (random access)
  Read and write branch record  (random access)
  Write message to terminal  (200 bytes)
Commit
```

Figure 1.11 TPC-A/B Transaction Program The program models a debit-credit transaction for a bank.

When running these benchmarks, a typical system spends more than half of the processor instructions inside the database system, and maybe another third of the instructions in message communications between the parts of the application. Only a small fraction of the processor directly executes the transaction program. This isn't really surprising, because the transaction program mostly just sends messages and initiates database operations. The transaction program itself does very little.

The TPC-C Benchmark

TPC-A/B are too simplistic compared to most of today's TP applications. Moreover, most vendors have such good TPC-A/B benchmark numbers that the benchmark is no longer a good differentiator when selecting systems. Therefore, the TP Performance Council has developed TPC-C as a better differentiator of today's systems.

TPC-C is based on an order-entry application for a wholesale supplier. Compared to TPC-A/B, it includes a wider variety of transactions, some "heavy weight" transactions (which do a lot of work), and a more complex database.

The database centers around a warehouse, which tracks its stock of items that it supplies to customers within a sales district, and tracks those customers' orders, which consist of order-lines. The database size is proportional to the number of warehouses (see Figure 1.12).

There are five types of transactions:

- New-Order—To enter a new order, first retrieve the records describing the given warehouse, customer, and district, and then update the district (increment the next available order number). Insert a record in the Order and New-Order tables. For each of the 5–15 (average 10) items ordered, retrieve the item record (abort if it doesn't exist), retrieve and update the stock record, and insert an order-line record.
- Payment—To enter a payment, first retrieve and update the records describing the given warehouse, district, and customer, and then insert a history record. If the customer is identified by name, rather than ID

Table Name	Number of Rows per Warehouse	Bytes per Row	Size of Table (in Bytes) per Warehouse
Warehouse	1	89	0.089K
District	10	95	0.95K
Customer	30K	655	19.65K
History	30K	46	1.38K
Order	30K	24	720K
New-Order	9K	8	72K
Order-Line	300K	54	16.2M
Stock	100K	306	306M
Item	100K	82	8.2M

Figure 1.12 Database for the TPC-C Benchmark The database consists of the tables in the left column, which support an order-entry application.

number, then additional customer records (average of two) must be retrieved to find the right customer.

- Order-Status—To determine the status of a given customer's latest order, retrieve the given customer record (or records, if identified by name, as in Payment), and retrieve the customer's latest order and corresponding order-lines.
- Delivery—To process a new order for each of a warehouse's 10 districts, get the oldest new-order record in each district, delete it, retrieve and update the corresponding customer record, order record, and the order's corresponding order-line records. This can be done as one transaction or 10 transactions.
- Stock-Level—To determine, in a warehouse's district, the number of recently sold items whose stock level is below a given threshold, retrieve the record describing the given district (which has the next order number), retrieve order-lines for the previous 20 orders in that district, and for each item ordered, determine if the given threshold exceeds the amount in stock.

The New-Order, Payment, and Order-Status transactions have stringent response time requirements. The Delivery transaction runs as a periodic batch, and the Stock-Level transaction has relaxed response time and consistency requirements. The workload requires that there be an equal number of

New-Order and Payment transactions, and one Order-Status, Delivery, and Stock-Level transaction for every 10 New-Orders.

The transaction rate metric is the number of New-Order transactions per minute, denoted *tpmC*, given all of the other constraints are met. Published results must be accompanied by a *full disclosure report*, which allows other vendors to review benchmark compliance and gives users more detailed performance information beyond the summary tpmC number.

The TPC-C workload is many times heavier per transaction than TPC-A/B and exhibits higher contention for shared data. Moreover, it exercises a wider variety of performance-sensitive functions, such as deferred transaction execution, access via secondary keys, and transaction aborts. It is regarded as a more realistic workload and has completely replaced TPC-A/B as the standard benchmark for TP systems.

1.6 Availability

Availability is the fraction of time the TP system is up and running and able to do useful work—that is, it isn't down because of hardware or software failures, operator errors, preventative maintenance, power failures, and so on. Availability is an important measure of the capability of a TP system because the TP application usually is offering a service that's "mission critical," one that's essential to the operation of the enterprise, such as airline reservations, managing checking accounts in a bank, or processing stock transactions in a stock exchange. Obviously, if this type of system is unavailable, the business stops operating. Therefore, the system *must* operate nearly all of the time.

Just how highly available does a system have to be? We see from Figure 1.13 that if the system is available 96 percent of the time, that means it's down nearly an hour a day. That's a lot of time for many types of businesses, which would consider 96 percent availability to be unacceptable.

An availability level of 99 percent means that the system is down nearly two hours per week. This might be tolerable provided that it comes in short outages of just a few minutes at a time. This is typically the range of availability you see in airline systems, say, 98.5–99.5 percent. That may be fine for an airline, but it is probably not so fine if you are running a stock exchange, where an hour of downtime can produce big financial losses.

An availability level of 99.9 percent means that the system is down for about an hour per month, or really just a few minutes per day. An availability level of 99.999 percent means that the system is down an hour in 20 years, or three minutes a year. That number may seem incredibly ambitious, but it is attainable; telephone systems in North America typically have that level of availability.

Today's TP system customers typically expect availability levels in the 98–99 percent range, although it certainly depends on how much money they're

Downtime	Availability (%)
1 hour/day	95.8
1 hour/week	99.41
1 hour/month	99.86
1 hour/year	99.9886
1 hour/20 years	99.99942

Figure 1.13 Downtime at Different Availability Levels The number of nines after the decimal point is of practical significance.

willing to spend. Generally, attaining high availability requires attention to four factors:

- Environment—making the physical environment more robust to avoid failures of power, communications, air-conditioning, and the like
- System management—avoiding failures due to operational errors by system managers and vendors' field service
- Hardware—having redundant hardware, so that if some component fails, the system can immediately and automatically replace it with another component that's ready to take over
- Software—improving the reliability of software and ensuring it can automatically and quickly recover after a failure

This book is about software, and regrettably, of the four factors, software is the major contributor to availability problems. Software failures can be divided into three categories: application failures, database system failures, and operating system failures.

Because we're using transactions, when an application fails, any uncommitted part of the transaction it was executing aborts automatically. Its updates are backed out because of the atomicity property. There's really nothing that the system has to do other than reexecute the transaction after the application is running again.

When the database system fails, all of the uncommitted transactions that were accessing the database system at that time have to abort because their updates may be lost during the database system failure. The system has to detect the failure of the database system and the database system has to be reinitialized. During the reinitialization process, the database system backs out all the transactions that were active at the time of the failure, thereby getting into a clean state, where it contains the results only of committed transactions.

A failure of the operating system requires it to reboot. All programs, applications, and database systems executing at the time of failure are now dead.

Everything has to be reinitialized after the operating system reboots. On an ordinary computer system all this normally takes between several minutes and an hour, depending on how big the system is, how many transactions were active at the time of failure, how long it takes to back out the uncommitted transactions, how efficient the initialization program is, and so on. Very high availability systems, such as those intended to be available in excess of 99 percent, are typically designed for very fast recovery. Even when they fail, they are only down for a very short time. They usually use some form of replicated processing to get this fast recovery. When one component fails, they quickly delegate processing work to a copy of the component that is ready and waiting to pick up the load.

The transaction abstraction helps the programmer quite a bit in attaining high availability because the system is able to recover into a clean state by aborting transactions. And it can continue from where it left off by rerunning transactions that aborted as a result of the failure. Without the transaction abstraction, the recovery program would have to be application-specific. It would have to analyze the state of the database at the time of the failure to figure out what work to undo and what to rerun. We discuss high availability issues and techniques in more detail in Chapter 7.

1.7 Styles of Systems

We've been talking about TP as a style of *application,* one that runs short transaction programs that access a shared database. TP is also a style of *system,* a way of configuring software components to do the type of work required by a TP application. It's useful to compare this style of system with other styles that you may be familiar with, to see where the differences are and why TP systems are constructed differently from the others. There are several other kinds of systems that we can look at here:

- Batch processing systems, where you submit a job and later on get output in the form of a file
- Time-sharing systems, where a display device is connected to an operating system process, and within that process you can invoke programs that interact frequently with the display
- Real-time systems, where you submit requests to do a small amount of work that has to be done before some very early deadline
- Client/server systems, where a client device, typically a PC or workstation, is connected via a network to a server system that performs work on behalf of the client
- Decision support systems, where you have reporting programs or ad hoc queries access data maintained to support periodic or strategic decisions

Designing a system to perform one of these types of processing is called *system engineering*. Rather than engineering a specific component, such as an operating system or a database system, you engineer an integrated system by combining different kinds of components to perform a certain type of work. Often, systems are engineered to handle multiple styles, but for the purposes of comparing and contrasting the different styles, we'll discuss them as if each type of system were running in a separately engineered environment.

Let's look at requirements for each of these styles of computing and see how they compare to a TP system.

Batch Processing Systems

A batch is a set of requests that are processed together, often long after the requests were submitted. Data processing systems of the 1960s and early 1970s were designed to be used primarily for batch processing. Today, batch workloads are still with us. But instead of running them on systems dedicated for batch processing, they usually execute on systems that also run a TP workload. TP systems can execute the batches during nonpeak periods, since the batch workload has flexible response time requirements. To make the comparison between TP and batch clear, we will compare a TP system running a pure TP workload against a batch system running a pure batch workload. But understand that mixtures of the two are now commonplace.

A batch processing system is typically uniprogrammed. That is, each batch is a sequence of transactions and is executed sequentially, one transaction at a time. Therefore there's no problem with serializability, as there is in a TP system, because you're executing the transactions serially. By contrast, in a TP system you're generally executing several transactions at the same time, and so the system has extra work to ensure serializability.

The main performance measure of batch processing is throughput, that is, the amount of work done per unit of time. Response time is less important. A batch could take minutes, hours, or even days to execute. In contrast, TP systems have important response time requirements because generally there's a user waiting at a display for the transaction's output.

Batch processing normally takes its input in the form of a record-oriented file, whose records represent a sequence of request messages. The output of the batch is also normally stored in a file. By contrast, TP systems typically have large networks of display devices for capturing requests and displaying results.

Batch processing can be optimized by ordering the input requests consistently with the order of the data in the database. For example, if the requests correspond to debit or credit transactions on a banking database, the requests can be ordered by account number. That way, it's easy and efficient to process the requests by a merge procedure that reads the account database in account number order. In contrast, TP requests come in a random order. Because you have a fast response time requirement, you can't take time to sort the data in an order consistent with the database. You have to be able to access the data randomly, in the order in which it's requested.

Batch processing takes the request message file and existing database file(s) as input and produces a new master output database as a result of running transactions for the requests. If the batch processing program should fail, there's no harm done because the input file and input database are unmodified—simply throw out the output file and run the batch program again. By contrast, a TP system updates its database on-line as requests arrive. So a failure may leave the database in an inconsistent state because it contains the results of uncompleted transactions. This atomicity problem for transactions in a TP environment doesn't exist in a batch environment.

Finally, in batch the load on the system is fixed and predictable, so the system can be engineered for that load. For example, you can schedule the system to run the batch at a given time and set aside sufficient capacity to do it because you know exactly what the load is going to be. By contrast, a TP load generally varies during the day. There are peak periods when there's a lot of activity, and slow periods when there's hardly any activity at all. The system has to be sized to handle the peak load and also designed to make use of extra capacity during slack periods.

Time-Sharing Systems

Before the widespread use of PCs, when time-sharing systems were popular, TP systems were often confused with time-sharing because they both involve managing lots of display devices connected to a common server. But they're really quite different in terms of load, performance requirements, and availability requirements.

A time-sharing system is often run as a computing utility and processes a highly unpredictable load. Users constantly make different demands on the system, exercising new features in different combinations all the time. By comparison, a TP load is very regular. It runs the same transaction types day in, day out, with similar load patterns every day.

Time-sharing systems have less stringent availability and atomicity requirements. Downtime has less expensive consequences. There's no concept of atomicity of application execution. If a time-sharing program crashes, you simply run it again. Only one user may be affected, or only those users running that particular program. Other users can still continue their work. The file system only needs to maintain some level of physical integrity, as opposed to a database in a TP environment, which has to support atomicity, isolation, and durability requirements.

For time-sharing systems, performance is measured in terms of system capacity, for example, in MIPS (millions of instructions per second) or number of on-line users. There are no generally accepted benchmarks that accurately represent the behavior of a wide range of applications. In a TP environment, the TPC benchmarks are widely used to compare TP system products.

Real-Time Systems

We can also compare TP to real-time systems, such as a system collecting input from a satellite or controlling a factory's shop floor equipment. TP essentially is a kind of real-time system, with a real-time response time demand of one to two seconds. It responds to a real-world process consisting of end users interacting with display devices, which communicate with application programs accessing a shared database. So not surprisingly, there are many similarities between the two kinds of systems.

Real-time systems and TP systems both have predictable loads with periodic peaks. Real-time systems usually emphasize gathering input rather than processing it; TP systems generally do both.

Because of the variety of real-world processes they control, real-time systems generally have to deal with more specialized devices than TP, such as laboratory equipment or factory shop floor equipment.

Real-time systems generally don't need or use special mechanisms for atomicity and durability. They simply process the input as quickly as they can. If they lose some of that input, they just keep on running. To see why, imagine for example that you're collecting input from a monitoring satellite. The data keeps pouring in. It's not good if you miss some of that data. But you certainly can't stop operating to go back to fix things up as you would in a TP environment because the data keeps coming in and you must do your best to keep processing it. By contrast, in a TP environment you can generally control whether input is coming or you can buffer the input for awhile. If you have a failure, you can stop collecting input, repair the system, and then come back and process input again. Thus, the fault tolerance requirements between the two types of systems are rather different.

Real-time systems are generally not concerned with serializability. In most real-time applications, processing of input messages involves no access to shared data. Since the processing of two different inputs does not affect each other, even if they're processed concurrently, they'll behave like a serial execution. No special mechanisms, such as locking, are needed. When processing real-time inputs to shared data, however, the notion of serializability is as relevant as it is to TP.

Our comparison of system styles so far is summarized in Figure 1.14.

Client/Server Systems

Today, a large fraction of computer systems are designed for the client/server environment, where a large number of personal computers communicate with shared servers. This kind of system is very similar to a TP environment, where a large number of display devices connect to shared servers that run transactions. Since client/server and TP systems have similar overall requirements, the internal structure of the operating system and the communications system supporting them is similar, too. In fact, one can say that TP systems were the original client/server systems with very simple desktop devices, namely, dumb terminals. As desktop devices have become more powerful, TP systems and personal computer systems have been converging into a single type of computing environment. PC servers and TP servers still offer rather different functions, but we anticipate the convergence of these system types will continue to the point where they are nearly identical.

	Transaction Processing	Batch	Time-Sharing	Real-Time
Isolation	serializable, multiprogrammed execution	serial, uniprogrammed execution	no transaction concept	no transaction concept
Workload	high variance	predictable	high variance	high variance or predictable, depending on application
Performance Metric	response time and throughput	throughput	no standard metric	no standard metric, missed deadlines?
Input	network of display devices submitting requests	record-oriented file	network of display devices submitting commands	network of display devices submitting commands
Data Access	random access	accesses sorted to be consistent with database order	unconstrained	unconstrained
Recovery	after failure, ensure database contains committed updates and no others	after failure, rerun the batch to produce a new master file	application's responsibility	application's responsibility

Figure 1.14 Comparison of System Types Transaction processing has different characteristics than the other styles and therefore requires systems that are specially engineered to the purpose.

A variation on client/server is the World Wide Web, where clients and servers communicate over the Internet. Clients run a web browser and servers offer access to pages expressed in HyperText Markup Language. Like client/server systems on local area networks, these Internet-based systems are quickly evolving into large-scale TP environments. We'll discuss this trend in Chapters 2, 5, and 11.

Decision Support Systems

TP systems process the data in its raw state as it arrives. *Decision support systems* collate and organize the data to provide information on which decisions can be made.

For example, a distribution company decides each year how to allocate its marketing and advertising budget. Sales orders are processed by a TP system that includes data for the geographical origin, type, and value of each order. When the company invests in advertising that targets a specific region or a specific product, executives can access the TP database to discover the effect on sales of their promotional activities, and therefore determine how best to allocate promotional resources.

In contrast to TP applications, which are typically quite short, decision support applications are typically long-lived, like batch applications, because they access large amounts of data. But unlike TP and batch, the data they access can be somewhat out-of-date, since decision support is looking for trends that are not much affected by the very latest updates. Thus, a decision support application can use a snapshot copy of the TP database, instead of the on-line database itself. Often it's important to run on a static database copy, so that the results of successive queries are comparable. Operating on a snapshot copy is also helpful to the performance of the TP database, which would be slowed down by a heavy decision support workload. For these reasons, companies often create *data warehouse* databases, containing snapshots of TP databases to be used for decision support.

Why Engineer a TP System?

Each kind of system that we looked at is designed for certain usage patterns: batch, time-sharing, real-time, client/server, and decision support. Although each system is engineered for a particular purpose, it actually can be used in other ways. For example, people have used time-sharing systems to run TP applications. These applications typically do not scale very well and do not use operating system resources very efficiently, but it can be done. People have built special-purpose TP systems using real-time systems. They have built batch systems to run on a time-sharing system. And so on.

By analogy, if you want to drive a nail into wood, there's a device designed for that purpose—namely, a hammer. You can use a stone or a drill, or a toaster for that matter, to drive in a nail. These tools were not designed for that purpose, but they will work after a fashion. Likewise, you can use a batch processing system or a time-sharing system for transactions. It's just that they aren't really designed for that purpose, and they don't work particularly well.

TP has enough special requirements that it's worth engineering the system for that purpose. The amount of money businesses spend on TP systems justifies the additional engineering work vendors do to tailor their system products for TP—for better performance, reliability, and ease of use.

1.8 Example Applications

To get a feel for the size and complexity of TP applications, we present two examples. These are abstracted from systems developed by, and used for, real businesses.

Automated Teller Machine

In the mid-1970s, automated teller machines (ATMs) were a leading-edge TP application. Today, it is considered a relatively simple application that doesn't require much computing resource.

The database consists of four tables. For each table, we describe its content and give a rule of thumb for estimating its size:

- AccountBalance—Has one row per account, including the account number (Acct#, 10 bytes) and account balance (Balance, 6 bytes). There are about 3000 rows for each ATM.
- HotCard—Lists the ATM cards that should not be honored. It has just one column, Acct#. There are about 100 rows per ATM.
- AccountVelocity—Has one row for each recently used account, including the Acct# and sum of recent withdrawals (4 bytes). The number of rows is proportional to the number of withdrawal transactions per day, about 150 for each ATM.
- PostingLog—Has a row for each message exchanged with each ATM, including the Acct#, ATM identifier (ATM#, 2 bytes), and amount deposited or withdrawn (Amount, 4 bytes). It has about 300 rows for each ATM.

Calculating the above, in a network of several hundred ATMs, the database size is about 25–50 megabytes, covering about a million customers.

There are two main kinds of transactions:

1. Deposit or Withdrawal—Input includes Acct#, ATM#, transaction type, PIN (personal ID number, i.e., password), unique transaction ID (generated by the ATM), and the amount of money.
   - Write the request to the PostingLog.
   - Check the validity of the PIN.
   - Check Acct# in the HotCard table. If it's there, reject the request.
   - Check Acct# in AccountVelocity table. If there's too much activity, reject the transaction.
   - For a withdrawal, update the velocity file.
   - Update Balance in AccountBalance to indicate the deposit or withdrawal.
   - Write a deposit or withdrawal record to the PostingLog.
   - Commit the transaction.
   - Send a message to the ATM to dispense the money.
2. RequestBalance—Input includes Acct#, ATM#, PIN, transaction type, and unique transaction ID.
   - Write the request to the PostingLog.
   - Check the validity of the PIN.
   - Read the balance from the AccountBalance table.
   - Send a message containing the Balance to the ATM.

TP systems are configured to handle their peak load. The peak load on this system is lunchtime, when each ATM may be generating one transaction per minute, which is one transaction per second (tps) for every 60 ATMs. Depending on how much is buffered in main memory, each transaction does about five disk I/O operations. One mirrored disk (i.e., two disks, performing the same load, for reliability) can handle about 5 tps, or about 300 ATMs. The database system's log is generally given its own pair of disks, since it is accessed sequentially and would otherwise create much contention with the disk that holds the database.

The PostingLog is run through a batch accounting system at night. This batch system is the "real money" database that is used to balance the financial books each day. Early systems would download a snapshot database to the ATM system every night. Today, many systems have the ATMs directly access an on-line "real money" database used by other applications.

When an ATM is reloaded with money each day, its balance is rectified. This is done by scanning the PostingLog to determine how much money was dispensed, and subtracting that from the amount that had been loaded into the ATM the previous day. The result should be the same as the amount in the ATM at the time it was reloaded. In large systems, ATMs are not necessarily rectified at the same time as each other, creating some accounting complexities.

Stock Exchange

This example is an automated trading system that connects a complex network of display devices to 10 stock exchanges throughout a large country. All dealers can trade in the same security in real time, despite their geographical distribution.

The database consists of the following tables:

- Users—Contains a row for each trader and market watcher. It is keyed on the UserID column and has about 1000 rows, 64 kilobytes (KB) per row, equaling 64 megabytes (MB).
- Stocks—Contains a row for each stock that's traded. It is keyed on the StockID column and has about 1000 rows, 100KB per row, equaling 100MB.
- BuyOrders and SellOrders—Contains a row for each order entered during the day. It is keyed on StockId, Price, and TimePriority. It has an average of 25,000 rows per table, 20KB per row, equaling 500MB.
- Trades—Contains a row for each trade executed during the day. It is keyed on StockId and Trade number and has about 60,000 rows, 5KB per row, equaling 300MB.
- Prices—Contains a row describing the buy and sell total volume and number of orders disclosed for each stock and price. It is keyed on

StockId and Price and has about 500,000 rows, 800 bytes per row, equaling 400MB.

- Log—Contains a row for each user request and system reply message. It is keyed on transaction ID and has about 200,000 rows, 320 bytes per row, equaling 640MB.
- NotificationMessages—Contains all messages sent to users during the day, most of which are notifications that a trade has executed. It is keyed on UserId and has 150,000 rows, 4KB per row, equaling 600MB.

The total database is about 2.6 gigabytes (GB).
The main types of transactions are the following:

1. GetStockServer
   - Read the server number that handles a given stock from the Stocks table. (For scalability, the application is partitioned across multiple server machines, each of which handles some of the stocks.)
   - Return it.
2. LogRequest
   - Check the validity of the transaction ID.
   - Write a transaction request to the Log table.
3. ExecuteTrade
   - Read information about the given stock from the Stocks table.
   - Get the timestamp.
   - Read the scheduled trading periods for the stock.
   - Check if the trading period is correct, the order is valid, and the book situation in the Prices table indicates that the trade can be executed.
   - If yes, then match the incoming order with those on the opposite side (i.e., buy with sell or sell with buy), according to its price, time priority, and quantity parameters. Update the Trades and NotificationMessages tables regarding the trade. Update Orders and Prices on the opposite side until the order is completely filled. Insert the order in the Orders table of its side, and update the Prices and Stocks tables.
   - If not, insert the order in the Orders table of its side, and update the Prices table and the Stocks table.
   - Write the system response to the incoming request in the Log.
   - Commit the transaction.
   - Call the Broadcast process, which sends the new orderbook situation for this stock.

The peak daily load is 140,000 orders. The peak-per-second load generates about 180 disk I/Os per second and consumes 300 million instructions per second.

1.9 Summary

A *transaction* is the execution of a program that performs an administrative function by accessing a shared database. Transactions can execute on-line, while a user is waiting, or off-line (in batch mode) if the execution takes longer than a user can wait for results. The end user requests the execution of a *transaction program* by sending a message called a *request message.*

A *transaction processing application* is a collection of transaction programs designed to automate a given business activity. A TP application consists of a relatively small number of predefined types of transaction programs. TP applications may run on a wide range of computer sizes, and may be centralized or distributed, running on local area or wide area networks. TP applications are mapped to a specially engineered hardware and software environment called a *TP system.*

The three parts of a TP application correspond to the three major functions of a TP system:

1. Obtain input from a display or special device and construct a request.
2. Accept a request message and call the correct transaction program.
3. Execute the transaction program to complete the work required by the request.

Database management plays a significant role in a TP system. TP monitors help get the best price/performance out of a TP system. TP monitors also provide a structure in which TP applications execute.

A transaction has four critical properties: atomicity, consistency, isolation, and durability. Consistency is the responsibility of the program. The remaining three properties are the responsibility of the TP system.

- *Atomicity*—Provided by database mechanisms. Successful transactions *commit;* failed transactions *abort.* Commit makes database changes permanent; abort undoes or erases database changes.
- *Consistency*—Each transaction is programmed to preserve database consistency.
- *Isolation*—Each transaction executes as if it were running alone. That is, the effect of running a set of transactions is the same as running them one at a time. This behavior is called *serializability* and is usually implemented by locking.
- *Durability*—The result of a committed transaction is guaranteed to be on stable storage, usually disk.

If a transaction updates multiple databases or resource managers, then the two-phase commit protocol is required. This ensures atomicity, that is, that the transaction commits at all resource managers or aborts at all of them.

Two-phase commit is usually implemented by a transaction manager, which tracks which resource managers are accessed by each transaction and runs the two-phase commit protocol.

Performance is a critical aspect of TP. A TP system must scale up to run many transactions per time unit, while giving one- or two-second response time. The standard measure of performance is the TPC-C benchmark, which compares TP systems based on their maximum transaction rate and price per transaction for a standardized order-entry application workload.

A TP system is often critical to proper functioning of the enterprise that uses it. Therefore, another important property of TP systems is *availability,* that is, the fraction of time the system is running and able to do work. Availability is determined by how frequently a TP system fails and how quickly it can recover from failures.

TP systems have rather different characteristics than batch, real-time, and time-sharing systems. They therefore require specialized implementations that are tuned to the purpose. These techniques are the main subject of this book.

CHAPTER 2

Transaction Processing Monitors

2.1 Introduction

A *TP monitor* is a software product used to create, execute, and manage transaction processing applications. Its main job is to provide an environment that takes applications written to process a single request and scale them up to run efficiently on large, often distributed, systems with many active users submitting requests and many servers processing requests. By making it possible to scale up the TP application to run on large systems, it increases the capacity and lowers the per-transaction cost of the application. From a business perspective, it increases the capacity and lowers the cost of retail sales, ticket reservations, funds transfers, and so on.

A TP monitor typically includes software in three major functional areas:

- An application programming interface (API) to a set of runtime functions that support transaction execution, such as transaction bracketing (Start, Commit, and Abort operations), communication between programs within a transaction, and communication to front-end programs that submit requests
- Program development tools for building transaction programs, such as a compiler that translates high-level operations in a specific programming language into the API just mentioned
- A system management interface and accompanying runtime functions to monitor and control the execution of transaction programs

From the user's point of view, a TP application is a serial processor of requests. It is a classic server that appears to be in an infinite loop whose body is an ACID transaction (see Figure 2.1). The TP monitor helps ensure some of the ACID properties. It also coordinates the flow of requests between the sources of the requests, which could be a display or other kind of device, and the transaction programs, which are the application programs that execute the transactions.

The control flow within a TP monitor for each request is the following:

- Translate the input from the display (or other) device, which is typically captured using one or more form and menu selections, into the standard message format that the TP monitor defines for requests.
- Examine the request header to determine what kind of transaction is being requested and which program should process the request.
- Start a transaction and invoke the program that corresponds to the type of transaction being requested. (The program typically invokes a database system to do some of its work.)
- Commit the transaction if it terminated successfully, or abort the transaction if it was unable to successfully complete the execution of the request.
- Finally, send some output back to the source of the request, which is the display (or other) device.

```
Do Forever
     /* the body of the loop is a transaction */
     receive a request
     do the requested work
     send a reply (optional)
End
```

Figure 2.1 TP Application Loop A TP application serially processes requests, which run as transactions.

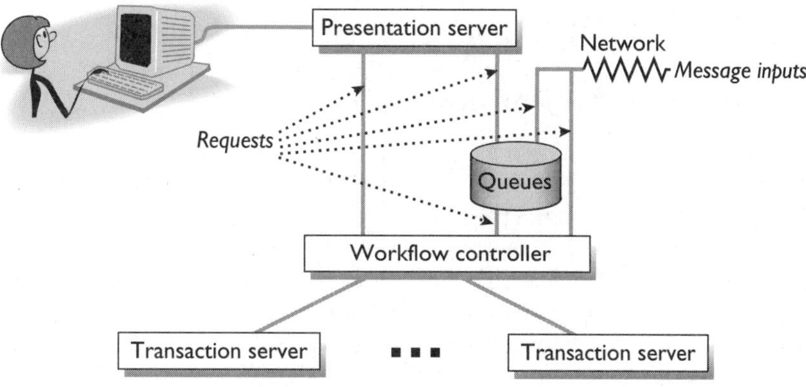

Figure 2.2 TP Monitor Components (The Three-Tier Model) The presentation server manages the user's display and outputs requests. The workflow controller processes a request by calling transaction servers, which access databases and other resources.

Much of the work of the TP monitor is to process requests efficiently when there are many active requests from a large number of display devices going to a large number of servers.

2.2 TP Monitor Architecture

A TP monitor implements its control flow using the set of software components illustrated in Figure 2.2. The figure also illustrates the process and communications structure for the control flow.

The display device in the upper left interacts with the component called the *presentation server*, which is responsible for translating the forms, menu selections, and other input into a message in a standard request format. Presentation services are increasingly being provided by fourth-generation languages (4GLs), such as Microsoft's Visual Basic, Powersoft's PowerBuilder, and Borland's Delphi. The request message coming from the presentation server can be temporarily stored on disk in a queue, or it can be forwarded directly for processing by the component called *workflow control*. The workflow con-

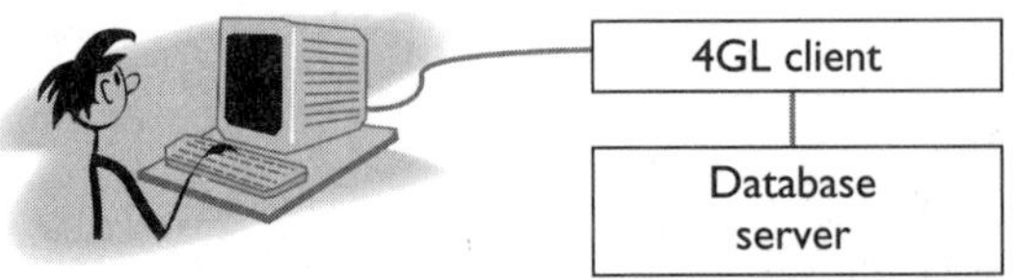

Figure 2.3 Two-Tier Model A 4GL front end communicates with a database server back end.

trol component routes the request message to the proper transaction server and invokes a transaction server program, which is the program that does the actual work of the request and is where the transaction is really executed.

Two-Tier vs. Three-Tier Systems

The system model in Figure 2.2 is often called a *three-tier model.* There's a *front-end tier* (presentation servers) that sits close to the user, a *back-end tier* (transaction servers) that sits close to the data resources, and a *middle tier* (workflow controllers) that routes work between the front and back ends.

By contrast, in a two-tier model, the presentation server communicates directly with a transaction server or a database server, and no TP monitor is required. A common configuration is a 4GL front end communicating directly with a database server back end (see Figure 2.3). The two-tier model is sometimes called "TP lite" because it doesn't have the extra weight of a TP monitor. We will compare TP lite to the three-tier model at the end of this chapter, after we have discussed each tier of the three-tier model and the detailed functions that each tier provides.

TP Monitor Functions

The TP monitor provides a software environment in which application programs run and in which users interact with the computer system. One way to think about a TP monitor is that it provides "glue" and "veneer": the glue ties together the underlying system components that are needed by all TP applications—the database system, communications system, and operating system—and the veneer papers over the components to provide a single, smooth interface, so that developers and end users don't need to deal with each of these components independently (see Figure 2.4). For example, a TP monitor may provide a consistent interface to all of these resources, including database management systems, communications systems, and display devices.

For each vendor's set of components, different amounts and kinds of glue and veneer are required, so TP monitors are often very different from one vendor's system to another. This is why many TP monitors are offered by computer system vendors rather than independent software vendors. TP applications tend to rely on functionality that is closely tied to the vendor's hardware architecture or to a particular operating system, to gain maximum performance and to ensure the highest possible degree of reliability. For exam-

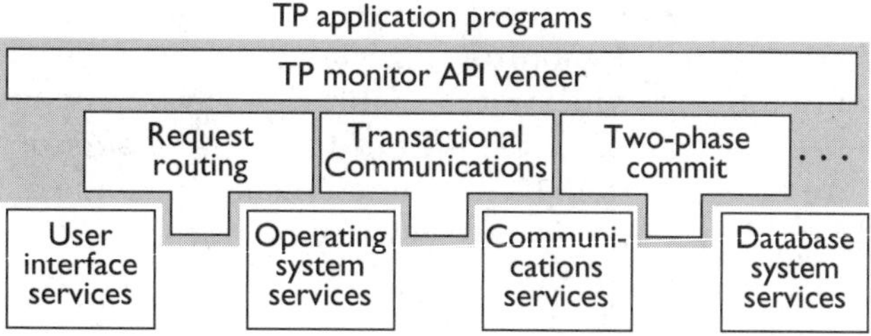

Figure 2.4 **Glue and Veneer** The TP monitor (in the shaded area) provides glue services, such as request management, transactional communications, and two-phase commit. Its API veneer provides a single smooth interface to application programmers.

ple, the TP monitor may use shared memory to communicate between processes if the operating system's messaging is too slow for high-performance TP. Or it may exploit hardware memory protection mechanisms to efficiently protect concurrently executing transactions from each other. Or it may use low-level disk I/O interfaces for high-frequency disk updates, such as those to a log. And so on.

Instead of writing application programs that talk independently to the operating system, communications system, forms system, and so on, you can write an application using a single language that talks to the TP monitor. The TP monitor then takes the responsibility of performing the right functions with the right underlying systems and provides runtime functions corresponding to each of the components in Figure 2.2 (the presentation server, the workflow controller, and transaction server).

Over the past decade, portable TP monitors have been developed to run on a variety of operating systems (e.g., Windows NT, OS/2, and many flavors of UNIX), communications systems, and database systems. We will describe some of these products in Chapter 5.

In addition to providing functions for running applications, the TP monitor usually provides system management functions by interpreting measurements from the operating system and database system in terms of TP abstractions. For example, instead of just telling the system manager that an operating system process failed, the TP monitor might say that the bank's loan server has failed, thereby giving the system manager a better idea where the problem is and what to do about it.

System management functions include load balancing, fault monitoring and repair, performance monitoring and tuning, and the ability to change the configuration by creating and destroying processes, creating and destroying communications sessions, and so on. For example, the TP monitor may store a description of which workflow controllers and transaction servers are running on which systems and, in the event of a failure, can recreate the failed components on other systems that have spare capacity. System management functions are also required to set up and maintain security mechanisms for protecting access to displays and to ensure that only authorized users can access sensitive transaction control programs. These system management capabilities distinguish a TP monitor from TP lite implementations.

The TP monitor also provides some application development tools to make it easier to write the code that maps onto the components of the three-tier architecture. We'll be describing these functions both for the application programmer and for the system manager as we go along.

Three-Tier Applications

The structure of a TP application is split into components that correspond exactly to the three main components of the three-tier TP monitor structure. The application consists of

- definitions of forms and menus, including data validation programs, that gather the input and turn it into a request (the definitions execute by talking to the presentation server)
- programs that map input request messages into calls to the appropriate transaction servers (these programs execute by talking to the workflow controller)
- transaction programs that actually do the work (these programs are the transaction servers)

Object-oriented application design has led to application structures that map nicely onto the three-tier TP monitor architecture (see Figure 2.5). In this style of design, one starts by defining "business objects" that correspond to elementary functions of the business that change slowly. For example, a business object might be Customer, which supports operations to create a new customer, change address, change phone number, and display itself in several different formats. An Account object might support operations to create a new account, debit or credit the balance, and associate it with a different customer. And so on. After defining the business objects in an application, one defines "business rules," actions that the business performs in response to things that happen in the real world. For example, the business rule for opening a new loan might involve creating a new customer object (if this is a new customer), checking the customer's credit history, and if the credit history is satisfactory, then creating an account. Business rules change more frequently than business objects because they reflect changes in the way the business operates in the real world. It is therefore useful to program business rules in separate modules than business objects.

One can map this object-oriented application design onto a three-tier TP monitor architecture by running business objects as transaction servers and business rules as workflow controller programs. This architecture is efficient because business objects make frequent access to the database that stores the object's state and can be colocated with the object. It is also a flexible structure, since business rules can be changed within workflow controllers without affecting the business objects (i.e., transaction servers) that they call.

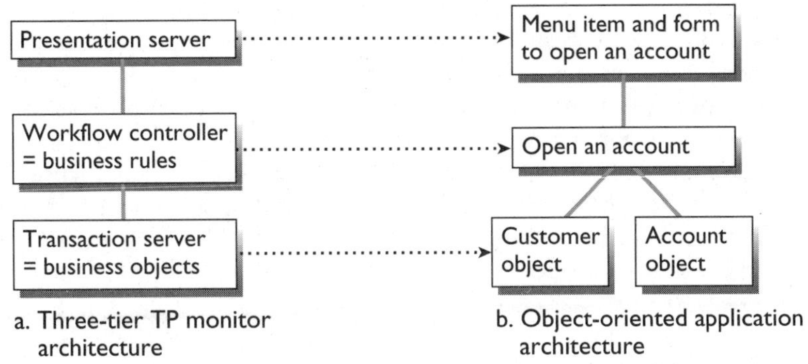

Figure 2.5 **Mapping Object-Oriented Application Architecture to Three-Tier Model** Business objects such as "Customer" and "Account" run in transaction servers, and business rules such as "open an account" run in workflow controllers.

In this chapter we discuss each of the three tiers in turn, looking at both the application programming interface for defining the application's functions, and the system implementation issues of building the underlying component—presentation server, workflow control, or transaction server—that has to support that part of the application.

Simple Requests

To begin with, we'll discuss simple requests. A *simple request* accepts one input message from its input device (a display or special device such as an ATM), executes the transaction, completes the transaction, and sends one message back to the input device. Examples are depositing into a bank account, placing an order, or logging a shipment. Each simple request is completely independent of every other simple request.

A given user interaction may actually require a sequence of related requests. For example, you might want to arrange a trip, which requires reserving airline seats, reserving a car, and reserving a hotel room. You may regard this as one user interaction, even though it may run as three separate requests. We'll look at multirequest interactions in Chapter 4. In this chapter, we'll assume that all requests are simple—one message in and one message out.

2.3 Presentation Server

Presentation Server Layers

The presentation server gathers the input from the user and sends it to the workflow controller as a request message in the TP monitor's standard format. From that point on, the TP monitor only deals with the standard request format. It doesn't need to know any details of the various devices, forms managers, and 4GLs that provide the input to the transaction and interpret the output of the transaction. Only the presentation server deals with that. We call this *presentation independence* because the presentation server makes the rest of the application independent of the presentation software and hardware that's interacting with the user.

The presentation server usually has two layers (see Figure 2.6), one that interacts with the user to gather input and display output, and one that deals with constructing request messages in the TP monitor's format. We'll describe each layer in turn.

Gathering Input

The presentation server generates a request message after gathering the required input from a display device. If the display device is a terminal, a PC, or a workstation, the presentation server generally interacts with the user via menus and forms. The user selects a menu item—perhaps by clicking on an icon or a command button, or highlighting an entry on a pull-down menu—to identify the type of transaction he or she wants to run. After the user selects the menu item, the presentation server generally displays a form in which the user enters the input data needed for this type of request. The presentation server usually performs some data validation on this form input to ensure that the input values make sense. This avoids the delay of executing the request before determining that the input is incorrect.

Application programmers write programs that direct the presentation server's menu management, forms management, and data validation functions. Application programmers generally use a forms manager to define the menus and how to navigate between them, to define the fields of each form and how they are laid out on the screen, and to identify the data validation routine to be called for each field on the form. Early TP monitors had a built-in presentation server to perform these functions, with a language for expressing how to lay out and display forms. In the 1980s, independent forms manager products became popular, which offered a WYSIWYG ("what you see is what you get") forms designer and callout functions to a standard programming language. Today, most developers use an independent 4GL or visual programming product to perform the presentation server aspects of the application.

Forms management software is still used when end user devices are dumb terminals. The forms manager compiles form and menu definitions into an internal representation that the presentation server interprets at runtime (see Figure 2.7). Using this internal representation as a guide, it talks to the display device to gather input being entered on the form, to validate that input, and to generate output to be placed on the form. Usually the presentation server does this in a way that can operate on a variety of display devices, so the programmer is often able to define the menu and forms format just once. For each kind of display device that is hooked up, the forms manager issues the right control signals and messages to tell that kind of device what to do.

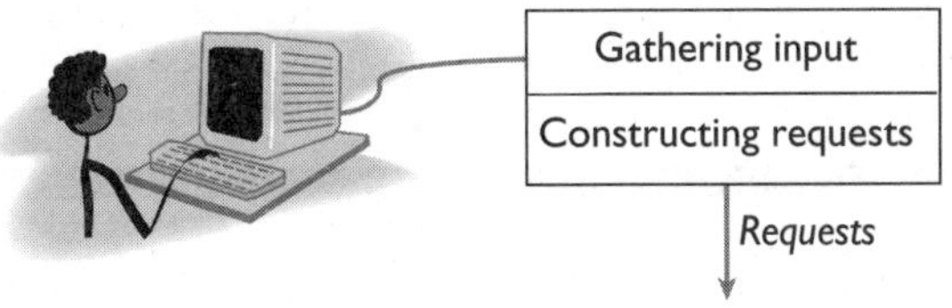

Figure 2.6 Layers of a Presentation Server The presentation server gathers input by communicating with the display, then translates that input into a request message.

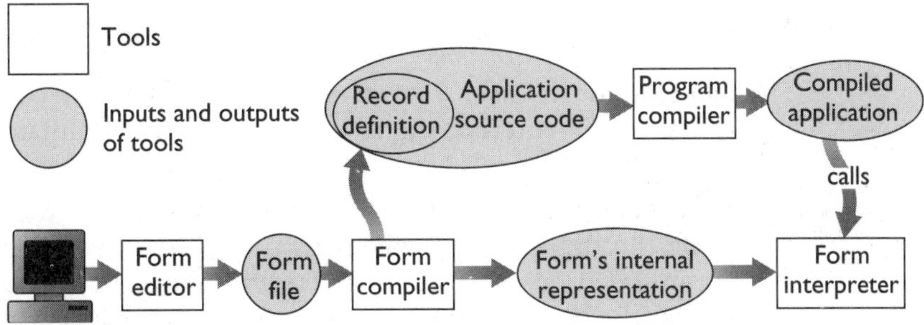

Figure 2.7 Forms Manager Tools To access the form, the compiled application calls the form interpreter, which uses the form's internal representation that was produced by the form compiler.

The forms software also usually generates a record definition that corresponds to the input/output fields within the form. This record definition can be included in the transaction program that processes the form, which saves programmers from having to figure out that format on their own.

Data validation is best done with a cached copy of valid data values that are compared to values that the user enters in the form. By contrast, it is usually a bad idea to compare the entered values directly with data in the database because the database accesses necessary to make those comparisons interfere with the execution of update transactions and seriously degrade performance. The cached copy is refreshed from the live database only periodically, so it usually isn't completely accurate. This is satisfactory for fields that don't change frequently, such as department names and product codes, but not for frequently changing fields, such as number of seats available on a flight. The latter fields can only be validated by executing the transaction itself, in the transaction server, which has direct access to the database.

Constructing Requests

Each TP monitor defines its own format for requests. At the moment, there is no standard format for a request message, although in the future we anticipate the widespread adoption of the remote procedure call marshaling mechanism,

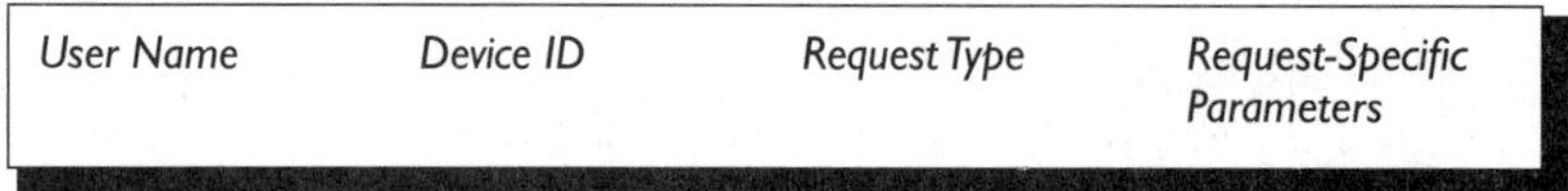

Figure 2.8 Typical Request Format It contains the name of the user entering the request, the user's device, the type of transaction being requested, and parameters to the request.

which is described at length in Chapter 3. Today, different monitors generally use different message formats, but there's certain information that each usually includes (see Figure 2.8):

- The identifier of the user, that is, the name of the user who is sitting at the device and is entering the request (assuming a human is doing this work).
- A device identifier, generally the network address of the device that's producing the input. The device identifier is generally mapped through the communications system to a certain device type. The TP monitor knows that the device connected at a certain address is of a certain type: a PC running a certain operating system, running a certain communication protocol, and so on.
- A request type, which is the identifier of the type of transaction that the request is asking to execute.
- Each request type generally requires a certain number of parameters as input. The rest of the message contains those request-specific parameters, which are different for each type of request.

After the presentation server has gathered the user's input, it must create a request message to send to the workflow controller. When a forms manager is tightly integrated with the TP monitor's presentation server, the request may be constructed by the presentation server with little application programming. By setting certain properties of the menu item and by tagging forms fields with the names of parameters required by the transaction, the application programmer can give the presentation server what it needs to translate that menu item and form into a transaction request.

When using a forms manager that isn't tightly integrated with the presentation server, the application programmer needs to issue calls to the presentation server layer that constructs the request, which we call the *request constructor* (there's no industry standard term for this). This is the common case with client/server 4GLs and with forms managers designed to interact with specialized devices, such as bar code readers, credit card authorization terminals, cash registers, gas pumps, robots, ATMs, and so on.

The interface to the request constructor is a simple Send-request and Receive-reply. The parameters to Send-request are the fields required by the request format and the input data. If the presentation server is allowed to have many requests outstanding, then Send-request returns a request identifier, which the presentation server can later use to identify the subsequent reply (to match it with the request). Receive-reply returns the results of running the request, in the TP monitor's reply format (analogous to the request format), in some cases including system control information for exception handling and transaction coordination. There are often functions to move very large parameters (e.g., a long input stream from a communication device or a large report to be displayed as output).

The presentation server may offer a cancel function, which attempts to kill the request before it actually executes. This operation cannot be guaranteed to succeed. If the request has already executed and committed at the time the cancel operation is received by the system, it's too late because once a transaction is committed, its results are permanent (except by running a compensating transaction).

Many TP monitors have implemented a request constructor layer that includes much communication machinery to actually move the request messages between the presentation server and workflow controller. Today, remote procedure call is becoming a ubiquitous system mechanism for such communication and greatly simplifies the implementation of the request constructor. We discuss the internals of remote procedure call mechanisms in some detail in the next chapter.

Authentication

Another function performed by the presentation server is *authentication,* the activity of determining the identity of the user and of the display device he or she is using to interact with the system. Authentication is usually done using a password entered by the user or by the system manager when the device is connected to the application. Whether or not authentication is done on the client system, a TP monitor usually requires an additional level of authentication on a server, since it doesn't entirely trust client authentication. As distributed computing architectures mature, robust and trustworthy client authentication schemes will become more common, allowing TP monitors to forgo authentication on the server.

Whenever the presentation server sends a request message to the workflow controller component of the TP monitor, the authenticated user name and device identifier is included, which proves to the rest of the TP monitor that the message came from a certain person operating a certain device, and allows authentication to be performed by the server (see Figure 2.9).

An additional level of security can be provided if the wire or network that connects the device to the system is encrypted, which reduces the threat of wiretapping. A good encryption algorithm makes it unlikely that a wiretapper would be able either to decrypt messages or to spoof the system by trying to convince the system that it's actually a qualified user from a qualified device.

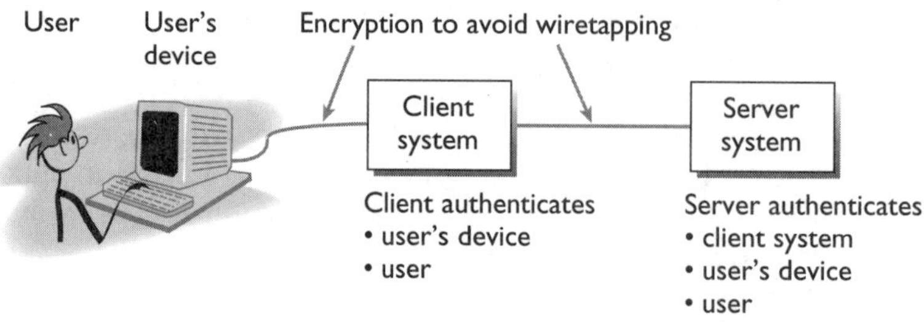

Figure 2.9 Authentication and Security Clients and servers authenticate the identity of users and devices that communicate with them. Additional security is provided by encrypting messages.

In many TP applications, it's quite important to know that a message arrived from a particular device, not just from any device at which a particular user logged in. This is called *geographic entitlement* because one is entitled to provide input based on one's geographic location. An example would be in the stock trading room of a brokerage house. When the traders show up for work, they have to display their identification cards to a guard before entering the trading room. They then sit down at their display devices and provide passwords to prove to the TP monitor that they are who they say they are. For this extra level of security to work, the system must know that the request actually came from a device in the secured trading room. If someone dials in from some other location, device authentication will tell the system which device entered the request, so the TP monitor can determine that the device is not entitled to enter requests, even if that person happens to know the password of an authorized user.

Specifying the security of the TP system and monitoring the presentation server's behavior creates requirements for a variety of system management functions within the presentation server. The presentation server has to allow a system manager to define information needed to authenticate devices and users, such as passwords and valid network addresses. For example, the presentation server might allow the system manager to set up a default password that the device owner or the user can change after logging in. The system manager may also specify that a user is only allowed to enter certain types of requests at certain times of day. Since there may be many users of the system, the complexity of this specification can be reduced by introducing the concept of *role* and assigning a role to each user. Then the system manager only needs to specify allowable requests and usage times for each role, rather than for each user.

Communication

The TP monitor translates various communication functions of the underlying system into more abstract, easier-to-understand messages. For example, it may translate the names of the lines between devices in the system into logical device names. This allows programmers to send messages to semantically meaningful device names, such as ATM_3 or $BranchServer_4$. It also enables system management functions to provide more meaningful reports, such as "ATM_3 in the Main Street branch isn't responding" instead of "device 14.3 on system 27 isn't responding." System parameters that control these devices can similarly be presented in a more abstract way, using logical names of recognizable real-world concepts, rather than low-level system identifiers that are much harder to interpret.

Logging

Some presentation servers are able to keep a record of all the work going on at the front end by logging messages. Sometimes the display devices themselves do this—for example, many ATMs have a logging device built right into the machine that monitors all of the message traffic going in and out. But for less functional devices, the presentation server may do the logging itself and provide an interface where system managers can go back and look at that log to reconcile any errors that might appear later on. We discuss some of those problems of messages and what might be done with that log in Section 4.6 on multitransaction requests.

2.4 Workflow Control

Each request contains a request type field, as we described. The main purpose of workflow control is to map that request type into the identifiers of the transaction server programs that can perform the request and to send the request message to one of those transaction servers so it will execute. If the transaction produces output, workflow control is responsible for routing the response back to the presentation server that sent the request. Usually the workflow control layer brackets the transaction; that is, it issues the Start, Commit, and Abort operations. And within the transaction, there may be calls to one or more transaction servers.

First we'll discuss the main system function of workflow control—routing. Then we'll talk about aspects of the programming interface for specifying workflow control—workflow logic, transaction bracketing, and exception handling.

Routing

Routing is the function of sending a request to a transaction server that can process it. Routing involves mapping request types to server identifiers and then sending the message on its way.

Directory Services

The routing function requires a place to store the map from symbolic request type names into server identifiers. This map is usually supported by a directory (or name) service, which is a specialized kind of database system that is used to store and retrieve entries that map names into server identifiers.

Mapping request type names into server identifiers has to be a dynamic function because the TP monitor has to support periodic reconfiguration. For example, if a server on one system fails, and the system manager recreates that server on another system, the mapping from request type names to server identifiers needs to be updated to reflect the new location of the server. The system manager may also want to move servers around to better balance the load across servers, for example, based on changing input patterns.

If a networkwide directory server is available, then it can be used to store request types and server identifiers, and the workflow controller retrieves this information when needed. The directory server is responsible for making its information available to systems throughout the network (including all workflow controllers). It does this by replicating its contents on many servers. For good performance, it provides a client layer that caches recently accessed information.

If a networkwide directory server is not available or cannot be counted upon, then the TP monitor has to implement it itself. To do this, it usually maintains a central copy of the type-to-server mapping, and each system keeps a cached copy that is periodically refreshed. This arrangement gives fast access to the cached mapping during normal operation. When a reconfiguration requires that the central copy be updated, the central copy must notify the other systems to refresh their cache.

The activity of mapping symbolic request type names into server identifiers is part of the work done by an object request broker (ORB), as in the Object Management Group's (OMG's) Common Object Request Broker Architecture (CORBA). The CORBA standard describes interfaces that help support this mapping but do not mandate a particular mechanism (such as a directory server) to implement it. If this type of mechanism were universally available in all distributed operating systems, then it could be used in place of TP monitor-specific mechanisms.

Parameter-Based Routing

Sometimes a given transaction server has so much work to do that it needs to be partitioned into independent servers. One convenient way to partition a server is to have different copies of the server handle different ranges of input parameters. For a debit-credit application dealing with retail banking, for example, you might split up the server into five servers, each of which handles a range of account numbers (see Figure 2.10). The database that supports each of these servers can be local to the system that supports those account numbers. So the first group of account numbers is stored on the same computer as the transaction server that supports those account numbers, and so on.

When the system is organized in this way, the workflow controller has to route each request to the correct server based not only on the identifier of the request type, but also on one or more of the input parameters. In the example, it would be the account number. This is called *parameter-based routing.*

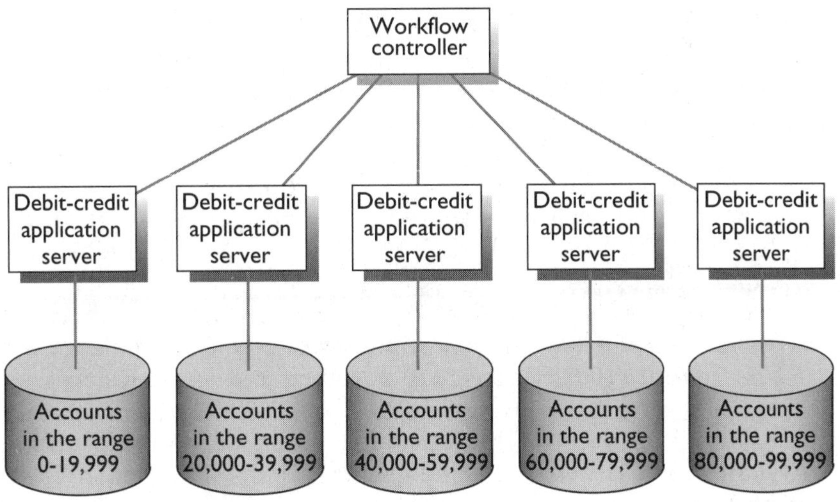

Figure 2.10 **Parameter-Based Routing** Workflow controller calls the right server based on the account number parameter in the request.

Although most systems support it, not all do. And the level of support varies, with the more sophisticated products providing more flexible partitioning, more automated routing, and more dynamic reconfiguration of the partitions.

Sessions and Security

Communications sessions are needed to cache state that is shared by the communicating parties. A session is created between two parties by exchanging messages that contain the state to be shared. The session state usually includes addressing information, to avoid costly lookups every time a message is sent. It may also include security information, so each party knows that the other one is authorized to be sending it messages, thereby avoiding some security checks on each message.

Even when sessions include some security state, per-message security checking is often needed in the workflow controller. A user may only have privileges for certain request types. Therefore, the workflow controller has to look at the request type and user identifier to determine if the user is authorized to make the request.

Some security checking can be eliminated in the transaction server if the workflow controller is treated as a trusted client. That is, if the transaction servers can trust workflow controllers only to send authorized requests, then they don't need another level of authorization checking on every call. Similarly, a database system may treat its transaction servers as trusted clients. There are significant performance gains to be had by avoiding these layers of security checks. However, these layers of checking are sometimes unavoidable to cover security holes that could lead to unauthorized access.

Minimizing Communications Sessions

Another function of workflow control is to reduce the number of communications sessions by providing a routing layer in between the clients (the presentation servers) that are the sources of the requests and the transaction servers where the requests actually execute.

In a two-tier architecture, if there are many presentation servers, it's too expensive for each presentation server to connect to all of the transaction servers. If each PC has a presentation server, there could be hundreds of thousands of presentation servers all connecting to the same set of transaction servers. This can result in a *polynomial explosion* in the number of sessions. For example, if each presentation server connects to all transaction servers, and there are 100,000 presentation servers and 500 transaction servers, each of the 500 transaction servers would have 100,000 communications sessions, resulting in 50,000,000 sessions overall (see Figure 2.11). Each session consumes some main memory and requires some setup time. When there are too many sessions, this session overhead can be troublesome.

Inserting a routing layer between the presentation servers and the transaction servers can greatly reduce the number of sessions and thereby solve the problem. This routing layer corresponds to instances of the workflow control function. Each router or workflow controller connects to a subset of the presentation servers and to all of the transaction servers. Each of the request managers connected to that router can send messages to all of the transaction servers by passing requests through the router (see Figure 2.12).

Now say you have 10 routers (workflow controllers) between the presentation servers and the transaction servers, and each presentation server is connected to one router. Each of the 10 routers would have 1000 sessions to their presentation servers and 500 sessions to all of the transaction servers, resulting in 5000 sessions with the transaction servers, 10,000 sessions with the presentation servers, or 15,000 sessions overall—a huge reduction from the 50,000,000 sessions required without the routing layer. This reduction in communications sessions is a major scalability benefit of TP monitors over two-tier client/server systems.

Grouping presentation servers by workflow controller is often based on geographical considerations. For example, all of the presentation servers on a given local area network might be serviced by the same workflow controller. More complex groupings may be needed for fault tolerance reasons. For example, the ATMs at a bank branch may be split across two workflow controllers over two separate communication lines, so the failure of one workflow controller still leaves half of the ATMs operating.

Workflow Logic

A request may require the execution of many transaction server programs, and possibly of many transactions. The program that decides which transaction servers to call, and in which order, is the application-specific part of a workflow controller—it's the part that controls the flow of work.

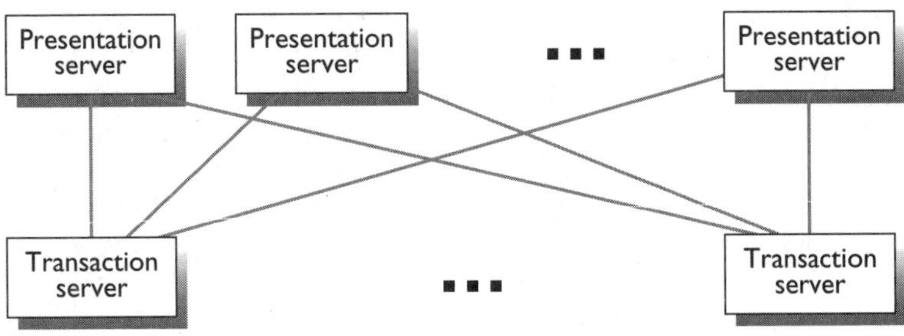

Figure 2.11 **Polynomial Explosion in Two-Tier Model** If there are p presentation servers and t transaction servers, then there are $p \times t$ sessions.

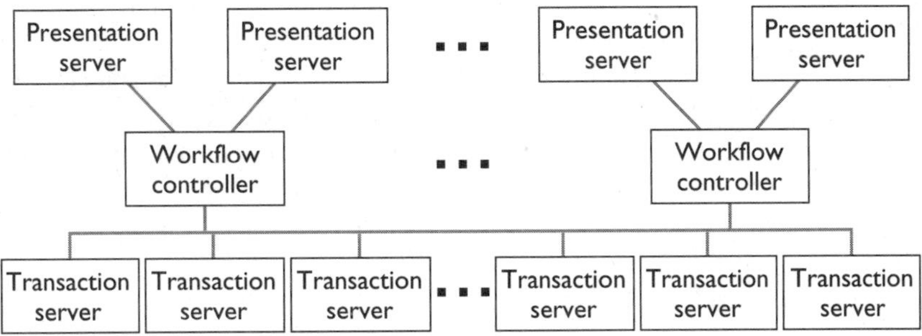

Figure 2.12 **Multilevel Routing** By introducing workflow controllers in between presentation servers and transaction servers, the overall number of sessions is greatly reduced, compared to the two-tier model of Figure 2.11.

On the face of it, there's nothing special about this application program. It simply accepts calls in the form of requests and calls subroutines (transaction servers) to do most of its work. For requests that execute as a single transaction, the application really is quite simple. When multiple transactions are required to process the request, there are complications, but we'll defer those until Chapter 4.

Some TP monitors support a special programming language in which to express the workflow logic. For example, one such language is Digital's task definition language (TDL) used in ACMS or the X/Open structured transaction definition language (STDL) implemented in ACMSxp. Tandem has a language called SCREEN COBOL in their Pathway/TS TP monitor. Some TP monitors simply include a library of function calls that can be issued from a program expressed in any language; for example, BEA Systems' TUXEDO and AT&T/NCR's TOP END TP monitors work this way. Some TP monitors may have no language at all; the mapping of request names into transaction server names may be specified simply by putting entries in a table or definition file.

In TP monitors that don't have a special workflow control language, the same language is used both for workflow control and transaction server functions. To get the benefits of a separate workflow control function, it's necessary to write the application so it has a root transaction server that performs the workflow control function independently of the functions of any transaction server. This preserves the three-tier application model, so that workflow control programs, which represent business rules, can be modified independently of business objects, which execute in transaction servers. It also makes it easier to port the application to a system that does have a specialized workflow language, since the workflow control logic, which would need to be rewritten, is modularized.

One distinguishing feature of languages for expressing workflow is whether they support parallelism. For example, consider an application program that automatically pays credit card bills out of a checking account. You might want to execute the credit card payment server in parallel with the debit checking account server, which in principle will respond to the user more quickly than executing the servers sequentially. If transaction servers are executing on different machines, the system is already partitioned nicely to benefit from this concurrency. Such concurrency is supported in STDL and in Transarc's Encina, but not in many other monitors.

Transaction Bracketing

The workflow controller generally brackets the transaction before it actually calls the program to do the work for the request—that is, it issues a Start operation to begin a transaction before it calls any transaction server programs. After all of the transaction servers that execute on behalf of the request have returned, it issues a Commit operation to indicate that the transaction is done and should be committed.

Request Message Integrity

One major complication related to transaction bracketing is ensuring the integrity of each transaction's request message (see Figure 2.13). If a transaction aborts, its request may be lost, making it impossible to reexecute the transaction, which is very undesirable. The user will never hear about the result of such a lost request—possibly not even receive an error report that the request failed to execute.

To avoid lost requests, the operation that gets a request as input (say, get-input-request) should execute within the transaction that performs the request. Usually, it's the first operation executed by the transaction. The system should make the get-input-request operation recoverable. That is, if the transaction aborts, then the get-input-request operation is undone, just like any other recoverable transaction operation, so the request message is restored and will cause another transaction to execute, as desired.

```
// Example A
Get-input-request;
Start;
  . . .
Commit;
```

```
// Example B
Start;
  Get-input-request;
  . . .
Commit;
```

Figure 2.13 **Ensuring the Integrity of Requests** In Example A, the get-input-request operation executes before the transaction, so if the transaction aborts, the request is lost. In Example B, get-input-request executes within the transaction, so if the transaction aborts, the get-input-request operation is undone and the request is restored.

```
void workflowController:
    { Start;
      Get-input-request (RequestMsg* req);
      . . .
    }
```

a. Pull model

```
void workflowController (RequestMsg* req);
    { Start;
      . . .
    }
```

b. Push model

Figure 2.14 **The Pull vs. Push Models** In the pull model, the workflow controller calls the presentation server to get an input request. In the push model, the workflow controller receives a call containing an input request from the presentation server.

The explicit get-input-request operation works well in a "pull model," where the program waits until a presentation server has an input request to offer (see Figure 2.14a). This is common practice with dumb display devices, which was the usual situation before the advent of PCs.

Client/server computing, with PCs as the display devices, has made the "push model" popular, where the presentation server on the client *calls* the program in the workflow controller (see Figure 2.14b). In this case, the operation that "catches" the client's call is the invocation of the called procedure. To avoid the message integrity problem, this "catch-the-client's-call" operation must be made explicit, so it can be undone if the transaction aborts. For example, in the STDL language, each procedure starts with a statement that explicitly "accepts" the input parameters and is undone if the transaction aborts. Some monitors finesse this problem. If the transaction aborts, they do not undo the implicit get-input-request operation in the catch-the-client's-call operation. In this case, it is up to the caller to decide what to do.

The details of how to recover a request if the transaction aborts are sufficiently complex that we devote an entire chapter to them, Chapter 4, and therefore do not discuss them further here.

Chained and Unchained Transactions

Some workflow controllers call the Start and Commit operations implicitly. In other words, the application programmer only needs to specify which data access programs in the transaction servers are called by the workflow controller, and the workflow controller automatically issues a Start before it calls the transaction servers and automatically issues a Commit or Abort when the transaction servers return. When the TP monitor language explicitly specifies the bracket of the transaction there are two ways to do this, called the chained and unchained programming models.

In the *chained* programming model, the program is *always* executing inside the body of a transaction. Rather than specifying where the transaction starts and commits, one simply specifies the boundary between each pair of transactions. This "boundary operation" commits one transaction and immediately starts another transaction, thereby ensuring that the program is always executing a transaction. The CICS verb called *Syncpoint* works in this way. In the STDL language, the program is always executing inside of a transaction. When you finish one you always start another.

The alternative is an *unchained* model, where after you finish one transaction, you need not start the execution of another transaction right away. In other words, you can say Commit, execute some more instructions, and then later say Start.

On the face of it, the unchained model sounds more flexible, since there may be times when you would want to do work outside of a transaction. However, in fact there's really very little purpose in allowing any of the application code to run outside of a transaction. If the code is accessing any shared data or other shared resources, then it's bad to do it outside of a transaction, since the updates will not be linked to the commit or the abort of a transaction, which is usually not what the user intends. For other kinds of operations, well, they're not affected by a transaction one way or another, so it really doesn't matter whether they're in the transaction or not. So the unchained model simply gives the programmer the opportunity to make a mistake by accidentally leaving statements that access shared data outside of a transaction.

The chained model is offered by most TP monitors, although they also typically offer an unchained model option for easy access to nonrecoverable data. In systems where a transaction has significant overhead even if it doesn't access recoverable data, the unchained model offers an opportunity to avoid this overhead.

Exception Handling

Transaction Exceptions

Since the workflow control part of the application specifies the boundaries of the transaction, it must also say what to do if the transaction fails and therefore aborts. For example, suppose the program divides by zero, or one of the underlying database systems deadlocks and aborts the transaction. The result would be an *unsolicited abort*—one that the application did not cause directly by calling the Abort operation. Alternatively, the whole computer system could go down. For example, the operating system might crash, in which case all of the transactions that were running at the time of the crash would be affected. Thus, workflow control must provide error handling for two types of exceptions—transaction failures and system failures.

For each type of exception, the application should specify an *exception handler,* a program that executes either when the transaction fails or after the system recovers from the error. To write an exception handler, we need to know exactly what state information is available to the exception handler, that is, the reason for the error and what state was lost because of the error. There are also issues of how the exception handler is called and what transaction it is running.

Information about the cause of the abort should be available to the exception handler, usually as a status variable that the exception handler can read. If the abort was caused by the execution of a program statement, then the program needs to know both the exception that caused the statement to malfunction and also the reason for the abort—they might not be the same. For example, it's possible that there was some error in the assignment statement due to an overflow in some variable, but the real reason for the abort was a database system deadlock. The exception handler must be able to tell the difference between these two kinds of exceptions.

When a transaction fails (i.e., aborts), all of the resources it accessed are restored to the state they had before the transaction started. This is what an abort means, undo all of the transaction's effects. Nonrecoverable resources—such as a local variable in the application program, or a communications message sent to another program—are completely unaffected by the abort. In other words, actions on nonrecoverable resources are not undone as a result of the abort.

It's generally best if the program is automatically caused to branch to an exception handler. Otherwise the application program needs an explicit test, such as an IF statement, after each and every statement, which checks the status returned by the previous statement and calls the appropriate exception handler in the event of a transaction abort.

In the chained model, the exception handler is automatically part of a new transaction because the previous transaction aborted and, by definition, the chained model is always executing inside of some transaction. In the nonchained model, the exception handler is responsible for demarcating the transaction. It *could* execute the handler code outside of a transaction, although as we said earlier this is usually undesirable. For example, the X/Open STDL language automatically branches to an exception handler on transaction failure and starts a special transaction.

If the whole system goes down, all of main memory is generally lost, which means that all of the transactions that were active at the time of the failure abort. Therefore, any state information that will be needed by an exception handler must be saved into a database or some other stable storage area, so it will be available to the exception handler at the time of recovery. Notice that the state of the application program is also lost, that is, the instruction counter that points to the instruction that was executing at the time of the failure. So at recovery time the system doesn't really know what instruction in the program the transaction was executing at the time of the failure. Therefore, it generally has to run an exception handler that applies to the transaction as a whole.

Savepoints

If the transaction periodically saves its state, at recovery time the exception handler can restore that state, instead of undoing all of the transaction's effects. This idea leads to an abstraction called savepoints.

A *savepoint* is a point in a program where the application saves all of its state, generally by issuing a *savepoint operation*. The savepoint operation tells the database system and other resource managers to mark this point in their execution, so they can return their resources to this state later on if asked to do so. This is useful for handling exceptions that only require undoing part of the work of the transaction, as in Figure 2.15.

A savepoint can be used to handle broken input requests. Suppose a transaction issues a savepoint operation immediately after receiving an input request, as in the program `Application` in Figure 2.16. If the system needs to spontaneously abort the transaction, it need not actually abort, but instead roll back the transaction to its first savepoint, as in `ExceptionHandlerForApplication` in Figure 2.16. This undoes all of the transaction's updates to shared resources, but it leaves the exception handler with the opportunity to generate a diagnostic and then commit the transaction. This is useful if the transaction "aborted" because there was incorrect data in the request. If the whole transaction had aborted, then the get-input-request operation would be undone, which implies that the request will be reexecuted. Since the request was incorrect, it is better to generate the diagnostic and commit. Indeed, it may be essential to avoid having the request reexecute incorrectly over and over, forever.

Some database systems support the savepoint feature. Since the SQL standard requires that each SQL operation be atomic with respect to failure, the database system does its own internal savepoint before executing each SQL update operation. That way, if the SQL operation fails, it can return to its state before executing that operation. If the database system is supporting savepoints anyway, only modest additional work is needed make savepoints available to applications.

```
void Application
     { Start;
       do some work;
       . . .
       Savepoint ("A");
       do some more work;
       . . .
       if (error)
          { Restore("A");
             take corrective action;
             Commit
          };
       else Commit;
     }
```

Figure 2.15 Using Savepoints The program saves its state at savepoint "A" and can restore it later if there's an error.

```
void Application
     { Start;
       get-input-request;
       Savepoint ("B");
       do some more work;
       Commit;
     }
```

```
void ExceptionHandlerForApplication
     { Restore ("B");
       generate diagnostic;
       Commit;
     }
```

Figure 2.16 Using Savepoints for Broken Requests The application's savepoint after getting the request enables its exception handler to generate a diagnostic and then commit. If the transaction were to abort, the get-input-request would be undone, so the broken request would be reexecuted.

In general, savepoints seem like a good idea, especially for transactions that execute for a long time, so that not all of their work is lost in the event of a failure. Although it's available in some systems, at the time of this writing, it's a feature that reportedly is not widely used, perhaps because application designers find it more intuitive and useful to use request queuing features, which are described in Chapter 4.

Persistent Savepoints

A *persistent savepoint* is a savepoint where the state of the transaction's resources is made stable (that is, put on disk where it won't be lost in the event of a system failure), and enough control state is saved to stable storage so that on recovery the application can pick up from this point in its execution.

Notice that a persistent savepoint is not a commit. It's possible that after issuing a savepoint the transaction subsequently aborts. A persistent savepoint offers the durability property of transactions without the atomicity property.

If the system should fail and subsequently recover, it can restart any transaction at the point at which it issued its last persistent savepoint operation. It doesn't have to run an exception handler because the transaction has its state and it can simply pick up from where it left off.

Persistent savepoints are tricky to implement efficiently, since they require that a consistent snapshot of control and data state be saved in stable storage. For this reason, it is not widely supported by TP monitors or database systems.

2.5 Transaction Servers

A *transaction server* is the application program that does the real work of running the request. It can be a self-contained program, or it might call other programs to do its work. Those other programs might execute on the same system as the transaction server or on a remote system, in which case a communications message is required to go from the caller to the callee.

For application portability, it's desirable that the transaction servers be written using a standard programming language such as C, C++, or COBOL, and that they access databases using standard data manipulation languages such as SQL or C-ISAM. This ensures that the transaction server part of the application can be ported to different TP monitors.

There is very little to say about transaction servers. In most respects, they are ordinary data access programs that execute under the control of the TP monitor. However, in two respects transaction servers are not ordinary data access programs—they need to scale to high request rates and they need to support transaction-based communications. This leads to two technical issues in the design of a transaction server interface and the underlying mechanisms that support it:

- The way that transaction server programs are mapped onto operating system processes
- How transaction servers communicate—how messages are sent between these programs, especially in the context of a transaction

Both of these issues apply to all three tiers of the TP monitor, not just to transaction servers, so we will treat them as separate topics. We discuss operating system process issues in the next section.

Communications in the context of a transaction is special for two related reasons. First, the transaction's context needs to be propagated along with the call. That is, if you start a transaction in one process, such as a workflow controller, and then send a message to another process, such as a transaction server, the transaction server needs to be told that it is operating in the same transaction as its caller. Second, all of the processes that were involved in the transaction have to be told when the transaction commits or aborts. This is only possible if the set of participants in the transaction is tracked while it executes. A lot of the work of a TP monitor is devoted to these activities.

They are sufficiently complex that we'll devote the entire next chapter to them (Chapter 3 on TP communications), as well as part of Chapter 9 on two-phase commit.

2.6 Operating System Processes

Why We Need Threads

All of the programs in a TP monitor—the presentation server, the workflow controller, and the transaction server—have to execute in some kind of processor context. That is, they need to access memory through an address space, and they need a place to save the processor's registers. The latter is generally called a *control thread*. The combination of an address space and control thread (or threads) is a *process*.

The whole architecture of a TP monitor is affected by which components share an address space, whether that address space has one thread or multiple threads executing, and whether there are hardware or operating system mechanisms to protect the application's and TP monitor's memory accesses from each other. For example, traditional time-sharing systems, such as UNIX systems, are structured so that each display device has its own process, each process has exactly one thread executing, and all programs that run on behalf of that display device execute in that one process. As we'll see, TP monitors don't work this way.

In the time-sharing model one could implement a TP monitor by combining all three monitor functions—the presentation server, the workflow controller, and the transaction servers—into one big sequential program, essentially the one shown in Figure 2.1. The monitor would simply be a sequential program that consists of an infinite loop that gets an input message from a display device, starts a transaction, calls the appropriate transaction server program to run the request, commits or aborts that transaction, and returns to the top of the loop to do it again. Each display device would be connected to a process that runs this program, thereby executing transactions on behalf of that display.

There are many disadvantages, however, of running in this model. The most important is that there are just too many processes. A system with tens or hundreds of thousands of display devices would have tens or hundreds of thousands of processes because it would need one process for each display device. Operating systems do not work well with such a large number of processes, for many reasons:

- Some operating system functions sequentially scan lists of processes. If the list is too long, it takes too long to perform these operating system functions.
- There is lots of context switching between these processes, which involves swapping out register values of one process and swapping in those of another process, including invalidating and reloading the processor's

cache memory. This overhead can greatly reduce effective processor speed.

- There's usually a certain amount of memory for each process that has to remain in physical main memory and can't be paged at all. When many processes are running, this high memory load may leave insufficient memory for all active processes. Many processes may have some of their virtual memory out on disk, which has to be paged in when the process's terminal invokes a transaction, adding extra delay.
- Distributing transactions on multiple nodes requires even more processes because each display device needs a process running on every system doing work on behalf of that display.
- It is difficult to control the load on such a system. The only operating system knob you can turn is to reduce the number of active processes. Since each process is associated with a display device, shutting down a process effectively turns off a display—bad news for the person using that display. It would be better to shut down only certain low-priority types of transactions, but this is hard to control because those transaction types are buried in the application. It would require some application assistance to control the load in this way.

Because of all these disadvantages, from a very early stage in the history of TP monitors, vendors started supporting multithreaded processes. A multithreaded process supports many *threads*, each of which is an independent path of execution through the process. All of the threads in the process execute the same program and use the same process memory. But each of them has a save area for register values and private variables (e.g., the process stack). (See Figure 2.17.) Thus, a multithreaded process has many executions of its program running concurrently, one for each of its threads.

Threads save memory, because the process's memory is shared by many threads. It avoids context switching, since a processor can switch between threads without switching address spaces. And it reduces the number of processes, since threads can be used instead of processes and there are many threads per process.

A thread can be used to execute a program on behalf of a display. When the process switches attention between display devices, it switches to a different thread. This reduces the number of processes and the number of context switches.

Initially, threads were dynamically allocated to display devices when the display was actively executing a request. Later, as the cost of processors and memory declined, a thread was statically allocated to each display device.

Implementing Threads

Threads can be implemented by the TP monitor or by the operating system. There are benefits to each approach.

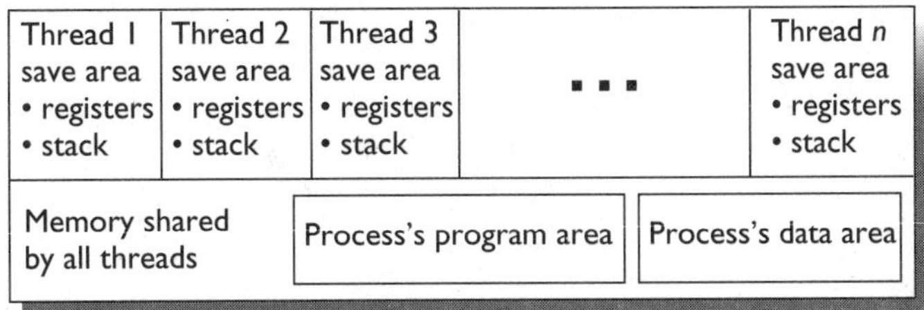

Figure 2.17 Memory Structure of a Multithreaded Process In addition to the usual program and data areas, there is a save area for each thread (instead of one save area for the whole process, as in a single-threaded process).

TP Monitor Threads

If threads are implemented by the TP monitor, then the operating system doesn't know about the threads. It's just running an ordinary process. Basically the TP monitor is fooling the operating system by turning the process's attention to different display devices by itself. However, this may produce interference between these two levels of scheduling. Since the operating system is scheduling processes and the TP monitor is scheduling threads within the process, they may end up working at cross-purposes.

There is one technical difficulty with having the TP monitor implement threads. If the transaction server, executing in a multithreaded process, tries to read data from disk or tries to read a communications message, and the data that it needs is not yet available, then the operating system ordinarily will put the process to sleep. If there's only one thread running, this is the right thing to do—put the process to sleep till it has some work to do. But if there are multiple threads running inside the process, then all of the threads, and therefore all of the displays, end up getting delayed. This is bad, because some of those other displays could do useful work while the first display's I/O operation is in progress.

For this reason, the TP monitor has to trap any of those synchronous I/O operations (generally reads). By trapping those calls, it can avoid putting the process to sleep; instead, it sends an asynchronous message to the disk, database system, or communications system and asks to get a software interrupt back when the operation is completed. After the message is sent, the TP monitor can continue operating by calling another thread that has useful work to do. When the I/O operation that corresponds to the message has finished, it will send a software interrupt to the TP monitor, which then wakes up the thread that was waiting for that result. For example, the mainframe version of IBM's CICS TP monitor has worked this way starting from its earliest implementations. The advantage is multithreading; the disadvantage is that all of the calls to I/O operations have to be intercepted by the TP monitor.

Digital's ACMS TP monitor uses multithreading in its presentation server and its workflow controller functions, as does Tandem's Pathway/TS TP monitor. They limit the multithreading capability to the presentation and workflow control functions and use languages that only offer control flow and communications functions. Indeed, this was a main reason for introducing separate workflow languages. The monitor does not have to intercept synchronous database operations because there aren't any. Database operations are only issued by transaction servers.

Operating System Threads

If the operating system supports multithreading, it keeps track of all the threads on its own. For example, Windows NT and many modern UNIX operating systems support this. When a thread issues a synchronous I/O operation, the operating system puts that *thread* to sleep. But it recognizes when there are other active threads that it can execute, and executes another thread that's ready to run (in that process), rather than putting the whole process to sleep. This avoids unnecessary context switching. Another benefit of operating system multithreading is that if the process is running on a shared-memory (i.e., symmetric) multiprocessor (SMP), it can assign the threads of the same process to different processors in the machine and thereby get parallelism between the threads of the process.

A difficulty of operating system multithreading, however, is performance overhead. Since it is the operating system that is involved in switching threads, this involves system calls. These are generally more expensive than thread operations executed at the user level, which is where the TP monitor is operating.

There is another disadvantage of multithreading, which is a problem whether it is implemented by the TP monitor or operating system. Since there are multiple threads running inside the same process, there's little or no memory protection between them. An error in the execution of one thread could potentially damage memory for the entire process, thereby causing all of the threads to malfunction. This could also lead to a security leak if one thread reads memory that is private to another thread. With operating system threads, this problem can be somewhat mitigated by providing a protected memory area for special subsystems, such as TP monitor functions, which can be protected from user level code, as is done in Windows NT.

In summary, multithreading offers significant efficiency improvements, but must be used carefully to avoid blocking during disk I/O operations, interference between TP monitor and operating system scheduling, performance overhead in thread context switching, and corrupting unprotected memory. Overall, for most applications, operating system multithreading is superior to TP monitor multithreading, since it avoids the first two of these problems and can benefit from SMP configurations.

Mapping Servers to Processes

Whether processes are single-threaded or multithreaded, there is the question of how to map presentation servers, workflow controllers, and transaction servers into processes. One natural way is to have each of the three functions run in a separate kind of process:

- The presentation server is run in a separate process, generally either on the desktop in a workstation or PC, or on LAN servers that are close to the display devices.
- Workflow controllers run in separate processes and communicate with the presentation servers via messages. They can run on LAN servers or on back-end systems.
- Transaction servers are distributed into processes, generally on back-end systems colocated with the data that they most frequently access. They communicate with workflow controllers and each other via messages.

Most modern TP monitors are structured in this three-tier architecture to get the full benefit of a client/server environment. That is, they run their presentation server and sometimes their workflow control functions close to the client and the transaction server functions close to the database server. This has the following benefits:

- Flexible distribution—One can move functions around in the distributed system because the different functions are already separated into independent processes that communicate by exchanging messages. Whether the messages are exchanged between processes that are nearby or far apart makes no functional difference to the software.
- Flexible configuration—One can locate the processes to optimize performance, availability, manageability, and so on.
- Flexible control—It offers independent control of the three functions. One can control the relative speeds of transaction servers by varying the number of threads in those servers without affecting the presentation server or workflow control functions, which are running in separate processes.
- Better memory protection—Since the different functions are running in different processes, errors in one function cannot corrupt the memory of other functions.

The main disadvantage of this kind of architecture is its impact on performance. The programs in the TP monitor and the application programs that run in those processes are communicating via messages instead of local procedure calls. A local procedure call between two programs in the same process is on the order of 50 machine language instructions; sending a message from a program in one process to a program in another process costs 1500–15,000 machine language instructions, depending on the system. Since even the simplest transaction requires a round-trip between presentation server and workflow controller and between workflow controller and transaction server, there's quite a lot of message overhead in this approach.

Server Classes

A good alternative to multithreading processes is to use a set of processes to emulate a pool of threads. That is, instead of having one multithreaded process, the system uses a set of single-threaded processes, all of which are running the same program (see Figure 2.18). This is often called a *server class* since this technique is most often used for transaction servers. In this case, for each transaction server program, there is a set of server processes that runs it.

If a transaction server is implemented by a server class, and the workflow control function calls a transaction server, it actually calls one of the processes in the server class. Any available process in the server class can handle the request.

Server classes have a number of nice features. Most of them stem from the fact that each process in the server class is an ordinary single-threaded process and therefore avoids the disadvantages of multithreading:

- Since the process is single-threaded, there's no harm in putting it to sleep if it blocked during a synchronous I/O operation. Therefore, there is no need for the TP monitor to trap synchronous I/O; the normal blocking behavior of the operating system is just fine.
- There's no possible conflict between process and thread scheduling and no possible memory corruption problems from threads in the same process.
- Processes in a server class fail independently. That is, a server class is largely unaffected by the failure of any individual process in the server class, since other processes continue to run. This is in contrast to a multithreaded process, where the failure of one thread can bring down the whole process if it corrupts the memory of other threads.

For these reasons, and to avoid the expense of implementing multithreading, server classes were quite popular in TP monitors before the advent of multithreaded operating systems, as in Digital's ACMS and Tandem's Pathway/TS TP monitors.

Server classes do require an additional mechanism to dispatch calls to the server class to a particular server process. This problem is how to balance the load across the servers in the server class. The caller could randomize its selection of server, thereby balancing the load across multiple servers, on the average. Or, the processes in the server class could share a queue of unprocessed requests. If a busy process receives a call, it simply adds it to the queue, where another process can pick it up. Or, the server class could have a single process that receives all requests and routes each one to an idle process. This is usually the easiest to implement, but costs an extra context switch, since each call has to invoke the server class's router process before going to a server.

A moment ago we complained that single-threaded processes result in too many processes. Why is it OK for transaction servers? The answer is that the number of transaction servers that are needed is proportional to the number of

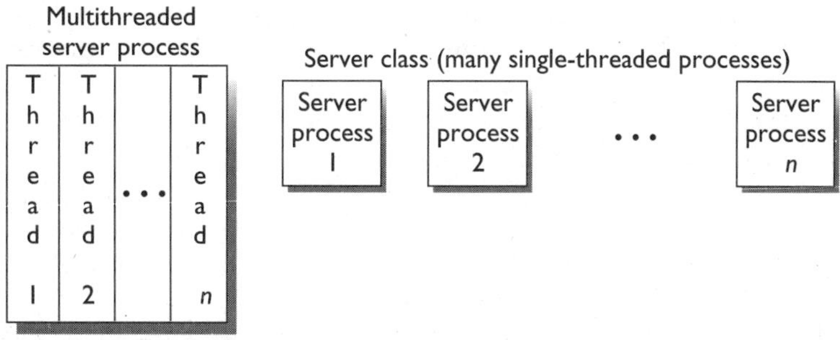

Figure 2.18 **Multithreaded Process vs. Server Class** In both cases, there is one server program and many threads executing it. The difference is whether the threads execute in one process (multithreaded server) or many processes (server class).

executing *transactions*, not proportional to the number of *display devices*. That is, one only needs enough transaction servers to handle requests that are executing at a given moment, which is a much smaller number than the number of active display devices.

Whether transaction servers are multithreaded or use server classes, there is still the need for multithreaded workflow controllers. Otherwise, the system ends up with one workflow controller process for each display device, and we run into the problem of too many processes and too many communications sessions. If the operating system doesn't support multithreading, which is often the reason for using server classes in the first place, then we're back to having the TP monitor do multithreading, but only for workflow controllers. This is why Digital's ACMS and Tandem's Pathway/TS support multithreaded workflow controllers along with server classes.

In an object request broker (ORB) based on the OMG CORBA architecture, a client can call a class of objects. The class could be implemented as a server class or as a multithreaded server. The same issues apply to the ORB's object classes as to transaction servers. Like the mapping of request type names to server identifiers (in the subsection on routing in Section 2.4), if an object class mechanism were universally available in an ORB, then it could be used in place of TP monitor-specific mechanisms (provided the ORB handles the complexities of transactional communication).

2.7 Database Servers vs. TP Monitors

A database server is a database system that offers many of the features of a TP monitor. It is a relational database system that also has a multithreaded server that supports stored procedures. These procedures are written in a general-purpose programming language and can issue SQL requests to the database system, just like a transaction server in a TP monitor. Clients can call stored procedures, much like presentation servers can invoke transaction server programs. And since it's a database system, the database server supports transactions. Since this configuration looks a lot like a TP monitor, it is sometimes called *TP lite*.

It's interesting to compare database servers to TP monitors, to see where these two technologies are similar and different. As shown in Figure 2.19, a TP monitor has a presentation server (which is a client program) that calls an application running in a multithreaded workflow control process talking to a single- or multithreaded transaction server. The transaction server talks to a database system, either locally or remotely.

Most relational database systems today offer this database server structure, including those from Oracle, Sybase, Informix, and Microsoft. So why should one buy a TP monitor if the database system supports most of the facilities that we've been discussing in this chapter? The answer is scalability and features.

Database servers offer a two-tier model—clients talk to multithreaded servers. When a large number of clients need to communicate with a large number of servers, the routing problems that we encountered in Section 2.4 become a serious problem. The solution is to add a middle tier, as offered by a TP monitor. Moreover, as explained in Section 2.2, the three-tier TP monitor architecture is a more natural fit for object-oriented system designs, which consist of business rules that call business objects.

The remaining issues that distinguish TP monitors from database servers are based on detailed features. These feature distinctions are changing with each new product release. What we say here is a snapshot of the current marketplace.

First, with a database server, you have to write your application using stored procedures. Today, these procedures are written in a proprietary language specific to each database system and are not portable across database systems. (This may change if the portable module language of the proposed SQL3 standard becomes widely adopted.) Often the stored procedure language is not as expressive as a general-purpose programming language. For example, some systems don't allow one application to call another; you can only call from the client to the database server. As another example, some languages have a limited set of data types. Others have proprietary data type extensions that can cause compatibility problems when using multiple database systems. In addition, it's another language to learn on top of your standard programming language, although this is a problem that some TP monitors have as well.

The database server offers limited debugging and development tools because it's running in this specialized environment. So you only have the debugging capability offered by this database system's runtime environment, which is often less than what's available in a complete program development environment.

By comparison, TP monitors generally give you a much wider choice of options. They use standard languages such as COBOL, C, or C++ for the transaction servers, they have a more complete set of tools for operating or debugging the program, and they generally use a compiled language that performs better for compute-intensive applications.

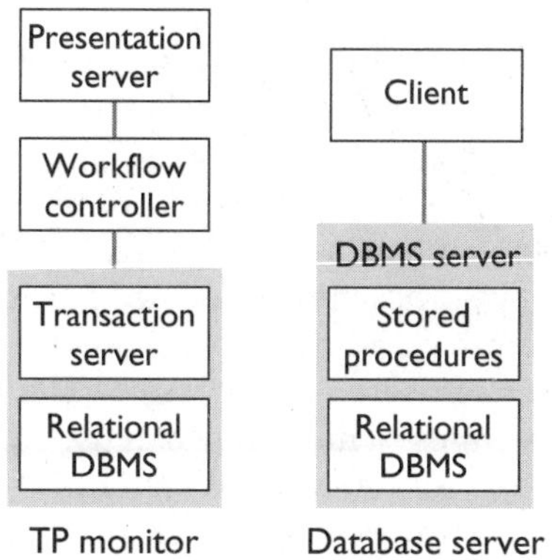

Figure 2.19 TP Monitor and Database Server Configurations The database server architecture does not use the workflow controller layer of the TP monitor.

A second feature difference between the two environments is their support of distributed transactions. Relational database systems generally support distributed transactions only for transactions that access data in that one product. For example, you could distribute an application that accessed several copies of a Sybase server, but you couldn't run a program that accessed a Sybase server in one machine and Oracle in another machine within a distributed transaction. By contrast, a TP monitor's implementation of distributed transactions can cover multiple database system products. In addition, it can cover other specialized kinds of resource managers, such as record-oriented file systems and queue managers.

The advantage you get from using a database server is that the protocols are tuned for the database system and therefore may run faster. But as for distributed transactions, the communication protocols are proprietary for each database product. Moreover, only a request-response communication paradigm is offered. You don't get more general message passing (e.g., peer-to-peer) or queue-based communication (which we'll describe in Chapter 4).

Other missing features in the database server approach are the abstraction of a request and any special features that involve formatting request messages. Request messages are an enabling technology for workflow systems because they represent steps in a multistep workflow. Request messages can carry parameters from one step of the workflow to the next, a capability unavailable in database servers.

In general, a TP monitor offers a richer system management environment than the one supported by a database server. TP monitors offer geographic entitlement. A TP monitor knows about different applications running on different nodes of the system. It can prioritize the applications, do application-based load control, remote name resolution, and application-based security, all of which are hard to do in the database server case because a database server considers the concept of an application to be the same as the concept of a database. In the TP monitor case you can, for example, shut down an application while leaving the database system running. This kind of system management feature is typically missing from a database server.

Although TP monitors have many features that make them desirable compared to database servers, the performance of database servers is catching up. Not long ago, database servers were not at all comparable to TP monitors. Now they are viable alternatives for some environments, particularly small-scale environments where the scalability and interoperability of a TP monitor is not so important and the number of users not too large. The database system vendors are generating huge revenues, which they can use to support their continued development of these client/server types of systems, suggesting that they might eventually catch up to the lower-volume TP monitor products in functionality, and perhaps eventually surpass them. In the short term, the TP monitors have well-established, thriving businesses that are not about to be completely subsumed by the capabilities of database servers, but this is a trend to watch. In the long term, it's really unclear which way it will work out.

2.8 Transactions over the Internet

The main function of a TP monitor is to scale up TP applications to run efficiently on large, distributed systems with many active users submitting requests and many servers processing requests. Today's quintessential example of this scale-up problem is the Internet, which connects tens of millions of clients and servers.

The World Wide Web (WWW) defines the most popular client/server architecture on the Internet. In TP terms, it consists of a presentation server (called a *web browser*) that displays messages expressed in HyperText Markup Language (HTML), and a communications protocol, HyperText Transfer Protocol (http), for moving these messages between web browsers and web servers. A web browser issues a request for an HTML page identified by an address, called a *uniform resource locator* (URL), and the web server for that URL returns the HTML page to the browser.

This architecture is reminiscent of using block-mode terminals, such as the IBM 3270, to access a TP system. A screen at a time is transferred between the terminal and the server, much as HTML pages are transferred between the web browser and web server. Some vendors believe the comparison to block-mode terminals is exact and are offering Internet terminals—a limited-function device that runs a web browser and interacts with the outside world through http.

Although web browsers were initially designed to read text pages in HTML from web servers, people quickly recognized the value of producing more active content. That is, the web page could be constructed on the fly, at the time it is accessed, by reading data from a database and using it to populate certain fields of an HTML page before returning that page to the browser. For example, access to stock price information could return up-to-the-minute information. Such an interaction looks a lot like executing a transaction.

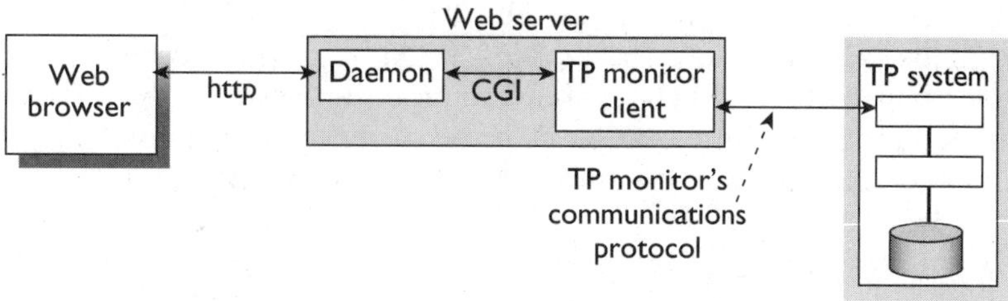

Figure 2.20 Using a Web Browser to Run Transactions The web browser behaves like a presentation server that provides input to the TP client program running in the web server.

Generalizing this scenario only slightly, we could use a web browser to access TP servers. The web browser functions as a presentation server, and the web server functions as either a gateway to the TP system or as a bona fide workflow controller.

Using a TP Monitor for Web Access

To be used as a TP display device, the web browser must be able to offer menu selections (to identify the transaction type to run) and forms (to capture the input parameters to the transaction). Menus can be offered straightforwardly as URLs. Each URL identifies a transaction type. When the user clicks on a URL displayed in an HTML page, the browser sends the URL to the server, which replies with an HTML page that describes the form. The user enters input in the HTML form, which causes another URL to be sent back to the server as input to the transaction. The form fields entered by the user appear as parameters in the URL.

The server is a web server that is communicating with the browser via http (see Figure 2.20). The web server daemon is a dispatcher, which listens for browser requests (URLs) and invokes the requested function. In the simplest case, it just returns the requested page. But it can also function as a gateway between the browser and a TP system. For example, a browser can submit a URL that identifies a TP monitor script. To process the URL, the server daemon calls the script, which in turn acts as a client of the TP system and calls it to execute a transaction. After it receives a reply from the transaction, it formats it in HTML and passes it back to the gateway, which forwards it to the web browser that submitted the request.

The Common Gateway Interface (CGI) was the first protocol commonly offered by web servers for web server daemons to call other applications, such as a TP monitor script. Using CGI, the daemon's call to an application causes a new process to be created to execute the application.

CGI essentially uses the time-sharing model of executing commands—namely, create a process for every call, connect to all the necessary resources (e.g., databases), and run the called program in that process. The approach is simple but expensive, so it has limited scalability. Therefore, newer interfaces have been developed to avoid the obvious inefficiencies. For example, Microsoft's Internet Server API (ISAPI) and Netscape Communication's Netscape Server API (NSAPI) avoid creating a process per call by allowing the called program to execute within the caller's (i.e., daemon's) context. Thus, in Figure 2.20, the daemon and TP monitor client can run in the same process.

Executing the URL request in the daemon's server process is essentially the TP monitor model: a server receives requests (in this case, coded as URLs) and processes them. That is, the web server is functioning as a workflow controller. If the web server system and TP system support a compatible transaction protocol, then the TP monitor client in Figure 2.20 can do all the usual workflow controller functions, such as bracketing the transaction and directly calling TP servers, rather than passing through another routing layer in the TP system. So the transformation of a web system into a TP system is complete: a presentation server (i.e., web browser) sends a request (i.e., URL) to a workflow controller (i.e., web server), which calls a transaction server.

This architecture can be used to run TPC benchmarks. In May 1996, Intergraph Computer Systems produced the first audited TPC-C benchmark using this type of configuration. They connected 1500 PCs to a small Intergraph server, which functioned as the web server, running Microsoft's Windows NT and Internet Information Server. The server was configured to maintain context for each browser and to keep socket connections alive after completion of each request, which is nonstandard behavior for web servers. The web server in turn called a larger Intergraph transaction server, which executed the transactions against a locally connected SQL server database. The resulting performance was highly competitive.

Using a TP monitor in this way to support transactions on the World Wide Web is not common at the time of this writing. However, given the massive upward scalability requirements of the Web, it is a good bet that they will be commonly used. Servers will need to be multithreaded and/or have server pools, support transactions, route requests to a variety of transaction servers, and so on.

2.9 Summary

A TP monitor is a software product used in the development, deployment, and management of TP applications. Its basic system architecture consists of three parts:

1. Presentation server—for interaction with an end user or special device
2. Workflow controller—for routing a request to the correct transaction program
3. Transaction server—to do the work necessary to fulfill the request, usually involving accesses to shared resources, such as databases, and typically returning results to the end user or input device

The presentation server is responsible for interacting with the end user via menus and forms, gathering input for the transaction request and the name of the transaction to be executed. After gathering input, the presentation server constructs the request message and sends it to the workflow controller. The presentation server also is responsible for authentication (checking the user name and password) and optionally geographic entitlement (checking that the device is authorized to submit requests).

The main goal of the workflow controller is to improve scalability by reducing the number of sessions that would be required if presentation servers directly connected to transaction servers. Its main job is routing. It decodes the request message, determines the location of the transaction program to be called, and makes the call. It locates the transaction program using some type of directory service that translates the symbolic request name to a server identifier. Optionally, it uses parameter-based routing to select the transaction program based on the contents of the request, not just the request name.

The workflow controller demarcates the transaction and handles exceptions. Transaction demarcation may be chained, where it identifies only the boundaries between transactions, or unchained, where explicit Start and Commit operations bracket the transaction. Exception handling must cope with transaction aborts and system failures.

The transaction server executes program logic to fulfill the request, such as retrieve data from a database or update data with new values provided by the request.

The three parts of a TP monitor may be mapped onto processes in various ways. Early monitors mapped all three parts into a single process. Today, it is more common for each part to be executed in a separate process. The trade-off is interprocess communications overhead versus flexibility of distribution and configuration of the components.

Multithreaded processes are another important architectural feature of TP monitors to reduce the number of processes. Threads may be implemented by the operating system, which makes more efficient use of SMP systems and avoids trapping synchronous I/O in the TP monitor, or by the TP monitor, which avoids the performance overhead of system calls for thread switches. Server classes are an alternative to multithreaded servers, in which a set of processes functions as a single logical server.

Many functions previously performed only by TP monitors are now features of database servers. TP monitors still provide features that database servers don't yet have, such as workflow control, server classes, transactions distributed across multiple types of resource managers, and certain system management and administrative functions for TP applications programs and systems. However, database servers are suitable for many applications, and their range of applicability is growing.

TP monitors are rapidly becoming relevant to the World Wide Web. A web browser functions as a presentation server, which sends requests (i.e., URLs) to a web server. Although originally designed to serve HTML pages to display on clients, this paradigm is rapidly evolving to support transactions. URLs take parameters, just like a transaction request. And for the server to scale to large numbers of clients, it needs to adopt the mechanisms used in today's TP monitors, such as processing each request in a long-lived server with transactional access to the servers and resources it needs.

CHAPTER 3

Transaction Processing Communications

3.1 Introduction

TP application programs communicate with each other when they run in a distributed setting on different computers. Even on a single computer, for modularity reasons it's often convenient to break up the application programs into separate processes. Application programs therefore have to communicate between processes, which means the programs have to exchange messages. There are three ways to do this:

1. Use remote procedure calls, which mimic the behavior of local procedure calls within a single process. When a program in one process calls a program in another process (in another address space), it does so by calling a procedure and getting a value returned just as if the two procedures were running within a single address space.
2. Explicitly send and receive messages, called peer-to-peer messaging. Rather than using a procedure call with a return, application programs issue operations that send and receive messages.
3. Move messages among queues. An application sends a message from one program to another by putting the message in a queue. The queue is a third object, with which both programs communicate. One program enqueues the message to the queue, and sometime later the receiver program dequeues the message from the queue.

These communications paradigms apply to all distributed applications, not just in TP. However, there are some aspects of these communications paradigms that are unique to TP. In any case, these communications paradigms are a core function of a TP monitor, and we need to review them here, even though they apply in other settings, too.

We cover the remote procedure call and peer-to-peer message-passing styles in this chapter. The queuing style is sufficiently different that we devote a separate chapter to that topic, Chapter 4.

3.2 The Remote Procedure Call Model

If all communicating programs involved in a TP application are executing within the same address space, that is, within the same process, then they can communicate with an ordinary procedure call. The idea behind remote procedure call (RPC) is that since this is a simple and commonly understood way to communicate between programs in the same process, it would be beneficial to offer the same behavior between programs in different processes. It effectively treats distributed programs running in two or more processes as if they were part of a single, sequential program by allowing the programs to communicate via a standard call and return mechanism.

In the classical design of RPC the calls and returns are synchronous. When the client executes a statement that calls a procedure, it stops and waits for the called procedure to execute and return control to the caller, at which point the caller receives the return and continues just as it would in a sequential program. From the time the caller makes the call until the time the caller gets the return, the caller is stopped. There are also asynchronous designs where the caller can continue after issuing a call and before receiving the return. These are hybrid designs that are similar to both peer-to-peer message passing and synchronous RPC. We don't discuss them further in this book.

RPC mechanisms are offered by many vendors. Probably the most widely used RPC is the one defined in the Open Software Foundation's Distributed Computing Environment (OSF DCE), whose source code and specifications are used by several major computer vendors.

RPC Programming Model

There are several benefits to programming in the RPC style. First, the programmer can still program and think about the program as if all of its procedures were linked together in a single process. Therefore, the programmer can focus on correctly modularizing the program and ignore the underlying communications mechanism. In particular, the programmer can ignore that the program is really distributed, which would add significant complexity to the programming task if it were made visible. Second, the RPC style avoids certain programming errors that arise when using lower-level styles such as peer-to-peer. For example, a program receives a return for every call. Either the caller receives a return message from the called procedure, or the system returns a suitable exception to the caller so it can take appropriate action.

Programming by explicitly sending and receiving messages, as in the peer-to-peer style, requires the programmer to handle the message sequences and errors directly. The programmer designs and creates a protocol. Each program must be ready to receive a message after it's sent. Programs have to cope with certain error conditions, such as waiting for a message that never arrives, or giving up waiting for a message and coping with that message if it does eventually arrive later. In RPC, these problems are dealt with by the RPC implementation rather than the application program. RPC implementations also usually hide the differences in parameter format between the languages in which the client's and server's program are written. For example, the client could be written in Visual Basic and the server in C++, or the client in C++ and the server in Pascal. RPC implementations also can hide differences among vendor platforms such as Intel x86, PowerPC, and Alpha.

To understand how RPC works, consider the example in Figure 3.1. This program consists of three applications:

1. `Pay_cc`, which pays a credit card bill
2. `Debit_dda`, which subtracts money from a checking or savings account—that is, a demand deposit account (dda), a banking term for a checking or savings account
3. `Pay_Bill`, which calls `Pay_cc` and `Debit_dda` to pay the credit card bill from the checking or savings account

```
Boolean Procedure Pay_Bill (dda_acct#, cc_acct#)
{ int     dda_acct#, cc_acct#;
  long    cc_amount;
  Boolean ok;

  Start;  /* start a transaction */
  cc_amount = pay_cc (cc_acct#);
  ok = debit_dda (dda_acct#, cc_amount);
  if (!ok) Abort; else Commit;
  return (ok);
}

long Procedure Pay_cc (acct#);
{ int  acct#;
  long amt;

  /* get the credit card balance owed */
  Exec SQL Select AMOUNT
           Into :amt
           From CREDIT_CARD
           Where (ACCT_NO = :acct#);
  /* set balance owed to zero */
  Exec SQL Update CREDIT_CARD
           Set AMOUNT = 0
           Where (ACCT_NO = :acct#);
  return (amt);
}

Boolean Procedure Debit_dda (acct#, amt);
{ int  acct#;
  long amt;

  /* debit amount from dda balance if balance is sufficient */
  Exec SQL Update ACCOUNTS
           Set BALANCE = BALANCE - :amt
           Where (ACCT_NO = :acct# and BALANCE ≥ :amt);
  /* SQLCODE = 0 if previous statement succeeds */
  return (SQLCODE == 0);
}
```

Figure 3.1 Credit Card Payment Example `Pay_Bill` brackets the transaction and calls two subprograms, `Pay_cc` and `Debit_dda`, by RPC.

Pay_cc takes a credit card account number as input, returns the amount of money owed on that account, and zeroes out the amount owed. The first SQL statement selects the amount of money from the credit card table, which contains the amount of money owed on each account number. The second statement zeroes out that amount (i.e., the entire balance is paid off) and returns the amount actually owed for the account.

Debit_dda (or "debit demand deposit account") subtracts a given amount of money from the account. The first SQL statement looks in the account table and returns the amount of money that's currently in that account. If the balance in that account is less than the amount of money to be debited, then the WHERE clause is false, so no action is taken. If there is enough money (i.e., the SQL statement succeeds and therefore sets SQLCODE to zero), it subtracts the amount of money to be debited from the account balance and returns true.

Each of these programs is useful by itself. The Pay_cc program can be used to process credit card bills. The Debit_dda program can be used for an automated teller machine to process debits and credits against a checking account. To offer a new automatic bill paying service, which automatically pays a customer's credit card bill out of their checking account on the appropriate date, we write a third program, called Pay_Bill, which uses the other two.

The Pay_Bill program takes a demand deposit account number and credit card account number and tries to pay the credit card bill out of the demand deposit account. The program starts a transaction, calls Pay_cc to pay the credit card bill (which returns the amount of money owed), and tries to debit that money from the demand deposit account. If the Debit_dda program returns true—meaning that there was enough money to pay the bill—the program commits. If it returns false, there wasn't enough money to pay the bill and the transaction aborts. In both cases the Pay_cc program updates the credit card table. But if the Pay_Bill program aborts the transaction, the abort automatically undoes that update, thereby leaving the bill for that credit card account unpaid. (If Debit_dda returns false, its SQL update failed and has no effect on the accounts table.)

Transaction Bracketing

Notice that Start, Commit, and Abort are issued by the Pay_Bill program and do not appear in the Pay_cc or Debit_dda programs. This is fine for the application that tries to automatically pay credit card bills, but how do you execute the Pay_cc program all by itself? Since the Pay_cc program updates the database and preserves database consistency, you might reasonably expect it would also have a Start, Commit, and Abort, too. But it doesn't. The reason is that when Pay_cc is called from another program such as Pay_Bill, it shouldn't start another transaction. Rather, it should run within the transaction of its caller.

An important aspect of programming style in transaction-based applications is not to have the elementary programs that do the work of the transaction contain the Start, Commit, and Abort operations (or other transaction bracketing operations in the chained transaction model), but rather have them be pure procedures. The caller of the program is the one that actually starts, commits, or aborts the transaction. That way the callee can be called from several different applications that may use the same procedure in different ways. For example, a simple wrapper program could be used to bracket the transaction and call the `Pay_cc` program, and do nothing else. Another program such as `Pay_Bill` could call the same `Pay_cc` program as part of a larger activity. That's why in this example the Start, Commit, and Abort operations are not in the `Pay_cc` or `Debit_dda` programs. This is a matter of programming style that facilitates the reuse of elementary transaction-based application programs. Another approach to the problem of reusing transaction programs is nested transactions, described in Chapter 11.

Transparent Transaction Identifiers

Notice that there are no transaction identifiers in Figure 3.1. When the system executes the Start operation, it assigns a transaction identifier to the program. This transaction identifier must somehow be associated with every RPC, so the called program knows what transaction it is executing, and with every database operation (in the example, every SQL statement), so the system will later be able to either commit or abort them all.

The application could manage all of this explicitly. That is, the Start operation could return a transaction identifier explicitly to the application, the application could pass that transaction identifier to every program it calls, and each of those programs could pass the transaction identifier to each of its database operations.

Most systems hide this complexity. That is, they automatically attach the transaction identifier to every RPC and every database operation. This is more convenient for application programmers (so they don't have to deal with it). It also avoids errors because if the application passes the wrong transaction identifier, the system could malfunction.

Binding Clients and Servers

The programs shown in Figure 3.1 don't include all of the complexity that an application programmer would really need to perform these functions. First of all, to make remote procedure call worthwhile in this situation, the `Pay_Bill` program would probably be running in a different process, possibly on a different system, than the `Pay_cc` or `Debit_dda` programs. To compile and run the programs on these different systems, `Pay_Bill` needs to reference the `Pay_cc` and `Debit_dda` programs. Otherwise, the compiler will produce an error for the `Pay_Bill` program, saying that the `Pay_cc` and `Debit_dda` programs don't exist. This is avoided by writing an *interface definition* (which is very similar to a header file in C) for each program to be called—in this case `Pay_cc` and `Debit_dda`.

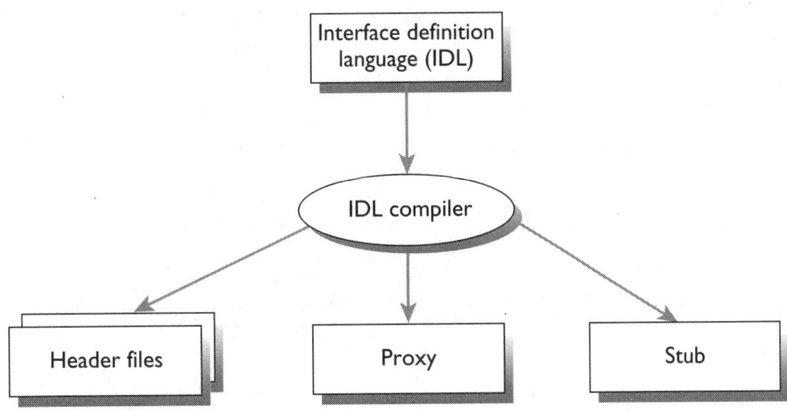

Figure 3.2 IDL Compiler Operation The IDL compiler produces header files for the caller and callee to use and proxy and stub procedures that provide an interface between the caller and callee and the underlying network.

Interface Definitions

An interface definition specifies the name and type of the program and its parameters. An interface definition is processed by a special compiler, called the *interface definition language (IDL) compiler* or *stub compiler*. The IDL compiler produces several outputs, one of which is a header file (consisting of data structures) for the caller to use. In this case the IDL compiler would produce header files for `Pay_cc` and `Debit_dda` that could be included with the `Pay_Bill` program so that it can be compiled. The IDL compiler also produces *proxy* and *stub* procedures, which are the programs that interface the `Pay_Bill` caller to the `Pay_cc` and `Debit_dda` servers via the network. The caller's program is linked with a proxy and the server's program is linked with a stub. The IDL compiler produces both the header files and the proxy and stub procedures. Figure 3.2 illustrates the IDL compiler operation.

IDLs have been defined for OSF RPC and for OMG's CORBA, which includes an RPC capability as part of its object broker function.

Marshaling

Another function of the proxy and stub procedures is to lay out the procedure name and parameters into a stream, which can be sent in a message. This is called *marshaling*. As part of marshaling parameters, the proxy can translate them between the format of the caller and the callee. In the previous examples, all the programs were written using the same language, but that needn't be the case. The `Pay_cc` and `Debit_dda` programs might have been written some time ago in one language, while the `Pay_Bill` program, added later to introduce the new service, was written in a different language. In this case the client proxy translates the parameters into a standard format that the callee can understand, and the server stub translates that into the appropriate format for the procedures being called—`Pay_cc` and `Debit_dda`.

Communications Binding

Besides linking in the proxy and stub, there is the issue of creating a communications binding between these programs so they can communicate over the network. The runtime system has to know where each server exists (e.g., `Pay_cc` and `Debit_dda`) so it can create bindings to each server when asked (e.g., by `Pay_Bill`). Two activities are involved:

1. Each server program must *export* its interface, to tell what interface it supports, and it must tell where on the network it can be found.
2. When the `Pay_Bill` program wants to connect to the server, it must create a communications connection using that information exported by the server.

In an RPC environment these activities are ordinarily supported by a directory service (described in Section 2.4). It is used to store and retrieve the names of objects in a distributed system and is accessible from any computer in the distributed system. For example, when the `Pay_cc` program is initialized in a process, the fact that the `Pay_cc` program is available in process 17315 of network node 32.143 is written to the directory service (step 1 in Figure 3.3). When the `Pay_Bill` program asks to connect to the `Pay_cc` program, it calls the directory service (one of the RPC runtime calls mentioned earlier) to find out where `Pay_cc` is located (step 2). The directory service returns the instances of `Pay_cc` it knows about (in this case, one). If there are any running, `Pay_Bill` may connect to any one of them (step 3). Some TP monitors automate server selection to balance the load across multiple identical transaction servers. Having received the network address of the server process number (in this case 32.143.17315), the `Pay_Bill` process can open a communications session with the server, so `Pay_Bill` can subsequently issue RPCs to `Pay_cc`.

Much of this work is done by the RPC runtime system, but some is exposed to the application. For example, the application may have to issue calls to get the network address and create a communications binding. Some systems hide some of this. A differentiating feature of RPC implementations is how much of this complexity is exposed to the application programmer.

Application Programmer's View

While the RPC style does simplify some aspects of application programming, it also introduces some new complexities. First, one has to write the interface definitions for the servers. This is a new programming task that isn't needed in the single-process case. Second, to support this synchronous paradigm where the caller waits for the server to reply, one needs a multithreaded client

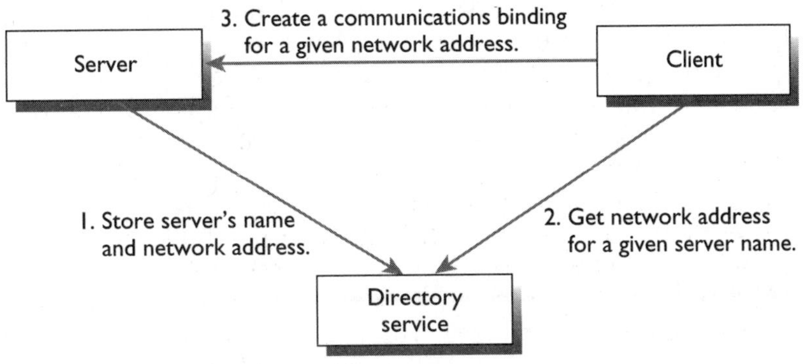

Figure 3.3 Using a Directory Service When it's initialized, the server stores its name and address in the directory service. Later, the client gets the server's address and uses it to create a communications binding.

so that blocking a caller doesn't stall the client process. To support many clients concurrently, one needs either a multithreaded server or a server class. Programmers have found it challenging to learn to program multithreaded servers and create "thread-safe" applications. Third, the client and server programs need startup code to connect up or *bind* the programs together before they first communicate. This includes importing and exporting interfaces, defining security characteristics, setting up communications sessions, and so on. While some of this can be hidden, often a lot of it isn't. For example, the RPC system in OSF DCE has more than 150 runtime calls for binding. Most of them aren't needed in common situations, but the very fact that they exist represents another dimension to think about, which adds complexity to the programming problem. Finally, communication failures generate some new kinds of exceptions, such as a return message that never shows up because of a communications or server failure. Such exceptions don't arise in the nondistributed case when the programs are running inside of the same process.

How to Compare RPC Systems

RPC has become a standard feature of distributed computing systems, whether or not those systems run transactions. For example, Microsoft's Windows NT and Sun's operating systems support RPC as a built-in function. To get RPC integrated with transactions usually requires buying a TP monitor, although in some operating systems (e.g., Tandem's Guardian, Digital's OpenVMS, or Microsoft's Windows NT) some of this integration is built in.

When shopping for a TP monitor, simply knowing that a system supports RPC, or even RPC with transactions, is not enough. You really have to go to the next layer of detail to understand the exact programming model and how difficult it is to write programs. Some of these interfaces are low level and hard to program; others are high level and relatively easy to program.

One thing to look for when evaluating RPC systems is which languages are supported and what data types can actually be handled. For example, some systems only support a generic proxy and stub procedure, which require application programming to marshal parameters. Most proxies and stubs are unable to translate complex data structures such as an array. Or they may handle it as a parameter, but only for a certain language. Bulk data transfer is difficult using some RPC systems, for example, scrolling through a long table a portion at a time.

When an RPC is coupled with transactions (often called a *transactional RPC*), additional data must be passed to coordinate a transaction, and transaction-related exceptions must be passed with the return. Sometimes this additional data is passed as "hidden" parameters, that is, as parameters that the TP system adds to the procedure's declared parameters. The hidden parameters can contain the transaction identifier and other information necessary to coordinate a transaction with the remote procedure, such as the name of the calling TP system, the exception code and location, and so on.

The hidden parameters allow a transactional RPC system to coordinate the data flow with the flow of the two-phase commit messages. Sometimes, the RPC mechanism itself is used to transmit the two-phase commit messages. In this case, the transaction identifier is used to correlate the two message flows, one for application data and the other for two-phase commit messages. We'll discuss these issues at length in Chapter 9 on two-phase commit.

3.3 An RPC Walkthrough

Now that we have explained the main components of an RPC system, let's walk through an example to see what happens, beginning to end. In Figure 3.4, the client application calls the server application. The client application could be the `Pay_Bill` program, for example, and the server application could be `Pay_cc`. As we discussed, there are proxy and stub programs and a runtime system along the path.

The client application issues a call to the server, say, `Pay_cc`. This "`Call Pay_cc`" statement actually calls the client's `Pay_cc` proxy (1). The proxy is a procedure with the same interface as the server application; so it looks exactly like `Pay_cc` to the client. Of course, the `Pay_cc` proxy doesn't actually do the work. All it does is send a message to the server.

The `Pay_cc` proxy takes the parameters of `Pay_cc` and marshals them into a packet (2). The proxy then calls the communications runtime for the RPC, which sends the packet as a message to the server process (3).

The RPC runtime uses the communications system to move messages between the client and server processes. To do this, the RPC runtime must create a communications binding between the two processes, which is a parameter to subsequent send and receive operations. In response to a send operation, the client communications system moves the message to the

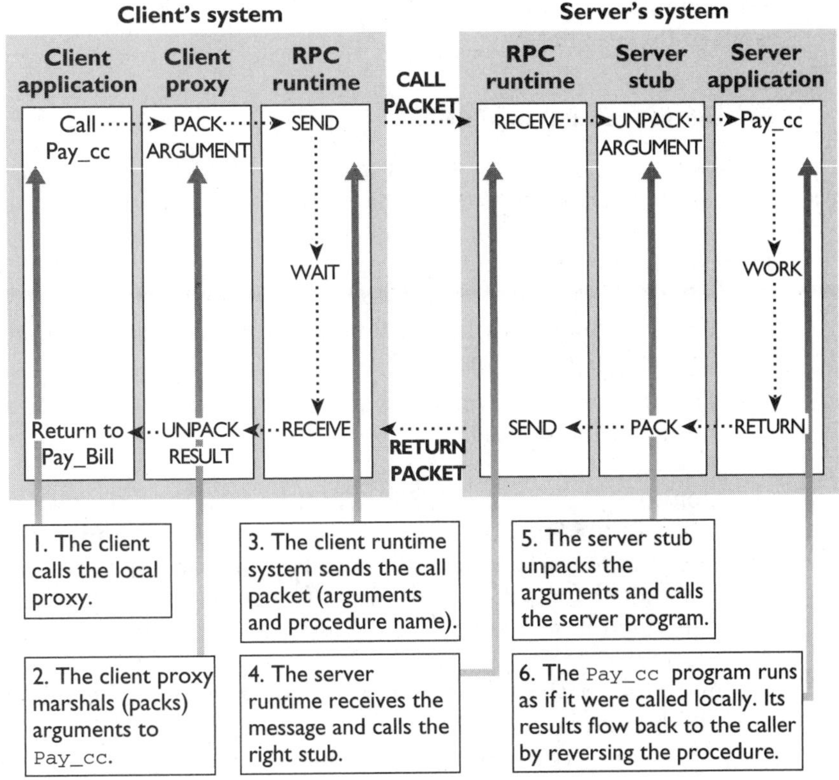

Figure 3.4 **RPC Implementation** The numbers indicate the sequence of actions to process a call from the client to the `Pay_cc` server program.

server *system*. Based on the communications binding, the server system's communications software hands the message to the right process.

The server process's RPC runtime system receives the message (4). It looks at the packet's header and sees that this is a call to the `Pay_cc` program, so it calls the `Pay_cc` server stub. The server stub unmarshals the arguments and performs an ordinary local procedure call to the `Pay_cc` program (5). The `Pay_cc` program takes the call and runs just as if it had been called by a local caller instead of a remote caller (6).

When `Pay_cc` completes, the whole mechanism runs in reverse: `Pay_cc` does a return operation to the program that called it. From `Pay_cc's` viewpoint, that's the server stub. When it returns to the server stub, it passes a return value and its output parameters. The server stub marshals those values into a packet and passes them back to the RPC runtime system, which sends a message back to the caller.

The caller's system receives the packet and hands it off to the correct process. The process's RPC runtime returns to the correct proxy for this call, which unmarshals the results and passes them back as part of its return statement to the original `Pay_cc` call, the client's call.

Parameter Translation in RPC

Suppose that the client and server applications are using different languages with different data formats. In that case, the client proxy and the server stub need to translate the parameters between the client's and server's format. There are two ways to do this:

1. Put the parameters into a standard, canonical format that every server knows how to interpret.
2. Ensure that the server's stub can interpret the client's format, known as *receiver-makes-it-right.*

Canonical forms include ASN.1/BER and NDR (both ISO standards) and XDR (used in the Sun RPC). When using a canonical format, the client proxy translates the parameters into the standard format, the server translates them out of standard format, and likewise for the return parameters—the server stub puts them into standard format and the client proxy puts them back into client format.

This is fine if the client and server are running different languages, but what if they're running the same language? For example, suppose they're using the same implementation of C++. The client proxy is going through all the extra work of taking it out of C++ format, putting it into standard format, and then the server is taking it out of standard format and putting it back into C++ format. For this reason, the receiver-makes-it-right technique is often used. The client proxy marshals the parameters in the client's format, not in a standard format, and tags them with the name of the format it's using. When the receiver gets the parameters, if it sees that they're in the same format that the server is using, it just passes them unmodified to the server. However, if they're not in the right format, it does the translation—either via a standard format or directly into the target format. This saves the translation expense in many calls, but requires the server to support format translations for every format it might see as input.

Even when the client and server are running the same language, some machine-dependent translation may be required. This arises because there are two different ways of laying out bytes in words in computer memory, sometimes called little-endian and big-endian. The difference is whether the bytes are laid out left-to-right (little-endian) or right-to-left (big-endian) within the word. In other words, the low-order bit is either in the first or last position of the word. When moving packets between systems, it may be necessary to translate between little-endian and big-endian format, even if both systems are running the same implementation of the same language. Again this can be hidden by the proxies and the stubs using one of the parameter translation mechanisms.

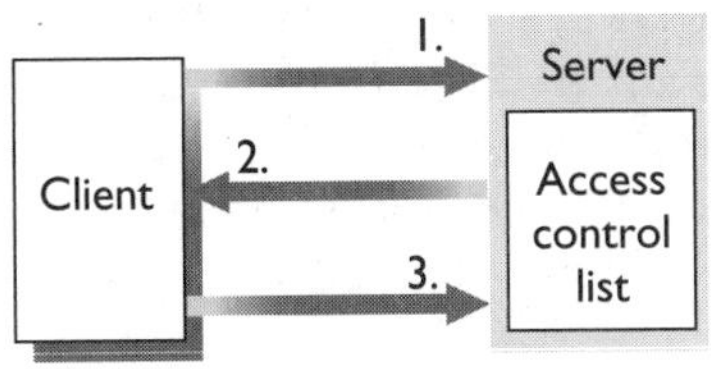
Client
Server
Access control list
1.
2.
3.
1. Create communications binding, passing in the authenticated client identity.
2. Acknowledge communications binding, passing back the authenticated server identity.
3. RPC to the server, which checks that the client is authorized to make this particular call.

Figure 3.5 RPC Security The communications system authenticates the client and server when it creates a communications binding between them. The server checks the client's authorization on subsequent calls for service.

Security of RPC

When the client binds to the server, the client first calls the runtime system to access the directory service to find the server's address and to create a communications binding to the server. A secure gatekeeper is needed to control the creation of these bindings, since not all clients should be able to connect to any server for any purpose. As an extreme example, it shouldn't be possible for any workstation to declare itself the networkwide electronic mail server, since it would allow anybody to eavesdrop on everyone's mail.

In general, when a client connects to a server, it wants to know who it is actually talking to—that the server is who it says it is. Moreover, the server wants to know that it's talking to an appropriate client. This requires authentication, a secure way to establish the identity of a system, a user, a machine, and so on, as was discussed in Section 2.3.

Thus, when binding takes place, the runtime system should authenticate the names of the client and the server (see Figure 3.5). This ensures, for example, that when the server comes up it can prove that it really is the mail server, and when the client binds to the server it can prove that it's really a client that's allowed to connect to this server.

Having authenticated the client, the server still needs to exercise *access control*, that is, to check whether a client is authorized to use the service and invoke specific operations. Access control is entirely up to the server. The server's TP monitor or operating system may help, by offering operations to maintain a list of authorized clients, called an *access control list*. But it's up to the server to check the access control list before doing work on behalf of a client.

Fault Tolerance in RPC

A common general fault tolerance problem (not just in RPC) is determining what to do if you issue an operation but don't get a reply that tells you whether the operation executed correctly. This problem arises in RPC when a client issues a call and does not receive a reply. The key question is whether it is safe to retry the operation.

Suppose the client calls a server that processes the call by updating a database, such as the `Debit_dda` program in Figure 3.1. If the client does not receive a return message, it's not safe to try the call again, since it's possible that the original call executed, but the return message got lost. Calling `Debit_dda` a second time would debit the account a second time, which is not the desired outcome.

The property that tells whether it is safe to retry is called idempotence. An operation is *idempotent* if any number of executions of the operation has the same effect as one execution. In general, queries are idempotent—it doesn't matter how many times you call, you always get back the same answer (if there were no intervening updates) and there are no side effects. Most update operations are not idempotent. For example, `Debit_dda` is not idempotent because executing it twice has a different effect than executing it just once.

A server is idempotent if all of the operations it supports are idempotent. It is useful if a server declares whether it is idempotent. If it is declared to be idempotent (its operations are all queries, for example), the RPC runtime system learns that fact when it creates a binding to the server. In this case, if the client RPC runtime sends a call but does not receive a return message, it can try to call again and hope that the second call gets through. If the server is not idempotent, however, it's not safe to retry the call. In this case, the client could send a control message that says, "Are you there?" or "Have you processed my previous message?" but it can't actually send the call a second time, since it might end up executing the call twice.

Even if it resends calls (to an idempotent server) or it sends many "Are you there?" messages (to a nonidempotent server), the caller might never receive a return. Eventually, the RPC runtime gives up waiting and returns an exception to the caller. The caller cannot tell whether the call executed or not. It just knows that it didn't receive a return message from the server. It's possible that a server will reply later, after the RPC runtime returns an exception. At this point, it's too late to do anything useful with the return message, so the RPC runtime simply discards it.

Looking at the issue a bit more abstractly, the goal is to execute an idempotent operation *at least once*, and to execute a nonidempotent operation *at most once*. Often, the goal is to execute the operation *exactly once*. Transactions can help. A call executes exactly once if the server is declared nonidempotent, and the RPC executes within a transaction that ultimately commits. We explore exactly once behavior further in Chapter 4.

Performance of RPC

RPC is a heavily used mechanism when a TP system is distributed. Each transaction that's split between two TP systems—for example, between a client PC and a server back end—needs at least one RPC to send the request and return the reply. It's very important that this executes quickly. If it isn't very fast, people will avoid using it, which completely defeats its purpose.

There are basically three parts to the execution, which were illustrated in Figure 3.4. One is the proxy and stub programs that marshal and unmarshal parameters. Second is the RPC runtime and communications software, which passes packets between the stub and the network hardware. And then there's the network transfer itself, which physically passes the messages through the communications hardware and over the wire to the other system.

In most RPC systems, the time spent performing a call is evenly split among these three activities, all of which are somewhat slow. The overall performance is typically in the range of about 10,000–15,000 machine language instructions per remote procedure call, which is several hundred times slower than a local procedure call, so it's very important to optimize this. There are lower-functionality stripped-down research implementations in the 1500–2000 instruction range, and vendors are hard at work trying to get this kind of speedup. Techniques to make the system run faster include avoiding extra acknowledgment messages, using the receiver-makes-it-right technique to make the proxies and stubs faster, optimizing for the case where all the parameters fit in one packet to avoid extra control information and extra packets, optimizing for the case where client and server processes are on the same machine to avoid the full cost of a context switch, and speeding up the network protocol.

System Management

We've discussed RPC assuming that both the client and server processes are already up and running, but of course somebody has to make all this happen to begin with. These are system management activities, to create (client and server) processes and communications sessions (to support RPC bindings). Sometimes these are dynamic functions that are part of the RPC system, such as in a CORBA object request broker. In TP systems, they are usually static functions that are part of initializing the application, done in the TP monitor.

The system manager also has to track the behavior of the system. This requires software to monitor all of the low-level system components and make them visible with abstractions that are intelligible to the system manager. For example, if someone calls the help desk saying, "I can't run transactions from my PC," the system manager has to check (among other things) whether the PC is communicating with the server, whether the server processes are running, whether the client and server are running compatible versions of the proxy and stub, and so on. Similarly, if there are performance problems, the system manager has to track the message load for each of the systems, determine whether the server has enough threads to run all of the calls that are coming in, and so on.

3.4 Peer-to-Peer Programming

An alternative to the RPC style of programming is peer-to-peer, where processes communicate by sending and receiving messages. Unlike RPC, in which there's a master/slave relationship between the caller and callee, in peer-to-peer the two communicating programs are peers, that is, on an equal footing. Each is able to both send and receive messages.

Programming Interfaces

A variety of command sets support peer-to-peer communications. The most popular one that supports transactional communications is based on an IBM SNA protocol called LU6.2. Two programming interfaces have been defined for this protocol:

- APPC—advanced program to program communications
- CPI-C—common programming interface for communications, a simplified version of APPC

These command sets are interesting for two reasons: First, they are good examples of peer-to-peer transactional programming. And second, the commands (which are called *verbs* in APPC and *calls* in CPI-C) correspond closely to the kinds of messages sent by the LU6.2 protocol. LU6.2 is a popular way to communicate with transaction programs running on IBM systems and therefore is of general interest, whether or not one expects to program using peer-to-peer communications commands.

IBM supports a specialized version of LU6.2 to emulate an RPC, called Distributed Program Link (DPL). DPL is used by IBM's CICS TP monitor (which is described in Chapter 5). DPL provides many RPC features by issuing a `SEND` immediately followed by a `RECEIVE`, transparently to the programmer. This emulates a synchronous procedure call, which calls a remote program (i.e., `SEND`) and then waits for a return message (i.e., `RECEIVE`). DPL does not support proxies, stubs, and marshaling. But it does simplify peer-to-peer programming for the common case of call-return style communications.

In the APPC model of peer-to-peer communications, the programs that want to communicate first establish a long-lived session called a *conversation*. The programs communicate by sending messages back and forth across the communications line. The basic operations are

- `ALLOCATE`—set up a conversation
- `SEND_DATA` and `RECEIVE_DATA`—send messages back and forth
- `DEALLOCATE`—break down the conversation

APPC includes transaction synchronization commands, notably Syncpoint. The behavior of these commands is intimately tied to the behavior of message communication. It is therefore essential that we discuss them together. This is called a *one-pipe* model, because synchronization messages (for two-phase commit) flow through the same session as application messages. In the alternative *two-pipe* model, synchronization and application messages flow through separate sessions. The one-pipe model ensures that certain application communication has completed before certain synchronization messages are sent, since they flow across the same session, which avoids some timing errors, particularly in recovery situations.

A conversation is half duplex, meaning that messages can flow in either direction but only in one direction at a time. IBM chose this model because it closely reflects the call-return style of most transactional communications. Therefore, at any given time, one of the conversation's participants is in *send mode* and the other is in *receive mode*. The sender can turn over control of the conversation to the receiver, so that the sender becomes the receiver and the receiver becomes the sender. The main way this happens is when the sender issues a `RECEIVE_DATA` call. This causes a signal, or *polarity indicator*, to be issued to the other participant, telling it that it's now the sender and the former sender is now the receiver.

Not all peer-to-peer communications mechanisms use half duplex, however. For example, the OSI TP protocol, which is an ISO standard peer-to-peer protocol, uses full duplex.

A peer-to-peer program issues the command `ALLOCATE(program_name)` to create a conversation to a new execution of the program `program_name`. Suppose program A allocates a conversation with program B, B allocates a conversation with C, and B also allocates a conversation with D. Then A is communicating with B, and B is communicating with both C and D. This creates a *conversation tree*, which is the set of communication paths between the executing programs, as shown in Figure 3.6. These programs can execute as part of the same distributed transaction. As we'll see, the conversation tree plays a role in determining the conditions under which a distributed transaction can commit.

Syncpoint Rules

LU6.2 supports three levels of synchronization: Levels 0, 1, and 2. The levels of synchronization (called Syncpoint Levels) indicate the degree to which operations among the communicating programs are coordinated. Level 2 supports transaction semantics. When operating with Syncpoint Level 2, if the sender program issues a Syncpoint operation, it is telling the receiver to commit the transaction that's currently executing.

The two weaker levels of synchronization, Levels 0 and 1, have no transaction context. Syncpoint Level 1 is application-level synchronization, meaning that the protocol supports a confirm command that each program can use to acknowledge the receipt of the previous message, to synchronize its processing with other programs. Syncpoint Level 0 means that the protocol supports no special synchronization at all—the programs just send and receive messages. For example, it could be used by a program that sends a message to read, but not update, a database.

When a product says it supports LU6.2, this does not necessarily mean that it supports transactional communications. Often, a product only supports Syncpoint Levels 0 and 1, in which no transactions are present. Since transactions are the main subject of this book, we'll assume Level 2 (i.e., transaction support) is present and will not look at Levels 0 and 1 further.

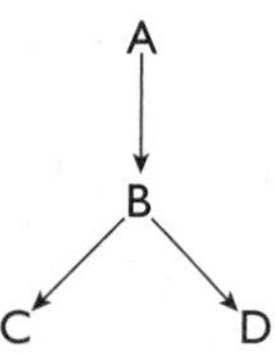

Figure 3.6 Conversation Tree Program A has allocated a conversation with program B, which in turn has allocated conversations with programs C and D.

Each program in a conversation tree must independently announce when it's finished with its piece of the transaction. It does this by issuing the Syncpoint operation. This causes a message to propagate to all of the programs that are adjacent to it in the conversation tree. To ensure that this message can propagate and that the receiver will be able to process it, a program that issues a Syncpoint operation must satisfy one of two rules:

1. All of its conversations are in send mode, and it has not yet received a Syncpoint from any other conversation, or
2. all but one of its conversations are in send mode, and the one that's in receive mode has already sent it a Syncpoint, which the program previously received.

Rule 1 is applicable if the transaction has not yet started to commit and the program whose conversations are in send mode is kicking off the commitment activity by sending a Syncpoint message to all of the programs with which it's communicating. Rule 2 is applicable if the program has received a Syncpoint message from a program on one of its conversations, and it is now propagating that Syncpoint by issuing a Syncpoint itself to all of the other conversations it's engaged in, all of which are in send mode. The application programmer, when issuing Syncpoint operations, has to be aware of these two rules to avoid sending a message at the wrong time and violating the protocol, which would produce a runtime error in the programs.

Although these rules eliminate some protocol errors, they don't eliminate all of them. For example, two programs in the conversation tree can independently issue a Syncpoint operation according to Rule 1. If they do, then another program will find itself stuck in a situation from which it can't complete. For example, in Figure 3.7 program A has a conversation with B, and B has a conversation with C. The conversation from A to B has A in send mode, and the conversation from B to C has C in send mode. Suppose that none of the three programs has yet issued a Syncpoint operation. In this situation, Rule 1 says that A and C can both issue a Syncpoint command. But if they do, program B will be stuck, because it will receive a Syncpoint command across two of its conversations, one from A and one from C. Program B will never be able to satisfy either Syncpoint rule. That is, two Syncpoint messages would collide at B, so the transaction would have to abort.

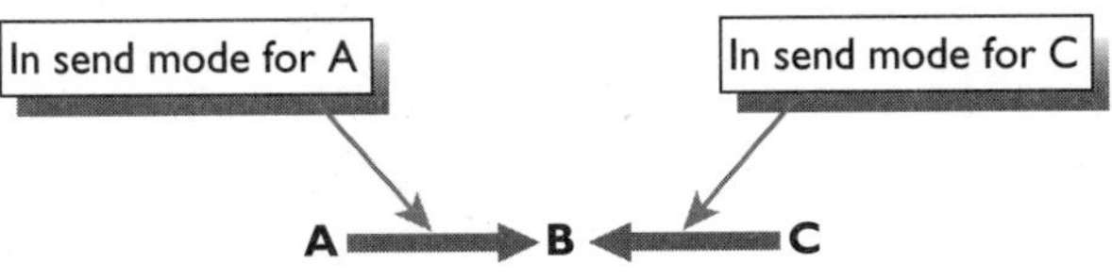

Figure 3.7 Possible Syncpoint Error A and C can both issue Syncpoint operations, leaving B stuck, unable to ever issue a Syncpoint according to Rules 1 or 2.

In LU6.2, you can start committing a transaction from any of the programs involved in the conversation. In Figure 3.6, program A, B, C, or D is allowed to start committing the transaction by issuing a Syncpoint operation, independently of which program originally allocated the conversation. This is different from the RPC model, in which the program that started all the work and issued the first RPC is normally the one that starts committing the transaction; after all of the program's RPCs have returned, it issues the Commit operation. In LU6.2, any of the programs can issue the Commit operation at any time. In this sense peer-to-peer is a more flexible paradigm than RPC.

When a program issues a Syncpoint operation, it says that *it* is ready to commit, but this does not guarantee that the transaction actually will commit. If anything goes wrong with another program or with messages between the programs, the transaction will abort. In that case, when the program gets control after the Syncpoint operation, there will be an error code indicating that the transaction actually aborted, even though the program had attempted to commit.

In LU6.2, a Syncpoint is a combination of a Commit operation followed immediately by a Start operation. In other words, LU6.2 implements the chained transaction model, in which there is always a transaction executing. When a program performs a Syncpoint operation, LU6.2 sends off the Syncpoint message, but the program itself stops until all of the other programs have also issued their Syncpoint operations and the entire transaction has committed. Whether the transaction commits or aborts, when the program gets control again, it is executing in a new transaction, which is the same new transaction as all other programs in the conversation tree. Thus, all programs in a conversation tree enter the next transaction cosynchronously.

An Example

In the following example (see Figure 3.8), we revisit the `Pay_Bill`, `Pay_cc`, and `Debit_dda` programs that appeared in the previous section on RPC, except that we implement them using peer-to-peer communications. We walk through each pseudoprogram step by step to illustrate how the peer-to-peer commands actually work.

```
Boolean Procedure Pay_Bill (dda_acct#, cc_acct#)
{ int           dda_acct#, cc_acct#;
  long          cc_amount;
  Boolean       ok;
  CONVERSATION conv_A, conv_B;

  /* Allocate the two conversations that are needed. */
  Allocate net_addr1.pay_cc Sync_level Syncpoint Returns conv_A;
  Allocate net_addr2.debit_dda Sync_level Syncpoint Returns conv_B;
  Send_data conv_A, cc_acct#;                /* call Pay_cc */
  Receive_data conv_A, cc_amount;            /* get reply from Pay_cc */
  Receive_data conv-A, What_received=Send; /* put conv_A in Send mode */
  Send_data conv_B, cc_acct#, cc_amount;     /* call Debit_dda */
  Syncpoint;                                 /* start committing */
  Receive_data conv_B;                       /* get Syncpoint from Debit_dda */
  If (What_received=Syncpoint) return(TRUE);
                                             /* committed */
  else return(FALSE);                        /* aborted */
  Deallocate conv_A;                         /* deallocate conversations */
  Deallocate conv_B;
}

void Procedure Pay_cc (acct#);
{ int           acct#;
  long          amt;
  CONVERSATION conv_C;

  Receive_allocate Returns conv_C;
  Receive_and_wait Gets acct#, Data_complete;
                                             /* get the call from Pay_Bill */
  Exec SQL Select AMOUNT into :amt           /* retrieve the amount owed */
           From CREDIT_CARD
           Where (ACCT_NO = acct#);
  Exec SQL Update CREDIT_CARD                /* pay the bill */
           Set AMOUNT = 0
           Where (ACCT_NO = acct#);
  Receive_and_wait What_received=Send;       /* put conv_A into Send mode */
  Send_data amt;                             /* send reply to Pay_Bill */
  Receive_data What_received=Take_Syncpoint;
                                             /* get Syncpoint from Pay_Bill */
  Syncpoint;
}
```

Figure 3.8 Credit Card Payment Example Using Peer-to-Peer Communication See the text for a walkthrough of this pseudocode.

```
void Procedure Debit_dda (acct#, amt);
{ int          acct#;
  long         amt;
  CONVERSATION conv_C;

  Receive_allocate Returns conv_C;
  Receive_and_wait Gets acct#, amt Data_complete;
                                          /* get the call from Pay_Bill */
  Receive_and_wait What_received=Take_Syncpoint;
                                          /* get Syncpoint from Pay_Bill */
  Exec SQL Update ACCOUNTS                /* debit the account by amt */
           Set BALANCE = BALANCE - :amt
           Where (ACCT_NO = :acct# and BALANCE ≥ amt);
  If (SQLCODE == 0) Syncpoint else Rollback;
}
```

Figure 3.8 (continued) **Credit Card Payment Example Using Peer-to-Peer Communication** See the text for a walkthrough of this pseudocode.

While following the explanation, notice that the communications mechanism is closely tied to the application logic. In other words, the application-to-application communications protocol appears in the application design in the peer-to-peer style, which contrasts with RPC, where the only protocol is the call-return style of procedure calls.

The `Pay_Bill` program first allocates a conversation with the `Pay_cc` program, called conversation A (`conv_A`), and then with the `Debit_dda` program, called conversation B (`conv_B`). Initially, it is in send mode on both conversations. It then sends a credit card account number over conversation A to the `Pay_cc` program (`Send_data conv_A, cc_acct#`). The `Pay_Bill` program then asks to receive the amount owed (`cc_amount`) from `Pay_cc` (`Receive_data conv_A, cc_amount`), so it waits for `Pay_cc` to send that message. This puts it into receive mode on conversation A.

Next, let's look at the `Pay_cc` program. After the program receives the request to allocate a conversation, it waits to receive an account number (`Receive_and_wait Gets acct#, Data_complete`). `Data_complete` means that it's expecting this to be all of the data. The program executes the same SQL commands as in the RPC example (Figure 3.1), which determine how much money was owed on that account and then zeroes it out. The `Pay_cc` program then performs a receive and wait operation, which asks the other program (`Pay_Bill`) to turn the conversation around so that `Pay_cc` is now the sender. At this point, `Pay_cc` calls `Send_data`, including the amount that's owed (this is the message that `Pay_Bill` is waiting for). The next operation, `Receive_data`, waits for a Syncpoint. There is no Syncpoint to be received, so it waits until one arrives. We'll come back to that in a moment.

Looking again at Pay_Bill, we see that the Receive_data on conversation A of cc_amount (Receive_data conv_A, cc_amount) will now execute because the message sent by Pay_cc has been received. Pay_Bill receives the data and completes the receive with a Receive_data operation (What received = send). It then sends data over conversation B to the Debit_dda program with the account number and the amount owed (send_data conv_B, cc_acct#, cc_amount).

Looking at Debit_dda, we see that it starts by receiving the message from Pay_Bill, including the account number and the amount owed, and then waits for a Syncpoint operation. Looking back at Pay_Bill, we can see that the next thing *it* does is send a Syncpoint operation that goes out over conversations A and B, which are both in send mode (for Pay_Bill). Pay_Bill is therefore performing a Syncpoint operation according to Rule 1.

The Debit_dda program receives the Syncpoint, which is a request to commit, and then performs the SQL to debit the account. The SQL return code tells whether the SQL succeeded, that is, whether there was enough money in the account to perform the debit. Debit_dda then tests the return code. If the SQL succeeded, it sends a Syncpoint, thereby committing the transaction. Otherwise it calls Rollback, thereby aborting the transaction. If Pay_Bill receives the Syncpoint, it knows the transaction committed and returns TRUE. Otherwise, it knows the transaction aborted and returns FALSE.

The ISO TP Protocol

The LU6.2 protocol is the basis of an international standard protocol—the ISO TP protocol—which incorporates the same ideas as LU6.2 with some small modifications. ISO TP uses a globally unique transaction identifier, whereas LU6.2 numbers transactions within a conversation tree beginning with 1, and then 2, 3, 4, and so on. In ISO TP, only the root of the transaction tree can issue the Commit operation. An application is allowed to exchange data in either full duplex (simultaneous) or half duplex (two-way alternate). Using full duplex, both parties to the conversation can send data at any time. ISO TP allows unchained transactions, in which a transaction program does not have to execute all of its operations within the transaction, as well as chained transactions. ISO TP does not specify the communications paradigm for the data transport—RPC and peer-to-peer implementations can both be used, as is the case with the various X/Open TP communications standards. And details of the actual protocol message exchange are different, which we'll discuss in the two-phase commit chapter later in the book.

3.5 Comparing RPC and Peer-to-Peer

The RPC and peer-to-peer models can be compared in four ways:

- The flexibility of the message sequences they allow

- The way in which programs announce the termination of a transaction
- The method by which the models manage the state of the transaction, which is distributed over several programs
- The extent to which the communications mechanism is reflected in the application design

Allowed Message Sequences

RPC protocols use a call-return model, where call and return messages are matched up and are properly nested.[1] That is, for every call message, there is eventually a return message. And within any call-return pair, a program can issue other calls, for which it must receive return messages before accepting the outer return. Looking at Figure 3.9, we see three programs (A, B, and C), which are communicating by RPC. Time is moving down the page, and diagonal arrows indicate messages. There's a message from A to B, which is a call, followed by a call from B to C. C then returns to B, B calls C again, and so on. The call and return messages are matched and nested.

By contrast, peer-to-peer protocols allow a more flexible message flow. Each program can send or receive at any time, within the limits of the half-duplex communications (in LU6.2). Messages are not matched as calls and returns, and they need not be nested in the sense of RPC. Thus, there are message sequences that are possible in peer-to-peer but that cannot happen in RPC, such as the following (see Figure 3.10):

1. Peer 1 sends a message to peer 2 (which could have been a call statement in RPC).
2. Peer 2 sends a message to peer 3 (which could also have been a call statement in RPC).
3. Peer 1 sends a message to peer 2. This could not happen in the RPC communication model. For that to happen, peer 3 would have had to return to peer 2, and peer 2 back to peer 1, which is not what happened here. This message sequence can happen with peer-to-peer but cannot happen with RPC.

The added flexibility of peer-to-peer message sequencing is certainly a good thing. You can get more parallelism, because the programs can freely exchange messages whenever they're ready to, rather than having to wait for replies to earlier messages. You can also reduce the number of messages, by batching up multiple calls in a single message. However, for this kind of message flow to work, each program has to know exactly what message sequences to expect from every other program. It can be quite challenging to handle all of

1 This is often called a "request-reply" model. We use "call-return" terminology instead, to avoid confusion with the technical meaning of "request" in other chapters, that is, a message that asks the system to run a transaction.

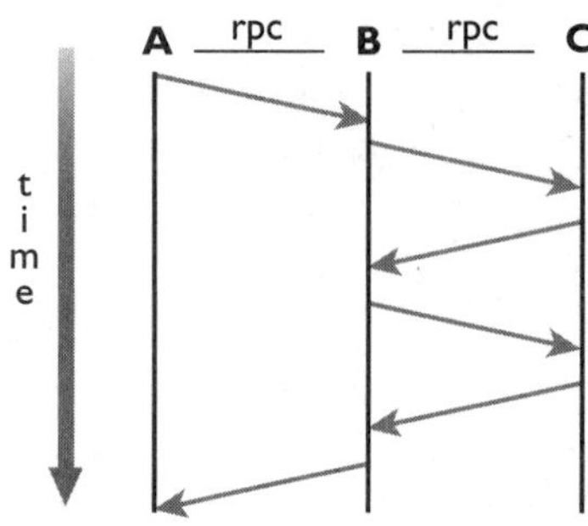

Figure 3.9 **Message Sequences in the RPC Model** Every call message has a return message, and call-return pairs are properly nested.

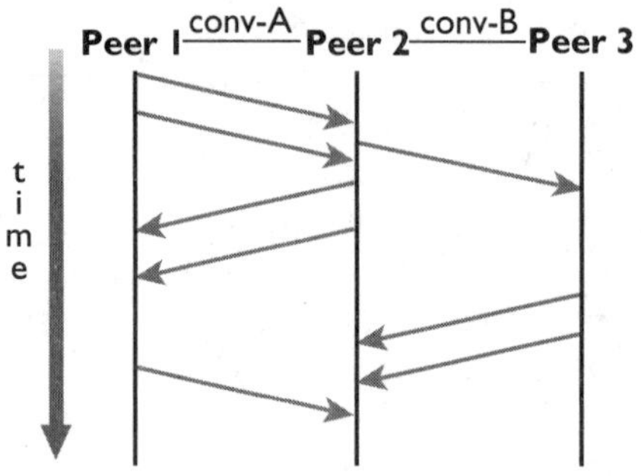

Figure 3.10 **Message Sequences in the Peer-to-Peer Model** Unlike RPC, there is no concept of call and return, so messages can be exchanged in orders that are not possible in RPC.

the possible error conditions correctly. So the flexibility comes at the expense of more programming complexity.

Termination Model

A second difference between the two models is the termination model. In the RPC model, a called program announces its termination simply by returning to its caller. It must not return to its caller until it has finished all of its work, including receiving responses from any calls that it made. So once it returns, it is obviously done. Ordinarily, a program using RPC does not commit its transaction until all its outbound calls have returned, so it does not start to commit until it has terminated.

In the peer-to-peer model, each program announces termination by invoking the Syncpoint operation. A Syncpoint operation may initiate the commitment of a program's transaction before other programs have terminated (see Figure 3.11). The Syncpoint rules avoid committing a program that still has work to do. They do this by delaying the commit of a program that receives a

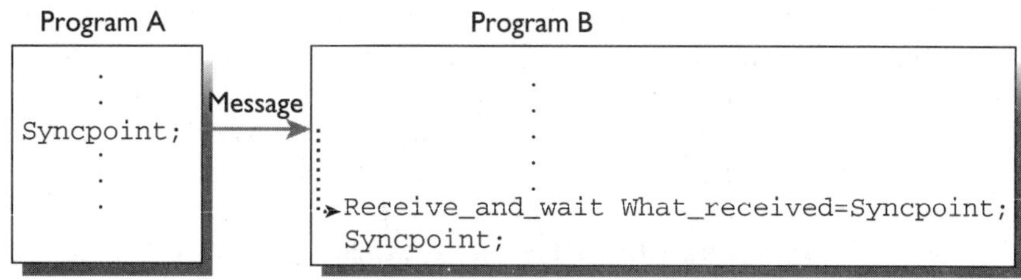

Figure 3.11 Flexible Syncpoint Timing Program A issues a Syncpoint before program B has finished its application functions. By contrast, in RPC, usually all programs finish application functions before any of them commit.

Syncpoint until the program itself has announced termination by invoking the Syncpoint operation itself.

Although the Syncpoint rules avoid committing an active transaction, they can unfortunately lead to certain programming errors that are not possible in the RPC protocol. For example, suppose program P1 invokes the Syncpoint operation, but program P2 is waiting for a message from P1. The programs are deadlocked because P2 will never receive the message that it's waiting for, and P1 will never return from its Syncpoint operation because it's waiting for P2 to issue a Syncpoint so the overall transaction can commit. This kind of termination error is the price that you pay for more flexible message passing. You get more parallelism, but there are more ways for the program to malfunction.

Connection Model

The third way in which the two models differ is that peer-to-peer is a connection-oriented communications model. The connection defines some shared state between communicating programs, which is the nature of any session-based communications. The shared state between the two communicating peer-to-peer programs includes the following:

- Direction of communications
- Direction of the link (i.e., send or receive mode)
- Transaction identifier of the current transaction being executed
- State of the transaction: whether it is active, committed, or aborted

Because programs hold connections across message exchanges, a program can rely on other programs' retained state from their last message exchange. Each program continues from where it left off, and other programs can count on that fact. For example, suppose program P1 has a connection to program P2, P1 is scanning a file owned by P2, and P1 maintains a cursor indicating P1's position in the file. In this example, P2 is counting on P1 to continue the scan from wherever it left off on each message exchange.

Peer-to-peer connections are generally not recoverable across failures of the system. Therefore, programs must reconstruct their retained state after they recover from a failure.

By contrast, RPC ordinarily uses a connectionless communications model, in which the client and server don't share any state. If the client and server want to share state, the server has to return the state to the client. For example, if P1 is calling a file service and expecting it to scan records on its behalf, then each time the file service returns it would have to give P1 the identifier of the last record that it looked at, which P1 can then give to the file service on its next call so the scan can pick up from where it left off.

Many RPC systems provide a general mechanism to do this. For example, in DCE and Microsoft RPC, a server can define a *context handle* as part of its interface. The context handle identifies state that is managed by the server and shared with the client. The client passes the context handle on each call, so the server can execute the call in the same state it had at the end of the previous call.

Some RPC systems also offer a connection-oriented variant, where the client can insist that all calls go to the same server. For example, the implicit and explicit binding options of DCE and Microsoft RPC allow this. However, these options do not prevent other clients from calling this server. Therefore, the server's state may change between calls from the same client. So a context handle is still needed by each client to ensure its state is unchanged by calls from other clients.

Current Trends

The simplicity of the RPC communications model is leading to a steady growth in its popularity for programming distributed applications. It is also widely used for systems programming, whenever communications requirements can be met by the call-return paradigm.

Database systems, TP monitors, and other system products sometimes need to exploit the flexibility offered by a peer-to-peer communications protocol. Developers of these products are willing to cope with the added programming complexity of a peer-to-peer protocol to get the benefits that this flexibility gives them—mainly, reducing the number of messages in cases where a reply is not needed for every send operation. Today, most database system vendors' communications protocols are connection-oriented peer-to-peer, such as Microsoft's and Sybase's TDS over TCP/IP, IBM's DRDA over LU6.2 and TCP/IP, Ingres's GCA over TCP/IP, and so on. An exception is Oracle's SQL*Net, which uses RPC.

3.6 Summary

The three TP monitor components (presentation server, workflow controller, and transaction server) can be mapped to separate operating system processes, in which case one of the following communications mechanisms is required in order to pass messages from one component to another: remote procedure call (RPC), peer-to-peer, or queuing. These communications paradigms are specifically adapted for use in a transactional environment, forming a core function of a TP monitor.

An RPC is a procedure call mechanism that executes across address spaces (from one process to another), either locally on the same node or remotely between different nodes. RPC is relatively easy to use because it allows the programmer to use the familiar procedure call mechanism for remote communications, and it transparently handles most aspects of communications. However, the RPC model also introduces some complexities, especially with respect to initial system setup, configuration, and performance. Some of the popular RPCs are those from Digital's ACMS, Microsoft RPC, OSF DCE, and Tandem's Pathway/TS.

An RPC mechanism employs client proxies and server stubs. The client proxy accepts the local procedure call from the calling program, binds to an appropriate server, marshals the procedure arguments into a message (translating them to the right representation for the server machine and programming language), and performs the communication required. The server stub turns the message received from the client into a local procedure call on the server procedure and sends the return message back to the client.

Some RPC systems only supply a generic proxy and stub, so marshaling must be done by the application. Others supply an interface definition language (IDL) for defining interfaces to the procedures that may be called remotely from another process. The IDL compiler generates the server-specific proxies and stubs, which include the marshaling code, and the required header files.

When a client is executing a transaction and calls a server, it must pass its transaction identifier to the server. This is usually hidden from the application programmer to simplify programming and avoid errors.

To call a remote server, a client must establish a communications binding to the server, usually by a lookup at a directory service. Security checks are also needed to authenticate the server and ensure the client is authorized to call the server.

RPCs execute several hundred times more instructions than a local procedure call. They must be carefully optimized to give satisfactory performance.

In the peer-to-peer model, programs send or receive messages in nearly arbitrary sequences, not just in call-return pairs. To communicate, programs first allocate a session (or conversation), after which they can exchange messages. Some of the popular peer-to-peer APIs are CPI-C and APPC from IBM, XATMI for TUXEDO, sockets for TCP/IP, and the TOP END communications manager.

LU6.2, the underlying communications protocol for IBM's peer-to-peer APIs, is a de facto standard, so most TP monitors provide an LU6.2 gateway for communication with IBM TP systems. LU6.2 operations include `ALLOCATE`, `DEALLOCATE`, `SEND`, and `RECEIVE`. A `SEND` followed immediately by a `RECEIVE` has essentially the same effect as an RPC. LU6.2 includes a

Syncpoint operation, which is a Commit immediately followed by a Start. A variant of LU6.2 is used in the OSI TP standard.

The LU6.2 protocol includes a variety of rules to synchronize the exchange of messages. For example, these rules control when a program can send or receive messages, and when it can issue a Syncpoint.

The peer-to-peer model offers more flexibility in message and termination sequencing than RPC. This flexibility comes at the cost of additional programming complexity.

CHAPTER 4

Queued Transaction Processing

4.1 Why Use Queues?

In direct transaction processing, a client sends a request to a server and waits, synchronously, for the server to run the transaction and return a reply. For example, in the RPC model, the client sends a request to the system as an RPC, which returns with a reply indicating whether or not the transaction ran. Similarly, in the peer-to-peer model, the client first issues a send-message operation; it then issues a receive-message operation to wait for the server to issue a send-message operation containing the reply. This is the TP model we discussed at length in Chapters 2 and 3.

Problems

Even though this direct TP model is widely used in practice, it has some limitations (see Figure 4.1). The first problem is dealing with the failure of a server or of client/server communications, which prevents a client from communicating with the server. If a client sends a request to this server, it immediately receives an error telling it that the server is down or disconnected and therefore is unable to receive the request message. At this point, either the client is blocked, waiting for a server to become available, or the user has to return later and resubmit the request to the client. A desirable alternative, which is not possible in direct TP, is simply to ask that the request be sent as soon as the server is available, without the user or client being required to wait on-line for the server to do so. For example, the user might want to log off and come back later to get the reply.

The second problem is the inverse of the first. The client may successfully send the request to the server. But the server, after executing the transaction, may be unable to send a reply to the client because the client failed, client/server communications failed, or the server failed after completing the transaction and before sending the reply. In each of these failure cases, the server's reply may be lost. So even after the failed component has recovered, the client still may not receive a reply. It therefore doesn't know whether its last request actually ran and hence whether it should resubmit the request.

A third issue is load balancing. In direct TP, if there is a pool of servers that can handle a client's request, then the mechanism for binding a client to a server must select one of the servers from the pool. As discussed in Section 2.6 on server classes, one approach is for the workflow controller to randomize the selection of a server, so, on average, the same number of clients are connected to each server. However, this randomization is just a guess. At any given moment, the actual load may not be equally balanced among the servers. That is, one server could receive many requests requiring a lot of work and thereby become overloaded. At the same time, other servers may not be receiving any requests at all. When the variance in workload is high, this type of situation is rather likely, leading to poor response time for some clients some of the time.

Finally, this whole model is based on first-come, first-served scheduling of requests. Whoever sends a request immediately gets that request processed.

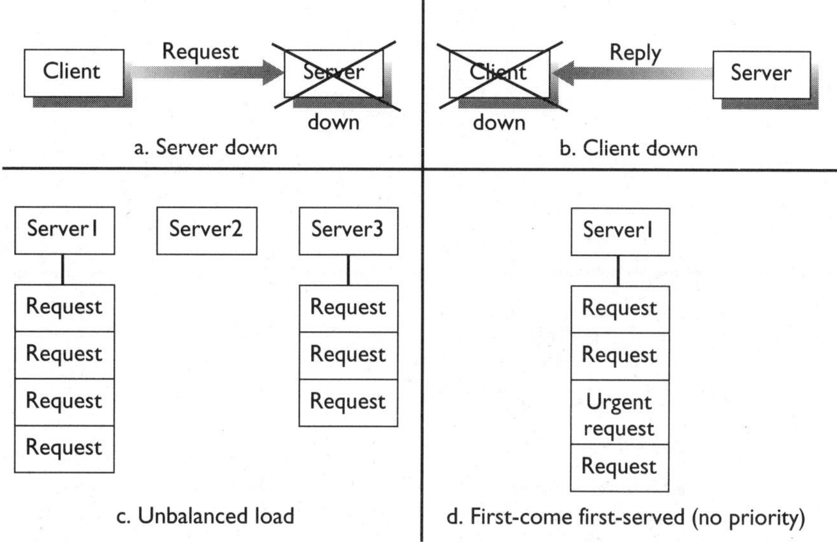

Figure 4.1 Problems with Direct TP (a) Sending a request to a down server. (b) Sending a reply to a down client. (c) Balancing the request load across many servers. (d) Scheduling requests.

There's no sense of priority in the system, in which high-priority requests are processed early and low-priority requests are delayed until later.

Queues as the Solution

This set of problems is solved by using a queue as a buffer for requests and replies between the client and the server (see Figure 4.2). Instead of sending a request directly to the server, a client sends it to a queue. And the server, instead of receiving requests directly from the client, receives those requests from the queue. Similarly, the server sends replies to a queue, and the client receives replies from the queue.

The queue is a transactional resource. So operations on the queue are made permanent or undone depending on whether the transaction that issued the operations commits or aborts. Usually, the queue is persistent and is stored on disk or some other nonvolatile storage device.

This queued TP model solves the problems that we just listed. First, a client can send a request even if the server is busy, down, or disconnected, as long as the queue is available. The client simply stores the request in the queue. If the server is available, it can execute the request right away. Otherwise, when the server becomes available, it can check the queue and run requests that were submitted while it was down.

Second, the server can send a reply to the client even if the client is down or disconnected, as long as the client's reply queue is available. The server sim-

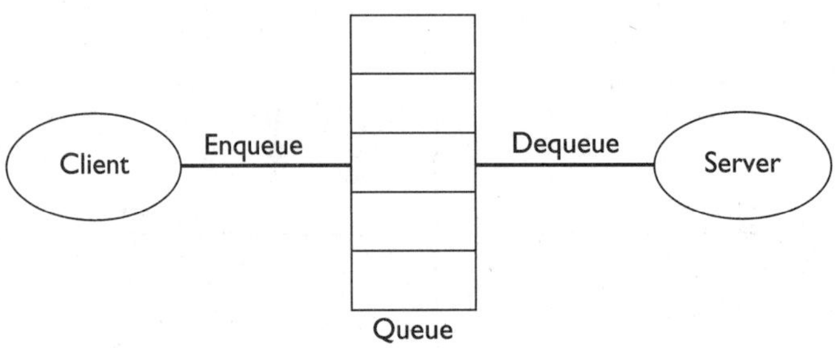

Figure 4.2 **Queued Transaction Model** In queued TP, clients send requests to queues, and servers receive requests from queues. This is in contrast to direct TP, where clients send requests directly to servers.

ply sends the reply to the queue. When the client reconnects to the system, it checks the queue to find any reply messages that are waiting.

Third, as shown in Figure 4.3, many servers can be receiving requests from the same queue, thereby balancing the load across many servers. This load balancing is fully dynamic. As soon as a server finishes processing one request, it can take another request from the queue. There is never a time when one server is overloaded while another is idle.

Fourth, queues can be used for priority-based scheduling. Each request can be tagged with a priority, which is used to guide the scheduling strategy. For example, each server can dequeue requests highest-priority-first. Alternatively, to ensure low-priority requests are given some service, one server can be given the job of servicing low-priority requests while all other servers use highest-priority-first. Or, each request's priority could be set to be its deadline, and requests are processed in deadline order. Requests can also be scheduled manually, by collecting them on a queue and running them under operator control. Once there is a queue in the picture, there is great flexibility in controlling the order in which requests are processed.

This is a long list of benefits for such a relatively simple mechanism. For this reason most TP monitors support queues as one way of moving requests and replies between clients and servers.

4.2 The Queued Transaction Processing Model

Server's View of Queuing

Let's look at how the queued TP model works in the context of a transaction from a server's perspective. In terms of our TP monitor model, the server is a workflow controller that is receiving requests from presentation servers, which are its clients. Since queues can be used outside the context of a TP monitor, we will use the more general client/server terminology, instead of

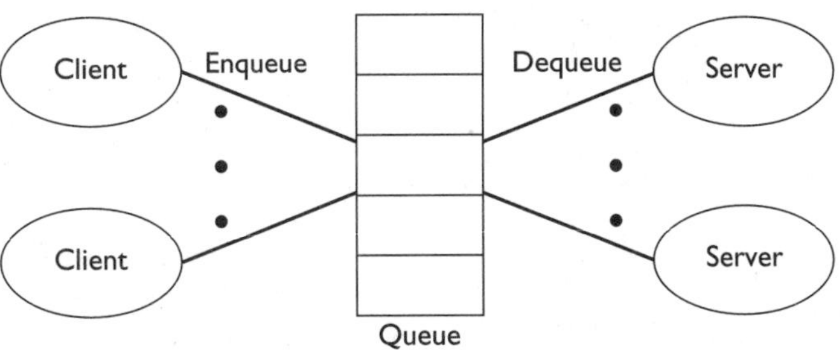

Figure 4.3 Load Balancing Using Multiple Servers When a server finishes processing one request, it takes another request from the queue. This dynamically balances the load across all servers.

presentation server and workflow controller terminology. However, to be concrete, you can think about it in the latter setting without being misled.

As in our description of direct TP in previous chapters, we will assume that each request is asking for just one transaction to be executed. In the queued TP model, the server program starts a transaction and dequeues the next request from the request queue (see Figure 4.4). The server then does the work that the request is asking for, enqueues the reply to the reply queue, and commits.

Since queues are transactional resources, if the transaction aborts, the dequeue operation that receives the request is undone, thereby returning the input to the request queue. If the abort happens at the very end, the enqueue operation to the reply queue also is undone, thereby wiping out the reply from the reply queue. Therefore, whenever the client checks the queues, either the request is in the request queue, the reply is in the reply queue, or the request can't be checked because it is currently being processed. In any case, there's never any ambiguity as to the request's state. It either has not yet been processed, has completed, or is in the midst of being processed.

Client's View of Queuing

In Figure 4.4 we looked at the queues from the server's viewpoint. Now let's look at the entire path from the client to the server in the queued TP model. In this model, each request executes as three transactions (see Figure 4.5). Transaction 1 receives input from the user, constructs a request, enqueues that request onto the request queue, and then commits. Then transaction 2 runs, just as described in Figure 4.4: It starts a transaction, dequeues the request, processes the request, enqueues the reply, and commits. At this point, the request is gone from the request queue, and the reply is sitting in the reply queue. Now, transaction 3 runs: It starts a transaction, dequeues the reply from the reply queue, translates it into the proper output format, delivers that output, and commits, thereby wiping out the reply from the reply queue.

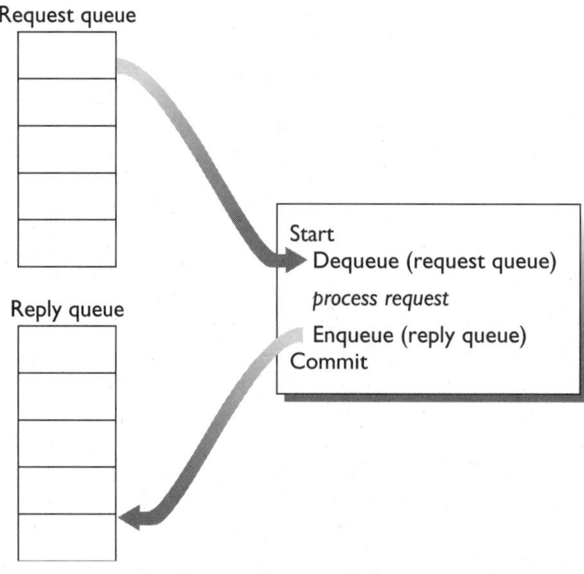

Figure 4.4 Managing a Queued Request within a Transaction The request is dequeued and the reply enqueued within a transaction. If the transaction aborts, the request isn't lost.

For example, to run a debit transaction, the client runs a transaction that enqueues a request on the request queue. The debit server runs a transaction that dequeues the request, debits the account, and enqueues a reply that confirms the debit. Later, the client runs a transaction to dequeue the reply and print a receipt. By contrast, if direct TP were used, the client would send the request directly to the server, and the server would send the reply directly to the client, without any queues in between.

Compare Figure 4.5 to the discussion of push and pull models in the subsection on request message integrity in Section 2.4. Here, the client uses a push model while the server uses a pull model. If desired, the server (transaction 2) can be turned into a push model by adding a dispatcher component that starts a transaction, dequeues the request, and then calls the rest of the transaction 2 code (i.e., starting with "process request" in Figure 4.5).

Because the queues are now under transaction control, they have to be managed by a database system or some other resource manager that supports transaction semantics. To optimize performance, TP monitors usually use a specialized queue manager, which is tuned for the purpose.

Notice that to run even a single request, the system executes three transactions. The client transactions may be rather lightweight, as transactions go. For example, in the simple case of Figure 4.5, they each do one access to a transactional resource, that is, a queue. But even so, queued TP uses more system resources than an ordinary direct TP system in which each request runs as a single transaction. Not only are there two client transactions, but the

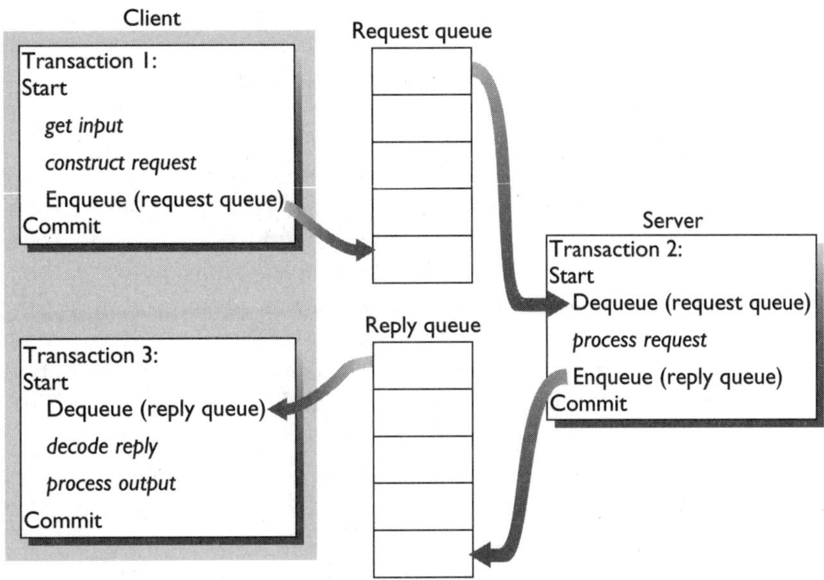

Figure 4.5 Running a Request as Three Transactions The client submits a request (transaction 1), the server processes the request and returns a reply (transaction 2), and the client processes the reply (transaction 3).

server transaction also has two additional accesses to transactional resources—the request and reply queues. In return for this extra overhead, the system offers the benefits that we talked about previously, that is, communication with unavailable servers and clients, load balancing across servers, and priority-based scheduling.

4.3 Client Recovery

An important reason to use queuing instead of direct TP is to address certain client and server failure situations. In this section, we systematically explore the various failure situations that can arise. We do this from a client's perspective, to determine what a client should do in each case.

We assume the request-reply model of Figure 4.5. That is, a client runs transaction 1 to construct and submit a request, and later runs transaction 3 to receive and process the reply. Its goal is to get exactly once behavior—that is, transaction 2 executes exactly once and its reply is processed in transaction 3 exactly once.

Unless the client fails, its behavior is pretty straightforward. After submitting a request, it waits for a reply. If it is waiting too long, then there is presumably a problem with the server—it is down, disconnected, or busy—and the client can take appropriate action, such as sending a message to a system administrator. The important point is that there is no ambiguity about the state of the request. It's either in the request queue, in the reply queue, or being processed.

Suppose the client fails, either because the client application or machine fails or because the client loses connectivity to the queues. Later it recovers. What recovery actions should it take?

To keep things simple, let's assume that the client processes one request at a time. That is, it processes the reply to each request before it submits another request, so it never has more than one request outstanding. In that case, at the time the client recovers, there are four possible states of the last request it submitted:

A. Transaction 1 did not run and commit. Either it didn't run at all, or it aborted. Either way, the request didn't get submitted. The client should resubmit the request (if possible), or else continue with a new request.

B. Transaction 1 committed, but transaction 2 did not. So the request was submitted, but it hasn't executed yet. The client must wait until the reply is produced and then process it.

C. Transaction 2 committed, but transaction 3 did not. The request was submitted and executed, but the client hasn't processed the reply yet. The client can process the reply right away.

D. Transaction 3 committed. The request was submitted and executed, and the client already processed the reply. The client should continue with a new request.

To determine what recovery action to take, the client needs to figure out which of the four states it is in.

If each client has a private reply queue, it can make some headway in this analysis. Since the client processes one request at a time, the reply queue either is empty or has one reply in it. So, if the reply queue is nonempty, then the system must be in state C, and the client should go ahead and process the reply. If not, it could be in states A, B, or D.

One way to disambiguate these states is to have the client mark each request with a globally unique identifier (GUID). The client records each request's ID in its local persistent storage before submitting the request, so it can use the ID at recovery time if need be. In addition, the queue manager keeps the IDs of the last request enqueued and the last reply dequeued by each client in the queue manager's persistent storage. The queue manager updates these IDs every time it performs an enqueue or dequeue for a client.

At recovery time, the client asks the queue manager for the IDs of the client's last request enqueued and last reply dequeued. This is the queue manager's view of the world, and it may differ from the client's.

- If the queue manager's request ID doesn't match the ID of the last request the client thinks it submitted, then the system must be in state A: that is, the client wrote its request's ID in persistent storage and submitted the request; but the server never got the request, so it still has the ID of the client's previous request as the last request enqueued. The client can either resubmit the request (if it has a copy) or start with a new request.

- If the queue manager's ID of the last reply dequeued matches the client's request ID, then the client dequeued (and presumably processed) the reply to the last request the client submitted, so the system is in state D.
- If the reply queue is nonempty, the client should dequeue the reply and process it (i.e., state C). Notice that in this case, the queue manager's and client's request ID must match and their reply IDs do not match, so the previous two cases do not apply.
- Otherwise, the client should wait until the reply appears before dequeuing it (i.e., state B).

The IDs of the last submitted request and the last dequeued reply can be represented as the state of a persistent session between the client and the queue manager. The client signs up with the queue manager by opening a session. The session information is recorded in the queue manager's persistent storage, so the queue manager can remember that the client is connected. If the client loses connectivity with the queue manager and later reconnects, the queue manager remembers that it already has a session with the client because it is maintaining that information in persistent storage. So when the client attempts to reconnect, the queue manager reestablishes the existing session. Since the session state includes the request and reply IDs, the client can ask for them to drive its recovery activity.

4.4 Handling Non-Undoable Operations

Although the analysis of the previous section appears to cover all the cases, it still leaves one problem open if the system is in state C. The transaction that processes a reply (i.e., transaction 3 in Figure 4.5) may perform a non-undoable operation, typically a message to some physical device to perform some action in the real world, such as dispense money or print an airline boarding pass. As we observed in Chapter 1, it isn't clear whether this operation should be done before or after the transaction commits. If the operation is done before the transaction commits, and it actually aborts, then the operation can't be undone, as it should be. If the operation is done after the transaction commits, but a failure happens after it commits and before the operation executes, then the operation is lost.

To solve this problem, the transaction must be able to read the state of the physical device, and the physical device must change its state as a result of performing the operation. That way, the transaction can record the device's state before it performs the operation and can determine if the operation ran by comparing the device's current state to the value it recorded. For example, the transaction might read the check number or boarding-pass number that is next to be printed. After printing the check or boarding pass, the transaction would read a different number for the new check or boarding pass sitting under the print head. If it reads the same number for the check or boarding pass, then it knows the printing operation did not execute.

Given that this device state is available, the transaction that processes replies should follow the procedure shown in Figure 4.6. To see why this works, suppose the client is recovering from a failure and through the previous analysis determines that it is in state C. It should therefore process the reply by running the above transaction. If this is its first attempt at processing the reply, then there is no earlier logged device state for this reply, so the transaction performs the device operation and commits. Otherwise, in step 3 it determines whether it's safe to rerun the device operation associated with this reply. If the state of the device has changed since the previous attempt to run the transaction, then the device operation for this reply appears to have executed, so it is *not* safe. At this point, the operator must get involved to determine what really happened. For example, did the boarding pass really get printed, or was it destroyed by the device, which caused the reply-processing transaction to abort after logging the device's state in step 4? In the latter case, the operator has to tell the transaction whether it's safe to reprint the boarding pass.

A clever technique for logging the device's state is to read the device state *before* dequeuing the reply (i.e., before step 2 in Figure 4.6) and to attach the device state to the log record for the dequeue operation. Since the queue manager has to log the dequeue operation anyway (since it might have to undo it), it can log the device state at the same time and thereby do one write to the log, instead of two.

There is one case where step 3 is not needed: if the device's operation is idempotent. For example, suppose the operation causes a robot arm to move to a certain position, or suppose it sends a mail message describing the transaction. In these cases, there may be no harm in executing the operation a second time. That is, the operation is idempotent. So there is no reason to log the state of the device and recheck it in steps 3 and 4.

Sometimes, an operation that is not normally idempotent can be made idempotent. This is important when it isn't possible to read the current state of the device. For example, sending a mail message that says, "you just bought 100 shares of IBM" is not idempotent. If you issued one request to buy 100 shares and got back two acknowledgment messages like this, you would be worried whether your request executed once or twice. Moreover, at recovery time, there is no device state that the client can read to tell if the message was sent. However, if the mail message says, "your request, with confirmation number 12345, to buy 100 shares of IBM, has executed," there's no harm in sending it twice. You would immediately recognize the second copy as a duplicate and ignore it.

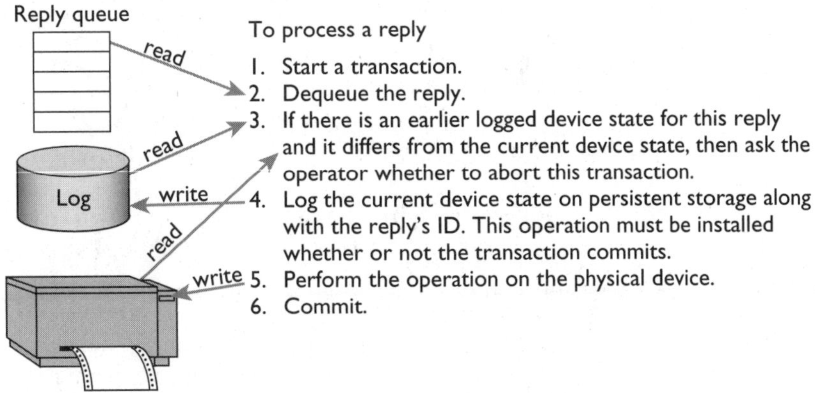

Reply queue
read
read
Log
write
read
write
To process a reply
1. Start a transaction.
2. Dequeue the reply.
3. If there is an earlier logged device state for this reply and it differs from the current device state, then ask the operator whether to abort this transaction.
4. Log the current device state on persistent storage along with the reply's ID. This operation must be installed whether or not the transaction commits.
5. Perform the operation on the physical device.
6. Commit.

Figure 4.6 Client Procedure for Reply Processing Step 3 determines whether the reply has already been processed. Step 4 logs the device state, in case this transaction aborts and restarts, so it can run step 3 the next time around.

4.5 The Queue Manager

To support a queuing model, the system or TP monitor needs a *queue manager* that stores and manages queues. A queue manager is a lot like a database system. It supports the storage abstraction of a queue database. Within a queue database, it supports operations to create and destroy queues and modify a queue's attributes (e.g., its owner, maximum size, user privileges). Most importantly, it supports operations on queue elements.

Operations on Queue Elements

The main operations on queue elements are enqueue and dequeue. The queue manager should also support operations to examine a queue, such as to determine if it's empty, and to scan a queue's elements one by one without dequeuing them. It might also support random access to queue elements, for example, to read or dequeue the third element in the queue.

Usually, the dequeue operation offers two options in dealing with an empty queue. If called with the nonblocking option, it returns with an exception that says the queue is empty. For example, this is useful if a server is polling several queues and does not want to be blocked on an empty queue since another one may be nonempty. If called with the blocking option, the dequeue operation remains blocked until an element can be returned. The latter is useful, for example, to dequeue a reply.

Priority Ordering

The elements of a queue may be ordered in a variety of ways, such as first-come first-served, in which case an enqueue operation places the new element at the end of the queue, or highest-priority-first, in which case an enqueue operation places the new element before the first element in the queue of lower priority.

Whatever the priority mechanism, the ordering is normally made fuzzy by the possible abort of a transaction that does a dequeue. For example, suppose transaction T_1 dequeues the first element E_1 from the queue and then T_2 dequeues the next element E_2 (see Figure 4.7). If T_1 aborts, then its dequeue operation is undone, so E_1 is returned to the queue. However, T_2 might commit, in which case E_2 ends up being processed before E_1, even though it should have been processed *after* E_1.

To avoid this anomaly, T_2 should abort, or possibly not even be allowed to dequeue E_2 until after T_1 commits. Unfortunately, this seriously reduces concurrency among transactions that dequeue from the same queue, in this case T_1 and T_2. This reduction in concurrency is only to prevent the relatively infrequent out-of-order dequeuing that results from an abort. For this reason, most systems allow concurrent dequeue operations and ignore the occasional out-of-order dequeuing. However, in some systems, this out-of-order processing is unacceptable, for example, for legal reasons. In a stock trading system, orders submitted at the same price (to buy or sell) are legally required to be processed in strict timestamp order. To obey this rule and get satisfactory concurrency, trading systems exploit the specific semantics of the trading transactions themselves, for example, by batching up a set of trades and committing them as a group (even though they were submitted separately).

Nontransactional Queuing

Most clients of the queue manager execute queue operations within a transaction. However, it should also be possible to execute operations as independent transactions, so the result is recorded whether or not the surrounding transaction aborts. A classic example is a security violation. Suppose a running transaction discovers that the request it is executing is illegal—for example, it includes an illegal password. It is often important to record such violations, so they can be analyzed later to find patterns of security break-in attempts. The transaction can do this by enqueuing a security violation message on a special queue. Even if the transaction aborts, the security violation should still be persistently recorded. Therefore, the operation to enqueue the security violation message should run as a separate transaction, which commits even if the transaction that called it aborts.

Queue Management

A queue manager usually supports operations to start and stop a queue. Stopping a queue disables enqueue and dequeue operations. While the queue is stopped, these operations return an exception. This is a way of taking a queue

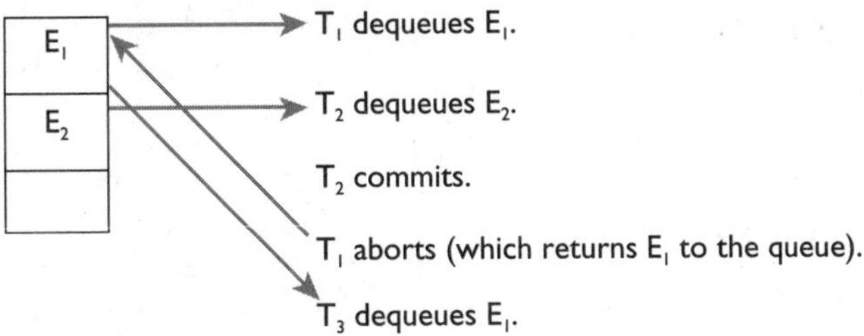

Figure 4.7 An Abort Destroys Priority Ordering Although E_1 is dequeued before E_2, since T_1 aborts, E_2 is processed before E_1.

off-line—for example, if it gets full, or if it's now low priority and should not accept any new work.

Persistent Sessions

If it's known that a queue will be used for requests and replies, then the queuing system can maintain persistent connections with users, including identifiers for the last request sent and the last reply received, as we discussed in Section 4.3. If this request-reply semantics is not built in, then the queue manager might not allow the submission of a request that has output parameters, and hence requires a reply. If it did, then the reply would simply be sent to the client's device and would be received by whoever happens to be using the device when the reply arrives.

Routing

A queue manager usually supports flexible routing. For example, it may support queue forwarding, to move elements from one queue to another. This is useful to reroute a client system's input queue to another server system when the server is overloaded or down. It can also be used to save communications by batching up requests on one system and sending them later in bulk to another system, rather than sending them one by one. Queue forwarding involves reading one or more elements from one queue, moving them to the other queue, storing them on disk, and then committing, thereby removing the elements from one queue and installing them on the other queue as one transaction.

A typical configuration that exploits queue forwarding is shown in Figure 4.8. The client can reliably enqueue requests locally, whether or not the server system is available. Requests on the local queue can subsequently be forwarded to the server's queue.

The transaction to forward a request adds a fourth transaction to the three-transaction model. Alternatively, a client could enqueue its requests directly to a server queue, without using a local queue as an intermediary. This saves the fourth transaction to forward the request. However, the client is unable to

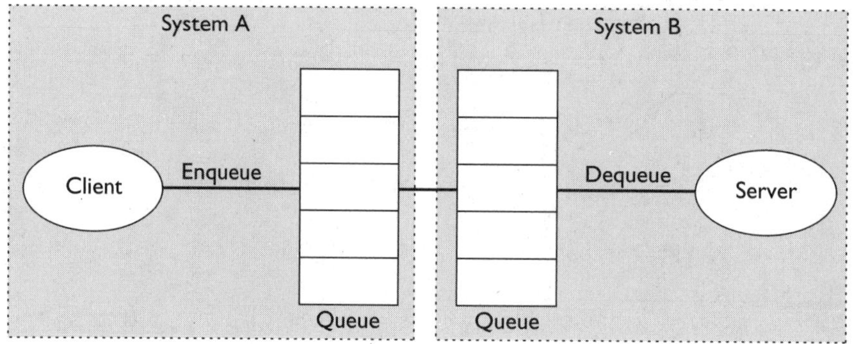

Figure 4.8 Forwarding with Local Enqueuing The client enqueues requests to its local queue. Those requests are transparently forwarded to the server's queue, where the server dequeues them locally.

submit transactions when the remote queue is unavailable. Some products offer both queue forwarding and remote queuing. This allows a hybrid scheme, where the client enqueues to the remote server queue when it's available, otherwise it uses a local queue.

Of course, for a client to support a local queue, it needs a queue database. This requires additional hardware resources and system administration—the price to be paid for the additional reliability.

IBM's MQSeries

A variety of queue manager products are on the market. One of the original implementations was in IBM's IMS TP monitor, where queued TP was the default behavior. Queuing is integrated with many other TP monitors, such as BEA Systems' TUXEDO, Transarc's Encina, and AT&T/NCR's TOP END. Some vendors offer queuing in independent products, such as Digital's DECmessageQ and IBM's MQSeries (MQ = Message Queuing). We briefly describe MQSeries as an example of such products.

IBM promotes MQSeries as an interoperability solution among various operating system and TP environments. Its API, called Message Queue Interface (MQI), can be used by applications running under IBM's TP monitors, CICS and IMS, and on any operating system supported by MQSeries, including IBM MVS/ESA, OS/400, AIX/6000, OS/2, and VSE/ESA, as well as AT&T/NCR UNIX, HP-UX, SCO UNIX, SunOS, Sun Solaris, Tandem NonStop Kernel, UnixWare, VAX/VMS, and Microsoft Windows NT.

The MQSeries queue manager accepts input from an application via the MQI verbs. The main verbs are `MQPUT` to enqueue a message and `MQGET` to dequeue a message. A named queue can support multiple concurrent enqueuers and dequeuers.

To process an `MQPUT`, the queue manager starts a transaction and places the message in the queue. The operation is committed along with the rest of the transaction (which can be the normal exit from the application) or can optionally run in its own transaction as described in the subsection on nontransactional queuing in this section. The enqueued message consists of application data and the *message context*, including a variety of parameters, such as system-generated message ID, an application-assigned message ID, a flag indicating whether the message is persistent, a message priority, the name of the destination queue, the ID of the reply queue (if any), message type (datagram, request, reply, report), correlation ID (to link a reply to a request), priority, expiry time, application-defined format type, code page identifiers (for language localization), and report options—whether the recipient should confirm on arrival (when it's enqueued), on delivery (when it's dequeued), on expiration (if the expiry time is exceeded), or on exception.

The queue manager integrates the transaction managers of many TP monitors, such as IBM's CICS and IMS, BEA Systems' TUXEDO, Transarc's Encina, and Hitachi's Open TP1 (actually, any TP monitor that supports the X/Open XA interface, as described in Chapter 9). Therefore, if the application is running within a transaction using one of these TP monitors, then MQI operations will participate in the transaction. If the application is executing outside a transaction, then the queue manager uses its own transaction manager, which allows the application to group MQI operations within a transaction by issuing explicit commit and abort operations.

The ability to enqueue persistent and nonpersistent messages in the same queue is a unique feature of MQSeries. Nonpersistent messages are more efficient but less reliable. They do not incur logging overhead and are normally handled in main memory, without being written to disk. Both types of messages obey transaction semantics and are guaranteed to be delivered at most once. However, a persistent message is delivered exactly once, while a nonpersistent message is delivered once (in the absence of failures) or not at all (if there is a failure).

Queue forwarding is handled by another component, which is much like an ordinary client that does `MQGET` from one queue manager and `MQPUT` to another, though it does have special access to the log for its sequence number management. So if `MQPUT` has a destination queue name that maps to a remote queue, this component forwards the message asynchronously and transactionally, using an intermediate node if necessary, to the node on which the remote queue exists (see Figure 4.9).

The queue forwarding component uses its own transaction (i.e., two-phase commit) protocol to coordinate updates to the source and target queues. This protocol runs on both LU6.2 (Syncpoint Level 0) and TCP/IP.

An application issues an `MQGET` to dequeue a message. The queue manager starts a transaction upon receipt of an `MQGET` verb, dequeues the message from the message queue, and, upon the commit from the application, the message is physically removed from the queue. If the transaction aborts, the queue manager returns the message to the queue. `MQGET` supports a blocking option, which blocks the caller if the queue is empty, and awakens it when a message is available or a timeout expires. Messages can be retrieved in order or by

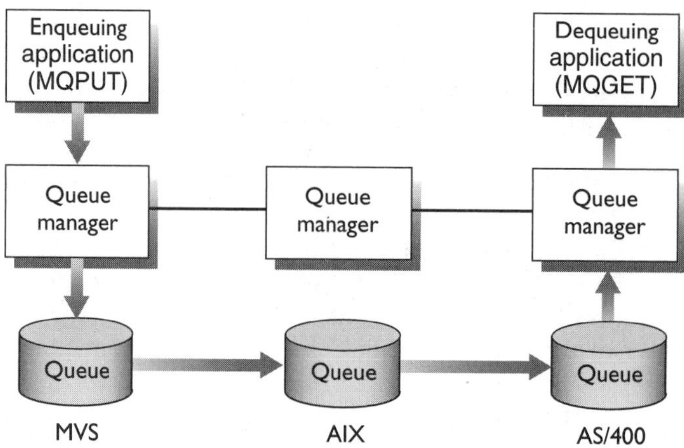

Figure 4.9 **MQSeries Architecture** Queue elements can be forwarded transparently between queue managers running on different platforms.

searching for a given ID or key. The queue can also be browsed, to examine the messages of the queue without deleting them.

MQSeries supports multiple named queues per queue manager. Each queue manager has the following components: a connection manager for managing the connections between the application and the queues; a message manager for remote communications; a data manager to manage the physical storage of the linked lists comprising the queue; a lock manager for locking queues and messages; a buffer manager for caching data, ordering writes, and flushing data to disk; a recovery manager for keeping track of active transactions in the event of a failure/restart; and a log manager for handling the recovery log. These components' names differ slightly in the different MQSeries products.

4.6 Multitransaction Workflow

Queuing techniques are valuable in running requests that require the execution of more than one transaction. We'll look at the general problem of managing such multitransaction requests and then explore how to solve the problem using queuing and other related techniques.

Motivation for Workflow Applications

Many requests require the execution of more than one transaction. These multitransaction executions are usually called *workflows*. A workflow consists of many *steps*. In a TP environment, each step executes as a transaction.

There are many examples of transactional workflow applications:

- Travel reservations—Arranging a trip may require making one or more flight reservations, car reservations, and hotel reservations.
- Insurance claim adjustment—When someone submits a claim, preliminary data must be captured. Later there is an inspection of the damage, which is recorded. After a while the claim is approved, and then, still later, a check is issued.
- Processing an order for some manufactured goods—This may involve a credit check on the customer, reserving the required material from stock, scheduling the shipment, giving commission credit to the salesperson, submitting a request for payment from a credit card company, performing the shipment, and then validating that the order was delivered.
- Money transfer—The source bank must approve the transfer and send a message to the target bank. The target bank must record the transfer, bill the account for the transfer fee, and send an acknowledgment to the source bank. The source bank bills the account for the transfer fee and sends a written acknowledgment to the customer.
- Bug reporting—A bug is reported in a software product. The problem is diagnosed and assigned to the appropriate engineer. The engineer fixes the problem. A test engineer checks that the repaired program indeed solves the problem. The repaired program is sent to the customer who reported the problem, and the bug is marked as repaired.

There are many reasons why a request should be executed as a multitransaction workflow rather than as a single transaction, such as the following:

- Resource availability—At the time the request is taken as input, only some of the people or systems that are necessary to execute the request may be available. For example, when a customer calls in a travel request, the agent might make a flight reservation immediately. But since the expert in hotel-car package discounts is busy, this step is delayed. As another example, one step in processing an expense claim may be getting a manager's approval, but the manager only sets aside time to approve claims once a day.
- Real-world constraints—Processing an automobile insurance claim may require the customer to bring in the car for damage inspection and get two estimates for the cost of the repair. This could take weeks.
- System constraints—When executing a money transfer between two banking systems (e.g., to automatically pay a credit card bill from a checking account), the two systems might not run compatible transaction protocols, such as two-phase commit. The transfer therefore has to run as multiple independent transactions on each system.
- Function encapsulation—Different business functions are managed independently by different departments. For example, in order processing, inventory management is done in manufacturing, scheduling a shipment

is done by the field service group, commission reporting is done in the sales system, credit approval is done by the finance department, and so on. Decomposing a workflow request into steps that are processed by these separate systems is more intellectually and organizationally manageable than designing it to run as one big transaction.

- Resource contention—A long-running transaction usually holds resources, such as a lock on data or a communications device. This causes contention for the resource and thereby slows down other transactions trying to use the resource. What starts as a performance problem, due to resource contention, may turn into an availability problem, since whole groups of transactions may be unable to run until the long-running transaction gives up its resources. For example, a money transfer between two banks could take a long time to run because the banks are connected by slow or intermittent communication. For this reason, the operation normally runs as (at least) two transactions: one on the source system, to debit the money from the source account, and then some time later a second one on the target system to credit the money to the target account.

Managing Workflows Using Queued Requests

Queuing is a natural mechanism to help manage multitransaction workflows. The workflow can be initiated by a request that is stored in a queue. Each step of the workflow produces requests for the succeeding steps of the workflow. Since the steps of the workflow are separated in time, some requests in a workflow may stay in a queue for a long time. However, since the queue is persistent, the request cannot be lost.

The top-level request that initiates a workflow often requires a reply that tells the user when the workflow is completed. For example, the reply might include the itinerary for a trip, the reimbursement for an insurance claim, or the acknowledgment of a money transfer. However, intermediate steps of the workflow often do not need to reply to the originator of the step's request. Rather than sending a reply to the previous step of the workflow, each intermediate step feeds a request to perform the next step of the workflow.

For example, consider the problem of moving orders from one office to another in a global enterprise. The Tokyo office runs a transaction to enqueue an order request (see Figure 4.10). The server recognizes the request as one that requires remote processing, so it runs a transaction that dequeues the order from the queue in Tokyo and enqueues it to another queue in New York. Now a server in New York dequeues the order, processes the order, and enqueues a shipping request. When the order ships, a transaction records that fact and enqueues a message containing an invoice and acknowledgment that the order was filled. A transaction forwards the reply from the queue in New York back to the queue in Tokyo. The Tokyo server prints the invoice and acknowledgment and mails it to the customer. That final step in Tokyo is effectively a reply to the original order request. The intermediate steps are a chain of steps where each step sends a request to perform the next step.

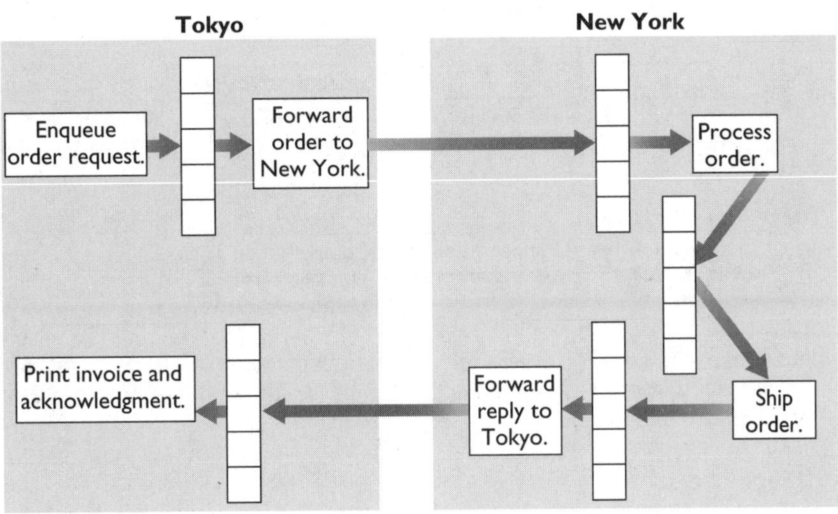

Figure 4.10 A Multitransaction Workflow Each boxed action runs as a transaction. An order is entered in Tokyo, forwarded to New York for processing, processed, and shipped, and a reply is forwarded to Tokyo, which prints an invoice for the order.

Workflow and Atomicity

While multitransaction workflows do solve many problems with long-running requests, they also create some problems. Once you split the execution of a request into multiple transactions, you no longer get the benefits of a single transaction. In particular, you lose the benefits of isolation (i.e., serializability) and atomicity (i.e., all-or-nothing behavior).

Isolation

Consider a money transfer operation as an example, debiting $100 from account A and then crediting that $100 to account B at another bank. If these run as separate transactions, then the money transfer request is not isolated from other transactions. For example, somebody could perform an audit of the two banks while the money is in flight, that is, after it is debited from account A and before it is credited to account B. If the auditor reads those accounts, it would look as if $100 had disappeared. Thus, the audit and money transfer "transactions" are not serializable; no serial execution of the two could result in the audit seeing partial results of the transfer. Moreover, the money transfer is not all-or-nothing. After the first transaction that debits account A commits, a failure may prevent the second transaction from ever being run.

Of course, running the money transfer as one transaction would eliminate the problem. But as explained earlier, there are many reasons why this may not be possible or desirable. Therefore, in contrast to single-transaction requests, multitransaction workflows require special attention to these atomicity and isolation problems.

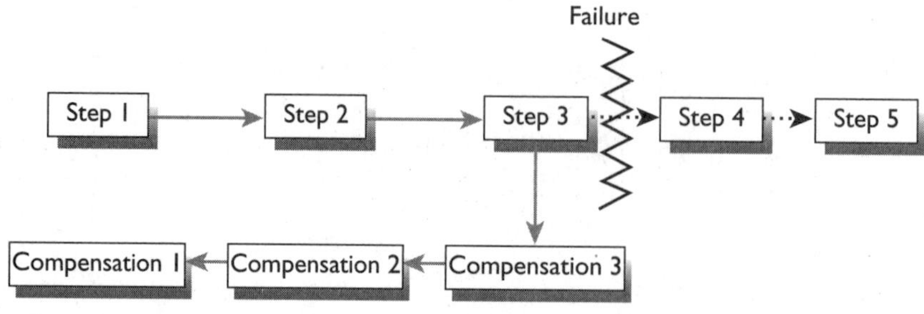

Figure 4.11 A Saga The saga has five steps, each of which is a transaction. Each step's program includes a compensating transaction. Since this execution of the saga cannot proceed past step 3, it runs compensations for the three steps that did execute.

The isolation problem of a multitransaction workflow usually requires application-specific solutions. For example, the bank audit program must have logic that can deal with in-flight money transfers. An alternative general-purpose solution is to lock data for the duration of the workflow. However, for long-running workflows, this creates major resource contention that is usually unacceptable.

All or Nothing

Unlike the isolation problem, semiautomatic solutions to the all-or-nothing problem are possible through automatic compensation. In this approach, all but the last transaction of a multitransaction request has an associated compensating transaction that reverses the effect of the original transaction. So in the money transfer example, the first transaction, which debits $100 from account A, has an associated compensating transaction that puts the money back into account A. If the system is unable to run the second transaction, which credits account B, it can run a compensation for the first transaction that debited account A.

Some research systems have proposed the concept of automated compensation. The system keeps track of the sequence of transactions that have run. If the system is unable to finish the entire sequence, it runs compensations for all of the transactions that already ran, and thereby brings the system back to its initial state (see Figure 4.11). The concept requires the application programmer to write the code for the compensating transactions for each step. The system automates the execution of those compensations by invoking them whenever some of the transactions in the request are unable to run. This is called a *saga*: a sequence of transactions that either runs to completion or that runs a compensating transaction for every committed transaction in the sequence.

In a saga, how does the system keep track of these multiple transaction steps to ensure that at any given time it can run the compensations if the saga

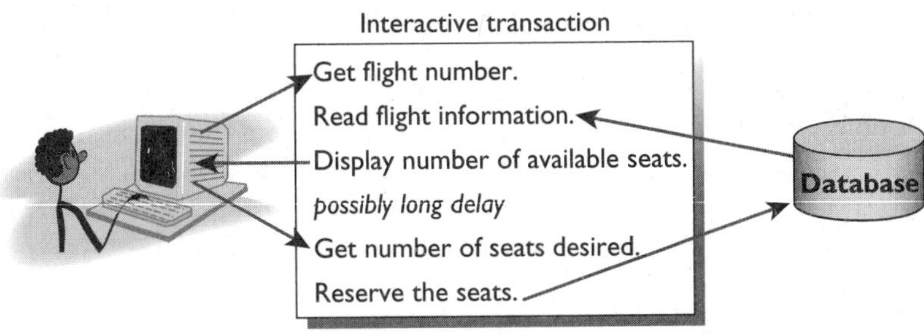

Figure 4.12 An Interactive Transaction During the delay while the user is deciding how many seats to reserve, the flight information is locked, preventing other users from accessing it.

terminates prematurely? One answer is to store the saga's state in queue elements. Each transaction in the saga creates a queue element, a request that incorporates or references the history of the steps that have run so far. If at any point the saga can't run the next step in the request, the system can look at that history and invoke the compensating transaction for each of the steps in the history. Because the queue elements are persistent, they can't get lost. Even if one of the steps is aborted many times, eventually the system will recognize the fact that the saga has not completed and will run the compensating transactions for those steps in the saga.

4.7 Multitransaction Requests without Queues

Another type of multistep request arises from an interactive request, where the resulting transaction interacts with a display device. As before, because of resource contention and availability, it is wise to break up the execution into several transactions, one for each point of interaction.

For example, consider an airline reservation transaction that gets a flight number as input from a display, reads the number of seats available on that flight from the database, and then displays that number and asks the user how many seats to reserve (see Figure 4.12). After the user says how many seats to reserve, this number is entered as input, the number of available seats is decremented, and the transaction commits. To make such transactions serializable, the system ordinarily holds a lock on that flight record for the duration of the transaction. This blocks other users from making reservations on that flight. The blocking delay could be significant while the user is deciding how many seats to reserve. For this reason, determining the number of available seats is usually run as a separate transaction from reserving the seats. That way, the flight record isn't locked while the user is deciding how many seats to reserve. Of course, this means that the number of available seats can change while the user is deciding. That's why ticket agents often reserve seats on the flight you inquire about, to make sure the seats don't go away while you're deciding; if you decide not to reserve them, they cancel the reservation.

In most ways, making this airline reservation is an ordinary multistep request, consisting of two transactions. The first displays the number of available seats, and the second makes a reservation. Like other multistep requests, one could implement it by moving requests between client and server queues. However, these sorts of interactive situations arise often enough that many systems have a special mechanism, called *pseudoconversations*, where the request is shuttled back and forth between client and server.

Pseudoconversations

With pseudoconversations, each time the server processes a request message, it saves some information that was gathered from that transaction step in the message that it returns to the client device (essentially a queued reply). Some of this information may be displayed to the user (e.g., number of available seats). Other information may be there just as context that can be sent back from the client to the next transaction step (e.g., the identifier of a partially completed reservation record). The message is saved in persistent storage on the client and the server. But since there's only one message ever in transit between them, the system doesn't need a mechanism as elaborate as queues. It just needs a disk block reserved for each client.

This way of exchanging messages is called a pseudoconversation because it looks as if it's a conversational transaction; that is, it looks interactive. In fact, it's just a sequence of noninteractive requests, each of which has one input and one output.

Fault-Tolerant Input Using Logging

Logging is another way to make interactive requests reliable, without a pseudoconversation or queuing. In this approach, the system runs the interactive request as one transaction (not a sequence of transactions), and logs to stable storage all of the transaction's input/output operations.

If the transaction aborts and restarts, then the system uses the log to service the transaction's input requests. That is, instead of reading from the display, it inputs the values produced during the previous execution, which are in the log (see Figure 4.13). It can continue to do this until the restarted transaction exhibits different behavior than the original transaction. For example, if the restarted transaction writes a different value than was recorded in the log during the original execution, then the restarted transaction has exhibited different behavior. This could happen because the restarted transaction read a different value from the database than the original transaction. At this point, the transaction is no longer following the same execution path that it did originally, so the system can no longer use the log to provide input to the restarted transaction.

The implementation of this approach can get quite complicated. There are many ways a transaction can perform input and output. Each type of input and output must be logged during the original execution. And for each type of operation the system must be able to reproduce the logged behavior and to detect when the restarted transaction has exhibited different behavior.

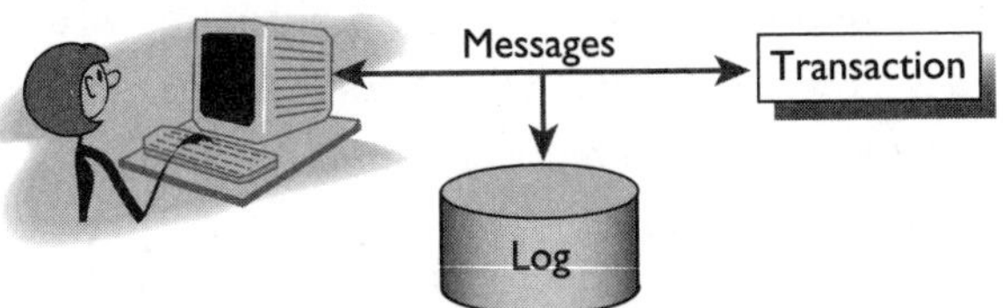

a. During normal operation, log all messages.

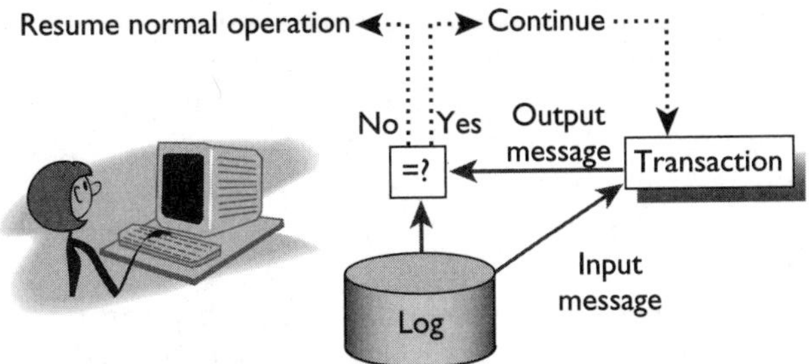

b. Use the log to recover from a transaction failure.

Figure 4.13 **Message Log for Transaction Recovery** During recovery, the transaction gets its input messages from the log and compares its output messages to the result of the previous execution.

This approach of replaying messages yields a similar level of fault tolerance as running multiple transactions, in that it avoids the user having to reenter input when a transaction aborts. However, since it runs the request as a single transaction, it doesn't avoid the problems of resource contention and availability. Thus, it's only suitable when the latter are not critical problems.

This message-replaying approach is used in Digital's RTR product, which maintains logs of client/server communications. In the event of a failure, RTR replays the log in order to bring the system back up to the state that it had at the time of the failure.

4.8 Summary

Queued TP is an alternative to direct TP that uses a persistent queue between client and server programs. The client enqueues requests and dequeues replies. The server dequeues a request, processes the request, enqueues a reply, and commits; if the transaction aborts, the request is replaced in the queue and can be retried.

The main benefits of queued TP are the following:

- A client can submit a request even when the server is down (by enqueuing the request).
- A server can reply to the client even when the client is down (by enqueuing the reply).

- Communication failures do not result in lost replies or uncertain results.
- Balancing the load among multiple servers is easier.
- Priority can be given to some requests relative to others.

The cost of these benefits is the additional transactions to enqueue requests and dequeue replies.

A client can determine whether or not a request executed by examining its queues. An unexecuted request is still in the client's request queue. An executed request has a reply in the client's reply queue. If the queue manager remembers the unique ID of the last request enqueued and reply dequeued by a client, then the client can recover from a failure by synchronizing its state with the state known to the queue manager. To cope with failures that make the result of non-redoable operations (such as printing a check) ambiguous, the client should read the state of the device and compare it to the state it logged before operating on the device.

A *queue manager* is needed to support the queued communication model. It may be an independent product or an integral component of a TP monitor. It provides operations for the storage abstraction of queues, including the following:

- Operations on queue elements, such as enqueue, dequeue, scan a queue, and keyed access
- Create and destroy queues
- Modify a queue's attributes (e.g., queue owner, size, privileges)
- Start and stop a queue

A queue manager may support routing, either by enqueuing to a remote server, or by enqueuing locally and forwarding elements to a remote server. This is useful to reroute requests to another server when a primary server is overloaded or down, or to batch requests that are processed only periodically. When forwarding is done transactionally, it adds a fourth transaction to the model.

Queuing is helpful in running workflow requests, which require executing multiple transactions, such as a travel reservation that includes transactions to reserve an airline seat, rental car, and hotel room. Each workflow step takes a queued request as input and produces one or more requests as output for the next workflow steps.

Breaking up a request into multiple transactions loses the benefits of isolation and atomicity. Therefore, multitransaction workflow applications require special attention to avoid incorrectly interpreting the result of a partially executed workflow and to invoke compensating transactions to cope with the failure of a partially executed workflow.

If a transaction requires interactive input, then it can be broken up into multiple transactions, where each interactive input is the input to a separate request. This is called a pseudoconversation and is another application of multitransaction requests. A related technique to cope with an interactive transaction is to log its I/O, so if the transaction fails in midstream, its I/O can be replayed at recovery time.

CHAPTER 5

Transaction Processing Monitor Examples

5.1 Introduction

In this chapter, we'll survey some popular TP monitor products and standards from the perspective of the three-tier TP monitor model described in Chapter 2. For each monitor, we'll describe its overall system architecture and the particular approaches it takes to TP communications, database system integration, and system management. We conclude each section with some source code examples, using the well-known debit-credit application.

For the most part, we use this book's terminology when describing each TP monitor product, rather than the terminology used by the product itself. For people who know a given product well, it may seem strange to see it described using unfamiliar terms. However, for a reader learning about the monitor for the first time, we hope this approach makes it easier to gain a basic understanding of how the monitor is structured and what features it offers, which is the main goal of this chapter.

We cover eight TP monitors: CICS and IMS from IBM, TUXEDO from BEA Systems, ACMS from Digital Equipment Corp., Encina from Transarc, TOP END from AT&T/NCR, Pathway/TS from Tandem, and Microsoft Transaction Server from Microsoft. We also describe the X/Open Distributed Transaction Processing (DTP) Model, which has influenced, and was influenced by, many of the above products, and we outline the Object Management Group's Object Transaction Service (OMG OTS). We close with Microsoft's Internet Informational Server and Netscape's HTTP Server to illustrate how TP monitor features are becoming integrated with the World Wide Web.

In many ways, the monitors offer very similar features, such as independent presentation servers, multithreaded transaction servers or server classes, transactional communications, queued TP, and two-phase commit. At a detailed level, these features have different capabilities, only some of which are highlighted in this chapter. One obvious difference is platform coverage—different monitors cover different operating systems. Another difference is programming interfaces and communication paradigms. Although the industry is shifting toward standardization on the call-return or RPC communication paradigm, its usage in TP monitor products is far from universal. The monitors conform to various X/Open standards, such as the Structured Transaction Definition Language and the XA interface, but no two monitors conform to the same ones.

The goal of this chapter is to give you a feeling for the state of the art in TP monitors, and some confidence that the technical issues discussed in Chapters 2–4 do give the necessary background to understand a TP monitor product.

It is not a goal to provide sufficiently detailed feature comparisons to help you select the TP monitor product that best suits your needs. Product features change with each succeeding product release, so we recommend that you evaluate the latest product information from the TP monitor vendor when making such a decision.

It is also not a goal to explain enough to enable you to use any of the monitors. For this reason, the example programs provide just enough to illustrate each product's approach. We avoid duplicating concepts, so the examples vary in length from one product to the next. We also omit most error handling and database operations.

5.2 CICS

CICS is IBM's most popular TP monitor product. By the usual measures (number of licenses and customers, and revenue), it currently has the largest market share by far of any TP monitor product.

Developed in 1968 to improve the efficiency of mainframe operating system environments, CICS is now a family of products running on several different platforms and operating systems, such as CICS/VSE, CICS/MVS, CICS/400 (for the AS/400), CICS for AIX, CICS for OS/2, and CICS for Windows/NT. These are supported by several code bases. Some of them have evolved from the original mainframe implementation (e.g., CICS/VSE, CICS/MVS). Others have been developed more recently, such as CICS for AIX, which uses a TP infrastructure supplied by Transarc. (Transarc also offers a TP monitor on this infrastructure, called the Encina Monitor, described later in this chapter.) CICS for AIX has also been ported to several other UNIX platforms, including Digital UNIX, HP-UX, and Sun Solaris. Although there is some variation of features between the implementations, the products all support essentially the same "command level" API.

System Architecture

CICS offers a process-like abstraction called a *region*. A region is an address space that can execute multiple threads. Mainframe CICS uses its own threading abstraction; newer versions of CICS use the appropriate process and memory abstractions available on each operating system. A region can own resources, such as terminals, programs, communications, and databases. Each resource type is described by a table, whose entries list resources of that type (see Figure 5.1). The failure of an application is scoped by a region; that is, when a failure occurs, it only affects the region. The unit of distribution likewise is a region.

In early mainframe versions of CICS, it was common practice to have all resources of a TP application be owned by a single region. Early communications mechanisms were limited and had high overhead, so this was the most efficient structure. It amounts to running the three tiers of a TP application in a single process. Today, communications capabilities are much improved, so the recommended practice is to partition an application into three regions that correspond roughly to our TP monitor model—a terminal region (the presentation server), an application region (workflow control), and a data region (transaction server). Recent enhancements balance application workload among collections of *cloned* application regions.

In a terminal region, the terminal table identifies the terminals attached to the region. When a user logs in, the user is authenticated via a password; later accesses to data resources are controlled via an access control list. The region can optionally also check that the user is authorized to operate from the given terminal (i.e., it supports geographical entitlement) within a given time period and to fulfill a given role (such as being the master terminal operator).

Each request entered by a user includes a four-character transaction code (*transaction* is the CICS term for a request). Using the region's transaction table, the request can be sent to a region that can process it. In CICS, this is called *transaction routing*. In our model, it corresponds to routing a request from a presentation server to a workflow controller.

Requests that arrive at a region are prioritized, based on request type, user, and terminal. Once the request is scheduled, the program table checks to see whether or not this request type can be processed locally, and whether the user and terminal are authorized to run this request. It then loads the application program if it's not already loaded (multiple tasks can share the same copy of a transaction program). Then CICS creates a *task*, which is the execution of a transaction program for a given user and request, assigns it an execution thread, and automatically starts a transaction (it uses the chained transaction model). Each execution thread is reclaimed for use by another program when the reply message is sent.

Presentation Server

Before the widespread adoption of PCs, most CICS systems were accessed by IBM 3270 block-mode terminals, which send and receive a screen of data at a time. This is still a popular mode of access, sometimes with 3270 emulation software running on a PC or with industry-specific devices that conform to the 3270's data stream communications protocol, such as ATMs, bar code readers, and shop floor controllers. Thus, one way for an external system to communicate with a CICS application is to emulate a 3270 terminal and communicate using the 3270 protocol. A client application running on an AIX or OS/2 system can use CICS's external presentation interface (EPI) to communicate with another CICS terminal region in this way (EPI is not currently supported on mainframe servers). Using EPI, the application must pack and unpack the 3270 data stream, and convert from the ASCII to EBCDIC character set, if necessary. A similar function, called the front end programming interface (FEPI), is supported within mainframe CICS.

Another way for an external system to communicate with a CICS application is via the external call interface (ECI), which provides a call-return communications option for clients wishing to connect with CICS servers, such as CICS clients on Windows platforms.

CICS has a built-in forms manager, called Basic Mapping Support (BMS), which maps between a device-oriented view of the data and program-oriented data structures. BMS can be used to interact with 3270 terminals and other types of devices, including EPI clients.

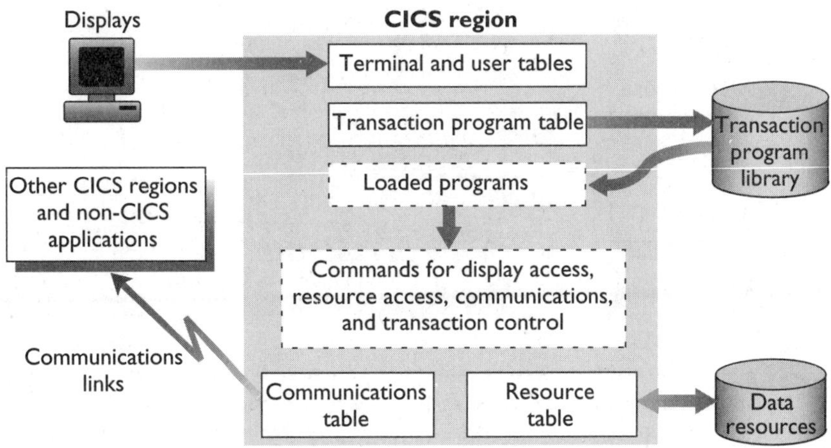

Figure 5.1 A CICS Region A region provides multithreading and controls application resources, including devices, transaction programs, data resources, and communications links.

TP Communications

CICS offers applications a variety of ways to call remote programs. We have already encountered three of them: transaction routing, ECI, and EPI. Some others are the following:

- Multiregion Operation (MRO) and Intersystem Communication (ISC), available on CICS/ESA, /MVS, and /VSE, are transport mechanisms that enable communications between regions running on the same mainframe (i.e., transaction routing and DPL can be implemented using MRO or ISC).
- Distributed Transaction Processing (DTP), which is the APPC interface to LU6.2 for peer-to-peer communications.
- Distributed Program Link (DPL), which is similar to a remote procedure call. DPL is synchronous (i.e., the application waits for the results). ECI is a DPL that accesses a CICS program from outside the CICS environment (see Figure 5.2).

DTP is considered hard to use because the programmer has to establish and break sessions, understand the many possible application states, and consider the state changes effected by each of the DTP commands. However, DTP can interoperate with transactional applications running outside a CICS region if they use LU6.2, which accounts for the popularity of LU6.2 gateways in other TP monitors.

DPL is an easier-to-use alternative to DTP, although DPL does not support all of the DTP state changes. For example, in DPL the called program can automatically run in the same transaction as the calling program, or optionally run as a separate transaction, which commits or aborts independently of the caller, but it cannot in any case issue a Syncpoint. Both DPL and DTP

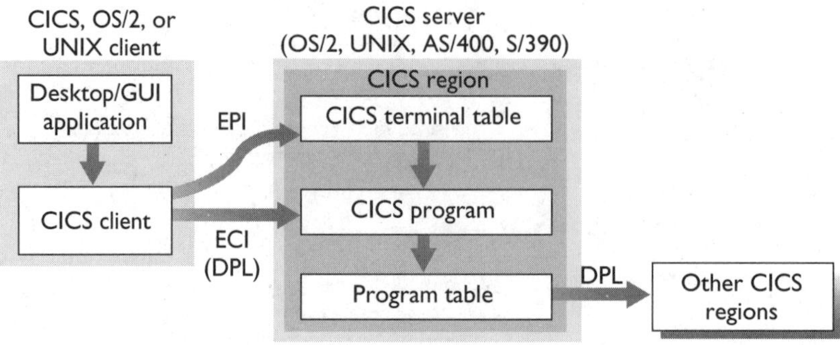

Figure 5.2 Communications from CICS Clients and External Interfaces CICS provides multiple communications options for distributed processing, including the integration of PCs and UNIX servers via the external call interface and the external presentation interface.

require the caller to map the program parameters and convert between the caller's and callee's data representations, though both DPL on AIX and OS/2 clients via the external call interface (ECI) offer data conversion utilities. Examples of DPL calls via the ECI interface are shown in Figure 5.3. (DPL and ECI are essentially the same, the main difference being that ECI executes outside a CICS region while DPL executes inside.)

The *commarea* is the standard place in main memory to put information to pass by ECI and other interregion communications facilities such as LINK and DPL.

The ECI is used by the IBM System Object Model (SOM)/Distributed System Object Model (DSOM) object request broker. It is also used by IBM's implementation of the Object Management Group's Object Transaction Service (OTS) to incorporate calls to CICS applications within CORBA-compliant object-oriented programs. The ECI cannot be used to invoke CICS programs that include terminal I/O, though this is not a serious limitation because programs called by the ECI are generally performing only workflow control or transaction server functions.

CICS offers several styles of queued transaction processing:

- Asynchronous processing—The CICS `START` operation issues a request to begin the execution of a transaction at a specified time or after a specified interval of time. Results are not returned to the caller. Execution of the transaction is not guaranteed in the event of system failure (i.e., the request is queued, but not persistently).
- Transient data—These are queues of data to be sent to a terminal, printer, or sequential file. It can be input to a report.
- Temporary storage—This can be used as a scratch pad for passing data between transactions. There is an option to write the data to a recoverable persistent temporary storage queue. CICS supplies operations for browsing and updating these queues.

An ECI call expressed in COBOL:

```
CALL '_CICS_ExternalCall'
USING BY REFERENCE ECI-PARMS
RETURNING ECI-RETURN-CODE.
```

An ECI call expressed in C:

```
ECI_PARMS           EciBlock;
cics_ushort_t       Response;
:
:
Response = CICS_ExternalCall(&EciBlock);
```

Figure 5.3 ECI Calls Expressed in COBOL and C Using the external call interface, a CICS program can be called from a program running outside a region.

Database Access

CICS was initially implemented on mainframe operating systems that did not support multithreading. Thus, multithreading was implemented by CICS. Recall from Chapter 2 that such an implementation must not allow application programs to issue blocking operations, since they would delay all the threads in the process. Therefore, applications issued all of their database operations to CICS, which could thereby switch threads if a database operation would ordinarily cause the process to be blocked. However, modern versions of CICS allow applications to issue the resource manager operations using the resource manager APIs and integrate those operations within a CICS transaction.

Early versions of CICS did most of their database processing through COBOL indexed files, accessing the VSAM (Virtual Sequential Access Method) file store. CICS and VSAM include services for buffer management, block management, indexed access, and optional logging for rollback. CICS was among the first TP systems to offer remote data access, using a facility called *function shipping*, which allows an application to access a remote VSAM file.

Later, support was added for IMS databases via the DL/I interface and, more recently, for relational databases including IBM's DB2 family and third-party systems, such as Oracle, Sybase, Ingres, and Informix. The AIX and UNIX versions of CICS support the X/Open transaction manager interfaces (described in Chapter 9) that allow other database systems to be added, too.

System Management

CICS provides many system management commands that cover starting and stopping regions, controlling transaction policy (such as starting a transaction on terminal input or message receipt), recovering regions, auditing, batch job scheduling, accounting, and performance monitoring. Many system management operations run as *system transactions* that manipulate the running system, executing in the same region as application program transactions. They are performed as transactions, so they are isolated from application transactions running on the same resources. CICS system management transactions allow multiple regions to be managed from a single point of control.

A CICS system includes a *master terminal* application to control the running system. The master terminal operator can respond to messages from programs; enable or disable CICS files, transactions, or interregion communications; turn on a debugging trace; or install a new copy of a transaction program.

CICS also provides many features that are often associated with operating systems, such as

- virtual storage within a region, such as dynamic storage for loading programs and input/output areas for data sets and workspaces
- timer services, to initiate the execution of a transaction program at a specified time or to send a signal after a specified time period has elapsed
- guarding against storage "leakage" (i.e., crashes due to overwriting system-level storage or out-of-bounds memory access)

Programming Example

Figure 5.4 shows the `PROCEDURE DIVISION` of a COBOL program that embeds CICS commands to execute a simplified debit-credit transaction. In all of the example programs of this chapter, calls to TP monitor services are shown in boldface.

The programming example illustrates the combination of CICS commands and COBOL functions to

- send a "map" or data entry form to the display device
- receive data from the display
- call a debit procedure to withdraw funds from one account
- call a credit procedure to deposit the funds into another account
- notify the display device of successful completion and display the account balance

The CICS `HANDLE CONDITION` command transfers control to the named COBOL section if an error occurs during processing. The example does not include explicit transaction start/commit/abort verbs because transaction control is handled automatically by the CICS system. The `LINK` command transfers control to another CICS program (actually mapping the new program into main storage along with the calling program). The `LINK` command function is nearly identical to the distributed program link (DPL) command, except that the DPL command executes a program in another CICS region.

```
PROCEDURE DIVISION.

001-MAIN SECTION.
      EXEC CICS HANDLE CONDITION
            LENGERR (001-LENGTH-ERROR)
            ERROR   (001-GENERAL-ERROR)
      END EXEC.
      PERFORM 001-SEND.
      PERFORM 001-RECEIVE.
      PERFORM 001-DEBIT.
      PERFORM 001-CREDIT.
      PERFORM 001-SUCCESS.
      EXEC CICS RETURN.
      END EXEC.

001-SEND SECTION.
      EXEC CICS SEND
            MAP ('MAPDBCR')
            MAPSET ('DBCRSET')
            MAPONLY
            ERASE
      END EXEC.

001-RECEIVE SECTION.
      EXEC CICS RECEIVE
            MAP ('MAPDBCR')
            MAPSET ('DBCRSET')
            INTO (INPUT-DBCR-AREA)
      END EXEC.

001-DEBIT SECTION.
      MOVE INPUT-CUST-NO TO CUST-NO.
      MOVE DB-ACCT-NO TO ACCT-NO.
      MOVE INPUT-AMT TO AMOUNT.
      MOVE 'DEBITPGM' TO PGM-NAME.
      EXEC CICS LINK
            PROGRAM (PGM-NAME)
            COMMAREA (PGM-COMAREA)
            LENGTH (24)
      END EXEC.
      MOVE BALANCE TO DB-ACCT-BAL.
```

Figure 5.4 **COBOL and CICS Program for Debit-Credit** This portion of the program defines the workflow control, sends a form to the terminal, receives input, and calls the debit program.

```
001-CREDIT SECTION.
      MOVE CR-ACCT-NO  TO ACCT-NO.
      MOVE 'CREDITPGM' TO PGM-NAME.
      EXEC CICS LINK
            PROGRAM (PGM-NAME)
            COMMAREA (PGM-COMAREA)
            LENGTH (24)
      END EXEC.
      MOVE BALANCE TO CR-ACCT-BAL.

001-SUCCESS SECTION.
      MOVE 'ACCOUNT BALANCES AFTER THE WITHDRAWAL ARE: '
            TO TXFR-MESSAGE.
      EXEC CICS SEND
            MAP ('MAPDBCR')
            MAPSET ('DBCRSET')
            FROM (OUTPUT-DBCR-AREA)
            DATAONLY
      END EXEC.

001-LENGTH-ERROR SECTION.
      MOVE 'INVALID ACCOUNT NUMBER LENGTH, PLEASE TRY AGAIN '
            TO TXFR-MESSAGE.
      EXEC CICS SEND
            MAP ('MAPDBCR')
            MAPSET ('DBCRSET')
            FROM (OUTPUT-DBCR-AREA)
            DATAONLY
      END EXEC.
      GOTO 001-MAIN.

001-GENERAL-ERROR SECTION.
      MOVE 'TRANSFER OPERATION NOT AVAILABLE AT THIS TIME, PLEASE
      TRY AGAIN LATER' TO TXFR-MESSAGE.
      EXEC CICS SEND
            MAP ('MAPDBCR')
            MAPSET ('DBCRSET')
            FROM (OUTPUT-DBCR-AREA)
            DATAONLY
      END EXEC.
      EXEC CICS RETURN.
      END EXEC.
```

Figure 5.4 (continued) **COBOL and CICS Program for Debit-Credit** This portion of the program calls the credit program and includes the CICS exception-handling mechanism.

By using ECI from a client outside of a CICS system (remember that ECI is effectively the same as using DPL), the COBOL program illustrated here could be called from outside of the CICS system, and the `SEND/RECEIVE` commands routed to and from the PC or other display device via 3270 protocol. The example highlights the major CICS API elements used to process a request within a single program, but these elements of the CICS API can easily be used in different programs in separate regions to support a wide variety of application structures, including a PC-based presentation server, integration with queued messaging systems, object-oriented wrappers, and so on.

The CICS *transaction definition* refers to the first application program called by CICS after receiving a request from a terminal (either directly or from a terminal-owning region via transaction routing) or from a program that issues a `START` transaction command. The transaction definition includes security, priority, and location information. The second-level programs themselves (such as those called via a `LINK`, ECI, or DPL) within a transaction also have their own definitions that include security and location information.

All of the CICS commands are translated via a preprocessor into COBOL calls to CICS routines. The `RETURN` command returns program control to the CICS system (or to the calling CICS application program), which is ready to receive the next transaction ID to start the next program.

5.3 IMS

IMS (Information Management System) is another popular TP monitor product from IBM. IMS/ESA V5 is the latest version, which runs on MVS/ESA. IBM says that IMS has 15 million end users and is used by 40 percent of the world's largest companies.

IMS was originally developed in the late 1960s. It was among the first products to offer on-line database and transaction processing at a time when nearly all data processing was done in batch. IMS runs in both on-line and batch modes, allowing the incremental conversion of an application from batch to on-line. Like many TP applications, most IMS applications still contain a large portion of batch programming.

IMS has always been a mainframe product. Today's IMS can interoperate with CICS and DB2, can be accessed from workstations and PCs outside the mainframe environment, and has object-oriented and SQL gateways.

IMS consists of both a TP monitor (which IBM calls a transaction manager) and a hierarchical-style database system, which together are called IMS DB/DC (for database/data communications). The TP monitor and database system are independent and can be configured separately, which allows considerable flexibility. For example, the IMS database manager can be used with the CICS TP monitor, or the IMS TP monitor can be used with DB2, IBM's relational database product. Multiple IMS systems can be configured to support distributed processing environments and as standby systems for high availability.

System Architecture

Applications run in a *system,* which contains the application program itself and the facilities required to support the application. In contrast to CICS on MVS, which manages its own address space, an IMS application runs in an operating system process and accesses TP monitor services such as threading, dispatching, and program loading through a call interface to a system library. Multiple applications can run in separate processes to take advantage of symmetric multiprocessing configurations.

The basic IMS model is queued. An end user (or operator) inputs some data on a terminal (see Figure 5.5). IMS adds a transaction ID, formats the input into a request message, and enqueues it on the input queue. If the application program is not running, IMS starts it. Then IMS dequeues the input message (starting the transaction), translates the transaction ID into the transaction program name, and routes the message to the application, which executes the transaction program using the input data. Dequeuing a message starts a transaction. When the transaction program completes, the application enqueues a reply message to the output queue associated with the input terminal or program. There are options to enqueue the reply message to a different terminal, another application, or a specific user, instead of or in addition to the input terminal.

IMS also offers a *fast path* optimization, which essentially allows the application to bypass the queuing system (i.e., workflow controller) and send simple request messages directly from the terminal to the transaction program, using a predefined mapping. The fast path routing information is kept resident in main memory. Requests that identify fast path transaction programs are automatically routed using the fast path, rather than going through the additional step of translating the transaction name into the destination of the transaction program. The fast path can also use a special main memory database with advanced concurrency control features, as described in Section 6.5 on hot spot locking.

Multiple systems can be configured for a single application and can share access to the same database. Systems can be distributed across multiple nodes, support database replication and partitioning, and can be configured for high availability using local or remote standby systems. An IMS system can communicate with a CICS region, and the IMS transaction manager can be coordinated with the CICS transaction manager for two-phase commit coordination between the two monitors. An IMS system can access a DB2 database and can coordinate a two-phase commit between the two database managers.

Recovery works at several levels. The system as a whole is designed to be recoverable. However, parts of it can be recovered separately. IMS automatically recovers from system crashes, database failures, or application program failures. It also provides several recovery facilities under the control of its users, such as checkpoints, recoverable queues, various logs, automatic abort, and utilities for managing the logs and recovery mechanisms.

A system is composed of regions that perform different types of operations or provide operational areas for the various system facilities. For example, the control region includes the database manager, data communications manager,

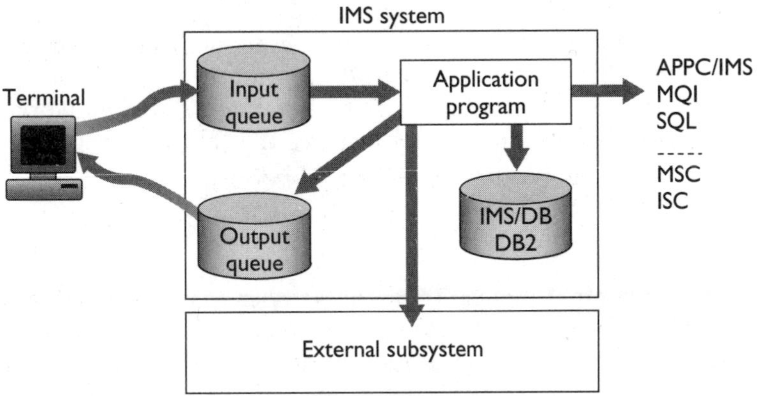

Figure 5.5 IMS System Architecture Request and reply messages move between a terminal and an application via queues. Modern systems connect to external communications and resource managers, in addition to terminals.

message manager, and transaction manager. A dependent region includes the application program, and a batch region includes the database manager and the batch program.

Multiple external subsystems can connect to IMS applications using the External Subsystem (ESS). The ESS provides the functions necessary to support two-phase commit between IMS and the external subsystems. For example, using the ESS, IMS can connect to DB2 or MQSeries.

Another interface, called the Open Transaction Manager Access (OTMA), allows multiple communications managers to connect to IMS. Using OTMA, IMS receives transaction requests from non-IMS sources and routes responses back. Examples of other subsystems that can use this interface are MQSeries, DCE RPC, SOM (object method requests), and TCP/IP sockets.

Some external facilities are accessible directly from an IMS program, such as communication with programs via APPC/LU6.2, MQSeries, Multiple System Coupling (MSC) for joining multiple IMS systems, and Intersystem Communication (ISC), which supports access to CICS programs. In addition, workstations can access IMS databases using either SQL or the native IMS Data Language/I (DL/I).

The MVS Workload Manager (WLM) is integrated with IMS to balance system resource requirements among requests in order to meet explicitly stated response time requirements.

Presentation Server

There is a built-in forms manager, called Message Format Service (MFS), and an optional Screen Definition Facility (SDF) that defines and formats IBM 3270 terminal screens and collects the input data and transaction ID for the request message.

The IMS Client/Server for Windows package provides a communications link to the Microsoft Windows or OS/2 windowing environment. It allows virtually any PC tool to emulate a 3270 terminal.

There is a separate option for changing the terminal network without reinitializing the system. It includes features that allow a program to send a reply message to a user ID instead of a device ID.

TP Communications

IMS is based on a queued TP model, rather than a direct TP model such as RPC or peer-to-peer. This has enhanced request recovery compared to most TP monitors, at the cost of extra transactions and I/O, as described in Chapter 4.

Applications access the input and output queues using calls to retrieve input messages, return output messages to the sending terminal, and send output messages to other application programs and terminals. MFS assists in translating messages between terminal format and the application program format.

An input message can be the following:

- A request to run a transaction program. This type of message (called a "transaction" in IMS, as it is in CICS) includes a transaction code that determines the transaction program to be executed.
- A message to be sent to a logical terminal, identified by logical terminal name.
- A command, identified by a system-unique first character (usually a forward slash), such as a system administration command entered by the master terminal operator.

Input messages are placed on an input queue according to the destination or transaction program name. Once the message is enqueued, the terminal is free to continue work, which is one of the advantages of the queued message model. An input message can be defined to be recoverable, which means it is transactional and therefore will survive a system or application failure. Once the input message is enqueued, it is guaranteed to be processed.

After the input message is processed, the system places the reply on the reply queue. The reply can be enqueued for the user who entered the input message, a different user, or an alternate destination. The reply is also recoverable.

Recent enhancements to IMS have modernized its interfaces, allowing it to accept a DCE RPC call from a PC or workstation, access an IMS database via SQL, use APPC for LU6.2 conversational communications, access the message queue interface (MQI) to interoperate with IBM's MQSeries, and to accept calls from a System Object Model (SOM) wrapper. IMS also supports TCP/IP sockets for LU6.2-style conversations. And IMS has for a long time supported Intersystem Communication (ISC), which allows communication among multiple IMS systems or between an IMS system and a CICS region, and Multiple Systems Coupling (MSC), which allows communication among multiple IMS systems.

Database Access

The native database system that comes with IMS is based on a hierarchical model, which preceded the development of relational database systems. Today's IMS applications can use DB2, in addition to or in place of the IMS DB database. The database access runs using the application's thread. A data propagation utility is available that moves data updates from IMS DB to DB2, or vice versa, automatically. Other middleware tools allow data to be moved between IMS and non-IBM relational databases.

System Management

A master terminal is used to control the running system. The master terminal operator can execute IMS commands that read and modify control parameters, which control the system's execution, or invoke an associated MVS job.

With these commands a system manager can control the placement of database and lock control blocks, modify region sizes, define buffer pools, preload a program list, or override the number of message queue buffers. You can also modify certain system attributes without bringing down IMS, such as database definitions and directories, application program definitions and descriptors, request definitions, terminals, message format options, security, and fast path routing code definitions.

Certain system administration functions are also available in a batch or offline environment. They can start and stop communications lines and message regions, monitor the system, or send messages to users periodically or at predetermined times.

The extended recovery facility (XRF) maintains a duplicate copy of the active system at a backup IMS system. If the active system becomes unavailable, the backup performs recovery procedures and takes over the workload of the active system, thereby providing higher availability than would a single IMS system. This supports the hot backup model described in Chapter 7.

The Remote Site Recovery (RSR) facility provides an alternative option for allowing a remote site to take over the application workload should problems with the primary site prevent its continued operation. RSR allows a remote site to receive a continuous transmission of database and transaction information to maintain a backup. The backup is made live under operator control, unlike XRF, which does this automatically.

Security options include terminal security (which controls the entry of IMS commands from most terminals), password security, and access control on transactions, commands, control regions, application programs, and so on.

Programming Example

The sample IMS program shown in Figure 5.6 reads an input transaction with the following request format:

```
TRANSACTION LENGTH
ACCOUNT ID
TRANSACTION TYPE: C = CREDIT, D = DEBIT
AMOUNT REQUESTED FOR CREDIT/DEBIT
```

For each transaction, a DL/I call is issued with a segment search argument (SSA) to qualify the search for the segment (i.e., record) in the IMS database. When the `ACCOUNT ID` segment is found, another DL/I call is issued to get the account balance. Each `GET UNIQUE` to the IMS message queue commits the previous transaction and starts a new transaction (if another request message is in the queue).

Like most IMS transaction programs, this one is written as a complete module, not as several independent communicating modules. Separate parts of the program handle the debit and credit operations. To complete the debit-credit transaction, therefore, two requests must be queued, one for the debit and another for the credit. Because IMS uses the chained transaction model, and because the queues are recoverable, the debit-credit operation is guaranteed to succeed once both messages are in the queue. Error checking is illustrated following the first IMS call only; in a typical program, the status of each call would be checked, and an appropriate error message output in a similar fashion.

5.4 TP Standardization—X/Open, OSI, OMG, and MIA/SPIRIT

There are several efforts to standardize APIs (and thereby gain application and database system portability across TP monitors) and to standardize protocols (and thereby gain interoperability between TP monitors). Like the products they intend to influence, these standards are evolving designs. They will change over time, and new standards will be added as products and customer requirements evolve.

Development of these standards is recent history. Most were started in the mid-1980s, in parallel with the growing popularity of "open" systems, long after CICS, IMS, and other proprietary monitors were well established. All of the monitors described later in the chapter influenced, or were influenced by, some of these standards efforts.

X/Open

X/Open is part of The Open Group, Inc. X/Open's goal is to promote application portability through the development of API standards. X/Open has developed a distributed transaction processing (DTP) model, which includes many of the standard functions offered by TP monitors. The first version was

```
PROCEDURE DIVISION.

ENTRY-LINKAGE.
    ENTRY 'DLITCBL' USING I-O-PCB DB-PCB.

MAIN PROGRAM.

    PERFORM GET-MSG-ROUTINE THRU GET-MESSAGE-ROUTINE-EXIT
                    UNTIL I-O-STATUS-CODE EQUAL 'QC' OR 'QD'.
    GOBACK.

GET-MESSAGE-ROUTINE.

    CALL 'CBLTDLI'  USING  GET-UNIQUE
                           I-O-PCB
                           TERM-IN.

IF I-O-STATUS-CODE EQUAL 'QC'
    GO TO GET-MESSAGE-ROUTINE-EXIT.

IF I-O-STATUS-CODE NOT EQUAL SPACE
    MOVE I-O-PCB TO MESSAGE-AREA
    PERFORM SEND-MESSAGE-ROUTINE
    GO TO GET-MESSAGE-ROUTINE-EXIT.

MOVE INPUT-ACCT-ID TO ACCT-ID-SSA.

CALL 'CBLTDLI'  USING  GET-UNIQUE
                       DB-PCB
                       I-O-AREA
                       ACCT-ID-SSA.

IF STATUS-CODE NOT EQUAL SPACE. . .

IF TRAN-TYPE NOT EQUAL CREDIT-TYPE OR DEBIT-TYPE. . .
    MOVE INPUT-AMOUNT TO ACCT-BALANCE-SSA.

CALL 'CBLTDLI'  USING  GET-HOLD-UNIQUE
                       DB-PCB
                       I-O-AREA
                       ACCT-ID-SSA
                       ACCT-BALANCE-SSA.
```

Figure 5.6 IMS COBOL Example The PROCEDURE DIVISION starts with a loop that executes until no more messages are found on the queue. The first time a request is issued for this program, IMS loads it and keeps it loaded until all requests for the program are completed. The main section of the program processes the request message and accesses the database using the common IMS service library.

```
IF TRAN-TYPE EQUAL CREDIT-TYPE
    ADD INPUT-AMOUNT TO ACCT-BALANCE

    CALL 'CBLTDLI'  USING  REPLACE
                           DB-PCB
                           I-O-AREA
                           ACCT-BALANCE-SSA.

    MOVE INPUT-AMOUNT TO ACCT-BAL-MESSAGE
    MOVE OUTPUT-MESSAGE TO MESSAGE-AREA
    PERFORM SEND-MESSAGE-ROUTINE
GO TO GET-MESSAGE-ROUTINE-EXIT.

IF TRAN-TYPE EQUAL DEBIT-TYPE
    SUBTRACT INPUT-AMOUNT FROM ACCT-BALANCE

    IF ACCT-BALANCE LESS THAN 0
        MOVE NO-MONEY-MESSAGE TO MESSAGE-AREA
        PERFORM SEND-MESSAGE-ROUTINE.

    CALL 'CBLTDLI'  USING  REPLACE
                           DB-PCB
                           I-O-AREA
                           ACCT-BALANCE-SSA

    MOVE INPUT-AMOUNT TO ACCT-BAL-MESSAGE
    MOVE OUTPUT-MESSAGE TO MESSAGE-AREA
    PERFORM SEND-MESSAGE-ROUTINE
    GO TO GET-MESSAGE-ROUTINE-EXIT.

GET-MESSAGE-ROUTINE-EXIT.
    EXIT.

SEND-MESSAGE-ROUTINE.

    CALL 'CBLTDLI'  USING  INSERT
                           I-O-PCB
                           TERM-OUT.

    IF I-O-STATUS-CODE NOT EQUAL SPACE
          ADD PACKED-ONE TO BAD-DATA.
```

Figure 5.6 **(continued) IMS COBOL Example** This section illustrates the processing for the credit and debit operations. At the completion of the request, the SEND-MESSAGE-ROUTINE is invoked to send the reply to the terminal.

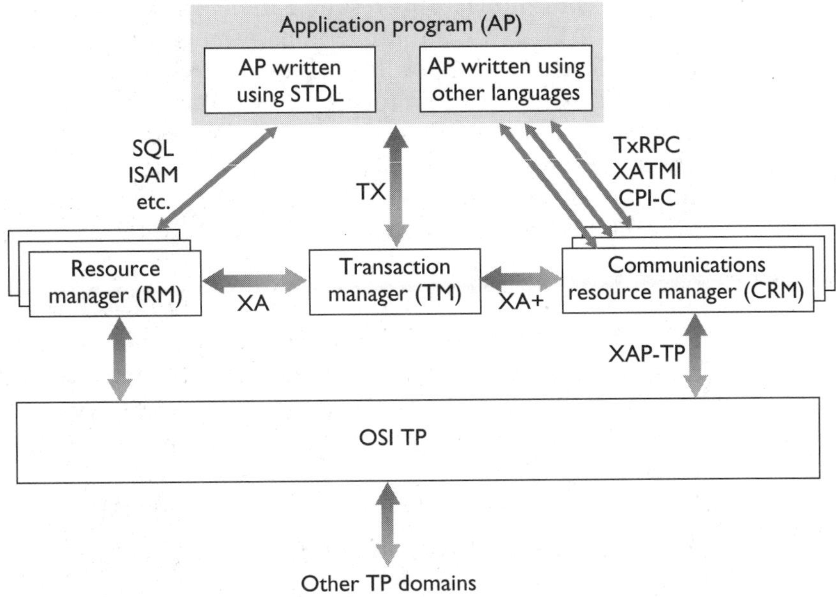

Figure 5.7 **X/Open DTP Model** An application program uses X/Open programming interfaces or STDL to access transaction and communications management services. The XA standard allows different vendors' TP monitors and resource managers to interoperate.

released in 1991, covering transaction demarcation and resource manager interfaces to transaction managers (for two-phase commit). The initial model has undergone steady development and is now quite detailed, including communications interfaces and a workflow control language, STDL.

The X/Open DTP model divides a TP system into components (transaction manager, database or other resource manager, and transactional communications manager) and defines interfaces between the components. Figure 5.7 illustrates the model.

The main components and interfaces in the model are the following:

- TX—Defines the interface between an application and the transaction manager. TX verbs start, end, and obtain status information about transactions. STDL optionally can be used instead of TX.
- XA—Defines the interface between a resource manager and the transaction manager. When a TP monitor and database system both support the XA interface, they can be plugged together and coordinate a transaction between them. The XA interface is the most influential of the X/Open specifications. It has broad industry acceptance, so users can rely on it to combine leading TP monitor and database products. The XA interface is described in more detail in Section 9.5.

- CRM—A communications resource manager (CRM) provides an application-level API to a communications protocol for remote, transactional communications. X/Open has adopted three CRMs: XATMI (based on the TUXEDO API and protocol), CPI-C (based on a CICS API and LU6.2 protocol), and TxRPC (based on the ACMS and Transarc RPC models). CRMs are interoperable only when communicating with CRMs of the same type; for example, an XATMI CRM can interoperate with another XATMI CRM, but not with a CPI-C or TxRPC CRM.
- XA+—Extends XA with an interface between a transaction manager and a CRM, so the CRM can tell the transaction manager that a subordinate node joined a distributed transaction.
- RM—Resource manager (RM) interfaces are "native," that is, they are defined by the resource manager products themselves and are therefore outside the scope of the X/Open DTP model, although typically the resource managers are recoverable.
- XAP-TP—Provides an API between a CRM and OSI TP.
- STDL (Structured Transaction Definition Language)—Provides a portable TP language. It is an optional interface to any of the CRM protocols; only the mappings to TxRPC are publicly available. (STDL is described further, below.)

Most of the TP monitors described in this chapter implement one or more of the X/Open DTP specifications, but they do not implement the same ones.

OSI TP

OSI TP is the only two-phase commit protocol developed by an independent standards body. However, it is not widely implemented or endorsed. The three CRM interfaces of the X/Open model are layered on OSI TP, but this is not widely deployed in today's products. (See the subsection of Section 3.4 on the ISO TP protocol.)

Object Transaction Service

The Object Management Group (OMG) is an industry consortium that developed the Common Object Request Broker Architecture (CORBA) specifications, which is an interface for remote object invocation. They have more recently published an Object Transaction Service (OTS) specification that defines a transactional service based on CORBA for an object-oriented programming environment. The specification builds on the X/Open specifications and assures compatibility between the OTS and X/Open DTP models, which requires coexistence of procedure-oriented X/Open-compliant TP systems and object-oriented OTS-compliant TP systems (the details of how this is provided are currently sketchy).

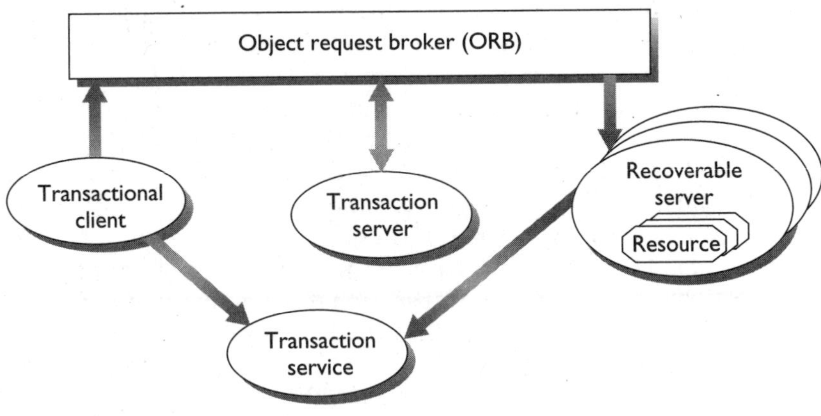

Figure 5.8 **The Object Transaction Service Defined by OMG** The transactional client calls a transactional server, which may be in the same address space as a recoverable server. The recoverable server registers recoverable resources as participants in the transaction and coordinates the transaction with the client via the transaction service object.

Many vendors have announced plans or intentions to support OTS. For example, Encina currently supports OTS, as described in Section 5.7. Like X/Open, OMG specifications allow a significant amount of flexibility in options and interpretation. For example, nested transaction support is not defined by X/Open, but it is optional in OTS (nested transactions are explained in Section 11.4). So the type and degree of OTS support will probably vary from vendor to vendor.

The OTS model includes a transactional client, transactional server, and recoverable server. A transactional client is a program that can invoke operations within a transaction and therefore corresponds to either a workflow controller or transaction server in our model. The transactional server and recoverable server abstractions in OTS correspond to the transaction server and resource manager in our model (see Figure 5.8). The concept of presentation server or nontransactional client is not explicitly called out in the OTS model.

The main difference between the object-oriented OTS model and the procedure-oriented X/Open model is that OTS casts all of the basic transaction operations as methods on objects. For example, instead of issuing a Start operation to the transaction manager, as in the X/Open model, one calls the Create method on the TransactionFactory interface of the Transaction Service object, which returns a Control object. The Control object can later be used to get a Terminator or Coordinator object that can be used to commit or abort the transaction.

A transaction is started and controlled by the transaction service. The transactional client and server communicate using the ORB, which propagates the transaction context from transactional client, to transactional server, to recoverable server. The transaction context can optionally be propagated explicitly by the application, instead of implicitly by the ORB. The client initiates the commit and rollback operations. The objects can, in theory, be placed anywhere in the network.

The transactional server does not access recoverable resources and therefore does not have to communicate with the transaction service. Also, a transactional server cannot communicate with another transactional server as a subordinate in a coordinated transaction.

The ORB performs many of the functions of a TP monitor. In effect, it is a model for TP monitor behavior in the OMG object architecture.

An object is defined as transactional via an attribute of the CORBA Interface Definition Language (IDL), which is similar to the DCE IDL. If an interface contains the transaction attribute, the ORB directs the transactional client call to the transactional server. When the client issues method invocations, the ORB manages the transaction context using the transaction service.

OTS does not specify a required two-phase commit protocol, which means interoperability depends on bilateral agreements between implementing vendors.

STDL

STDL was developed by the Multivendor Integration Architecture (MIA) Consortium, led by Nippon Telegraph and Telephone (NTT), with the collaboration of Digital, Fujitsu, Hitachi, IBM, and NEC. The goal of MIA was to provide a standard API for TP monitors and have it be implementable on a variety of TP monitor products (see Figure 5.9). Following the development of the original STDL specification, the Service Providers' Integrated Requirements for Information Technology (SPIRIT) Consortium—a follow-on to MIA, organized within the Network Management Forum (NMF)—produced an enhanced version of STDL, including additional contributions from Bellcore, BT, France Telecom, Hewlett-Packard, and Telecom Italia. This version of STDL was subsequently adopted as an X/Open standard.

An STDL compiler—or more typically, precompiler—translates STDL syntax into API calls for the TP monitor it supports. The (pre-)compiled application program is then submitted to the normal TP monitor compiler or preprocessor to produce executable programs. Thus, most vendors can offer an STDL interface without rewriting their TP monitor infrastructures. Communications mechanism transparency is provided by STDL's interface definition languages, called *group specifications*, that define procedure interfaces separately from the procedures themselves.

STDL does not impose an underlying process model and therefore can be supported on single or multitier systems, with or without multithreading. The underlying communications mechanism is assumed to be RPC; no peer-to-peer statements exist in the language. Of course, the RPC semantics can be emulated using peer-to-peer messaging, and some vendors support STDL using this approach. From a purely functional level, STDL features strongly resemble those of CICS, including chained transactions, concurrent execution, transient data queues, and transactional files.

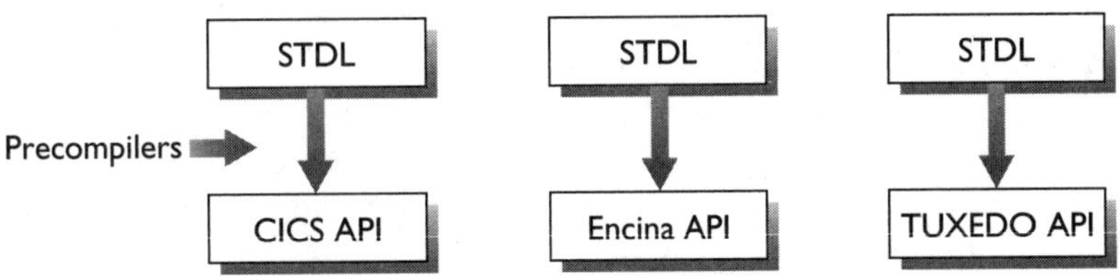

Figure 5.9 **STDL Precompilers Emit TP Monitor APIs** STDL defines a common language for TP monitors that can be mapped to existing products.

MIA also developed a companion specification for interoperability, called the Remote Task Invocation (RTI) protocol, for invoking remote STDL tasks. The MIA RTI specification was later adopted by X/Open as the basis of its transactional RPC (TxRPC) specification.

Today in Japan the original MIA vendors offer STDL- and RTI-compliant products, as do Unisys, Sun, Tandem, AT&T/NCR, and HP. Digital and AT&T/NCR offer STDL-compliant products worldwide.

5.5 TUXEDO

TUXEDO is BEA Systems' portable TP monitor. It is offered on more than 15 operating systems, including a wide variety of UNIX platforms and Windows NT. The product is sold directly by BEA Systems, who purchased the rights for TUXEDO from Novell in 1996, and by many resellers who customize the product for their own platforms. AT&T's Bell Laboratories created TUXEDO in 1984, primarily to service telecommunication applications, which is still its largest market. The TUXEDO design is based on IMS and was originally intended to replace IMS at the U.S. telephone companies (who are large IMS users). The current version is TUXEDO 6.1.

TUXEDO is the basis for many of the X/Open DTP standards, including the DTP model itself, XA, TX, and XATMI.

System Architecture

The TUXEDO API, called the *Application to Transaction Manager Interface* (ATMI), is a collection of runtime services that are called directly by a C or COBOL application. These runtime services provide support for communications, distributed transactions, and system management. In contrast to the CICS API, which was developed 15 years earlier, ATMI relies more heavily on underlying operating system and database system services.

TUXEDO's services are implemented using a shared *bulletin board*, which contains configuration information (similar to CICS tables) that supports many TP monitor functions. For example, it contains transaction service names, a mapping of transaction service names to transaction server addresses, parameter-based routing information, and configuration options for transaction services and servers.

One system is designated as having the *master* bulletin board. The bulletin board at each node is loaded into shared memory from a configuration file when TUXEDO boots. Later changes to the master bulletin board are written to the configuration file, which propagates to a machine the next time TUXEDO boots on that machine or when a running instance of TUXEDO reloads the file. Servers and services can be added, modified, or removed dynamically.

A TUXEDO system consists of *client* and *server* processes. Clients typically provide presentation services to users. That is, they interact with devices that issue requests and do not access transactional resource managers. Unlike our TP monitor model, they are allowed to issue a Start operation, which may optionally be forwarded to the server (workflow controller or transaction server) to actually start the transaction.

TUXEDO systems are configured in a *domain*, which defines the scope of computers in the network that participate in a given application. The domain concept is similar to the cell concept used by DCE and Encina.

Like CICS, a TUXEDO server can perform the functions of workflow control, transaction server, or both. This flexibility allows one to structure an application in the three-tier fashion described in Chapter 2, but it doesn't require it.

A *service* is the name of a server interface. A service can be supported by many transaction servers, and a transaction server can support many services. The mapping of services to transaction servers is recorded in the bulletin board (see Figure 5.10). When a client calls a service, the bulletin board forwards the call to a server that supports the service, similar to the way in which IMS routes a queued message to a transaction program. The server might be on a different node than the client, in which case the bulletin board routes the request via a bridge to the other node. The bulletin board serves as a type of temporary queue space while the message is being routed. When a service becomes available, the server advertises the service by posting the service name to the bulletin board. A service is similar to the concept of request type in our TP monitor model.

Each process has a main memory queue that is used for incoming messages (see Figure 5.11). A call to a service causes a message to be put into its queue. As in IMS, the server dequeues messages sent by the client and does the requested work, optionally in priority order. When it's done, the server sends a reply message to a message queue associated with the client, which includes a status that tells whether the call completed successfully or resulted in an error. The client dequeues the message and processes the reply.

TUXEDO offers programmers the usual transaction control primitives—`tpbegin`, `tpcommit`, and `tpabort`. In addition, flags can be set in the client program (for example in Data Entry System options, explained below) and in the configuration file to place the execution of transaction programs in automatic transaction mode. In automatic transaction mode, a transaction is automatically started when the transaction program receives control from the presentation server (or client program, in TUXEDO terminology) and is auto-

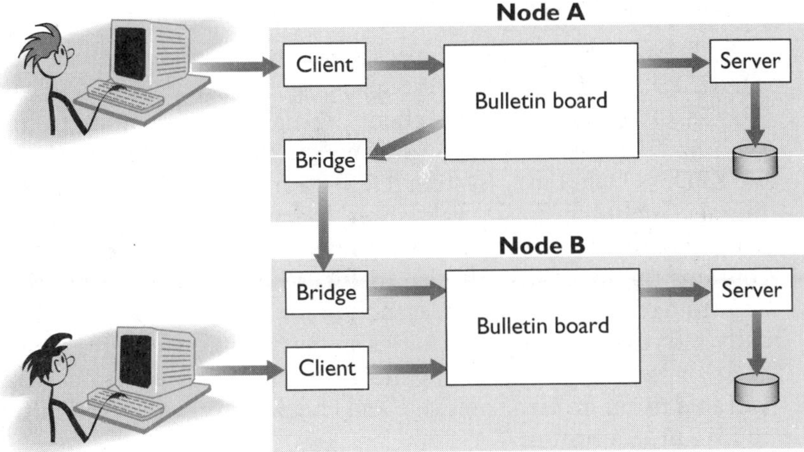

Figure 5.10 TUXEDO Client/Server Architecture Requests are routed to the correct server process using the bulletin board, whether on a local or remote node.

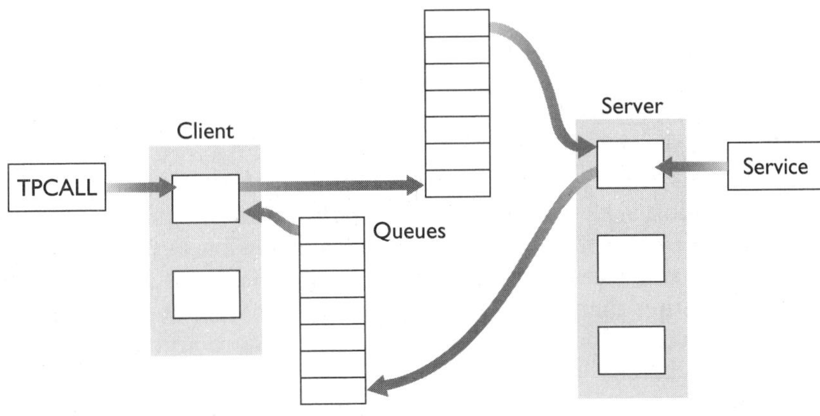

Figure 5.11 TUXEDO Request Message Flow Requests are routed between client and server processes using input and output queues.

matically committed if the execution of the server program is successful. If the client program starts a transaction, automatic transaction mode detects the existing transaction and includes the transaction program in the same transaction. An execution error (that is, return of bad status) results in an automatic transaction abort. This is similar to the way CICS handles transactions for DPL-invoked programs. Another option is asynchronous commit processing, where an application can continue without waiting for the second phase to complete in a two-phase commit operation.

Presentation Server

In addition to the System/T package, which supports all the server functions, TUXEDO offers a System/WS package for presentation servers that access TUXEDO servers from PC clients. This allows custom front-end packages, such as client/server 4GLs, to issue service calls. Alternatively, one can use TUXEDO's Data Entry System (DES) for menus and forms on character cell terminals, including basic validation functions. The form input contains the desired transaction type's service name and a typed buffer (described below) that contains the input data. It also includes flags that select various options, such as automatically starting a transaction for the server being called and automatically retrying the transaction after an operating system interrupt signal.

Error handling is at the application level. The program examines a global variable to get an error message and checks this error status after every call, as in IMS programming.

TUXEDO supplies some system servers: BQ for background jobs (batch emulation); FRMRPT, which prints a copy of a data entry form; and AUTHSVR, a client authentication server. Features for /Q, IBM connectivity, and the event system are described below.

TP Communications

Processes can communicate using either peer-to-peer message passing, remote procedure calls, or an event posting mechanism, all of which TUXEDO layers on their peer-to-peer protocols. As in CICS, an RPC can be synchronous (i.e., the application waits for the results) or asynchronous (i.e., the application asks sometime later for the results). Using peer-to-peer, the programmer can establish a conversational session between the client program and the transaction server and exchange messages in an application-defined order, rather than in the strict request-reply style of RPC. There is a subscription service to put events on the bulletin board and an event posting mechanism, whereby a server can raise an event, which sends an unsolicited message to one or more clients (in the case of multiple clients, this represents a type of broadcast facility).

Communications messages can be constructed using TUXEDO's Field Manipulation Language (FML). This creates *typed buffers*, which are similar to the CICS commarea. TUXEDO also provides language bindings for the X/Open TxRPC Interface Definition Language (IDL) and a nontransactional DCE RPC gateway. For the event service, the fulfillment of a subscription to raise an event includes TUXEDO functions such as calling a service, enqueuing a message, or logging a message to a file. All three methods of communication are optionally transactional.

Unlike Pathway/TS or ACMS, the RPC client cannot retain a long-lived connection with a server that maintains context across RPCs. Instead, the client and server must use send-message and receive-message calls within the bracket of a call-return pair. Essentially, the call creates the connection, which is held until the server issues a return.

When a server calls another server, the caller can specify whether the callee runs in the same transaction or outside of the transaction context.

Transaction servers can also forward control to another transaction program while keeping the same return address of the original client program. For example, A calls B, B forwards the call to C, C services the call and returns to A (not B, which called it).

TUXEDO has a gateway to CICS/MVS via APPC/LU6.2, but without Syncpoint Level 2 processing (i.e., no transaction semantics).

An optional mechanism, called System/Q, supports a basic queued message-passing capability through persistent storage. Instead of submitting a request to a transaction server's main memory queue, a client enqueues the request to a disk-based queue manager. Queued requests are optionally forwarded to the appropriate server via a forwarding agent. Although TUXEDO does not directly support pseudoconversational programming, an application can get the same effect by explicitly exchanging persistently queued messages.

Database Access

TUXEDO has a built-in transaction manager that supports two-phase commit. It can use any XA-compliant resource manager, such as Oracle, Sybase, Ingres, or Informix.

System Management

System management changes are significant in the latest version with the introduction of a TUXEDO Management Information Base (TMIB). The TMIB maintains a virtual repository of configuration and operational information about a running TUXEDO application. The TMIB uses an entity/attribute typed buffer to support operations such as `get` and `set` configuration information. The TMIB also reports exceptions in the running TUXEDO application using the system-level brokered events. The TMIB supplies a graphical user interface (GUI).

The system manager controls the system configuration via the bulletin board's master node. There are commands to start up and shut down the system, compile the configuration file, load the bulletin board from the configuration file, add or remove services, move servers between nodes, change server priorities, and so on. There is built-in support for a backup master node in case the original one crashes.

Security is either supplied externally to TUXEDO—for example, by the underlying operating system platform—or by using optional application-specific authentication and authorization mechanisms.

Data-dependent routing is accomplished by matching data included in a `tpcall` statement against a predefined table that determines the location of the called service. Load balancing is performed by examining statistics kept by the system on the usage of services and on the amount of load on the process queues, so that a call can be routed to a lightly loaded queue.

```
main ()
{
char *rbuf;
char *reqfb;
long reqlen, r1len, r2len;
. . . // construct reqfb, which contains parameters to the call to DBCR
reqfb=tpcalloc("FML", "", 200);  /* allocate typed buffer for request */
tpcall( "DBCR", (char *)reqfb, 0, (char **)&reqfb, (long *)&reqlen,
        TPSIGRSTRT);
. . . // construct the input buffer, rbuf, for the next call
tpcall("PRINTER", rbuf, r1len, &rbuf, &r2len, TPNOTRAN)
}
```

Figure 5.12 A Client Program Using TUXEDO's ATMI Note the buffer allocation before issuing the tpcall to the DBCR and PRINTER services.

Programming Example

This section shows a simplified debit-credit example programmed using ATMI and C.

The client program (Figure 5.12) calls the DBCR server to debit one account and credit another and then calls a print service to print the result. It uses the tpcall primitive, which does a remote procedure call. Notice that parameters are passed and returned in a character buffer reqfb, which must be allocated and constructed by the client before the call. The server returns its parameters in the same buffer, along with a length, reqlen. For simplicity, the example leaves out the steps for initialization, joining the application, allocating buffer space, and error checking. The example illustrates the service-based approach of TUXEDO, which models its API after a UNIX system service library.

As an alternative to tpcall, the client could use tpacall ("tp asynchronous call") to issue the request and later use tpgetreply to get the result. Using tpcall is equivalent to using tpacall immediately followed by tpgetreply.

The server program DBCR (Figure 5.13) calls two other server programs within the transaction. It uses the primitives tpbegin, tpcommit, and tpabort to bracket the distributed transaction. Like the client, it uses tpcall to call servers, but since it is running within a transaction, those calls transparently propagate its transaction context. If the DEBIT and CREDIT servers are running on different databases, the execution of tpcommit runs TUXEDO's two-phase commit protocol.

The TPSVCINFO buffer contains the request information, including the service name (as posted on the bulletin board), service attribute flags (i.e., whether in transaction mode or not), request parameters and length, connection descriptor (if it's a conversational connection), application authentication key, and a client ID (so the service can issue a tpnotify to the client if desired).

```
void DBCR (TPSVCINFO *buf);
{
...
tpbegin()
ret1=tpcall ("DEBIT", (char *)reqfb,0, (char **)&reqfb, (long *)&reqlen,
             TPSIGRSTRT);
... // check for errors and construct next request
ret2= tpcall ("CREDIT", (char*)reqfb,0, (char **)&reqfb, (long *)&reqlen,
             TPSIGRSTRT);
... // check for errors
if (ret1 == -1 || ret2 == -1) tpabort(); else tpcommit();
... // construct the reply buffer
tpreturn (TPSUCCESS, 0, buf->data, sizeof(struct aud), 0);
}
```

Figure 5.13 A Server Program Using TUXEDO's ATMI Note the transaction bracketing around the calls to the DEBIT and CREDIT programs and the tpreturn that returns the buffer to the client.

The complete DBCR program would be included in the server Main procedure provided by System/T. Each service is called using a service template such as tpservice, which enrolls the server process as a server, advertises its services (on the bulletin board), and calls an application-supplied initialization procedure. The server Main then initiates a loop that checks the message queue for requests. When it finds a request, it dequeues it and calls the subroutine that implements the requested service. When the service subroutine is finished, it returns to the server Main, which sends a reply. On server shutdown, Main calls an application-supplied cleanup routine. In other words, TUXEDO provides a server Main that includes the dequeue loop programmers typically include at the top of an IMS program.

Some other functions of the ATMI API not shown in the example are the following:

- tpgetlev, which indicates whether or not the subroutine is currently in transaction mode
- tpcancel, which attempts to cancel an outstanding tpacall
- tpgprio, which gets the priority of the last request
- tpsprio, which sets priority of next request

In addition to the call-return style illustrated above, a subroutine can be conversational, where it exchanges additional messages in an application-specific order (rather than strict call-return). Of course, the client program that calls the service must use the conversational ATMI primitives and the application-specific message order.

TUXEDO optionally supports the X/Open TX verbs, which are derived from ATMI. One main difference is that TX supports chained transactions, while ATMI normally does not.

5.6 ACMS

ACMS (Application Control and Management System) is Digital Equipment Corporation's most popular TP monitor product. ACMS was originally developed in 1984 as part of the integrated VAX Information Architecture product set along with Rdb (relational database system), DBMS (CODASYL database system), TDMS (original forms system), DECforms (a newer forms system), CDD (Common Data Dictionary), and Datatrieve (query and report writer for record-oriented files and databases). The workflow control language of ACMS, called the Task Definition Language (TDL), is the basis of X/Open's Structured Transaction Definition Language (STDL) (see Section 5.4 on X/Open and STDL). ACMS runs on the OpenVMS platform on both the VAX and Alpha processors.

ACMS recently was updated by Digital for the UNIX, Windows NT, and OpenVMS platforms in the ACMSxp product ("xp" for cross-platform) and integrated with a new set of component products. ACMSxp implements the same basic system architecture as the original ACMS on OpenVMS, but provides STDL (not TDL) layered on the OSF DCE services, integration with the Encina toolkit transaction manager and recoverable file system, and a new system management facility.

The current versions are ACMS 4.1 and ACMSxp 2.1.

System Architecture

ACMS uses a three-process TP monitor model in which each of the three tiers is mapped to a different operating system process: presentation server, workflow control, and transaction server (see Figure 5.14). The processes communicate via RPC.

ACMS applications accept a request for the execution of a transaction from a terminal or other display device connected to the presentation server process, called the *command process*. It is multithreaded to handle multiple devices concurrently. The presentation server sends a request message to the workflow controller process, called the *task server*. (A *task* is a program in a workflow controller that controls a request.) The workflow controller is also multithreaded to route multiple request messages concurrently. The workflow controller calls the transaction server, called the *procedure server*.

Since the transaction server is single-threaded, it is typically deployed as a server class consisting of multiple server processes. ACMS monitors the workload on transaction servers to determine whether enough server instances are active to handle the application workload. If there are too few, it automatically starts another server instance. If a server is idle for too long, ACMS automatically deletes it to conserve system resources.

ACMS was originally designed for use in application control and management, including process creation and application startup, monitoring, control, and maintenance. Its RPC mechanism was used to offload its front-end forms-handling processes onto small MicroVAXes for better price/performance than

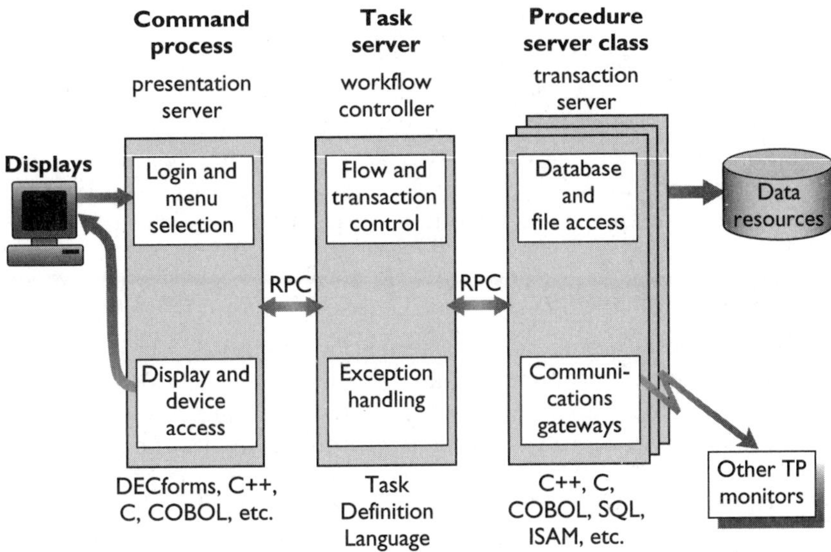

Figure 5.14 ACMS Three-Process Model Remote procedure calls communicate among predefined processes tuned for specific types of application work. The Task Definition Language defines the workflow.

the mainframe-oriented solutions that were popular at the time. True transaction capability (with start, commit, abort) was added later.

Unlike CICS and TUXEDO, ACMS has a specialized language, TDL, for specifying workflow control. TDL was developed to support features that were required by the ACMS model but not present in traditional third-generation languages (3GLs), such as RPC, multithreading, transaction control, and structured exception handling. It was later found to be suitable as a portable language, one that could be translated into the runtime functions of different TP monitors. It therefore became the basis of STDL, developed by the Multivendor Integration Architecture (MIA) Consortium (see Section 5.4).

ACMS includes an option for enqueuing requests to persistent queues. A task scheduler dequeues them and calls the appropriate workflow controller. ACMSxp extends this to include forwarding the deferred requests from one task queue to another, including remote queues and queues on other vendors' systems that support STDL. It also has data queuing for exchanging information between processes, similar to the CICS transient data facility.

When an exception occurs, control is passed to the exception handler portion of the task procedure. Certain exceptions automatically abort the transaction before branching to the exception handler, as in CICS or automatic transaction mode of TUXEDO.

ACMS was among the first TP monitors to offer an open, call-level interface to its RPC, called the Systems Integration interface, so that its built-in menu/forms presentation server could be replaced by application-specific or device-specific code.

Presentation Server

ACMS and ACMSxp support character cell terminals via Digital's DECforms software and support personal computers (including DOS, Windows, Windows NT, and Apple's Macintosh) via Digital's ACMS Desktop software. ACMS supports special devices (such as point-of-sale terminals, gas pumps, shop floor controllers, etc.), using the Systems Interface. ACMSxp supports special devices via the STDL customer-written client interface.

TP Communications

All process-to-process communication is via RPC. It simplifies programming with a pure procedure call abstraction that avoids any special considerations for the remote case, such as data conversion, and explicit reply. It uses RPC for the local case, too—calling a procedure in another process on the same machine. The presentation server process can be moved from one node to another dynamically by reconfiguring the RPC address of the task server.

The TDL and STDL compilers build stub programs for the RPC caller and callee. This allows callers to use standard procedure call syntax, rather than explicitly constructing a specially formatted buffer and then passing it in the call (as in CICS and TUXEDO). Information about the request, such as the security context and display identifier, is automatically placed in hidden arguments and is forwarded transparently to the server, where it becomes part of the server's context. Although the ACMS use of RPC does simplify application programming, there is some additional work in writing procedure interface definitions and in learning an extra programming language (that is, TDL or STDL), and a trade-off between the simplification of a predefined application structure and the greater flexibility of another approach.

Unlike CICS and TUXEDO, ACMS and ACMSxp do not provide peer-to-peer messaging. Any of the standard peer-to-peer APIs can be included in 3GL procedures in the presentation server and transaction server, but such an API is not included in the product.

In ACMS, transactional RPC is available from workflow controllers to transaction servers on the same machine. ACMSxp adds remote transactional RPC between workflow controllers and supports both the DCE RPC and X/Open TxRPC protocols for interoperability with other open TP monitors. Neither product supports transactional RPC between transaction servers (although X/Open STDL supports transactional communication from transaction servers to workflow controllers).

ACMS and ACMSxp use cluster technology to support high availability for applications by automatically redirecting an RPC from a failed node to a surviving node. They also use the OpenVMS transaction manager, DECdtm, for two-phase commit. ACMSxp uses the Encina transaction manager on Digital UNIX and the Microsoft Distributed Transaction Coordinator on Windows NT.

As mentioned previously, ACMSxp supports the STDL language for workflow control, replacing ACMS's TDL. STDL programs are compiled into calls on OSF DCE services for RPC, naming, and security, much as the ACMS TDL

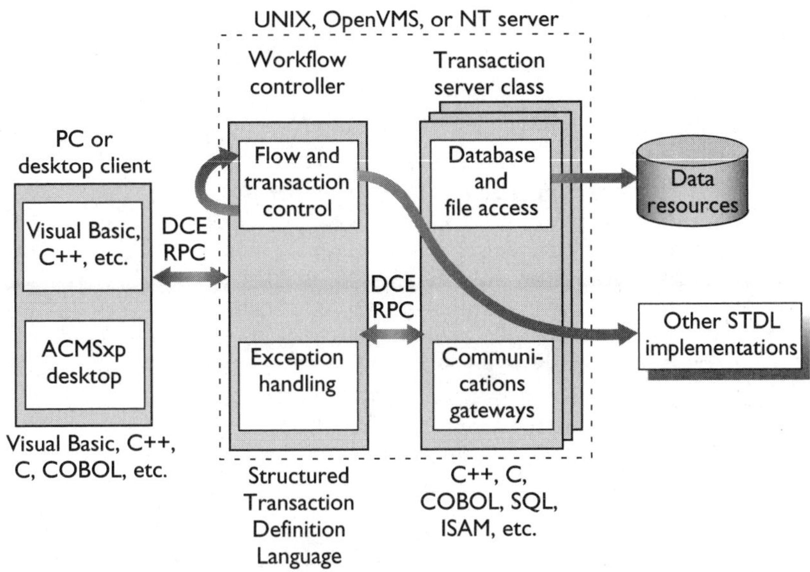

Figure 5.15 ACMSxp Model (Shown with ACMSxp Desktop) The updated ACMS product uses STDL and DCE RPC for communication. The presentation server process is typically a PC or desktop client.

compiler produces calls on the proprietary RPC, naming, and security services of ACMS. ACMSxp uses components from the Encina toolkit for transaction management and recoverable files on the UNIX platform and Microsoft TP components on the Windows NT platform.

Figure 5.15 illustrates ACMSxp. Also shown is the Desktop component, which is a presentation server that connects desktop devices to both ACMS and ACMSxp. For ACMSxp, ACMS Desktop has been updated to use DCE RPC and can be replaced by an application-specific presentation server, much like TUXEDO's System/WS and CICS EPI.

Database Access

Transaction server programs directly access any database or resource manager. Certain specialized databases are directly accessible in TDL and STDL. For example, ACMS includes a queue manager for durable request queue operations. ACMSxp adds a recoverable workspace manager for accessing program variables under transaction control and a recoverable data queuing resource manager.

If a transaction is bracketed within a TDL program (in a workflow controller), then ACMS controls the commitment activity with the platform's transaction manager (ACMS does not provide its own transaction manager). If it is bracketed within the transaction server, then ACMS is uninvolved in the commitment process. This is useful for database systems that are not inte-

```
TASK GROUP SPECIFICATION dbcr_example
    UUID IS 8C2A59A4-C5D3-11CE-828A-9E621218AA77;
    VERSION IS 1.0;

    TASK debit_credit
      USING customer_record PASSED AS INPUT
            account_record PASSED AS INOUT;

    COMPOSABLE TASK debit
      USING customer_record PASSED AS INPUT
            account_record PASSED AS INOUT;

    COMPOSABLE TASK credit
      USING customer_record PASSED AS INPUT
            account_record PASSED AS INOUT;

END TASK GROUP SPECIFICATION;
```

Figure 5.16 STDL Example, Interface Definition An STDL `TASK GROUP SPECIFICATION` defines the interface to a group of related task procedures. ACMSxp generates DCE IDL from the task group, processing group, and presentation group specifications (the processing group and presentation group specifications are omitted). The UUID and version number are passed directly to DCE.

grated with the OpenVMS transaction manager (DECdtm), or that offer specialized options that can only be set in the transaction bracket statements.

Like TUXEDO, ACMSxp supports the X/Open XA interface and therefore integrates with any XA-compliant resource manager. ACMSxp requires the XA interface for transactions started using STDL but allows any resource manager to be accessed from a transaction server.

System Management

ACMS system management facilities help configure, start, and monitor the execution of ACMS-controlled processes. They include utilities to define tables of terminals to be controlled, define user authentication and authorization, analyze error log information, start and stop application servers, and display runtime performance statistics.

The ACMS Central Controller (ACC) starts the system, including presentation servers, workflow controllers, and transaction servers configured for startup. After startup, system management is a passive observer that monitors load and responds to operator requests.

ACMSxp offers similar capabilities to ACMS. It unifies the management of DCE and ACMSxp components in one utility and uses the DCE RPC protocol for executing management operations in a distributed environment.

```
TASK debit_credit
      USING customer_record
            account_record

      BLOCK WITH TRANSACTION

      CALL TASK debit IN dbcr
            USING customer_record
                  account_record;

      CALL TASK credit IN dbcr
            USING customer_record
                  account_record;
      END BLOCK;

      EXCEPTION HANDLER
            RAISE EXCEPTION no_luck;
      END EXCEPTION HANDLER;
END TASK;

COMPOSABLE TASK debit
      USING customer_record, account_record;
      CALL PROCEDURE db_update USING customer_record, account_record;
END TASK;

COMPOSABLE TASK credit
      USING customer_record, account_record;
      CALL PROCEDURE db_update USING customer_record, account_record;
END TASK
```

Figure 5.17 Debit-Credit Tasks Written in STDL The `debit` and `credit` tasks are called as subtasks from the `debit_credit` task. The `CALL TASK` procedure statements are enclosed by a block-structured transaction with associated exception handler. The `COMPOSABLE` keyword indicates the called task procedures execute within the transaction of a calling task.

Programming Example

The STDL example in Figure 5.16 illustrates the use of a task group specification for a simple debit-credit application. (Recall that a task is a program that executes a request.) The `debit_credit` task in Figure 5.17 contains a "transaction block," which brackets a transaction. Within the transaction block are procedure calls to the `debit` and `credit` tasks, which in turn call C or COBOL procedures to access the respective account records to be adjusted. All operations on recoverable resource managers must be contained within a transaction block.

The example does not show the client program because it's ordinary C, C++, or COBOL with a procedure call to an STDL task, using a client stub generated by the STDL compiler. The input to the task is the `customer_record` and `account_record` arguments.

The transaction is started within the STDL procedure, and then the called C, C++, or COBOL processing procedure joins the transaction. Multiple procedure calls can be enclosed within a transaction block, including transactional calls to remote task procedures. The example does not include the processing procedure because, like the client program, processing procedures are normal C, C++, or COBOL programs linked to a server stub generated by the STDL compiler.

The ACMSxp STDL compiler uses STDL's version of an IDL (the *group specification*) to generate the required client and server stubs for communication among the three processes.

5.7 Encina

Encina is a portable TP monitor offered by Transarc, which was founded in 1989 by several Carnegie-Mellon University researchers, and was purchased by IBM in 1994. The product is available on multiple UNIX platforms and Microsoft Windows NT; Encina clients are available for Microsoft Windows 3.1 and IBM's OS/2. Encina implements the following standards: OSF DCE; X/Open XA, TX, and TxRPC; and OMG OTS. RPC, threading, and Kerberos are exploited for communication, concurrency, and security. The current version is Encina 2.0.

System Architecture

Encina communications is synchronous, based on DCE RPC with its Interface Definition Language (IDL). The Encina Monitor is linked with popular 4GL tools, such as Visual Basic, to provide the presentation server. Workflow control is implemented using RPC-based communications, which routes requests to the transactional servers. The transactional servers are integrated with transactional resource managers, and a transactional version of the Encina RPC (TRPC) provides two-phase commit.

The Toolkit

The Encina Monitor is built from a modular toolkit of enabling technology, which has also been incorporated into the CICS for UNIX and ACMSxp TP monitors in various ways. Each toolkit component has well-defined interfaces and minimal dependence upon other components, which allowed IBM and Digital to use only the selected toolkit components they required. All components are thread-safe, designed for high concurrency, and support nested transactions, which provides isolation to threads working on behalf of the same transactions. The components work as follows (see Figure 5.18):

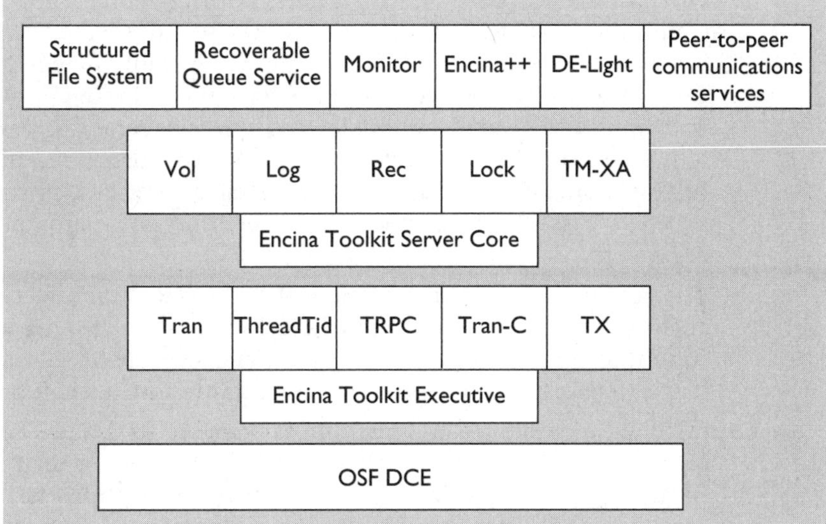

Figure 5.18 **Encina Component Architecture** The Encina Monitor is constructed of components from the Toolkit Server Core and Executive, layered on DCE, and is one of several Encina products. The CICS for AIX and ACMSxp monitors also incorporate Encina components and layer on DCE.

- The communications, authentication, data privacy, and operating system-independent and machine-independent execution environment is provided by OSF DCE.
- The Encina Toolkit Executive offers the basic set of services for all processes running within the Encina environment. Within the Executive are Tran, a library allowing processes to initiate, participate in, and commit distributed transactions; ThreadTid, a library for attaching transaction contexts to threads; TRPC, a compiler and library supporting TIDL, an extension of the DCE RPC IDL to include transaction context; Tran-C, a collection of macros and a runtime library providing C language extensions for transaction demarcation, concurrency management, and exception handling; and TX, a library providing the X/Open TX transaction demarcation API.
- The Encina Toolkit Server Core contains the modules necessary for building servers with ACID properties. It includes Vol, a disk management library for organizing mirrored data storage; Log, an append-only stable storage module for recording transactional modifications and state; Rec, a recoverable storage facility with write-ahead logging, which restores the storage state after transaction and system failures; Lock, a two-phase locking manager with conventional read/write and intention locks within nested transactions; and TM-XA, an adapter for communicating transaction information between the Encina Transaction service and X/Open XA-compliant resource managers, such as relational database systems.

- Encina includes two data managers, both of which support call-return communication with transactional RPCs and nested transactions: the Structured File System (SFS) and the Recoverable Queue Service (RQS). The SFS supports a collection of file formats including ISAM (B-tree) files with multiple secondary indices and offers several degrees of isolation: browse, cursor stability, and repeatable reads (described in Section 6.6). RQS is a queue database supporting first-in-first-out, prioritization, and keyed access. RQS queues can have one or many enqueuers and dequeuers.
- The Peer-to-Peer Communications (PPC) service contains two products: a client library and an SNA gateway. The PPC is used for mainframe system communications using SNA LU6.2 Syncpoint Level 2, tying the mainframe transaction and the Encina transaction into a single transaction.
- DE-Light provides a small client library and an RPC and TRPC interpreter gateway, which allows applications to dynamically invoke TRPCs to Encina application servers and demarcate transactions with an X/Open-compliant TX interface. Small clients running on Windows 3.1 and in Java interpreters can invoke Encina services through this interpreter.

The Monitor

An Encina administrative domain is called a *cell,* which is very similar to a DCE cell. All resources managed by the Encina Monitor belong to a single monitor cell. Each monitor cell consists of a cell manager that stores and disseminates the cell's configuration data and node managers that monitor and control resources on each machine.

The cell manager stores the configuration data in an object repository, which uses class hierarchies and inheritance to group characteristics of a set of related servers.

A node manager on each machine supports process management operations to start, restart, and stop processes. It also manages a shared log for recoverable application servers (application servers managing durable data).

Client/Server Binding and the Encina Monitor Client

The Encina Monitor client library integrates with presentation services such as Microsoft's Visual C++ and Visual Basic and Powersoft's PowerBuilder. It contains the necessary security context, binding, and caching logic to avoid some server communication. Under normal operation, the client application's call to a server is performed with a single RPC directly to the selected application server.

Encina++ is a collection of tools and class libraries encapsulating Encina and DCE communication and call-return binding code. It supports object interface definition with DCE IDL, Transarc's Transactional IDL, and the Object Management Group's (OMG) Object Transaction Service (OTS).

The Encina Monitor performs simple load balancing with a weighted random selection of servers and DCE RPC. Clients bind and communicate syn-

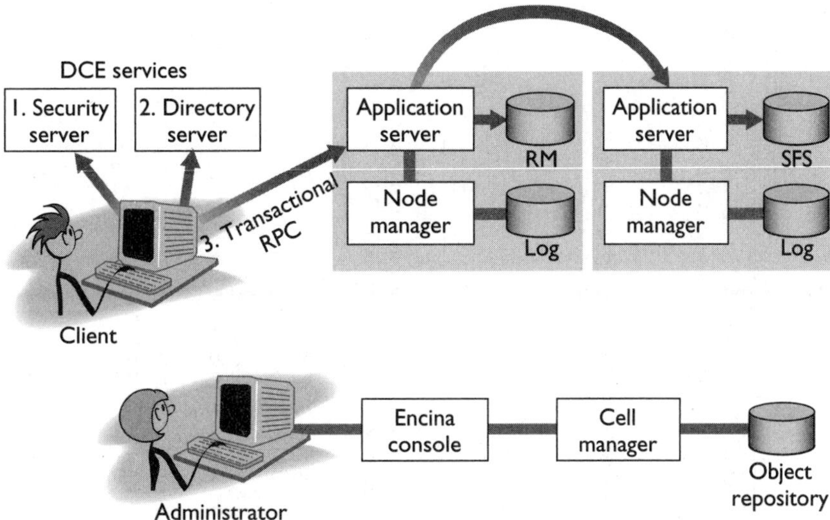

Figure 5.19 Simple Encina Monitor Cell Encina concepts are based on DCE, using directory services to locate the application server for the client and DCE security to authorize the client for access to the server. The TRPC propagates transactional context via DCE RPC to one or more servers.

chronously with the desired application servers or can use the monitor's Queue Request Facility (based on the RQS) for queued messages for later delivery to servers.

The Encina client library generates and caches communications bindings for use in TRPCs. When caches are empty, such as at login time, the client establishes a user context by contacting a DCE security server. Then the client issues an RPC to a name server to establish bindings for each server with which it will communicate. During normal operation, the bindings are cached and the client communication flows with a single RPC, as shown in Figure 5.19. The RPC can optionally be transactional and can include a second TRPC to another application server within the same transaction.

Transaction Server

Tran, the Encina transaction service, is a library linked into processes that participate in Encina transactions. Applications usually invoke Tran by using one of the several transaction demarcation APIs that are translated into Tran calls. Applications written with different transaction demarcation APIs can participate in the same transaction. Figure 5.20 illustrates the various models.

TP Communications

Encina supports several programming models: C or COBOL with conventional RPC and call-return binding; C++ with object methods and named-object binding; dynamic RPC invocation; and CPI-C peer-to-peer communication. Figure 5.21 illustrates each one.

`...`
`tx_begin();`
`...`
`tx_commit();`
	X/Open TX API supports chained and unchained transactions. Transarc extensions support nested transactions, too.

`Transaction{`
`   ... */ }`
`   transaction{ /* sub transaction`
`     onAbort { /* compensate without`
`     aborting top-level transaction. */ }`
`   ...`
`}`
`...`
	Tran-C and Tran-C++ extend the C and C++ programming languages through C macros and C++ class libraries. They support nested transactions.

`Commit();`
`.....`
`Commit();`
	CPI-RR is part of IBM's SAA, providing interoperability with mainframe systems. It is a nonnested chained transaction API.

Figure 5.20 **Encina Transaction Demarcation APIs** The APIs support the X/Open TX API, proprietary extensions to C and C++, and IBM's CPI-RR for interoperability with mainframe systems.

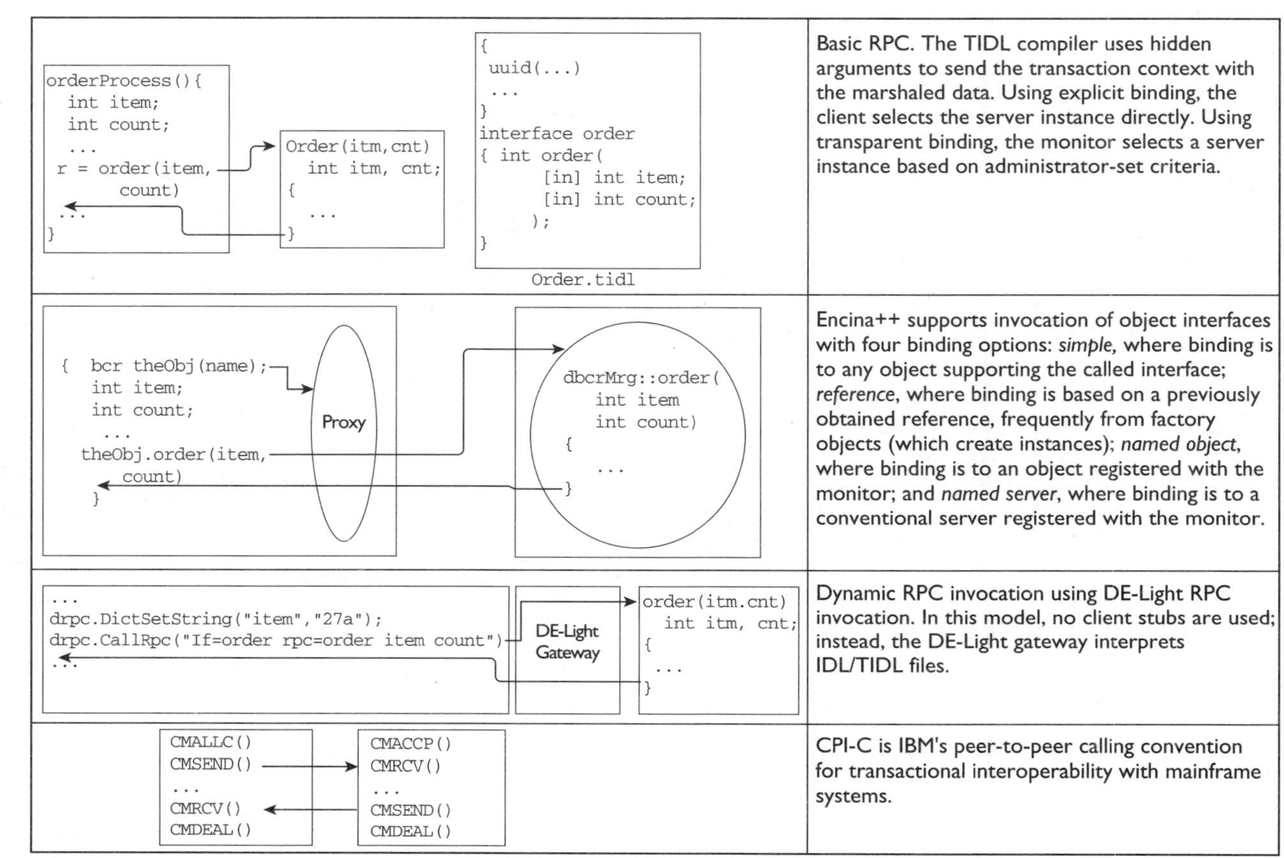

orderProcess(){
int item;
int count;
...
r = order(item,
count)
...
}
Order(itm,cnt)
int itm, cnt;
{
...
}
{
uuid(...)
...
}
interface order
{ int order(
[in] int item;
[in] int count;
);
}
Order.tidl
Basic RPC. The TIDL compiler uses hidden arguments to send the transaction context with the marshaled data. Using explicit binding, the client selects the server instance directly. Using transparent binding, the monitor selects a server instance based on administrator-set criteria.
{ bcr theObj(name);
int item;
int count;
...
theObj.order(item,
count)
}
Proxy
dbcrMrg::order(
int item
int count)
{
...
}
Encina++ supports invocation of object interfaces with four binding options: simple, where binding is to any object supporting the called interface; reference, where binding is based on a previously obtained reference, frequently from factory objects (which create instances); named object, where binding is to an object registered with the monitor; and named server, where binding is to a conventional server registered with the monitor.
...
drpc.DictSetString("item","27a");
drpc.CallRpc("If=order rpc=order item count")
...
DE-Light Gateway
order(itm.cnt)
int itm, cnt;
{
...
}
Dynamic RPC invocation using DE-Light RPC invocation. In this model, no client stubs are used; instead, the DE-Light gateway interprets IDL/TIDL files.
CMALLC()
CMSEND()
...
CMRCV()
CMDEAL()
CMACCP()
CMRCV()
...
CMSEND()
CMDEAL()
CPI-C is IBM's peer-to-peer calling convention for transactional interoperability with mainframe systems.

Figure 5.21 **TP Communications in Encina** There are four options: basic RPC, object-oriented invocation via Encina++, dynamic RPC using DE-Light, and CPI-C for communication with mainframes.

```
[ uuid(8c2a59a4-c5d3-11ce-828a-9e621218aa77),
  version(1.0),
  exceptions(invalid_account, illegal_amount)
]

interface dbcr
{ void withdraw([in] long account,
                [in] long amount);

  void deposit([in] long account,
               [in] long amount);

  [transaction_optional] long query([in] long account);
}
```

Figure 5.22 dbcr.tidl in Encina++ Interface definitions for the functions `withdraw` and `deposit`.

```
#include <ots/otsClient.H>
#include "dbcrTC.H"

void DBCR(char *nameOfObjToUse, long from, long to, long amount)
{   dbcr theObject(nameOfObjToUse);

    transaction { theObject.withdraw(from, amount);
                  theObject.deposit(to, amount); }
    onCommit { cout << "Transfer succeeded" << endl;}
    onAbort  { cout << "Transfer failed because " << abortReason()
               << endl;}
}

main(int argc, char **argv)
{   OtsClient theClient;
    long      from, to, amount;

    cout << "Withdraw from account? ";
    cin >> from;
    cout << "Deposit to account? ";
    cin >> to;
    cout << "Amount? ";
    cin >> amount;

    DBCR(argv[1], from, to, amount);
}
```

Figure 5.23 Client.C in Encina++ The debit-credit program, `DBCR`, and the client (`Main`) that calls it.

```
#include <ots/otsServer.H>
#include "dbcrTS.H"

main(int argc, char **argv)
{   OtsServer theServer;
    dbcrMgr theObject(argv[1]);
    theServer.RegisterResource(...);
    theServer.Listen();
    return(0);
}

void dbcrMgr::withdraw(idl_long_int account, idl_long_int amount)
{   if (amount <= 0) throw illegal_amount();
    EXEC SQL
      ...
    END EXEC
}

void dbcrMgr::deposit(idl_long_int account, idl_long_int amount)
{   if (amount <= 0) throw illegal_amount();
    EXEC SQL
      ...
    END EXEC
}
```

Figure 5.24 Server.C in Encina++ The server programs, withdraw and deposit.

Database Access

In addition to SFS and RQS, applications can call resource managers that have an X/Open XA-compliant interface. Encina's TM-XA module provides several extensions for mapping nested transactions to XA transactions, allowing the use of some of the nested transaction functionality.

System Management

The cell manager's object repository stores configuration data and runtime state information, including the number of threads per process, number of processes per machine, and process start and stop times. Runtime state includes audit and trace data. All the data are stored dynamically in class hierarchies.

Security options include client authentication, data tampering detection, and data privacy. The monitor can also be configured to restrict access to any of the services it manages. It maintains access control lists (ACLs) for application servers, interfaces, and individual RPCs.

Programming Example

The program in Figures 5.22, 5.23, and 5.24 illustrates the Encina++ interface for the debit-credit example. The method is defined in the TIDL file. This example shows how one might use a named object for binding.

The Encina approach is very flexible, allowing many programmer options and not imposing any predefined application structure. Like STDL, Encina uses a transactional version of an IDL (although the Encina TIDL is derived more closely from the DCE IDL). The Encina TIDL is the basis of the X/Open TxRPC IDL.

5.8 TOP END

TOP END was developed by NCR as a distributed TP environment for UNIX systems. It was first released in 1991. When AT&T acquired NCR, TOP END became AT&T's strategic TP monitor, replacing TUXEDO (which was sold to Novell along with UNIX System Laboratories). AT&T is currently divesting itself of NCR, but TOP END remains a strategic TP monitor product for NCR and has gained a significant share of the UNIX TP market.

The TOP END design encourages programmers to create *building blocks* of application services tied together via a communications network. One of TOP END's strengths is system management.

TOP END is the basis of the X/Open XA+ specification. It also supports the TX and XA specifications from X/Open and provides an STDL option.

TOP END currently runs on more than 10 platforms. AT&T/NCR certifies each port of TOP END code to ensure consistency. The current version is 2.03.02, which runs on various UNIX systems and Windows NT.

System Architecture

The TOP END architecture is based on the concept of a *node manager,* which is a collection of processes that coordinates TP application functions in a network, including request scheduling, dialog management, transaction management, and communications management. These processes fulfill similar functions to the TUXEDO bulletin board mechanism.

Applications are written using TOP END services that interact with the various TOP END system processes to perform application functions. Application components are typically mapped to a single process, called an *application server,* which functions as a transaction server.

Figure 5.25 illustrates the control flow within the TOP END system to process a request to execute a transaction. The workstation or other display device performs the presentation server function and is connected to the TOP END system via a *network agent*. The network agent communicates with the node manager, which acts as a workflow controller to determine the location of the transaction program to execute the request and to route the request to that program's transaction server. The transaction server that runs the transaction program may be on the same node as the node manager or on a remote node. When it is on a remote node, the node manager routes the request via the TOP END network interface to the remote node's node manager, which

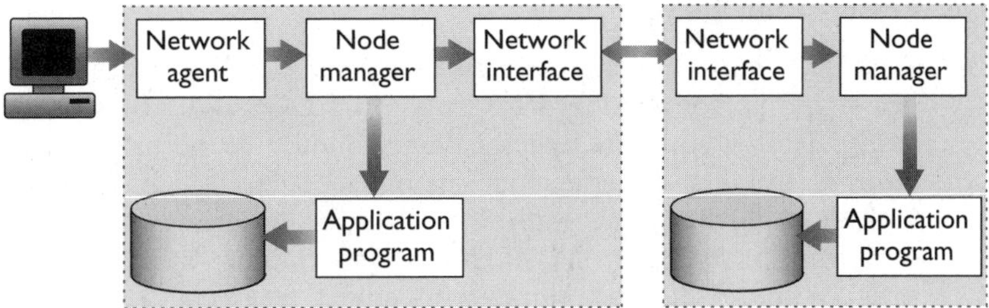

Figure 5.25 **TOP END Request Flow** Programs are configured as peers without using a master configuration file. Requests are routed across the network via the network interface and node manager to the correct transaction program.

passes the request to the transaction server on the remote node. Results are returned using the same path. Since a node manager can access remote servers, a system can be configured in three tiers, where presentation servers on workstations issue requests to an intermediate node manager, which performs workflow control to route requests to transaction servers. Each tier can run in a separate processor.

The programming model encourages programmers to create modular application components and use TOP END services to distribute the components across a network of servers. The components can be configured in networks of thousands of servers. The network interfaces are responsible for knowing where components are located, so node managers and components can communicate. To track component locations, network interfaces dynamically exchange information about application components during server startup, shutdown, and failure. In contrast to TUXEDO, components act as peers, allowing the network of components that comprise an application to be configured without a master or backup master node.

TOP END supports two types of servers:

- Standard applications, which incorporate TOP END services in any structure the programmer creates
- Managed server applications, which are subroutines wrapped by a TOP END supplied main program

Standard applications can be written in C or C++. COBOL applications run as managed server applications.

To locate transaction programs within application components efficiently, TOP END uses a two-tier naming structure, <product.function>, where a product is a group of functions.

The API allows a client to assign a request ID, which can be used for returning the reply or for other application-level message routing.

Presentation Server

TOP END supports character cell terminals, 3270 terminals, UNIX workstations, and personal computers (including DOS, Windows, Windows NT, and OS/2). It also supports special devices, such as point-of-sale terminals, gas pumps, and bar code readers, using a special client program gateway. It includes a *format management* facility for defining character cell screen layouts, similar to DES in TUXEDO. It also includes a line of optional products, called *remote clients*, that extend client services to the various desktops, including security, message passing, and transaction control services.

TP Communications

The TOP END communications manager implements a peer-to-peer paradigm with some optimizations, such as the ability to start a session and invoke a service in the same call. Similarly, a flag on a service call can be set to tell the communications manager to drop the session immediately after the service completes (that is, when the client executes the receive operation). This optimization produces call-return functionality, but with the send/receive verbs that TOP END uses throughout.

Another unique customization of the peer-to-peer communications model is that client and server programs use different versions of the send and receive functions, producing a model that is closer to call-return than fully symmetric peer-to-peer. For example, communication services include a context flag that lets the server know it is maintaining context for the client in anticipation of a subsequent call.

TOP END also offers a transactional queued message communications option called Recoverable Transaction Queuing (RTQ). RTQ can be used to support standby replicated database systems. It is an XA-compliant resource manager, capable of participating in a coordinated transaction with other RMs.

TOP END supports a DCE gateway for interoperability with other vendors via DCE RPC and an LU6.2 gateway for interoperability with CICS, but without Syncpoint Level 2 processing (i.e., no transaction semantics).

System Management

TOP END uses a PC-based system management environment with an advanced graphical user interface that, for example, changes colors to alert system managers of trouble in the network. Any number of PCs can be configured to manage the entire system.

There is an interactive system definition tool that provides a step-by-step icon and menu interface for defining, modifying, and upgrading the system configuration. The tool runs on a PC and downloads the resulting configuration definition to server nodes. A system generation component on server nodes automatically does the necessary linking to create transaction server executables.

```
/* call tp_initialize to sign on to the dialogue */
init = tp_initialize(&appl_info, NULL, 0L);

/* allocate data structures */
client_space = tp_csi_alloc(TP_DIF_ALL);

/* set the request parameters and initiate a dialogue */
tp_user_dialogue_id = USER_DIALOGUE_ID;
tp_user_message_id  = 0L;
tp_system_dialogue_id.tp_sys_dialogue = 0L;
tp_flags = TP_NOFLAGS;

status = tp_client_signon(tp_user_dialogue_id, tp_user_message_id,
      tp_system_dialogue_id, tp_userid, tp_password, tp_endpoint,
      tp_flags, 0L, NULL, NULL, 0, NULL);

/* receive response from the TOP END system */
status = tp_client_receive (...);

/* send a request to the debit-credit server and receive the reply */
status = tp_client_send(...flags, ACCOUNT, TRANSFER,
            ... dialogue_id, user_message_ID);
status = tp_client_receive(...flags, output format, buffer length
            ... buffer area, etc.);
```

Figure 5.26 TOP END Client Program for Debit-Credit Example Note the data structure allocation, request parameters, and use of control flags on the tp_client_send and tp_client_receive services.

At runtime, the system management utility monitors and controls the running application, including dynamic server startup and shutdown, managing audit and recovery capabilities in the event of failure, activating communications links among servers, and automatically distributing software updates.

In the event of a failure to the global system management station, local system management capabilities can take over and keep the application running.

Database Access

TOP END supports the X/Open XA interface to allow integration with XA-compliant resource managers, such as Informix, Oracle, Sybase, and SQL Server (on Windows NT). Both client and server processes can access XA-compliant resource managers, including multiple XA-compliant resource managers in a single process. There is also an XA *veneer* to integrate non–XA-compliant resource managers. The LU6.2 gateway can be used to access CICS and IMS applications.

Programming Example

A debit-credit example is shown in Figures 5.26 and 5.27. As in some previous examples, presentation services are not shown because their use is not a dis-

```
/* initialize product and function names and allocate storage */
function_array[0].tp_function_name = "TRANSFER";
function_array[1].tp_function_name = "CREDIT";
function_array[2].tp_function_name = "DEBIT";
appl_info.tp_product_name = "ACCOUNT";

status = tp_csi_alloc(TP_DIF_ALL);

/* initialize the resource manager */
status = tx_open();

/* receive the server request */
status = tp_server_receive(flags, service, input_format, location,
            source_info, &msglen, AirMsgIn);

/* start transaction */
status = tx_begin();

/* signon & execute debit service */
status = tp_client_signon(...<debit service>...);
status = tp_client_receive(...<signon status>...);
status = tp_client_send(...<execute debit>...);
status = tp_client_receive(...<receive results>...);

/* signon & execute credit service */
status = tp_client_signon(...<credit service>...);
status = tp_client_receive(...<signon status>...);
status = tp_client_send(...<execute credit>...);
status = tp_client_receive(...<receive results>...);

/* commit the transaction and return results to the client */
status = tx_commit();
status = tp_server_send(...<results>...);
```

Figure 5.27 TOP END Server Program for Debit-Credit Example Within the transaction (bracketed using X/Open TX verbs), the debit and credit services sign on and exchange messages.

tinguishing characteristic of TOP END. The example is divided into client and server programs.

When the client is launched, it sets up a session (called a *dialog*) with the server (see Figure 5.26). Then for each request, it sends the request and later receives a reply.

When the server is launched, it initializes itself (see Figure 5.27). Then for each request, it receives the request, starts a transaction, calls the relevant servers, commits, and sends the reply. The example illustrates TOP END's use of the X/Open TX interface for transaction start and commit.

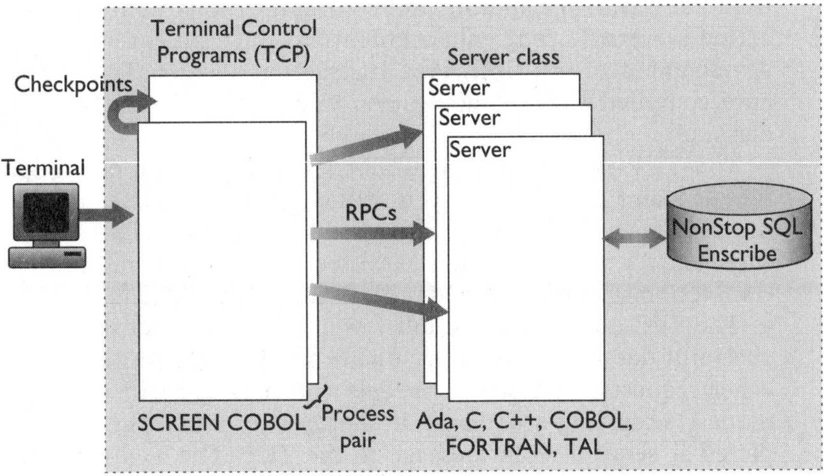

Figure 5.28 **Pathway Monitor Two-Process Model** The Terminal Control Program interprets SCREEN COBOL programs to interact with the display, format requests, and call servers via RPC. The servers access the Tandem resource managers. TCPs are implemented using process pairs for fault tolerance.

5.9 Pathway/TS

Pathway/TS (Transaction Service) is Tandem Computers' TP monitor product, originally released in the mid-1980s for Tandem's Guardian operating system running on their fault-tolerant platform. Pathway/TS supports a call-return interprocess communications and the transaction abstraction using Tandem's TP services infrastructure. That infrastructure includes Transaction Services/Massively Parallel (TS/MP) and Transaction Manager/MP (TM/MP), which provide TP monitor services and transaction management services, respectively. The same infrastructure now supports a subset of the CICS API and the TUXEDO API in addition to Pathway.

Tandem has recently teased apart its operating system into a kernel portion, the NonStop Kernel (NSK), with two layers on top: one that supports the Guardian API and one that supports a POSIX (UNIX) API, called Open System Services (OSS). In addition, they supply a native UNIX operating system, NS-UX, which supports a native port of TUXEDO.

System Architecture

Pathway uses a two-process model that uses call-return communications, which they call requester/server (see Figure 5.28). The client is a multithreaded Terminal Control Program (TCP), which handles multiple simultaneous interactions with end users. It supports both presentation server and workflow controller functions. The TCP interpretively executes programs written in Tandem's COBOL dialect, SCREEN COBOL, which includes features for terminal handling and communications with single-threaded transaction servers. Recent enhancements to the Tandem environment allow the development of multithreaded transaction servers. Transaction servers execute compiled object code written in a standard language and run in server classes.

The TCP interprets a SCREEN COBOL application program to display menus, paint and read a screen, validate the input data, and format a request message with the name of the target server class. The application program then starts a transaction and executes a `SEND` command to issue an RPC to a transaction server in the server class named by the request.

The RPC mechanism establishes a link to a server in the requested server class if it doesn't already have one or if all existing links are busy processing other requests. The server accepts the message and does the work of the request, accessing a database if appropriate. When the server program completes, it sends a reply message to the TCP. The TCP's application program can invoke many such RPCs before forwarding the reply to the terminal and committing the transaction. Finally, the reply message is displayed.

The Guardian operating system implements software fault tolerance through *process pairs*, a mechanism by which a given operating system process has a second, shadow process as a backup to each primary process. A configuration option tells Pathway to run each TCP as a process pair. At the beginning of each transaction, Pathway checkpoints the display context (essentially, the request), which means that it copies this state from the primary process to its backup process. It checkpoints again just before commit (essentially, the reply). If the primary fails during the transaction execution, the transaction aborts and the backup can reexecute the transaction using the checkpointed display context, without asking the user to reenter the data. If the transaction executes without any failures and commits, then the precommit checkpoint replaces the start-of-transaction checkpoint and can be sent to the display. The checkpoints play a similar role to queue elements in queued TP. A more complete description of the general process pair technique is presented in Section 7.4.

Servers are typically context free, which allows successive calls to a server class within the same transaction to be handled by different servers. The TS/MP API, called PathSend, has been developed to allow any process to send a request to a server class, not just the TCP. The PathSend API is similar to the ACMS systems interface because it makes the Tandem RPC available to external clients. An internal version of the PathSend API supports context-sensitive conversational communications mechanisms for the TUXEDO and CICS API subsets. Single-threaded clients can use the PathSend API in synchronous or asynchronous mode, as in native TUXEDO.

Transactions are managed by the Tandem transaction manager, called the TM/MP. Updates to data are logged to an audit file, from which TM/MP manages various types of recovery. There is one log per node. TM/MP provides a system logging service for both itself (as a TM), and for all the resource managers (NS SQL, Enscribe, NS TUXEDO /Q, etc.). All updates for a transaction are

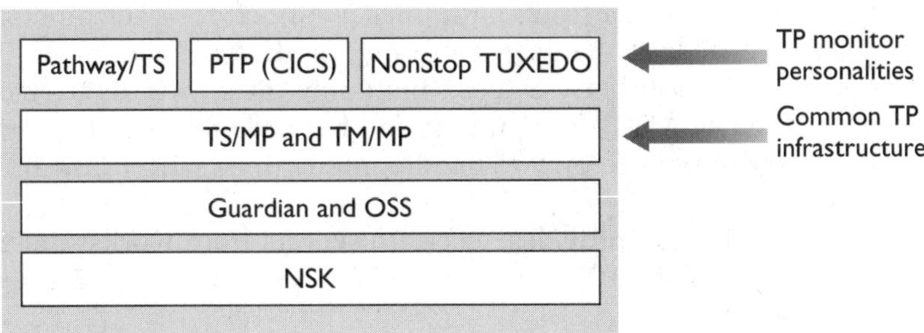

Figure 5.29 **Tandem Support for Multiple TP Monitor Personalities** TS/MP and TM/MP provide TP monitor and transaction management services for Pathway/TS, NonStop TUXEDO, and the PTP (CICS) API. Guardian and Open System Services operating systems are layered on a common NonStop Kernel.

written as a single log write, no matter how many resource managers are involved, thereby minimizing the number of I/Os per transaction to improve performance and scalability.

Tandem's resource managers provide fault tolerance through disk mirroring and hot backup and provide upward scalability through data partitioning and parallel processing. System server processes typically run as process pairs to ensure high availability.

Tandem supports the TUXEDO and CICS programming interfaces on NSK, using Tandem's fault-tolerant and parallel processing capabilities to provide high availability, performance, and scalability (see Figure 5.29). They also interoperate with implementations of those TP monitors outside of the Tandem environment. By using a common set of services, the various TP monitor options can interoperate with each other and get the benefits of Tandem's communications mechanism and server classes.

The Parallel Transaction Processing Services (PTP) for the CICS API environment reproduces the CICS MVS/ESA V3.3 API within the Guardian environment. PTP supports the CICS intersystem communication facility, including transaction routing, distributed program link, function shipping, and program-to-program communications. It can interoperate with other implementations of CICS via LU6.2, but does not support Syncpoint.

NonStop TUXEDO is implemented in the OSS environment. TUXEDO servers, like PTP and Pathway servers, are implemented using server classes that access Tandem resource managers and interoperate with TUXEDO on other platforms. All three TP monitor environments interoperate within the Tandem environment and share the same transaction manager and TP monitor services.

Presentation Server

Pathway was introduced in the days of low-function terminals. So its presentation server, TCP, supported Tandem's terminal devices via a multithreaded process, where each thread maintained a context for a terminal and initiated a request on behalf of the user. Later on, Tandem opened up the TCP interface for access from other devices, including PCs, workstations, and special devices such as ATMs, gas pumps, and bar code readers. Tandem created special adaptations of the TCP to handle interactions with these different types of devices.

Pathway/TS also provides access to servers from workstations via a client-only product called Remote Server Call (RSC), which is analogous to TUXEDO's /WS.

The NonStop TUXEDO option provides access to PCs and workstations via the TUXEDO /WS option. The PTP option handles IBM 3270 terminals via SNA LU2 and supports CICS BMS maps, as well as communications via any of the other intersystem communications functions that support displays.

TP Communications

A Tandem system (or node) is a loosely coupled cluster of 2 to 16 processors, connected by a high-speed bus. Tandem's wide area networking product, called Expand, can connect up to 255 nodes (for a total of 4080 potential processors). Processors do not share memory, but this architecture is supported by a common operating system environment and provides high performance, availability, and scalability.

Tandem's operating system uses a transactional remote procedure call mechanism for interprocess communications, both between processes on the same node and processes on remote nodes. The remote procedure call mechanism is implemented using the PathSend API. There is also support for TCP/IP and OSF DCE within OSS.

Tandem uses its own transaction manager and supports communication gateways with other TP protocols such as TUXEDO's ATMI and CICS's LU6.2.

Database Access

Tandem supplies an SQL-compliant resource manager called NonStop SQL and a transactional file system called Enscribe. Both resource managers support parallel processing and distributed processing features of the Tandem platform. When it was released in the mid-1980s, NonStop SQL was the first distributed, parallel relational database system product.

Mirrored disks are supported for local backup, and the Remote Duplicate Data Facility (RDF) supports a remote hot backup. RDF uses a process pair to forward log records from the primary database to the remote replica, where another process pair applies the log records to the database replica (see also Section 10.2).

Multiple processors can execute separate SQL requests simultaneously or divide a large single request for parallel processing on multiple processors. The resource managers support the standard locking and logging approaches described in Chapters 6 and 7, including record locking, relaxed isolation levels for improved read performance, and logs for undo-redo recovery. On-line reconfiguration is supported for such things as moving a partition or splitting an index.

System Management

The Tandem environment supports numerous system management tools. Some are generic to the operating system infrastructure, such as the transaction manager and the recovery utility. Others are specific to each of the TP monitor environments. A single view of the system is supported so that all processors in the network can be managed from a single management station.

Process management tools in TS/MP include facilities for starting and stopping TCPs and servers and for monitoring the processes and links between processes. They manage processes for Pathway, NonStop TUXEDO, and PTP.

The link management tool allocates requests to servers and establishes links between the client and server processes. TS/MP performs load balancing by linking each client request to the least loaded process in a server class (which can be distributed across multiple processors in a node). The number of processes in a server class varies between a configured minimum and maximum. Processes are dynamically started and stopped in response to load. Requests are serviced as promptly as possible (queuing is minimized), and completed as fast as possible by fully utilizing all available processors.

Automatic restart is supported for failed processes, and the system management utility reports on status information and system errors. The entire system can be shut down, or parts of the system can be shut down individually.

Programming Example

The example illustrates the Pathway/TS two-process model. The client (i.e., requester) program is written using SCREEN COBOL, which is interpreted by a TCP and calls a server written using standard COBOL (see Figure 5.30). A failure, such as a deadlock, causes an automatic transaction restart, which aborts the current transaction, obtains a new transaction ID from the transaction manager, and uses checkpointed input data to start the transaction again. The example illustrates Tandem's modification to the COBOL language to support display manipulation and to call server procedures.

Data items accepted from the display device are moved to fields in the corresponding output message, which is written as a record (`DBCR-MSG`) to a file shared between the client and server processes. Included in the write is information pertinent to the request, such as the transaction ID and the address of the originating thread within the TCP so that the reply message can be routed correctly. The transaction brackets both RPCs, and therefore the two update operations are coordinated.

Deadlocks are detected via timeout on the `SEND`. If the `SEND` times out, the transaction is aborted, and is automatically restarted at `BEGIN-`

```
PROCEDURE DIVISION.

000-BEGIN SECTION.
ACCEPT INPUT-MSG.
  BEGIN-TRANSACTION.

  MOVE ACCOUNT-ID OF INPUT-MSG TO ACCOUNT-ID OF DBCR-MSG.
  MOVE AMOUNT OF INPUT-MSG TO AMOUNT OF DBCR-MSG.

  SEND MESSAGE DBCR-MSG TO /LOCAL
      REPLY CODE STATUS.

  MOVE BALANCE OF DBCR-MSG TO BALANCE1 OF CONFIRM-MSG.

  SEND MESSAGE DBCR-MSG TO /REMOTE
      REPLY CODE STATUS.
  END-TRANSACTION.

  MOVE BALANCE OF DBCR-MSG TO BALANCE2 OF CONFIRM-MSG.
  MOVE "Successful transfer, new balance is:" TO DISPLAY-TEXT OF
     CONFIRM-MSG.
  DISPLAY CONFIRM-MSG.

END PROGRAM.
EXIT.
```

Figure 5.30 **SCREEN COBOL Example** The program accepts input from the display, begins a transaction, and sends messages to two servers, one locally for the debit operation and the other to a remote node for the credit operation.

TRANSACTION. On transaction abort the server program is free to accept a call from another client.

On the server side, two separate programs are called within the transaction, one on the local node and another on a remote node. The DEBIT program is shown in Figure 5.31; the CREDIT program would be similar. Updates are coordinated by TM/MP. Communications between client and server is accomplished using a special system file called $RECEIVE. The client writes the message to the file, and the server reads the message from the file.

5.10 Microsoft Transaction Server

Microsoft Transaction Server[1] is a new component-based TP monitor product from Microsoft. It is heavily object-oriented, which distinguishes it from most of the other TP monitors in this chapter. In addition to standard TP monitor functions, such as transaction management and transactional RPC, it includes attributes of object request brokers and message-oriented middleware.

1 At press time, the product name was not yet final. However, the description presented here is technically accurate.

```
PROGRAM DEBIT.
PROCEDURE DIVISION.

  READ INPUT-MSG.

  MOVE ACCOUNT-ID OF INPUT-MSG TO ACCOUNT-ID.
  MOVE AMOUNT OF INPUT-MSG TO AMOUNT.

  OPEN CURSOR...       EXEC SQL...FETCH ACCOUNT-REC FOR ACCOUNT-ID
  SUBTRACT AMOUNT FROM BALANCE OF ACCOUNT-REC.
      EXEC SQL...UPDATE ACCOUNT-REC.
  MOVE BALANCE OF ACCOUNT REC TO BALANCE OF OUTPUT-MSG.
  CLOSE CURSOR...

  WRITE OUTPUT-MSG.
END PROGRAM.
```

Figure 5.31 **DEBIT Server Program** The server program reads messages from its input file. When the server finishes processing the call, it writes the reply message back to the file. The reply message is received by the SCREEN COBOL program, and the reply status field is updated to show whether or not the communication completed successfully.

Its main goal is ease of use, to make it easier to develop, deploy, and administer reliable, distributed, and scalable component-based applications.

In April 1996, Microsoft Transaction Server shipped its transaction manager, the Microsoft Distributed Transaction Coordinator (MS DTC), embedded in SQL Server 6.5. The application execution portion of the product is planned for shipment by early 1997. It supports component-based applications that may be installed in a single-machine network, a large client/server environment, or in Internet and Intranet environments accessed by intelligent clients and simple browsers. Microsoft Transaction Server and MS DTC run on Windows NT with support for clients in Windows 95 and interoperate with X/Open XA transaction managers and resource managers.

Microsoft's Component Object Model

Microsoft Transaction Server provides a programming environment for component-based applications. It supports components written to Microsoft's COM (Component Object Model), the foundation technology for Microsoft's Object Linking and Embedding (OLE). COM is a binary standard that describes component-to-component calling conventions in a language-neutral fashion. Thus, components written in one language can seamlessly call components written in another language. We give a brief summary of the main concepts and capabilities of COM that are relevant to Microsoft Transaction Server.

A *component* is an executable program image. It can have multiple *interfaces*, where each interface is a collection of methods. An *object* is an instance of a component.

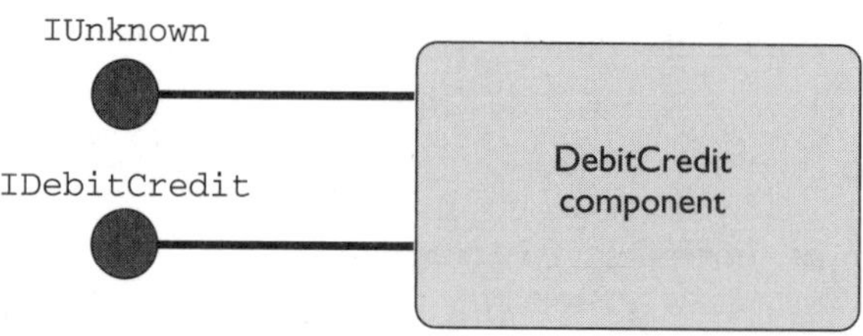

Figure 5.32 **Representation of a COM Component** An interface is depicted as a lollipop attached to a component. A component can have multiple interfaces. All COM components support the `IUnknown` interface.

An interface's specification includes its method names, the parameters expected by those methods, and a globally unique *interface identifier* (IID), which is a 128-bit standard universal unique identifier. An interface's specification is immutable. Therefore, if a component writer wants to enhance an interface, he or she must implement a new interface with another IID. By convention, interface names begin with *I*. See Figure 5.32 for the graphical representation of a component with multiple interfaces. Methods are ordinarily not shown in this representation; for example, the `IDebitCredit` interface supports the `Debit` and `Credit` methods, which are not shown in the figure.

Every COM component, and hence instances of that component, support the interface `IUnknown`. The method `QueryInterface` on `IUnknown` allows a client to ask a COM object if it supports a particular interface, given the interface's unique IID. If the object supports the IID, the client knows exactly what behavior the object will provide, because interface definitions are immutable. Thus, in Figure 5.32, an instance of `DebitCredit` would respond positively to a call on `QueryInterface` given `IDebitCredit`'s IID and therefore supports all the methods specified for `IDebitCredit`.

The `QueryInterface` mechanism helps cope with versioning components in a client/server environment, as follows:

- Since interface definitions are immutable, to change the behavior of an interface, one must define a new interface. Over time, one may have several different interfaces that are effectively versions of each other.
- A component can support several different interfaces each providing a different version.
- A client can be written to cope with multiple versions of a component interface as follows: The client queries for the IID of its preferred version, and the component replies yes or no. If the answer is no, the client can try its second favorite interface, and so on. The client and component can interoperate if the client can find an interface that it knows how to use and that the component supports.

This mechanism allows clients and server components to be independently upgraded even in a distributed environment. A client won't always be able to

Type of Object	Shares Data ?	Durable Data ?	Description
Client	Optional	Optional	Application code in the presentation server to interact with end users via a 4GL, terminal interface, Internet browser, and so on.
MTx object	No	No	Application business logic for workflow control and/or a transaction server. It consists of methods in a single-user nonpreemptive component with private member data (not shared by other objects) and is therefore easy to program.
Resource dispenser	Yes	No	Providers of shared nondurable resources, such as ODBC connections or memory heaps, which are shared by objects in a single process. Resource dispensers require more skill to implement than MTx objects as they involve sharing and, hence, require synchronization to provide correct behavior.
Resource manager	Yes	Yes	Resource managers, such as Microsoft SQL Server, provide shared durable state, participate in two-phase commit, and provide isolation.

Figure 5.33 **Pieces of a Microsoft Transaction Server Application** A Microsoft Transaction Server application consists of client code and MTx objects, which access shared resources from resource dispensers and resource managers.

offer access to a new server, and a server won't always support old clients, but neither program will break as a result of the version mismatch. The client will just report the version mismatch and return an error to its caller.

Every component has a *class factory*, which can create instances of the component. The class factory returns a pointer to an interface on the object. After receiving this pointer, a client can call methods on that object (locally, or remotely using Distributed COM [DCOM]) or can use `QueryInterface` to find other interfaces on the object and call methods on them.

Many application programming tools are available for producing COM components, such as Microsoft's Visual Basic, Visual C++, and Visual J++ (Java compiler); Borland's Delphi; Powersoft's PowerBuilder; and MicroFocus's Visual Object COBOL. It is expected that many users of Microsoft Transaction Server will program components and clients in Visual Basic.

System Architecture

A Microsoft Transaction Server application consists of client code, Microsoft Transaction Server objects (MTx objects, which are component instances), resource dispensers, and resource managers, which are described in Figure 5.33. Client code is any program that calls MTx objects, such as a presentation server. An MTx object can be a workflow controller or transaction server. As in TUXEDO and Encina, there is no forced architectural distinction between these roles, as there is in ACMS and Pathway, so distinguishing these roles is a matter of programming style. A resource manager is the same concept used throughout this book.

A resource dispenser supports a shared nondurable resource. Resource dispensers are usually supplied by system software vendors, but can be developed by a user, if appropriate. Though most TP monitors offer some types of resource dispenser, Microsoft Transaction Server is unique in making it an extensible mechanism, so that third parties can add their own.

To deploy and manage a component, Microsoft Transaction Server requires a component specification consisting of a dynamic link library (`.dll` file), definitions of the interfaces to the component, and some additional configuration information such as whether the component must run inside a transaction. The latter information says whether transactions are *not supported* (don't run the object within a transaction), *supported* (the object can execute within its creator's transaction), *required* (if the object's creator isn't running a transaction, then start one for the object when it's created), or *requires new* (when the object is created, start a new transaction even if its creator is running a transaction). These declarative properties of components are used to automatically create and manage transactions on behalf of application developers. By using this mechanism, many applications are not expected to use explicit transaction control mechanisms (e.g., Start, Commit, and Abort).

In the client programming model, a client creates an object that it needs and then calls methods on it. The client can start a transaction before creating the object, the object can start a transaction at the time it is created, or there may be no transaction in the picture, depending on the client's wishes and the transaction specification of the object's component.

Microsoft Transaction Server enhances the COM programming model by supporting component context. Context is inherited from an object's creator and may be influenced by attributes defined for the object's class. Example context information includes the transaction for the object and security identity (see Figure 5.34).

A component is a pure application that knows nothing of its runtime configuration. This allows the assembly of components purchased from independent companies and their deployment in a wide variety of system environments, without modifying the component at all.

A component can run in the same process as the object or client code that creates it. The same component can be deployed to run in a different process than its creator without recompiling. In this case, the process can be on the same node (local) or different node (remote) than its creator. The choice to run inside a process with another object is a trade-off between performance (inter-object calls are faster within a process, but a remote object may be placed close to the data it accesses) and protection against faults in the other object (objects are better protected if they're in different processes).

MTx objects usually run inside server processes, which are managed by Microsoft Transaction Server. DCOM is responsible for marshaling method

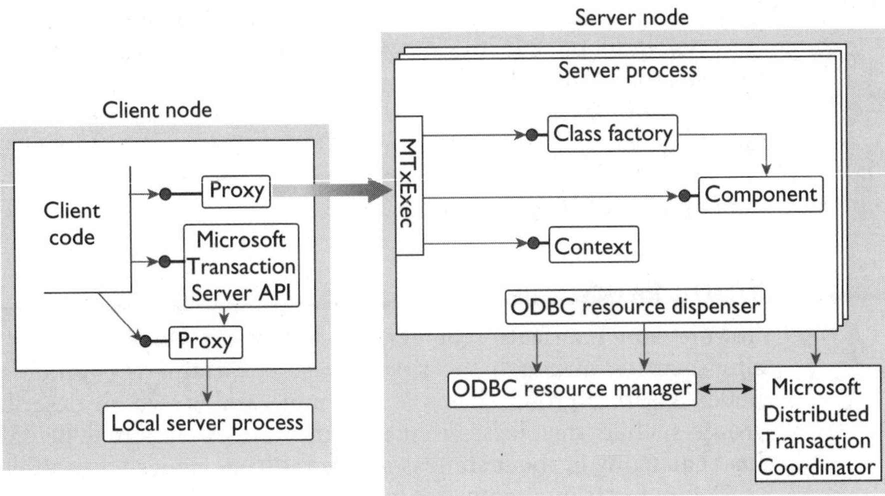

Figure 5.34 **Microsoft Transaction Server Architecture** Server applications and the Microsoft Transaction Server API itself are COM components. The MTxExec implements most Microsoft Transaction Server semantics; it manages threads and contexts, automatically starts and commits transactions, recycles objects, and so on.

calls from clients into the MTx objects running in the server process. The MTxExec propagates transaction context and manages the assignment and execution of threads in a server process.

Presentation Server

A presentation server application uses COM APIs to create and access server objects that perform the desired work. It therefore has few restrictions, other than being written in a language that supports COM. It can be a client application running on a personal computer, an HTML-based application running in a browser, an HTML application enhanced with a script, or an Active-X component embedded in HTML pages to provide interactive behavior across http. Components running on desktop clients may invoke applications on servers using http as the communications medium. (See Sections 2.8 and 5.11.)

TP Communications

Clients and components communicate via method calls, which are the object-oriented equivalent of RPC. The application is designed to be unaware of any distribution that may occur between its components. Calls can be made to an in-process object, to an object in another server process running on the caller's node, or to an object running on a different node.

The first shipment of Microsoft Transaction Server includes support only for synchronous execution of applications. Queued communications is planned for a later release.

Microsoft Transaction Server has a built-in transaction manager, MS DTC. ACMSxp, Encina, TOP END, and TUXEDO have all announced support for MS DTC (with MS DTC playing the role of a resource manager). ACMSxp also supports MS DTC as a transaction manager.

System Management

In Microsoft Transaction Server, a *server group* is a set of nodes managed as a single entity, although the first release constrains this group to be a single node. A server group shares a common catalog, which describes the server group, such as the classes that can run in it. A class may be defined to allow load balancing of the instances across multiple nodes within the server group.

Components are grouped into *packages*, which are similar to task groups in STDL. A package defines a unit of trust for a collection of components. Components in the package must trust each other, because if one of the components has a fault, it can corrupt the other components. Each package runs in a server process, which contains all of the components of a package and no other components.

An explorer provides a graphical interface for administering applications. It can be used to configure which components belong to which packages and where packages run within the server group. MS DTC also has an easy-to-use graphical explorer that displays statistics, transaction information, and tracing information. Both the Microsoft Transaction Server and MS DTC explorers are components that can be integrated into other administration frameworks. For example, the MS DTC explorer is integrated into SQL Server's Enterprise Manager Administration Console as well as the Microsoft Transaction Server Explorer.

Database Access

An application can use any resource manager that interoperates with MS DTC. The resource manager can use the OLE Transactions or XA interface. Today, Microsoft's SQL Server is the only resource manager that supports these on NT. It is expected that other products that store durable data will be implemented.

Programming Example

The program in Figures 5.35 through 5.38 illustrates the Microsoft Transaction Server interface for the debit-credit example. As in some previous examples, presentation services are ignored, and error handling is omitted.

In Figure 5.35, the nontransactional client creates a `TransferMoney` object, which runs the actual transaction.

```
// All the #include statements are omitted for readability

HRESULT DBCRclient(long from, long to, long amount)
{ HRESULT hr = S_OK;
  CLSID TransferMoneyClsid;
  ITransferMoney* pTransferMoney = NULL;

  // Create an object of the Transfer server component
  CLSIDFromProgID(L"TransferMoney.Server.1", &TransferMoneyClsid);
  CoCreateInstance(TransferMoneyClsid, IID_IDBCR, (void**)&pTransferMoney);

  // Transfer calls debit and credit within the same transaction
  hr = pTransferMoney->Transfer(from, to, amount);

  // Release the TransferMoney object and return
  pTransferMoney->Release();
  return hr;
}
```

Figure 5.35 Debit-Credit Client for Microsoft Transaction Server The `DBCRclient` program would be called by a main program that interacts with the presentation device. It calls the `debit` and `credit` methods via an intermediate `TransferMoney` object. Note that the client uses generic COM code, with nothing specific to Microsoft Transaction Server.

The `TransferMoney` class, in Figure 5.36, is configured with "transaction required." Since the client invokes it from outside a transaction, the Start, Commit, and Abort methods are invoked automatically by the runtime environment, similar to automatic transaction mode in TUXEDO. The transaction context is transparently passed in the two server calls, which are ordinary RPCs, with no special Microsoft Transaction Server syntax, for example, `pFromAcct->debit(amount)`.

The `DBCR` server, in Figure 5.37, receives its transaction context from the library function `GetObjectContext`. After doing its work, it tells Microsoft Transaction Server whether it's willing to commit using the methods `SetComplete` or `SetAbort` on its context object. `SetCommit` or `SetAbort` also tell the runtime that the object has no residual state and therefore can be reused. This allows the `Transfer` method in `TransferMoney` to use *just-in-time activations* to reuse a single `DBCR` (debit-credit) instance (`pAccount`) for both the source (`from`) and destination (`to`) accounts. Only the `debit` program is shown; the `credit` and `initNew` programs are similar.

The server class, `DBCR`, has an interface definition, shown in Figure 5.38, similar to that in Encina++. First the debit-credit interface is defined (`IDBCR`) by listing the signatures of its methods. The phrase `interface IDBCR : IDispatch` means that `IDBCR` inherits from `IDispatch`. `IDispatch` is the interface that supports OLE Automation, the dynamic call interface for OLE, which is used by Visual Basic. Then the `DBCR` class (coclass) is defined by listing its interfaces, in this case, just `IDBCR`. The `TransferMoney` class definition is similar and is therefore omitted.

```
STDMETHODIMP TransferMoney::Transfer(IN long from, IN long to, IN long amount)
{ HRESULT hr;
  IObjectContext* pContext = NULL;
  IDBCR* pAccount = NULL;

  // Get reference to my context
  GetObjectContext(&pContext);

  // Create the DBCR object via my context and transaction
  CLSIDFromProgID(L"DBCR.Server.1", &DBCRClsid);
  pContext->CreateInstance(DBCRClsid, IID_IDBCR, (void**)&pAccount);

  // Use the same reference to call 2 different objects via
  // "just-in-time activations"
  pAccount->initNew(from);
  hr = pAccount->debit(amount);
  if (SUCCEEDED(hr)) {  // reuse the same object for a different account
      pAccount->initNew(to);
      hr = pAccount->credit(amount);
  }

  // The transaction automatically commits or aborts upon return
  if (SUCCEEDED(hr)) pContext->SetComplete();
  else pContext->SetAbort();
  return hr;
}
```

Figure 5.36 **`TransferMoney`** **Server for Microsoft Transaction Server** The `TransferMoney` server should be declared as "transaction required." Thus, it need not bracket the transaction with an explicit Start method.

5.11 Web Servers

Server software products specifically designed for use with the World Wide Web (WWW) are starting to incorporate traditional TP monitor features, including Microsoft's Information Server API (ISAPI) and the Netscape Server API (NSAPI). This section presents a brief overview of these two products to illustrate the relationship between the emerging web server technology and TP monitors. The market for web servers is new and changing fast. The description below is a snapshot of early releases of these rapidly changing products.

As mentioned in Section 2.8, the WWW architecture, using web browsers and web servers, is very similar to that of TP monitors. When a client (browser) issues a request to a web server, the server transfers HTML pages back to the client using the http protocol. The web browser acts as a presentation server, and the web server acts as a workflow controller and/or transaction server.

```
HRESULT DBCR::debit(IN long amount)
{ HRESULT hr;
  IObjectContext* pContext = NULL

  // get reference to my context
  GetObjectContext(&pContext);

  if (amount <= 0)
    hr = E_INVALIDARG;
  else {
    // do the requested work here
    hr = S_OK;
  }

  if (SUCCEEDED(hr))
     // This object is done for now and agrees to commit
     pContext->SetComplete();
  else
     // This object is done for now and will not agree to commit
     pContext->SetAbort();
  return hr;
}
```

Figure 5.37 Debit Server for Microsoft Transaction Server The `debit` program for the DBCR server called by the `TransferMoney` class in Figure 5.36.

Given the similarity of WWW and TP monitor architectures, it isn't surprising to find features in web server products that closely match those of workflow controllers and transaction servers in a TP monitor. For example, web servers are long-lived processes that take requests from a large number of clients. For each request, the server replies with an HTML page. To access secure information, such as information that requires a paid subscription, a client must be authenticated, so its authorization to access information can later be checked. Such a server should support multithreading and dynamic procedure loading for good performance, error logging for diagnosis, and a system management console that provides functions to control performance parameters and other aspects of server operation. These are typical server functions of a TP monitor and can be included in web servers.

The Common Gateway Interface (CGI) was the first protocol commonly offered by web servers for web server daemons to call other applications and can be used to call a TP monitor (as was done by the IBM Internet Connection Server product). CGI essentially uses the time-sharing model of executing commands, namely, create a process for every call. The CGI approach has limited scalability, which gives rise to the extensions offered by ISAPI from Microsoft and NSAPI from Netscape.

```
[       object,
        uuid(27870601-E1A7-11CF-B899-0080C7394688),
        dual,
        helpstring("IDBCR Interface"),
        pointer_default(unique)
]

interface IDBCR : IDispatch
{       import "oaidl.idl";
        HRESULT initNew(             [in] long Account);
        HRESULT debit(               [in] long Amount);
        HRESULT credit(              [in] long Amount);
};

[       uuid(27870600-E1A7-11CF-B899-0080C7394688),
        version(1.0),
        helpstring("DRCR 1.0 Type Library")
]
library DBCRLib
{       importlib("stdole32.tlb");

        [       uuid(27870605-E1A7-11CF-B899-0080C7394688),
                helpstring("DBCR Class")
        ]
        coclass DBCR
        {
                [default] interface IDBCR;
        };
};
```

Figure 5.38 Interface Definition for the Debit-Credit Server This is processed by the IDL tool to produce marshaling code and the type library (`DBCR.tlb`), which provides runtime access to type information.

ISAPI and NSAPI support programmer-defined web server functions such as database and file access, logging, access to external applications, and customized responses (see Figure 5.39). The server daemon loads a dynamic link library (DLL) in ISAPI or function in NSAPI as an *in-process* application for better scalability and resource sharing, a principle in use for a long time by TP monitor products. Parameters are exchanged between the web server daemon and DLL using a data structure, called an *Extension Control Block* (ECB) in ISAPI or *parameter block* in NSAPI, whose function is similar to the commarea of CICS or the typed buffers of TUXEDO. Using ISAPI or NSAPI, a programmer can implement a multithreaded server that uses a web browser as a display, calls out to a database server or TP monitor program, or accesses data on the local platform directly. Furthermore, once a resource manager is mapped to the web server process, it can be reused by later requests.

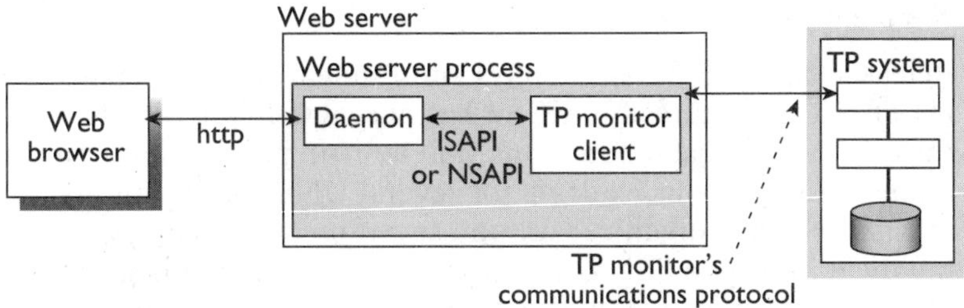

Figure 5.39 ISAPI and NSAPI for In-Process Calls These two web server APIs improve on CGI by calling DLLs or functions in the same process as the http server. The DLLs or functions can call TP systems or perform any local function such as starting a transaction (assuming a TM is available) or accessing a local database.

In addition to web servers, other products are coming to market that integrate the TP monitors described in this chapter with various other Internet technologies. Some examples are Digital's TP Internet Server (integrating ACMSxp with secure Internet tunnels), BEA Systems' Jolt (integrating TUXEDO and Java), and IBM's Internet Connection Server (integrating CICS and CGI). These products are not specifically web server products but instead rely on the TP monitors themselves to provide server features.

Microsoft Internet Information Server

The Internet Information Server (IIS) product was released by Microsoft in 1996 for the Windows NT platform. Most IIS features are implemented as extensions to native Windows NT functions, such as security, system administration, and performance monitoring. IIS is therefore tightly integrated with the Windows NT GUI, which enhances ease of use.

Windows NT file protection mechanisms secure access to HTML files and improve file availability via disk mirroring and striping. NT Server directory services can set password access to certain areas of a web site. Access control lists for authentication and the NT user manager provide multiple layers of protection against unauthorized access to HTML files. IIS security includes secure sockets for encrypting the transmission between web browser and server, auditing mechanisms, and various levels of access control that can be set on users, files, and communications links.

A GUI is provided for installation and setup. Microsoft's focus on ease of management and quick response time utilizes the native features of the Windows NT server for Internet and web setup, management, and performance optimization. For good performance, IIS supports multithreaded processes (using NT's kernel threads) and runs programs as dynamic link libraries (DLLs) within the web server process.

IIS is integrated with the Microsoft Back Office product and provides an Internet Database Connector for ODBC-compliant resource managers.

Netscape HTTP Server

Released in 1996 by Netscape Communications Corporation, the Netscape HTTP Server features NSAPI for better scalability, easier access to other applications, customizable functions, and built-in public functions for typical operations. The server is available for several UNIX platforms and Windows NT.

The NSAPI is organized around seven predefined *steps,* or types of actions, involved in responding to an http request. Each step is performed once for all of the *objects* invoked by the request. An object is a collection of HTML and related files. Steps include authentication and authorization, file location and operation, and customization of the response. The NSAPI approach to security anticipates the use of secure http protocol.

NSAPI initializes servers during startup with static data common to server modules, maintains an internal table of available functions, and loads code modules into the server at runtime. All operations must be thread-safe, and a certain amount of context is maintained for the functions, including the IP address and DNS name of the client and the full text of the client's request for logging purposes.

5.12 Summary

All of the TP monitor products surveyed here support the three-tier TP monitor model described in Chapter 2, but they do it with a variety of architectural designs. They all provide connectivity to modern desktop devices, which now replace the character cell terminals originally dominant in TP applications. They support several kinds of APIs—a specialized high-level language, a command-based API, or a system service library type of API. Most of the monitors now support the UNIX and Windows NT operating systems. Only two monitors, ACMS and Pathway/TS, define an application structure. Most of the monitors support the X/Open XA interface for integrating resource managers and can interoperate via IBM's LU6.2 protocol, but they vary widely in their support for other TP standards.

CICS

CICS is the most popular of the products by a wide margin. It has been implemented in several products on multiple platforms. CICS is designed around the concept of a *region,* which is an address space specifically designed and adapted for TP. A defining aspect of a region is that it owns and manages resources and controls access to them, typically via CICS commands embedded in C or COBOL programs. Resources include terminals, programs, communications links, and data resources.

CICS uses a command-based API that includes multiple features for distributed TP and communications among regions, including routing a transaction request to another region, accessing a data resource owned by another region, and executing a program owned by another region. CICS implements a direct communications model using peer-to-peer communications, with an optional call-return programming model. Recent extensions to CICS support integration of desktop devices and object-oriented programs. System administration is done by creating and updating tables or lists of the resources owned by a region and ensuring that the resources are available to applications that need them.

IMS

IMS is another popular TP monitor from IBM. It is based on the queued TP model. IMS applications run in a *system*, which is configured to include the resources required for an application. Like CICS, applications contain transaction programs, but instead of running in a region, they run in an MVS operating system process. A terminal enqueues a message containing the transaction program ID to the input queue. After the transaction program executes, a message is enqueued to a reply queue for the terminal or, optionally, to another terminal or to another application.

The IMS API is based on an external service library that supplies both database and TP monitor functions. IMS applications can access some services external to the system directly, while others require the use of its external subsystem, which maps external functions such as the System Object Model (SOM) to the equivalent or requested function with the IMS system itself. PCs and workstations can be added to IMS applications this way, even though the applications still run only on mainframes. Presentation servers are restricted to 3270 terminals or emulation.

TP Standards

Various efforts have been made to establish standards for two-phase commit, transactional communication, and programming interfaces. X/Open has defined a widely accepted reference model, the Distributed Transaction Processing (DTP) model, which divides TP systems into functional components for transaction management, resource management, and communications management. Applications use component interfaces directly or use the Structured Transaction Definition Language (STDL) to access transaction management and communications management services. STDL elements include an interface definition language for communications manager transparency. Resource manager interfaces are native to the resource managers. The XA standard allows different vendors' TP monitor and database products to interoperate. Most modern TP monitors implement at least XA as well as some of the other X/Open interfaces or STDL, but no two monitors implement the same set of standards.

X/Open transactional communications standards rely on the OSI TP two-phase commit standard. OSI TP is based on LU6.2, but it is not widely available. The Object Management Group's Object Transaction Service (OTS) integrates the X/Open specifications with object-oriented technology but does not mandate a particular two-phase commit protocol. OTS implementations are beginning to appear on the market.

TUXEDO

TUXEDO, from BEA Systems, is based on the IMS model of queued communications, optimized for a call-return paradigm and using a simplified service-based API. TUXEDO also offers a language-based version (based on X/Open's TxRPC IDL). TUXEDO was designed for use with UNIX operating systems, and today is the leading UNIX-based TP monitor. TUXEDO has also been ported to the Windows NT operating system.

TUXEDO's architecture relies on a shared memory construct called a bulletin board, which contains configuration information and routes request messages between client and server programs. One system is defined as the master, from which configuration information is propagated to bulletin boards at systems within a given domain. The domain is an administrative boundary around participating client and server processes in the network. Typically there is one TUXEDO system on each node of the domain, managing a collection of client and server processes.

ACMS

ACMS was created by Digital Equipment Corporation as an integration framework for applications built using its VAX Information Architecture product set, which also included a file query tool, two database systems, two forms systems, and a central data dictionary. ACMS features the Task Definition Language (TDL), a TP-specific high-level language on which the X/Open STDL is based. ACMS has recently been updated by Digital into a new cross-platform version called ACMSxp, which implements STDL.

The ACMS architecture is based on a three-process model: presentation, workflow, and data access. Interprocess communication uses a remote procedure call mechanism, which hides differences between local and remote calls from the programmer. TDL is compiled and generates stubs that handle communications, security, and name services in a distributed environment. ACMSxp implements the same architecture on open systems using STDL, DCE, XA-compliant resource managers, and Encina toolkit components.

Encina

The Encina Monitor is offered by Transarc Corporation (a subsidiary of IBM). It is one of several products based on Transarc's Encina Toolkit, which is a modular collection of TP and related functional components.

The Encina Monitor architecture is based on the OSF DCE. Encina uses a transactional RPC mechanism for communication (based on DCE) and DCE services for security and naming. It also includes nested transactions, full Syncpoint, and a transactional file system. Encina supports an implementation of the OMG OTS, provides a C++ class library to ease development, and supplies a lightweight DCE-derived protocol for small desktop devices.

Each administrative domain, called a cell, has a cell manager that stores configuration information in an object repository. Node managers monitor and control resources on each machine.

TOP END

TOP END is a TP monitor product from AT&T/NCR. Like TUXEDO, TOP END offers a system service style of API that accesses a library of transaction management and communications functions. Unlike TUXEDO, TOP END provides a flat system management structure that does not require a master configuration file. System servers communicate via node manager processes and exchange configuration information dynamically.

The TOP END system servers handle the application distribution functions. Application communications is based on the peer-to-peer model with several optimizations, such as the ability to start a session and send a request in the same message, and to reply and destroy the session at the same time, essentially emulating the call-return paradigm. TOP END services are designed to be integrated at the application level as components in large networks of servers, distributing information and processing work.

Configuration information is interactively defined and uploaded to servers from a PC. A sophisticated system management facility also is provided on a PC platform.

Pathway/TS

Pathway/TS from Tandem is a TP monitor that runs on the fault-tolerant Tandem platform. A multithreaded Terminal Control Program handles the display interaction while single-threaded server programs execute in a server class to process requests. The Terminal Control Program can be implemented using process pairs that periodically checkpoint their state from a primary to a backup process, which can continue processing a request if the primary fails.

Defining characteristics of the Tandem platform include high availability, loosely coupled multiprocessor nodes, integrated wide area networks for distributed processing, database replication and partitioning, and backup system configuration. Tandem recently reengineered its platform, breaking up the services on which Pathway/TS and the fault-tolerant features are based to allow support for TUXEDO and CICS TP monitor *personalities* (API subsets) on the same platform.

Microsoft Transaction Server

Microsoft Transaction Server is the newest of the TP monitor products described here, based on a new architecture integrated with Microsoft's Component Object Model (COM). Applications can be developed using any combination of products and languages that support Microsoft's OLE standard. Its main goal is to make it easier to develop, deploy, and administer component-based applications.

A client program can start a transaction and call server objects, which run in server processes that are managed by Microsoft Transaction Server. Microsoft Transaction Server transparently marshals method calls to server objects, propagates transaction context, and manages threads. System management of server processes and server groups is supported by a graphical explorer interface.

Microsoft Transaction Server includes a separately accessible transaction manager, called the Microsoft Distributed Transaction Coordinator, which supports a native Microsoft API as well as the X/Open XA standard. MS DTC was originally bundled with Microsoft's SQL Server product but later repackaged with the Microsoft Transaction Server TP monitor.

Web Servers

Web servers are an emerging technology that is beginning to implement TP monitor concepts to improve the performance, reliability, and security of World Wide Web applications. Microsoft's Internet Server API (ISAPI) and Netscape's Netscape Server API (NSAPI) provide mechanisms for loading customized web server programs into the same multithreaded operating system process that's serving the browser requests for HTML files. This reduces the cost of invoking the application (compared to CGI, which spawns a process for each request), just as TP monitor products have traditionally done. The new APIs provide better performance when connecting web browsers to TP applications or routing a request from a browser, and they are integrated with products that provide system management capabilities similar to TP monitor products.

CHAPTER 6

Locking

6.1 Introduction

Recall that one of the key properties of transactions is that they are *isolated*. Technically, this means that the execution of transactions has the same effect as running the transactions serially, one after the next, in sequence, with no overlap in executing any two of them. Such executions are called *serializable*, meaning "has the same effect as a serial execution."

The most popular mechanism used to attain serializability is locking. The concept is simple:

- Each transaction reserves access to the data it uses. The reservation is called a *lock*.
- There are read locks and write locks.
- Before reading a piece of data, a transaction sets a read lock. Before writing the data, it sets a write lock.
- Read locks *conflict* with write locks, and write locks *conflict* with write locks.
- A transaction can obtain a lock only if no other transaction has a conflicting lock on the same data item. Thus, it can obtain a read lock on x only if no transaction has a write lock on x. It can obtain a write lock on x only if no transaction has a read lock or write lock on x.

Although the concept of locking is simple, its effects on performance and correctness can be complex, counterintuitive, and hard to predict. Building robust TP applications requires a solid understanding of locking.

Locking affects performance. When a transaction sets a lock, it delays other transactions that need to set a conflicting lock. Everything else being equal, the more transactions that are running concurrently, the more likely that such delays will happen. The frequency and length of such delays can also be affected by transaction design, database layout, and transaction and database distribution. To understand how to minimize this performance impact, one must understand locking mechanisms and how they are used, and how these mechanisms and usage scenarios affect performance.

Locking also affects correctness. Although locking usually strikes people as intuitively correct, not all uses of locking lead to correct results. For example, reserving access to data before actually doing the access would seem to eliminate the possibility that transactions could interfere with each other. However, if serializability is the goal, then simply locking data before accessing it is not quite enough. The timing of unlock operations also matters.

Correctness and the Two-Phase Rule

To see how unlock operations affect correctness, consider two transactions, T_1 and T_2, which access two shared data items, x and y. T_1 reads x and later

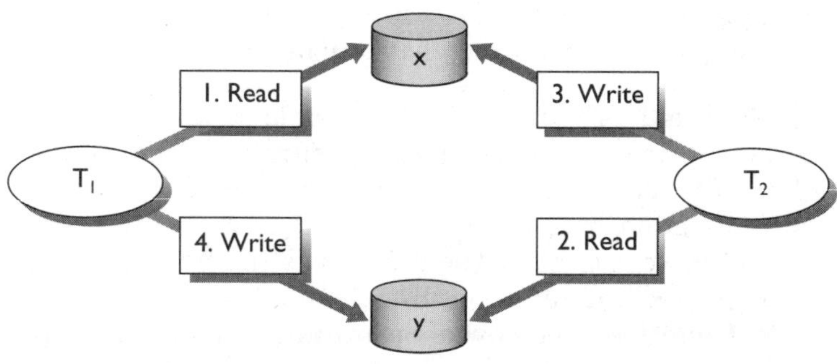

Figure 6.1 **A Nonserializable Execution, E', That Uses Locking** The numbers 1–4 indicate the order in which operations execute.

writes *y*, and T_2 reads *y* and later writes *x*.[1] For example, *x* and *y* could be records that describe financial and personnel aspects of a department. T_1 reads budget information in *x* and updates the number of open requisitions in *y*. T_2 reads the current head count and updates the committed salary budget.

To describe executions of these transactions succinctly, we'll use $r_1[x]$ to denote T_1's read of *x*, $w_1[y]$ to denote T_1's write of *y*, and similarly for T_2. We'll denote lock operations in a similar way—$rl_1[x]$ to denote T_1's setting a read lock on *x*, and $ru_1[x]$ to denote T_1's unlocking *x*. Given this notation, consider the following execution E of T_1 and T_2:

$$E = \underbrace{rl_1[x]\ r_1[x]\ ru_1[x]}_{T_1 \text{ reads } x}\ \underbrace{rl_2[y]\ r_2[y]\ wl_2[x]\ w_2[x]\ ru_2[y]\ wu_2[x]}_{T_2 \text{ reads } y \text{ and writes } x}\ \underbrace{wl_1[y]\ w_1[y]\ wu_1[y]}_{T_1 \text{ writes } y}$$

In execution E, each transaction locks each data item before accessing it. (You should check this for each operation.) Yet the execution isn't serializable. We can show this by stripping off the lock and unlock operations, producing the following execution (see Figure 6.1):

$$E' = r_1[x]\ r_2[y]\ w_2[x]\ w_2[y]$$

Since execution E has the same read and write operations as execution E', and the operations are in the same order, E and E' have the same effect on the database (the only difference between them is the lock operations). To show that E' isn't serializable, let's compare it to the two possible serial executions of T_1 and T_2 (T_1T_2 and T_2T_1) and show that neither of them could produce the same result as E':

- In the serial execution $T_1T_2 = r_1[x]\ w_1[y]\ r_2[y]\ w_2[x]$, T_2 reads the value of *y* written by T_1, which isn't what actually happened in E'.

1 The example is a bit contrived, in that each transaction updates a data item it didn't previously read. The example is designed to illustrate a variety of concurrency control concepts discussed throughout the chapter.

- In the serial execution $T_2T_1 = r_2[y]\ w_2[x]\ r_1[x]\ w_1[y]$, T_1 reads the value of x written by T_2, which isn't what actually happened in E'.

Since T_1T_2 and T_2T_1 are the only possible serial executions of T_1 and T_2, and E' doesn't have the same effect as either of them, E' isn't serializable. Since E has the same effect as E', E isn't serializable either.

Each transaction in E got a lock before accessing the corresponding data item. So what went wrong? The problem is the timing of T_1's unlock operation on x. It executed too soon. By releasing its lock on x before getting its lock on y, T_1 created a window of opportunity for T_2 to ruin the execution. T_2 wrote x after T_1 read it (making it appear that T_2 followed T_1), and it read y before T_1 wrote it (making it appear that T_2 preceded T_1). Since T_2 can't both precede and follow T_1 in a serial execution, the result was not serializable.

The locking rule that guarantees serializable executions in all cases is called *two-phase locking*. It says that a transaction must get all of its locks before releasing any of them. Or equivalently, a transaction cannot release a lock and subsequently get a lock (as T_1 did in E). When a transaction obeys this rule, it has two phases (hence the name): a growing phase during which it acquires locks, and a shrinking phase during which it releases them. The operation that separates the two phases is the transaction's first unlock operation, which is the first operation of the second phase.

Two-Phase Locking Theorem If all transactions in an execution are two-phase locked, then the execution is serializable.

Despite the simple intuition behind locking, there are no simple proofs of the Two-Phase Locking Theorem. The original proof by Eswaran et al. appeared in 1976 and was several pages long. The simplest proof we know of is by Ullman (1982) and is presented in the appendix at the end of this chapter.

Automating Locking

An important feature of locking is that it can be hidden from the application programmer. Here's how:

When a transaction issues a read or write operation, the data manager that processes the operation first sets a read or write lock on the data to be read or written. This is done without any special hints from the transaction program, besides the read or write operation itself.

To ensure the two-phase rule, the data manager holds all locks until the transaction issues the Commit or Abort operation, at which point the data manager knows the transaction is done. This is later than the rule requires, but it's the first time the data manager can be sure the transaction won't issue any more reads or writes, which would require it to set another lock. That is, if the data manager releases one of the transaction's locks before the transaction terminates, and the transaction subsequently issues a read or write, the system would have to set a lock and thereby break the two-phase rule.

Thus, a transaction program only needs to bracket its transactions. The data manager does the rest.

Although a data manager can hide locking from the application programmer, it often gives some control over when locks are set and released. This gives a measure of performance tuning, often at the expense of correctness. We'll discuss this in more detail later in the chapter.

Notice that we used the term "data manager" here, instead of the more generic term "resource manager" that we use elsewhere in this book. Since there is such a strong connotation that locking is used by database systems, we find it more intuitive to use the terms "data manager" and "data item" in this chapter, rather than "resource manager" and "resource." But this is just a matter of taste. We use the terms as synonyms, to mean a database system, file system, queue manager—any system that manages access to shared resources.

6.2 Implementation

Although an application programmer never has to deal directly with locks, it helps to know how locking is implemented, for two reasons. First, locking can have a dramatic effect on the performance of a TP system. Most systems offer tuning mechanisms to optimize performance. To use these mechanisms, it's valuable to understand their effect on the system's internal behavior. Second, some of those optimizations can violate correctness. Understanding locking implementation helps to understand when such optimizations are acceptable and what alternatives are possible.

An implementation of locking in a data manager has three aspects: setting and releasing locks, implementing a lock manager, and handling deadlocks. We discussed setting and releasing locks in the previous section. We discuss lock managers and deadlocks below.

Lock Managers

A lock manager is a component that services the operations:

- Lock(transaction-id, data-item, lock-mode)—Set a lock with mode *lock-mode* on behalf of transaction *transaction-id* on *data-item.*
- Unlock(transaction-id, data-item)—Release transaction *transaction-id's* lock on *data-item.*
- Unlock(transaction-id)—Release all of transaction *transaction-id's* locks.

It implements these operations by storing locks in a *lock table.* This is a low-level data structure in main memory, much like a control table in an operating system (i.e., not like an SQL table). Lock and unlock operations cause locks to be inserted into and deleted from the lock table, respectively.

Each entry in the lock table describes the locks on a data item. It contains a list of all the locks held on that data item and all pending lock requests that can't be granted yet.

To execute a lock operation, the lock manager sets the lock if no conflicting lock is held by another transaction. For example, in Figure 6.2, the lock manager would grant a request by T_2 for a read lock on *z* and would therefore add [$trid_2$, read] to the list of locks being held on *z*.

If the lock manager receives a lock request for which a conflicting lock is being held, the lock manager adds a request for that lock, which it will grant after conflicting locks are released. In this case, the transaction that requires the lock is blocked until its lock request is granted. For example, a request by T_2 for a write lock on *z* would cause [$trid_2$, write] to be added to *z*'s list of lock requests and T_2 to be blocked.

Any data item in a database can be locked, but only a small fraction of them are locked at any one time because only a small fraction of them are accessed at any one time by a transaction that's actively executing. Therefore, instead of allocating a row in the lock table for every data item in the database, the lock table is implemented as a hash table, whose size is somewhat larger than the maximal number of locks that are held by active transactions. The hash key is the data item identifier.

Lock operations on each data item must be atomic relative to each other. Otherwise, two conflicting lock requests might incorrectly be granted at the same time. For example, if two requests to set a write lock on *v* execute concurrently, they might both detect that *v* is unlocked before either of them set the lock. To avoid this bad behavior, the lock manager executes each lock or unlock operation on a data item completely before starting the next one on that data item. That is, it executes lock and unlock operations on each data item atomically with respect to each other. Note that lock operations on different data items can safely execute concurrently.

The lock manager could become a bottleneck if lock operations execute for too long. Since lock and unlock operations are very frequent, they can consume a lot of processor time. And since lock operations on a data item are atomic, lock requests on popular data items might be delayed because another lock operation is in progress. For these reasons, lock and unlock operations must be very fast, on the order of a hundred machine language instructions per operation.

Granularity

The lock manager is oblivious to the size or kind of data being locked. It just takes a data item identifier and lock mode and does its job. It's up to higher levels of the data manager to choose the size of data items to lock, called the *locking granularity*. The data manager could lock at a coarse granularity, such as files or storage segments, or at a fine granularity, such as records or fields. Both approaches have their benefits and liabilities.

Data Item	List of Locks Being Held	List of Lock Requests
x	[$trid_1$, read], [$trid_2$, read]	[$trid_3$, write]
y	[$trid_2$, write]	[$trid_4$, read] [$trid_1$, read]
z	[$trid_1$, read]	

Figure 6.2 **A Lock Table** Each entry in a list of locks held or requested is of the form [transaction-id, lock-mode].

If it locks at a coarse granularity, the data manager doesn't have to set many locks because each lock covers so much data. Thus, the overhead of setting and releasing locks is low. However, by locking large chunks of data, the data manager is usually locking more data than a transaction needs. For example, even if a transaction T accesses only a few records of a file, a data manager that locks at the granularity of files will lock the whole file, thereby preventing other transactions from locking any other records of the file, most of which are not needed by transaction T. This reduces the number of transactions that can run concurrently, which both reduces the throughput and increases the response time of transactions.

If it locks at a fine granularity, the data manager only locks the specific data actually accessed by a transaction. These locks don't artificially interfere with other transactions, as coarse grain locks do. However, the data manager must now lock every piece of data accessed by a transaction, which can generate a lot of locking overhead. For example, if a transaction issues an SQL query that accesses tens of thousands of records, a data manager that does record granularity locking would set tens of thousands of locks, which can be quite costly. In addition to the record locks, collateral locks on associated indexes are also needed, which compounds the problem.

There is a fundamental trade-off between the amount of concurrency and locking overhead, depending on the granularity of locking. Coarse-grained locking has low overhead but low concurrency. Fine-grained locking has high concurrency but high overhead.

One popular compromise is to lock at the file and page granularity. This gives a moderate degree of concurrency with a moderate amount of locking overhead. It works well in systems that don't need to run at high transaction rates, and hence are unaffected by the reduced concurrency, or ones where transactions frequently access many records per page (such as engineering design applications), and hence are not artificially locking more data than transactions actually access. It also simplifies the recovery algorithms for Commit and Abort, as we'll see in Chapter 8. However, for high-performance TP, record locking is needed because there are too many cases where concurrent transactions need to lock different records on the same page.

Multigranularity Locking

All but the most primitive data managers need to lock data at different granularities, such as file and page granularity, or database, file, and record granularity. For transactions that access a large amount of data, the data manager locks coarse-grain units, such as files or tables. For transactions that access a small amount of data, it locks fine-grain units, such as pages or records.

The trick to this approach is in detecting conflicts between transactions that set conflicting locks at different granularity, such as one transaction that locks a file and another transaction that locks pages in the file. This requires special treatment because the lock manager has no idea that locks at different granularities might conflict. For example, it treats a lock on a file and a lock on a page in that file as two completely independent locks, and therefore would grant write locks on them by two different transactions. The lock manager doesn't recognize that these locks "logically" conflict.

The approach used for coping with different locking granularities is called *multigranularity locking*. In this approach, transactions set ordinary locks at a fine granularity and *intention locks* at coarse granularity. For example, before read-locking a page, a transaction sets an intention-read lock on the file that contains the page. Each coarse-grain intention lock warns other transactions that lock at coarse granularity about potential conflicts with fine-grain locks. For example, an intention-read lock on the file warns other transactions not to write-lock the file, because some transaction has a read lock on a page in the file. Details of this approach can be found in Bernstein, Hadzilacos, and Goodman (1987) and Gray and Reuter (1992).

There is some guesswork involved in choosing the right locking granularity for a transaction. For example, a data manager may start locking individual records accessed by a transaction, but after the transaction has accessed hundreds of records, the data manager may conclude that a coarser granularity would work better. This is called lock *escalation* and is commonly supported by database systems.

6.3 Deadlocks

When two or more transactions are competing for the same lock in conflicting modes, some of them will become blocked and have to wait for others to free their locks. Sometimes, a set of transactions are all waiting for each other; each of them is blocked and, in turn, is blocking other transactions. In this case, if none of the transactions can proceed unless the system intervenes, we say the transactions are *deadlocked*.

For example, reconsider transactions T_1 and T_2 that we discussed earlier in execution $E' = r_1[x]\ r_2[y]\ w_2[x]\ w_1[y]$ (see Figure 6.3). Suppose T_1 gets a read lock on x (Figure 6.3a), and then T_2 gets a read lock on y (Figure 6.3b). Now, when T_2 requests a write lock on x, it's blocked, waiting for T_1 to release its read lock (Figure 6.3c). When T_1 requests a write lock on y, it too is blocked, waiting for T_2 to release *its* read lock (Figure 6.3d). Since each transaction is

$r_1[x]$

Data Item	Locks Held	Locks Requested
x	T_1,read	
y		

a.

$r_1[x]\ r_2[y]$

Data Item	Locks Held	Locks Requested
x	T_1,read	
y	T_2,read	

b.

$r_1[x]\ r_2[y]\ wl_2[x]$-{*blocked*}

Data Item	Locks Held	Locks Requested
x	T_1,read	T_2,write
y	T_2,read	

c.

$r_1[x]\ r_2[y]\ wl_2[x]$-{*blocked*} $wl_1[y]$-{*blocked*}

Data Item	Locks Held	Locks Requested
x	T_1,read	T_2,write
y	T_2,read	T_1,write

d.

Figure 6.3 Execution Leading to a Deadlock Each step of the execution is illustrated by the operations executed so far, with the corresponding state of the lock table below it.

waiting for the other one, neither transaction can make progress, so the transactions are deadlocked.

Deadlock is how two-phase locking detects nonserializable executions. At the time deadlock occurs, there is no possible execution order of the remaining operations that will lead to a serializable execution. In the previous example, after T_1 and T_2 have obtained their read locks, we have the partial execution $r_1[x]\ r_2[y]$. There are only two ways to complete the execution, $r_1[x]\ r_2[y]\ w_1[y]\ w_2[x]$ or $r_1[x]\ r_2[y]\ w_2[x]\ w_1[y]$, both of which are nonserializable.

Once a deadlock occurs, the only way for the deadlocked transactions to make progress is for at least one of them to give up its lock that is blocking another transaction. Once a transaction releases a lock, the two-phase locking rule says that it can't obtain any more locks. But since each transaction in a deadlock *must* obtain at least one lock (otherwise it wouldn't be blocked), by giving up a lock it is bound to break the two-phase locking rule. So there's no point in having a transaction just release one lock. The only alternative is to abort the transaction entirely. That is, the only way to break a deadlock is to abort one of the transactions involved.

Deadlock Prevention

In some areas of software, such as operating systems, it is appropriate to prevent deadlocks by never granting a lock request that can lead to a deadlock. For transaction processing, this is too restrictive because it would overly limit concurrency. The reason is that transaction behavior is unpredictable. For example, in the execution in Figure 6.3b, once the system grants T_1's request for a read lock on *x* and T_2's request for a read lock on *y*, deadlock is unavoidable; it doesn't matter in which order T_1 and T_2 request their second lock. The only way to avoid deadlock is to delay granting T_2's request to read lock *y*. This is *very* restrictive. This amounts to requiring that T_1 and T_2 run serially; T_1 must get all of its locks before T_2 gets any of its locks. In this case, a serial execution of T_1 and T_2 is the only serializable execution. But, usually, transactions can be interleaved a fair bit and still produce a serializable execution.

The only way to prevent deadlocks and still allow some concurrency is to exploit prior knowledge of transaction access patterns. All operating system techniques to prevent deadlock have this property. In general-purpose TP, it is inappropriate to exploit prior knowledge. It either overly restricts the way transactions are programmed (e.g., by requiring that data be accessed in a predefined order) or overly restricts concurrency (e.g., by requiring a transaction to get all of its locks before it runs). For this reason, all commercial TP products that use locking allow deadlocks to occur. That is, they allow transactions to get locks incrementally by granting each lock request as long as it doesn't conflict with an existing lock, and they detect deadlocks when they occur.

Deadlock Detection

There are two techniques that are commonly used to detect deadlocks: timeout-based detection and graph-based detection. *Timeout-based detection* guesses that a deadlock has occurred whenever a transaction has been blocked for too long. It uses a timeout period that is much larger than most transactions' execution time (e.g., 15 seconds) and aborts any transaction that is blocked longer than this amount of time. The main advantages of this approach are that it is simple, and hence easy to implement, and it works in a distributed environment with no added complexity or overhead. However, it does have two disadvantages. First, it may abort transactions that aren't really deadlocked. This mistake adds delay to the transaction that is unnecessarily aborted, since it now has to restart from scratch. This sounds undesirable, but as we'll see later when we discuss locking performance, this may not be a disadvantage. Second, it may allow a deadlock to persist for too long. For example, a deadlock that occurs after one second of transaction execution will be undetected until the timeout period expires.

The alternative approach, called *graph-based detection*, explicitly tracks waiting situations and periodically checks them for deadlock. This is done by building a *waits-for graph*, whose nodes model transactions and whose edges model waiting situations. That is, if transaction T_1 is unable to get a lock because a conflicting lock is held by transaction T_2, then there is an edge $T_1 \rightarrow T_2$, meaning T_1 *is waiting for* T_2. In general, the data manager creates an edge $T_i \rightarrow T_j$ whenever transaction T_i is blocked for a lock owned by transaction T_j, and it deletes the edge when T_i becomes unblocked. There is a deadlock whenever the deadlock graph has a cycle, that is, a sequence of edges that loops back on itself, such as $T_1 \rightarrow T_2 \rightarrow T_1$ (as in Figure 6.4), or $T_1 \rightarrow T_7 \rightarrow T_4 \rightarrow T_2 \rightarrow T_1$.

Any newly added edge in the waits-for graph could cause a cycle. So it would seem that the data manager should check for cycles (deadlocks) whenever it adds an edge. While this is certainly correct, it is also possible to check for deadlocks less frequently, such as every few seconds. A deadlock won't disappear spontaneously, so there is no harm in checking only periodically; the deadlock will still be there whenever the deadlock detector gets around to looking for it. By only checking periodically, the system reduces deadlock

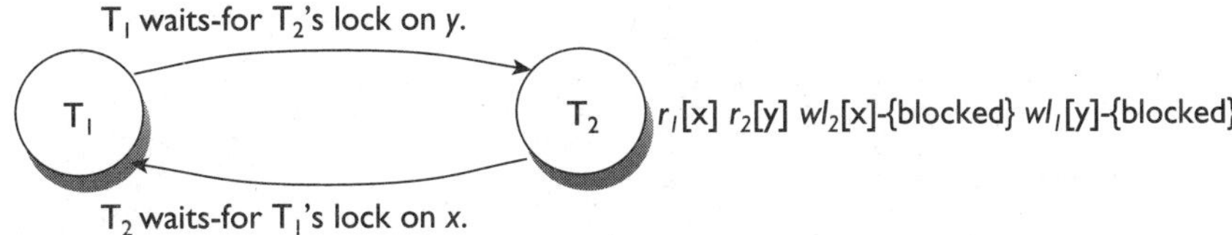

Figure 6.4 **A Waits-For Graph** The graph on the left represents the waiting situations in the execution on the right (see also Figure 6.3). Since there is a cycle involving T_1 and T_2, they are deadlocked.

detection cost. Like timeout-based detection, it allows some deadlocks to go undetected longer than necessary. But unlike timeout, all detected deadlocks are real deadlocks.

Distributed Deadlock Detection

To understand distributed deadlock detection, we must first examine distributed locking. In a distributed system, there are multiple data managers on different nodes of the network. A transaction may access data at more than one data manager. Data managers set locks in the usual way, as if the transaction were not distributed. That is, when a transaction accesses a data item at a data manager, the data manager sets the appropriate lock before performing the access.

As in the nondistributed case, sometimes a lock request becomes blocked. These blocking situations can exist at multiple data managers, which can lead to a deadlock that spans data managers yet is not detectable by any one data manager by itself. For example, let's reconsider our favorite transactions T_1 and T_2, and suppose x and y are stored at different data managers, DM_x and DM_y (see Figure 6.5). T_1 reads x at DM_x, setting a read lock, and T_2 reads y at DM_y, setting a read lock. Now, as before, T_1 tries to write y at DM_y but is blocked waiting for T_2, and T_2 tries to write x at DM_x but is blocked waiting for T_1. This is the same deadlock we observed in Figures 6.3 and 6.4; T_1 is waiting for T_2 at DM_y, and T_2 is waiting for T_1 at DM_x. However, neither DM_x nor DM_y alone can see the deadlock. They each see only one waiting situation.

There are a variety of algorithms to detect distributed deadlocks. The simplest is to designate one node *N* as the distributed deadlock detector and have every other node periodically send its waits-for graph to node *N*. *N* has a complete view of waits-for situations across all nodes and can therefore detect distributed deadlocks. Other, more complex algorithms have also been used. But the most popular approach to distributed deadlocks is timeout-based detection, which works surprisingly well. We will see why in the next section.

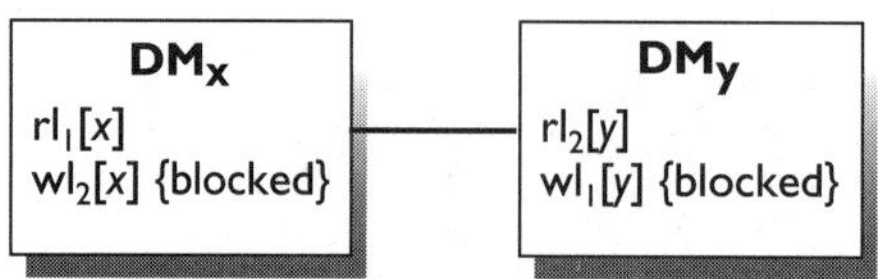

Figure 6.5 **A Distributed Deadlock** DM_x and DM_y are independent data managers, perhaps at different nodes of the network. At DM_x, T_2 is waiting for T_1, which is waiting for T_2 at DM_y. The transactions are deadlocked, but neither DM_x nor DM_y alone can recognize this fact.

6.4 Performance

Locking performance is almost exclusively affected by delays due to blocking, not due to deadlocks. Deadlocks are rare. Typically, fewer than 1 percent of transactions are involved in a deadlock.

There is one situation, however, that can lead to many deadlocks: lock conversions. A *lock conversion* is a request to upgrade a read lock to a write lock. This occurs when a transaction reads a data item, say *x*, and later decides to write it, a rather common situation. If two transactions do this concurrently, they will deadlock; each holds a read lock on *x* and requests a conversion to a write lock, which can't be granted. This problem can be prevented if each transaction gets a write lock to begin with. But how does the data manager know to do this? There are two possibilities. Either the transaction gives the data manager an explicit hint when it reads *x*. Or, the transaction issues its request in a higher-level language so the lock conversion can be anticipated. For example, if the request is an SQL update statement, then the SQL compiler can recognize that the compiled request will read and later write the data item, and can therefore ask for a write lock to begin with. Although getting write locks early can reduce concurrency, the overall performance effect is beneficial since it prevents a likely deadlock. All commercial SQL data managers that we know of use this approach.

Lock Thrashing

By avoiding lock conversion deadlocks, we have dispensed with deadlock as a performance consideration, so we are left with blocking situations. Blocking affects performance in a rather dramatic way. Until lock usage reaches a saturation point, it introduces only modest delays—significant, but not a serious problem. At some point, when too many transactions request locks, a large number of transactions suddenly become blocked, and few transactions can make progress. Thus, transaction throughput stops growing. Surprisingly, if enough transactions are initiated, throughput actually decreases. This is called *lock thrashing* (see Figure 6.6). The main issue in locking performance is to maximize throughput without reaching the point where thrashing occurs.

One way to understand lock thrashing is to consider the effect of slowly increasing the *locking load*, which is measured by the number of active trans-

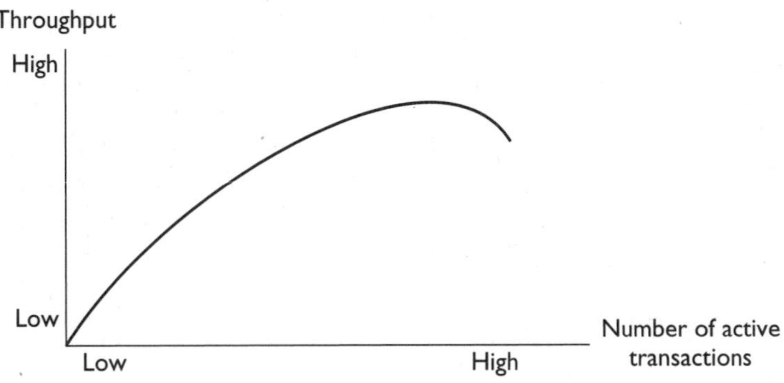

Figure 6.6 Lock Thrashing When the number of active transactions gets too high, many transactions suddenly become blocked, and few transactions can make progress.

actions. When the system is idle, the first transaction to run cannot block due to locks, because it's the only one requesting locks. As the locking load grows, each transaction has a higher probability of becoming blocked due to transactions already running. When the number of active transactions is high enough, the next transaction to be started has virtually no chance of running to completion without blocking for some lock. Worse, it probably will get some locks before encountering one that blocks it, and these locks contribute to the likelihood that other active transactions will become blocked. So, not only does it not contribute to increased throughput, but by getting some locks that block other transactions, it actually reduces throughput. This leads to thrashing, where increasing the workload decreases the throughput.

There are many techniques open to designers of data managers, databases, and applications to minimize blocking. However, even when all the best techniques are applied, if the transaction load is pushed high enough, lock thrashing can occur, provided other system bottlenecks (such as disk or communications bandwidth) don't appear first.

Tuning to Reduce Lock Contention

Suppose a transaction holds a write lock L for t seconds. Then the maximum transaction rate for transactions that set L is $1/t$ (i.e., one transaction per t seconds). To increase the transaction rate, we need to make t smaller. Thus, most techniques for minimizing blocking attempt to reduce the time a transaction holds its locks.

One approach is to set lock L later in the transaction's execution, by accessing L's data later. Since a transaction releases its locks when it completes, the later in its execution that it sets a lock, the less time it holds the lock. This may require rearranging application logic, such as storing an update in a local variable and only applying it to the database just before committing the transaction.

A second approach is to reduce the transaction's execution time. If a transaction executes faster, it completes sooner, and therefore holds its locks for a shorter period. There are several ways to reduce transaction execution time:

- Reduce the number of instructions it executes, called its *path length.*
- Buffer data effectively, so a transaction rarely has to read from disk. If data must be read from disk, do the disk I/O *before* setting the lock, to reduce the lock holding time.
- Optimize the use of other resources, such as communications, to reduce transaction execution time.

A third approach is to split the transaction into two or more shorter transactions. This reduces lock holding time, but it also loses the all-or-nothing property of the transaction, so one has to use one of the multitransaction request techniques discussed in Section 4.6. This can complicate the application design, the price to be paid for reduced lock contention. For example, instead of one all-or-nothing transaction, there are now two transactions; there needs to be recovery code for the case where one succeeds and the other doesn't, something that wasn't required when there was just one transaction.

Recall that lock granularity affects locking performance. One can reduce conflicts by moving to finer-granularity locks. Usually, one relies on the data manager to do this, but there are cases where a database or application designer can affect granularity. For example, suppose a data manager uses record granularity locking. Consider a file that has some frequently accessed fields, called *hot* fields, and other infrequently accessed ones, called *cold* fields. In this case, it may be worth splitting the file "vertically" into two files, where each record is split in half, with its hot fields in one file and its cold fields in the other. For example, the file may contain information about customer accounts, and we split it with customer number, name, and balance (the hot fields) in one file, and customer number, address, and phone number (the cold fields) in the other (see Figure 6.7). Note that customer number, the key, must appear in both files to link the two halves of each record.[2] Before splitting the file, transactions that used the cold fields but not the hot ones were delayed by locks held by transactions accessing the hot fields. After splitting the file, such conflicts do not arise.

When a running system is on the verge of thrashing due to too much blocking, the main way to control the problem is to reduce the transaction load. This is relatively straightforward to do: reduce the maximum number of threads allowed by each data manager. One good measure for determining that the system is close to thrashing is the fraction of active transactions that are blocked. From various studies, a value of about 30 percent is the point at which thrashing starts to occur. This fraction can be determined in most systems, which expose the number of active and blocked transactions.

---

2 In a relational database system, you could make the original table available as a view of the partitioned tables. This avoids rewriting existing programs and offers more convenient access to a transaction that requires both hot and cold fields.

Customer Number	Name	Address	Balance	Phone Number

a. Original table

Customer Number	Name	Balance

Customer Number	Address	Phone Number

b. Partitioning into two tables, with hot fields on the left and cold fields on the right

Figure 6.7 Splitting Hot and Cold Fields to Avoid Contention By moving the cold fields, address and phone number, into a separate table, accesses to those fields aren't delayed be locks on the hot fields, name and balance, which are now in a separate table.

Recall that detecting deadlocks by timeout can make mistakes by aborting transactions that are not really deadlocked. However, if a transaction is blocked for a long time, this suggests that the locking load is too high, so aborting blocked transactions may be good to do. Of course, to get the full benefit of this load reduction, the aborted transaction should not be immediately restarted, which would keep the transaction load at too high a level. But even if it is restarted immediately, aborting it may have a positive effect by unblocking some transactions that are waiting for the aborted transaction's locks.

A Mathematical Model of Locking Performance

Some fairly deep mathematics has been applied to locking performance. While it isn't necessary to understand the math to know how to reduce lock contention, the formulas do help explain the observed phenomena. The mathematics is based on a model where each transaction issues requests for K write locks with an average time T between lock requests. The overall database has D data items that can be locked, and there are N transactions running at any given time (see Figure 6.8).

Assuming all data items are equally likely to be accessed by all transactions, and using probability theory, the following formulas have been derived based on the above parameters:

- the probability of a conflict is proportional to K^2N/D.
- the probability of a deadlock is proportional to K^4N/D^2.

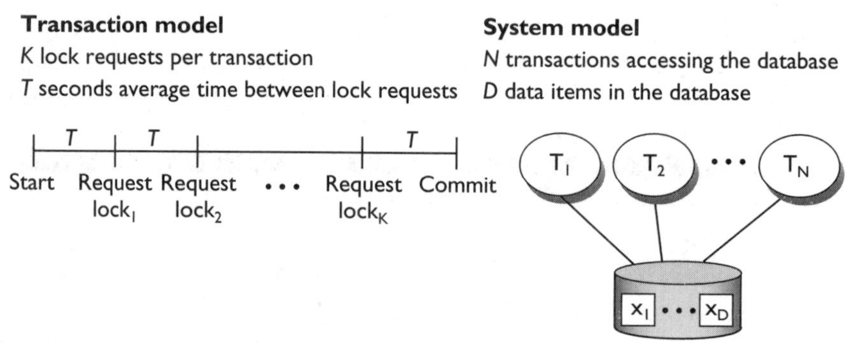

Figure 6.8 Mathematical Model of Transactions Using this model, formulas can be derived for probability of conflict and deadlock and for throughput.

Since a typical application might have a K of 20 (for an average transaction) and a D of one million, you can see from the previous two formulas why deadlock is so rare relative to conflict—a deadlock is K^2/D as likely as a conflict, or only .0004 as likely.

- The throughput is proportional to $(N/T')*(1 - AK^2N/2D)$, where
  T' = (total transaction time) – (time spent waiting for locks)
  = transaction's actual execution time
  and A = ratio of transaction waiting time per lock conflict to total transaction time, typically $^1/_3$ to $^1/_2$.

Looking at throughput, we see that using finer-grain locks increases D, which decreases K^2N/D, thereby increasing throughput (assuming that transactions are really accessing fine-grained data, so that K is unaffected by decreasing lock granularity). Shortening transaction execution time decreases T', which increases N/T', and hence increases throughput.

6.5 Hot Spots

Even when a system locks fine-grained data items, some of those data items are so frequently accessed that they become locking bottlenecks. Such data items are called *hot spots* (i.e., they are so frequently accessed that the data metaphorically "gets hot"). Some common kinds of hot spots are

- summary information, such as the amount of money in a bank branch, since every debit and credit transaction needs to update that value
- the end-of-file marker in a file being used primarily for data entry, since each insert operation moves (i.e., updates) that end-of-file marker and therefore needs to lock it

- the next serial number to be sequentially assigned, such as order number or transaction number, since many transaction types need to assign such serial numbers

In these cases, the hot spot is already a fine-grained data item, so moving to a finer granularity to relieve the bottleneck is not an option. Other techniques are needed.

There are four main techniques to relieve hot spot bottlenecks:

1. Keep the hot data in main memory. Since accesses to main memory are fast, the transaction accessing the hot data will hopefully execute quickly and therefore not hold onto its lock for too long.
2. Delay operations on the hot spot till just before the transaction commits. That way, the transaction holds its lock on the hot data for the minimum amount of time.
3. Replace read operations by verification operations that can be delayed until just before the transaction commits.
4. Group operations into private batches and apply the batch to the hot spot data only periodically.

Often, these techniques are used in combination.

The first technique is relatively automatic. Since the data is hot, the data manager's cache management algorithm will probably keep the data in main memory without any special attention. Still, some systems make a special point of nailing down hot data in main memory, so it can't be paged out even if it hasn't been accessed in awhile.

Delaying Operations Until Commit

The second technique can be implemented by carefully programming a transaction so that its updates come at the end. One can automate this approach. Instead of executing operations on data items when they occur, the data manager simply writes a description of each operation in a log. When the transaction is finished and ready to start committing, *then* the data manager actually executes the operations in the transaction's update log. The data manager gets locks for the operations only during this actual execution. Since this execution is at the very end of the transaction, the lock holding time will be quite short.

For example, consider a data entry application that is adding records to the end of a file. Each transaction must lock the end-of-file marker from the time it starts its insertion until after it commits. Since every transaction is adding a record, the end-of-file marker is likely to be a lock bottleneck. One can avoid this problem by delaying record insertions until the transaction is ready to commit, thereby reducing the lock holding time on the end-of-file marker. This technique is used in IBM's IMS Fast Path system for data that is declared to be a Data Entry database.

One problem with this technique is read operations. A transaction program usually cannot delay read operations until the end because the values it reads affect its execution—they affect the values it writes and they affect its control flow via IF statements and the like. For any read operation that must be executed when it is issued (and not delayed till the end of the transaction's execution), the data manager must set a read lock.

Optimistic Methods

One way to circumvent this problem of read operations is to build reads into higher-level operations that don't return data item values to the calling program. For example, consider an operation Increment(x, n), which adds a constant n to data item x. To increment x, it needs to read the current value of x, but it need not return that value to the caller. It therefore can be deferred until the transaction is ready to commit. However, if Increment(x, n) also returned the current value of x to its caller, then it could not be deferred.

This leads us to the third technique. Consider an operation Verify(f), where f is a predicate formula that references data items and evaluates to True or False. This operation *can* be deferred until the end of the transaction by logging not only the operation, but also the value it returns (i.e., True or False). As for other operations, the data manager does not set locks when it executes the Verify (see Figure 6.9). When the operation is replayed at the end of the transaction, along with other logged operations, it sets locks on any data items it accesses. If it evaluates to the same value it did during normal execution, then all is well. If not, then the transaction is aborted. Effectively, the data manager is saying: "If I did set a lock during normal execution, then f would evaluate to the same value during the replay as it did during normal execution. So, if it doesn't evaluate to the same value, then it is as if some other transaction violated this transaction's locks (the ones it didn't set during the normal execution of Verify). So, the execution is broken and the transaction must abort."

This Verify operation is useful in combination with Increment and Decrement operations. For example, consider an inventory application that is keeping track of the number of items in stock. It can accept orders for an item until there are none in stock. So, suppose that for each inventory item i, it stores the quantity in stock, *Quantity(i)*. A transaction that processes an order for n units of item i should decrement *Quantity(i)* provided that it doesn't make *Quantity(i)* negative. It can do this by calling:

1. EnoughAvailable = Verify(*Quantity(i)* $\geq n$)
2. If EnoughAvailable then Decrement(*Quantity(i)*, n) else Print("Insufficient stock.")

This idea of executing an operation without setting locks, and checking that the operation is still valid at commit time, is called *optimistic concur-*

```
void OptimisticTransaction;
  { Start;
      .
      .
      .
      b = verify(f)  ←— System logs "verify(f)" and the value returned.
      .
      .
      .
    Commit  ←———— System replays the log. If "verify(f)" returns a different value
                  than was previously logged, then abort, else commit.
  }
```

Figure 6.9 Using a Verify Operation with Optimistic Locking No locks are set when verify(f) first executes. During the replay of verify(f), the system sets locks, but aborts if the result changed since the original execution.

rency control. It is considered to be optimistic because you have to be optimistic that the check at commit time is usually OK. If it fails, the penalty is rather high—you have to abort the whole transaction. In the previous inventory application, for example, the technique would work well only if most items are usually in stock. This method, using a restricted form of the Verify operation combined with the previous two techniques, is used in IMS Fast Path, in its Main Storage Database feature.

Batching

Another technique that is used to relieve hot spots is batching. Instead of having each transaction update the hot data when it needs it, it batches its effect across a set of transactions. For example, in a data entry application, instead of appending records to the shared file in each transaction, each transaction appends the record to a local batch (one batch for each thread of executing transactions). Since each thread has a private batch, there is no lock contention for the batch. Periodically, the batch is appended to the shared file. As another example, consider the problem of assigning serial numbers. Instead of reading the latest serial number within each transaction, a batch of serial numbers is periodically set aside for each thread. The thread assigns serial numbers from its private batch until it runs out, at which time it gets another batch.

Batching is effective at relieving hot spots, but it has one disadvantage—failure handling requires extra work. For example, after a failure, the private batches of appended records must be gathered up and appended to the file. Similarly, if it's important that all serial numbers actually be used, then after a failure, unused serial numbers have to be collected and reassigned to threads. Sometimes, the application can allow the failure handling to be ignored—for example, if the lost serial numbers are not important.

6.6 Query-Update Problems

Another major source of concurrency bottlenecks is queries, that is, read-only requests for decision support and reporting. Queries typically run much longer than update transactions and they access a lot of data. So, if they run using two-phase locking, they often set many locks and hold those locks for a long time. This creates long—often intolerably long—delays of update transactions.

Degrees of Isolation

In the face of this problem, many systems just give up on serializability for queries. In such a system, if a transaction is declared to be a query, then it uses weaker locking rules than two-phase locking. One such rule is called *cursor stability* (sometimes called *degree 2 isolation*). If a query executes with cursor stability, then the data manager only holds a read lock on a data item while the query is actually reading the data. As soon as the data is read, it releases the lock.

Cursor stability is weaker than two-phase locking, which requires the transaction to hold read locks until it has obtained all of its locks. Cursor stability does ensure that the query only reads data that was produced by transactions that committed. That is, if an active update transaction is currently modifying a data item and is using two-phase locking, the query running with cursor stability will not be able to lock it until that updater has committed or aborted. However, it does not ensure serializability. For example, if the query reads data items *x* and *y*, and an updater is updating those data items, one quite-possible scenario is the following:

1. The query reads *x* and then releases its lock on *x*.
2. The updater updates *x* and *y*, and then commits and releases its locks.
3. The query reads *y*.

The query looks like it executed before the updater on *x* but after the updater on *y*, a result that would be impossible in a serial execution.

Customers are surprisingly accepting of cursor stability locking. Even though the answers could be incorrect, people don't seem to mind very much. There is no satisfactory technical explanation for this, though there is an intuitive explanation that might be true: Queries often produce summary results about a database. If the database is being updated frequently, then it doesn't matter that there are small discrepancies based on serializability errors because the result is somewhat outdated anyway, almost immediately after being presented to the user. Moreover, since this is only a summary for decision support purposes, it doesn't matter that the data isn't exactly right.

One can run queries in an even weaker locking mode, where it holds no locks at all (called *dirty reads* or *degree 1 isolation*). In this case, queries can read uncommitted data, too—that is, data that may be wiped out when a transaction aborts. This delays queries even less than cursor stability, at the cost of further inconsistencies in the values that are read.

Degree of Isolation	Technical Term	Behavior
1	dirty reads	don't set read locks
2	cursor stability	read only committed data
3	repeatable reads	serializability

Figure 6.10 **Degrees of Isolation** Degrees 1 and 2 provide less than serializable behavior, but better performance.

Notice that both with cursor stability and with no locking by queries, update transactions are still serializable with respect to each other, as long as they obey two-phase locking. Therefore, the database state is still the result of a serializable execution of transactions. It's just that queries might read inconsistent versions of that state.

Many database systems offer the option of running update transactions using cursor stability or even dirty reads. Running a transaction at one of these lower consistency levels violates two-phase locking and can produce a nonserializable execution. The performance may be better, but the result may be incorrect.

When discussing degrees 1 and 2, serializability is often characterized as degree 3. This is sometimes called *repeatable reads* because, unlike cursor stability, reading a data item multiple times returns the same value since read locks are held throughout a transaction.

A summary of the levels is in Figure 6.10. The degree-of-isolation terminology is used inconsistently in the literature. We've glossed over many of the finer points here. A more thorough discussion of the various terms and their subtle differences appears in Berenson et al. (1995).

Multiversion Data

One good technique for ensuring that queries read consistent data without slowing down the execution of updaters is *multiversion data*. With multiversion data, updates do not overwrite existing copies of data items. Instead, when an updater modifies an existing data item, it creates a new copy of that data item, called a new *version*. So, each data item consists of a sequence of versions, one version corresponding to each update that was applied to it. For example, in Figure 6.11, a data item is a row of the table, so each version is a separate row. There are three versions of employee 3, one of employee 43, and two of employee 19.

To distinguish between different versions of the same data item, each version is tagged by the unique identifier of the transaction that wrote it. Each version of a data item points to the previous version of that data item (the "previous transaction" field in Figure 6.11), so each data item has a chain of versions beginning with the most recent and going back in time. In addition,

Transaction Identifier	*Previous Transaction*	*Employee Number*	*Name*	*Department*	*Salary*
174	null	3	Tom	Hat	$20,000
21156	174	3	Tom	Toy	$20,000
21153	21156	3	Tom	Toy	$24,000
21687	null	43	Dick	Finance	$40,000
10899	null	19	Harry	Appliance	$27,000
21687	10899	19	Harry	Computer	$42,000

Figure 6.11 An Example Multiversion Database Each transaction creates a new version of each row that it updates.

the data manager maintains a list of transaction IDs of transactions that have committed, called the *commit list*.

The interesting capability of multiversion data is *snapshot mode,* which allows a query to avoid setting locks and thereby avoid locking delays. When a query executes in snapshot mode, the data manager starts by reading the current state of the commit list and associating it with the query for the query's whole execution. Whenever the query asks to read a data item, say *x*, the data manager selects the latest version of *x* that is tagged by a transaction ID on the query's commit list. This is the last version of *x* that was committed before the query started executing. There is no need to lock this data because it can't change. An updater will only create new versions, and never modify an existing version.

When a query executes in snapshot mode, it is effectively reading the state of the database that existed at the time it started running. Thus, it reads a consistent database state. Any updates that execute after it started running are from transactions that are not on the query's commit list. These updates will be ignored by the data manager when it executes reads on behalf of the query. So although it reads a consistent database state, that state becomes increasingly out-of-date while the query is running.

Multiversion Implementation Details

There are two technical issues in making this type of mechanism run efficiently. A user of the mechanism need not be aware of these issues, but for completeness, we describe them here.

First, it is too inefficient to represent the entire commit list as a list of transaction IDs. We can keep the commit list short by assigning transaction IDs sequentially (e.g., by using a counter to generate them) and periodically discarding a prefix of the commit list. We can do this by exploiting the following observation:

1. If all active transactions have a transaction ID greater than some value, say T-Oldest, and
2. no new transaction will be assigned a transaction ID smaller than T-Oldest, and
3. for all transactions with transaction IDs ≤ T-Oldest (which, by (1), have terminated), their updates have already been committed or have been aborted and wiped out from the database,
4. then queries don't need to know about transaction IDs smaller than T-Oldest.

To see why the commit list need only contain transaction IDs greater than T-Oldest, suppose the data manager processes a read operation for a query on data item *x*. If the transaction ID of the latest version of *x* is smaller than T-Oldest, then by (3) it must be committed, so the data manager can safely read it. If its transaction ID is greater than T-Oldest, then the data manager reads the last version whose transaction ID is on the query's commit list. To keep the list short, the data manager should frequently truncate the small transaction IDs off of the commit list based on the above rule.

A second issue is that the database can become cluttered with old versions that are useless because no query will ever read them. A version of data item *x* is *useless* if

1. it is not the latest version of *x*, and
2. all active queries have a commit list that contains the transaction ID of a later version of *x* (either explicitly or its T-Oldest value is greater than or equal to the transaction ID of some later version of *x*).

In this case, no active query will read a useless version of *x*; they'll only read later ones. No new query will look at this version of *x* either, because it will use an even more up-to-date commit list, which won't include smaller transaction IDs than currently running queries. So this version of *x* can be thrown out.

This type of multiversion technique is used in Oracle's Rdb/VMS product.

6.7 Avoiding Phantoms

In the standard locking model that we have been using in this chapter, insert and delete operations are modeled as write operations. We don't treat them specially. However, inside the system, the data manager must be particularly careful with these operations to avoid nonserializable results.

To see the potential problem, consider the database in Figure 6.12. The Accounts table has a row for each account, including the account number, branch location, and balance in that account. The Assets table has the total balance for all accounts at each branch location. Now, suppose we execute the following sequence of operations by transactions T_1 and T_2:

1. T_1: Read Accounts 1, 2, 3.
2. T_1: Identify the Accounts rows where Location = B (i.e., 2 and 3) and add their balances (= 150).
3. T_2: Insert a new Accounts row [4, B, 100].
4. T_2: Read the total balance for location B in Assets (returns 150).
5. T_2: Write Assets [B, 250].
6. T_2: Commit.
7. T_1: Read Assets for location B (returns 250).
8. T_1: Commit.

Transaction T_1 is auditing the accounts in location B. It first reads all the accounts in the Accounts table (step 1), adds up the balances in location B (step 2), and then looks up the Assets for location B (step 7) to make sure they match. They don't, because T_1 didn't see the Accounts row inserted by T_2, even though it did see the updated value in the Assets table for location B, which included the result of the insertion.

This execution is not serializable. If T_1 and T_2 had executed serially, T_1 would either have seen T_2's updates to both the Accounts table and the Assets table, or it would have seen neither of them. However, in this execution, it saw T_2's update to Assets but not its update to Accounts.

The problem is the Accounts row [4, B, 100] that T_2 inserts. T_1 didn't see this row when it read the Accounts table, but did see T_2's effect on Assets that added 100 to B's total balance. The Accounts row [4, B, 100] is called a *phantom* because it's invisible during part of T_1's execution but not all of it.

The strange thing about this execution is that it appears to be allowed by two-phase locking. In the following, we add the lock operations required by two-phase locking:

1. T_1: Lock rows 1, 2, and 3 in Accounts. Read Accounts 1, 2, 3.
2. T_1: Identify the Accounts rows where Location = B (i.e., 2 and 3) and add their balances (= 150).
3. T_2: Insert a new Accounts row [4, B, 100] and lock it.
4. T_2: Lock location B's row in Assets. Read the total balance for location B (returns 150).
5. T_2: Write Assets [B, 250].
6. T_2: Commit and unlock location B's row in Assets and row [4, B, 100] in Accounts.

ACCOUNTS

Account Number	*Location*	*Balance*
1	A	50
2	B	50
3	B	100

ASSETS

Location	*Total*
A	50
B	150

Figure 6.12 Accounts Database to Illustrate Phantoms Each row of the Assets table contains the sum of accounts in a location.

7. T_1: Lock location B's row in Assets. Read Assets for location B (returns 250).
8. T_1: Commit and unlock location B's row in Assets and rows 1, 2, and 3 in Accounts.

Is it really true that two-phase locking doesn't guarantee serializability when there are insertion operations? Fortunately not. Some hidden behavior here causes an extra lock to be set, which isn't shown in the execution. It all hinges on how T_1 knew there were exactly three rows in the Accounts table. There must have been a data structure of some kind to tell it: an end-of-file marker, a count of the number of rows in the file, a list of pointers to the rows in the file, or something. Since it read that data structure to determine that it should read exactly rows 1, 2, and 3, it had to lock it. Moreover, since T_2 added a row to the Accounts table, it had to lock that data structure, too, in write mode, so it could update it. It would be prevented from doing so by T_1's read lock on that data structure, and thus the above execution could not occur.

So, the phantom problem is not a problem, provided that the data manager sets locks on all data it touches, including system structures that it uses internally on behalf of a transaction's operation.

Performance Implications

This example brings up yet another common scenario that leads to performance problems, one that's closely related to the query-update problems we saw in the previous section. Here we had one transaction, T_1, that scanned a file (essentially a query), and another transaction, T_2, that inserted a row and therefore was blocked by the scan operation. Since T_1 needs to compare the values it reads in the Accounts table to the values it reads in the Assets table, it must run in a serializable way. Cursor stability locking isn't good enough. This means that T_1 must lock the entire table in read mode, which delays any update transaction that wants to write an existing row or insert a new one. This reduction in concurrency is bound to cause some transaction delays.

Database systems that support SQL reduce this problem somewhat by locking ranges of key values. In the example, since T_1 only wants to read rows in location B, the system would set a key-range lock on rows with "Location = B." Transaction T_2 would have to get a key-range lock on "Location = B" to insert its new row, and would be blocked as before. But other update transactions that operate on rows in other locations would be permitted to run because they get key-range locks on other key ranges. That is, a key-range lock on "Location = B" does not conflict with one on "Location = A."

Key-range locking works well in SQL because the `WHERE` clause in SQL has clauses like `Accounts.Location = B`, which gives the system a strong hint about which lock to set. In an indexed file system, such as COBOL ISAM implementations, it is much harder to do, since the operations issued by the program don't give such strong hints to the file system to figure out which key-range locks to set. For this reason, key-range locking is widely supported in SQL database systems, but not in many other kinds.

6.8 Other Techniques

There are many other tricks that are used internally by data managers to reduce the frequency of locking conflicts between transactions. For example, some of them leverage knowledge of how index structures are organized and accessed—locking a node n of a B-tree implicitly locks the nodes below n because all search operations to nodes below n must pass through n. Such approaches are technically interesting and do improve performance, but they are also complicated. Fortunately, they can be completely hidden from the application programmer, other than their effect on performance. We therefore don't cover them in this book. Details of the methods can be found in Bernstein, Hadzilacos, and Goodman (1987) and Gray and Reuter (1992), along with references to other articles on this subject.

6.9 Summary

Locking is the most popular mechanism to achieve transaction isolation, that is, to ensure that every execution of transactions is serializable. Each transaction sets read and write locks on data items that it reads and writes, respectively. And it follows the two-phase rule, meaning that it obtains all of its locks before releasing any of them. Locks are generally set and released automatically by data managers, and are therefore hidden from the application programmer.

A write lock conflicts with a read or write lock on the same data item. Two transactions cannot concurrently hold conflicting locks on the same data item. If a transaction requests a lock that conflicts with one owned by another transaction, it is delayed. This leads to two problems: deadlock and thrashing.

A deadlock occurs when a set of transactions are waiting for each other to release locks. Deadlocks are usually handled automatically by a detection mechanism. The system can use timeouts to identify a transaction that has been waiting too long and is suspected of being in a deadlock. Or it explicitly maintains a waits-for graph and periodically checks for cycles. The system breaks a deadlock by aborting one of the transactions involved in the deadlock.

The main application design problem created by locking is performance delays created by lock conflicts. If too many transactions request conflicting locks, transaction throughput decreases. This is called lock thrashing. To solve it in a running system, the number of active transactions must be decreased by aborting them. Alternatively, you can modify the application, database, or system design to reduce the number of conflicts. The latter is a design activity that involves adjusting the locking granularity or using special locking techniques that reduce the level of conflict, such as the following:

- Use finer-grained locks, thereby increasing concurrency, at the expense of more locking overhead, since more locks must be set.
- Reduce the time that locks are held by shortening transaction execution time or delaying lock requests until later in the transaction.
- Use a hot spot technique, such as delaying operations until commit time, using operations that don't conflict, or keeping hot data in main memory to shorten transaction execution time.
- Use a weaker degree of isolation, such as degree 2 consistency, allowing inconsistent reads by releasing each read lock immediately after reading.
- Use multiversions, so that queries can access old versions of data and thereby avoid setting locks that conflict with update transactions.

Insert and delete operations require special techniques, such as key-range locking, to avoid phantom updates and thereby ensure serializable executions.

Appendix Proof of Two-Phase Locking Theorem

One standard way to prove serializability is using a graph that represents the execution of a set of transactions. As in Section 6.1, we model an execution as a sequence of the read, write, and commit operations issued by different transactions. To simplify matters, we do not consider aborted transactions in this analysis, although they can be included with some modest additional complexity to the theory.

The graph that we build from the execution is called a *serialization graph*. It has one node for each transaction. For each pair of conflicting operations by different transactions, it has an edge from the earlier transaction to the later

$r_1[x]\ r_2[x]\ w_1[x]\ r_3[x]\ w_2[y]\ c_2\ w_1[y]\ c_1\ w_3[x]\ c_3$

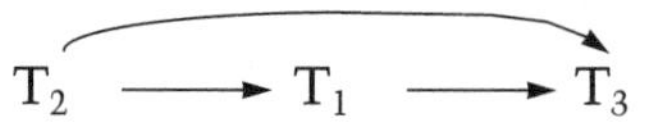

$T_2 \rightarrow T_1 \rightarrow T_3$ (with an additional edge $T_2 \rightarrow T_3$)

Figure 6.13 **An Execution and Its Serialization Graph** The execution graph on the left is modeled by the serialization graph on the right.

one. For example, consider the execution in Figure 6.13. In this execution $r_2[x]$ conflicts with and precedes $w_1[x]$, so there is an edge from T_2 to T_1 in the serialization graph. Two conflicts can lead to the same edge. For example, $r_2[x]$ conflicts with and precedes $w_1[x]$, and $w_2[y]$ conflicts with and precedes $w_1[y]$, both of which produce the same edge from T_2 to T_1.

The fundamental theorem of serializability theory is that an execution is serializable if its serialization graph is acyclic. So, to prove that two-phase locking produces serializable executions, we need to show that any execution it produces has an acyclic serialization graph.

Consider the serialization graph of a two-phase locked execution, and examine one edge in this graph, say $T_i \rightarrow T_j$. This means there were two conflicting operations, o_i from T_i and o_j from T_j. T_i and T_j each set locks for o_i and o_j, and since the operations conflict, the locks must conflict. (For example, o_i might have been a read and o_j a write on the same data item.) Before o_j executed, its lock was set, and o_i's lock must have been released before then (since it conflicts). So, in summary, given that $T_i \rightarrow T_j$, T_i released a lock before T_j set a lock.

Now, suppose there is a path $T_i \rightarrow T_j$ and $T_j \rightarrow T_k$. From the previous paragraph, we know that T_i released a lock before T_j set a lock, and T_j released a lock before T_k set a lock. Moreover, since T_j is two-phase locked, it set all of its locks before it released any of them. Therefore, T_i released a lock before T_k set a lock. Avoiding the rigor of an induction argument, we can repeat this argument for paths of any length, so for a path of any length $T_i \rightarrow \ldots \rightarrow T_m$, T_i released a lock before T_m set a lock.

To prove that the two-phase locked execution is serializable, we need to show that its serialization graph is acyclic. So, by way of contradiction, suppose there *is* a cycle in the serialization graph $T_i \rightarrow \ldots \rightarrow T_i$. From the previous paragraph, we can conclude that T_i released a lock before T_i set a lock. But this implies T_i was *not* two-phase locked, contradicting our assumption that all transactions were two-phase locked. Therefore the cycle cannot exist and, by the serializability theorem, the execution is serializable.

CHAPTER 7

High Availability

7.1 Introduction

A critical requirement for most TP systems is that they be up all the time, that is, highly available. Such systems are often called "24 by 7" (or 24 × 7), since they are intended to run 24 hours per day, 7 days per week. Defining this concept more carefully, we say that a system is *available* if it is running correctly, yielding the expected results. The *availability* of a system is defined as the fraction of time that the system is available. Thus, a highly available system is one that, most of the time, is running correctly and yielding expected results.

Availability is reduced by two factors. One is the rate at which the system fails. By *fails,* we mean the system gives the wrong answer or no answer. Other things being equal, if it fails frequently, it is less available. The second factor is recovery time. Other things being equal, the longer it takes to fix the system after it fails, the less it is available. These concepts are captured in two technical terms: mean time between failures and mean time to recovery. The *mean time between failures* (MTBF) is the average time the system runs before it fails. MTBF is a measure of system reliability. The *mean time to repair* (MTTR) is how long it takes to fix the system after it does fail. Using these two measures, we can define availability precisely as MTBF/(MTBF + MTTR), which is the fraction of time the system is running. Thus, availability improves when reliability (MTBF) increases and when repair time (MTTR) decreases.

7.2 Causes of Computer Failure

Failures come from a variety of sources. We can categorize them as follows:

- Environment—Effects on the physical environment that surrounds the computer system, such as power, communications, air-conditioning, fire, and flood
- System management—What people do to manage the system, including vendors doing preventative maintenance and system operators taking care of the system
- Hardware—All hardware devices including processor, memory, I/O controllers, and so on
- Software—The operating system, communications systems, database systems, TP monitors, other system software, and application software

Let's look at each category in turn.

Environment

One dimension of the environment is communications systems that are not under the control of the people building the computer system, such as long-distance communications provided by the phone company. Sometimes, you can pay more to buy more reliable lines. Otherwise, about all you can do to improve the reliability is to lease more communications lines than are needed to meet functional and performance goals. For example, if one communications line is needed, lease two independent lines instead, so if one fails, the other one will still be operating. This is often done to support automated teller machines at banks. Half of the teller machines use one line, the other half use a second line, so if one line fails, only half of the teller machines become unavailable.

A second aspect of the environment is power. In North America, the MTBF of urban power is about two months. Most outages are quite short; 90 percent of them are less than five minutes. Given this failure rate, it's often appropriate to have battery backup. In the event of power failure, battery backup can at least keep main memory alive, so the system can restart immediately after power is restored without rebooting the operating system, thereby reducing MTTR. Batteries may be able to run the system for a short period, increasing MTBF. To keep running during longer outages, an uninterruptible power source (UPS) is needed. A full UPS generally includes a gas- or diesel-powered generator, which can run the system much longer than batteries.

A third environmental issue is air-conditioning. An air-conditioning failure can bring down the computer system, so when a computer system requires an air-conditioned environment, a redundant air-conditioning system is often advisable. More and more computer systems are now being designed for warm environments, in part because of the current popularity of CMOS semiconductor technology. Buying such systems to avoid special cooling is another way to circumvent cooling problems.

Finally, there are acts of God and other random events that cause systems to fail, such as fire, flood, earthquake, and vandalism. There are things you can do to defend against each of these: build buildings that are less susceptible to fire, that are able to withstand strong earthquakes, and that are secured against unauthorized entry. How far one goes depends on the cost of the defense, the benefit to availability, and the cost of downtime to the enterprise. When the system is truly "mission critical," as in certain military, financial, and transportation applications, an enterprise will go to extraordinary lengths to reduce the probability of such failures. One airline system is housed in an underground bunker. One California bank built an extra computer facility east of the San Andreas fault, so they can still operate if their Los Angeles or San Francisco facility is destroyed by an earthquake.

System Management

System management is another cause of failures. People are part of the system. Everybody has an off day; everyone occasionally has lapses of attention. It's only a matter of time before even the best system operator does something that will cause the system to fail.

There are several ways to mitigate the problem. One is to simply design the system so that it doesn't require maintenance, such as using automated procedures for functions that would normally require operator intervention. Hardware manufacturers have done a lot in this direction. For example, disk reliability has improved greatly since the advent of sealed disks that don't require any hardware maintenance. Even preventative maintenance, which is done to increase availability by avoiding failures later on, may be a source of downtime. Such procedures should be designed to be done while the system is operating.

Simplifying maintenance procedures also helps if maintenance can't be eliminated entirely. So does building redundancy into maintenance procedures, so an operator has to make at least two mistakes to cause the system to malfunction. Training is another factor. This is especially important for maintenance procedures that are infrequently needed. It's like having a fire drill, where people train for rare events, so when they do happen, people know what actions to take.

Software installation is often a source of planned failures. The installation of many software products requires rebooting the operating system, which amounts to a failure. Developing installation procedures that don't require rebooting is a way to improve system reliability.

Many operation errors involve reconfiguring the system. Sometimes moving a disk to a different processor or changing the tuning parameters on a database system causes the system to malfunction. It may only degrade performance, rather than cause the system to crash, but the effect is the same from the end user's perspective. You can avoid unpleasant surprises by using configuration management tools that simulate a new configuration and demonstrate that it will behave as predicted, or by having test procedures on a test system that can prove that a changed configuration will perform as predicted. Moreover, it is valuable to have reconfiguration procedures that can be quickly undone, so that when a mistake is made, you can revert to the previous working configuration quickly.

If a system is not required to be 24×7, many of the above problems can be handled during scheduled downtime, such as preventative maintenance, installing software that requires a reboot, or reconfiguring a system. However, from a vendor's viewpoint, offering products that require such scheduled downtime limits their market to customers that don't need 24×7.

Hardware

The third cause of failures is hardware problems. To discuss hardware failures precisely, we need a few technical terms: A *fault* is an event inside the system that is believed to have caused a failure. A fault can be either transient or permanent. A *transient* fault is one that does not reoccur if you retry the operation. A *permanent* fault is not transient; it is repeatable.

The vast majority of hardware faults are transient, more than 90 percent. If the hardware should fail, simply retry the operation; there's a very good chance it will succeed. For this reason, operating systems have many built-in recovery procedures to handle transient hardware failures. For example, if the operating system issues an I/O operation to a disk or a communications device and gets an error signal back, it normally retries that operation many times before it actually reports an error back to the caller.

Of course, some hardware faults are permanent. The most serious ones cause the operating system to fail, making the whole system unavailable. In this case, rebooting the operating system may get the system back into a working state. The reboot procedure will recognize that some hardware component is dead and try to reconfigure around the dead component and continue to operate. If it can't, then repairing the hardware is the only option.

Software

This brings us to software failures. As for hardware failures, the most serious type of software failure is an operating system crash, since it stops the entire computer system. Since many software problems are transient, a reboot often repairs the problem. This involves rebooting the operating system *and* repairing disk state that might have become inconsistent due to the failure, recovering communications sessions with other systems in a distributed system, and restarting all of the application programs. These steps all increase the MTTR, and therefore reduce availability, so they should be made as fast as possible. For example, highly available communications systems have operating systems that can reboot in under a minute, worst case. Taking this goal to the extreme, if the repair time were zero, then failures wouldn't matter, since the system would recover instantaneously, and the user would never know the difference. Clearly reducing the repair time can have a big impact on availability.

There are less serious kinds of software failures than operating system failures. An application process or database system can fail, leaving the operating system functioning correctly. In this case, only that application or database system process needs to be recovered. This is where techniques that are specific to transaction processing become relevant. We set the stage for discussing these techniques by looking first at application and database behavior from a general client/server perspective and then delving into the types of failures that can arise and what to do about them.

7.3 Availability in the Client/Server Model

Client/Server Architecture

In the basic client/server model, a client process communicates with a server process, and the server process uses underlying resources, typically a disk or possibly a communications line (see Figure 7.1). We use RPC terminology when talking about client/server communications, namely, that the client *calls* the server, and the server *returns* a result. However, whether the

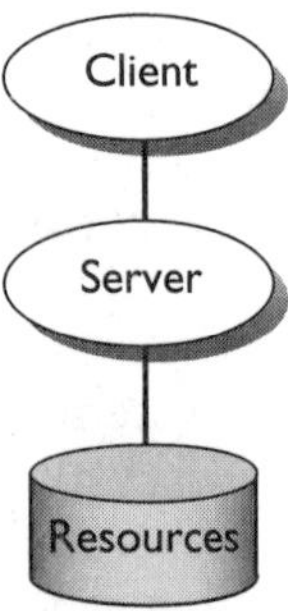

Figure 7.1 Basic Client/Server Model A client process communicates with a server process, and the server process uses underlying resources, such as a disk or communications line.

communications are based on RPC, peer-to-peer, or any other paradigm, is unimportant to the availability issues that we consider here.

A common configuration is to have the client running on a desktop machine and the server on a larger shared machine. In some cases, the client is running on a shared server, which is calling another shared server. The client and server might even be running on the same machine. Whatever the configuration, the possible technical approaches for keeping the client and server available and communicating with each other remain the same. Which approach to select depends on the configuration, workload, application requirements, cost, and many other factors. We therefore focus on overall approaches and are deliberately vague about the type of machine where the client and server run.

Detecting Process Failures

We would like each process to be as reliable as possible. But of course, no matter how reliable it is, there are times when the process will fail. When a process does fail, some agent outside of the process has to observe that fact and ask to recreate the process. Usually that's done by the operating system, database system, or TP monitor.

The TP monitor or database system usually has one or more monitoring processes that track when application or database processes fail. There are several ways that are commonly used to detect failures:

- Each process could periodically send an "I'm alive" message to the monitoring process (see Figure 7.2); the absence of such a message warns the monitoring process of a possible failure.
- The monitoring process could poll the other processes for "I'm alive" messages.

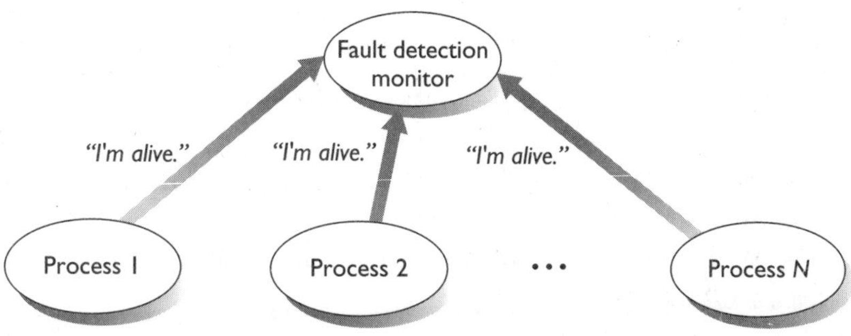

Figure 7.2 Fault Detection Monitor The monitor detects process failures, in this case by listening for "I'm alive" messages. When it doesn't hear one within its timeout period, it assumes the process has failed.

- Each process could own an operating system lock that the monitoring process is waiting to acquire; if the monitoring process is granted the lock, it recognizes that the process being monitored has failed (thereby releasing its lock).

Whichever approach is taken, it is important to optimize the time it takes for a monitoring process to detect the failure, since that time contributes to the MTTR, and therefore to unavailability.

After a process failure is detected, some agent needs to recreate the failed process. The operating system is generally designed only to recreate processes that it needs to keep the system operating at all, such as the file system (if it runs as a process) and system monitor processes. The operating system generally does not automatically recreate application processes, except those that the system administrator lists in the operating system's boot script; this doesn't help when a server fails without crashing the operating system. Therefore, detecting application or database system process failures and recreating them is generally a function of TP monitors and database systems.

Client Recovery

There are several points of failure in this system: the client, the client/server connection, the server, the server/resource connection, and the resource. If the client fails and later recovers, it needs to reconnect to the server and can start calling it again. Or, if the client loses communication with the server, either because the communication or server failed, the failure will eventually be repaired and the client will later reestablish that communication and resume calling it. In either case, at recovery time, the main issue for the client is to reestablish its state relative to the server.

The state of the client relative to the server consists of the set of outstanding calls. Therefore, to recover its state, it needs to determine the following:

- What calls were outstanding at the time it failed or lost connectivity with the server?
- What happened to those calls while it was down or not communicating with the server?
- What does it have to do to finish those calls properly before proceeding with new calls?

These are exactly the issues we discussed in Chapter 4 on queuing. If there is a persistent queue between the client and server, then the client can find out the state of all outstanding calls (called "requests" in Chapter 4) by examining the queue. If not, then it has to use some application-specific technique, such as looking at the database state on the server to determine whether or not the client's previous calls completed, or reissuing in-doubt calls with the same serial number and relying on the server to discard duplicate calls. These techniques too were discussed in Chapter 4.

The remaining issues all focus on server availability, which is the subject of the rest of this section.

Server Recovery

After a server has been recreated, it runs its recovery procedure to reconstruct its state before starting to process new calls. If this is the first time the server has ever run, then the recovery procedure is trivial—the server just initializes its state. If not, then it has some work to do.

To explore how a server reconstructs its state, let's begin from first principles. Suppose the server is a sequential processor of calls and there are no transactions in the picture. The server just receives a call from a client, does what is requested, and later returns a result. At the time it failed, the server might have been in the middle of processing such a call.

As we discussed in the previous subsection on client recovery, it is up to the client to determine the state of its outstanding calls. It's always possible that a server (or communications) failure causes a call to get lost, so the client must be able to cope with that fact. Since the client has to be able to deal with lost calls, it would seem that a recovering server could just ignore whatever call it was working on at the time it failed and start afresh. It's up to the client to figure out what to do.

The problem is that in the course of processing its last call before the failure, the server may have performed a non-redoable operation. For example, it may have printed a check, transferred money, credited a bank account, dispensed cash, shipped a product, and so on. If the client concludes that the server did not execute the call, it will reissue it, thereby causing the server to redo the work. Therefore, if the server performed a non-redoable operation on behalf of the call it was processing at the time of failure, it must not reexecute the call. Rather, it must complete the call and return a result.

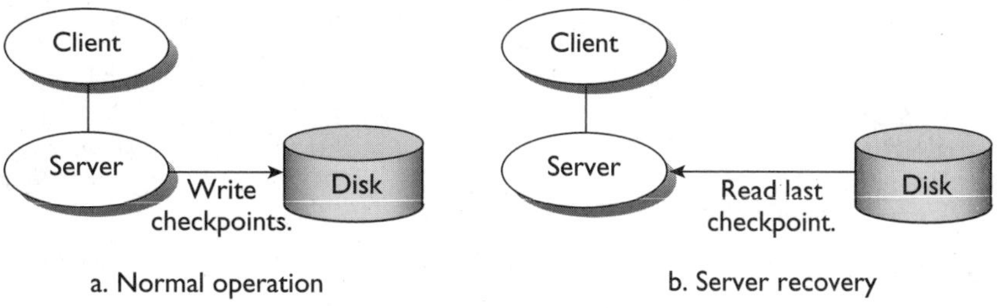

Figure 7.3 **Server Checkpointing** During normal operation, the server periodically takes a checkpoint. After a failure, it uses its last checkpointed state to recover.

The details of recovering a partially executed call are complex and are not commonly used in systems that support transactions. However, to appreciate how much easier things are when transactions are available, let us examine what the server would have to do if it could not rely on transactions.

Checkpoint-Based Recovery

Suppose all of the work that the server did for the call it was processing at the time of failure is redoable. In that case, at recovery time the server can simply reprocess the call from the beginning. If it redoes work that it did before the failure, there's no harm done because all of that work is redoable.

Suppose the server did perform non-redoable work for the last call. Then it must recover itself to a state that is consistent with having done the last non-redoable operation that it executed before the failure. That is, it must recreate a state that came *after* that last non-redoable operation. So, for example, if the server printed a check before the failure, then it must be recovered to a state after the time that it printed the check. If the server continued processing from a state before it printed the check, then it would repeat that operation (i.e., print the check again), which is exactly what should not happen. Recreating this state requires some careful bookkeeping before the failure, so the recovering server can look up what was going on at the time of failure to figure out what it should do.

One general way to prepare for this type of recovery is to have a server save its memory state on some nonvolatile device (e.g., a disk) before it executes a non-redoable operation. That way, when it recovers, it can recreate that state. Saving memory state is an example of checkpointing (see Figure 7.3). In general, *checkpointing* is any activity that is done during normal processing to reduce the amount of work to redo after a recovery. Saving memory state is a kind of checkpointing because it ensures that when the server recovers, it won't have to redo any work that it did before saving its state.

Saving the state of the server's memory is not cheap, especially if it has to be done every time a non-redoable operation is performed. As we'll see in a moment, transactions help reduce this cost.

```
Server Program
    ...
    Checkpoint;
    // Recovery procedure branches to next line
    Recover: If RestartFlag
    { RestartFlag = 0;
      If (check wasn't printed before the failure) print check;
    }
     else print check
     ...
```

```
Server Recovery Procedure:
   RestartFlag = 1;
   Find last checkpoint on disk;
   Restore checkpoint's memory state;
   Go to Recover; // statement after Checkpoint
```

Figure 7.4 Checkpoint-Based Recovery Procedure The server program checkpoints before its non-redoable "print check" operation. The server recovery procedure recovers the last checkpoint state and branches to the line after the statement that created the checkpoint. The server program then executes the non-redoable operation "print check" only if it wasn't done before the failure.

To recover from a failure, the server restores the last checkpoint state it saved before the failure (see Figure 7.4). It must then determine if the non-redoable operation that followed its last checkpoint actually ran. For example, if the server checkpoints its state right before printing a check, then at recovery time reconstituting the server state requires determining whether or not the check was printed. This is the same question we asked in the earlier subsection on client recovery. That is, in this situation, the server is a client that may have issued a call (the non-redoable operation) before it failed. As we said before, solutions to this problem were given in Chapter 4. Therefore, when the server recovers, it can determine whether that non-redoable operation ran, and if so, it can skip over it.

To summarize: if a server performs non-redoable operations, then it reconstitutes its state at recovery time to one that comes after the last non-redoable operation that it performed before the failure. The idea is to start running the process from that state, so that non-redoable operations it does from that point on don't cause a problem.

Transaction-Based Server Recovery

Transactions simplify server recovery by focusing clients' and servers' attention on the *transactions* executed by each server, rather than on individual calls within a transaction. That is, the server does all of its work within transactions. The client tells the server to start a transaction, the client makes some calls to the server within that transaction, and then the client tells the server to commit the transaction.

If a server that supports transactions fails and subsequently recovers, its state includes the effects of all committed transactions and no effects of transactions that aborted before the failure or were active at the time of the failure. Comparing this behavior to a nontransactional server, it is as if the transactional server performs a checkpoint every time it commits a transaction, and its recovery procedure discards all effects of aborted or incomplete transactions. Thus, when a transactional server recovers, it ignores which *calls* were executing when it failed and focuses instead on which *transactions* were executing when it failed. So instead of recovering to a state as of the last partially executed call (as in checkpoint-based recovery), it recovers to a state containing all the results of all committed transactions and no others.

For this to work, the server must be able to undo all of a transaction's operations when it aborts. This effectively makes the operations redoable when the transaction is reexecuted. That is, if an operation was undone, then there's no harm in redoing it later. This avoids a problem that was faced in checkpoint-based recovery—the problem of returning to a state after the last non-redoable operation. This isn't necessary because there are no non-redoable operations.

If all operations in a transaction must be redoable, then the transaction cannot include the non-redoable operations we encountered in the earlier subsection on server recovery, such as printing a check or transferring money. To cope with such a non-redoable operation, the transaction should enqueue a message that contains the operation. It's safe for the transaction to contain the enqueue operation because it is undoable. The program that processes the message and performs the non-redoable operation should use the reply-handling techniques in Section 4.3 to get exactly once execution of the actual operation (printing the check or sending a money-transfer message).

Transactions not only simplify server recovery, they also speed it up. A memory checkpoint is expensive, but transaction commitment is relatively cheap. The trick is that the transactional server is carefully maintaining all of its state on disk, incrementally, by writing small amounts to a log file, thereby avoiding a bulk copy of its memory state. It is designed to suffer failures at arbitrary points in time and to reconstruct its memory state from disk using the log, with relatively modest effort. The algorithms to reconstruct its state in this way are what gives transactions their all-or-nothing and durability properties; either all of a transaction executes or none of it does, and all of its results are durably saved in stable storage, even if the system fails momentarily after the transaction commits. These algorithms are the main subject of the next chapter, on database system recovery.

Stateless Servers

When transactions are used, servers are usually split into two types: application servers and resource managers (see Figure 7.5). An application server receives client requests, performs application logic, and sends messages to recoverable resource managers. It is a pure application processor, which does not directly access shared resources, such as a database. Resource managers handle the state being shared by transactions—databases, recoverable queues, and so on.

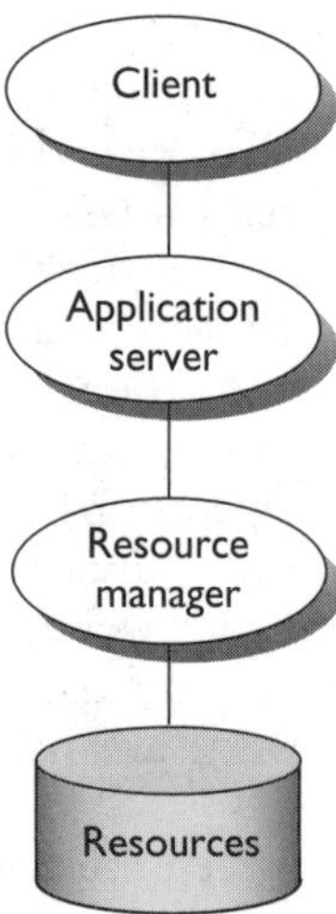

Figure 7.5 Stateless Servers An application server stores all of its state in resource managers and is therefore stateless.

A resource manager behaves just like a transactional server described in the previous subsection on transaction-based server recovery. That is, it executes all calls within a transaction. And its recovery procedure returns its state to one that includes the effects of all committed transactions and no others.

Application servers can use a simpler recovery procedure than resource managers because they don't have any state that might be needed after recovery. We say that a server is *stateless* if it executes each client operation within a transaction and maintains all of its state in resource managers. That is, it doesn't have any local state. A typical kind of stateless server is an application running under a TP monitor. It receives a request to run a transaction (from its client), starts a transaction, executes operations that manipulate local memory or call a database system or another application server, commits the transaction, and sends a reply back to the client. At this point, it has no state worth remembering. It simply processes the next request that it receives as if it had just been initialized.

A stateless server doesn't have to do very much to recover from a failure. It just reinitializes its state and starts running transactions again, completely oblivious to whatever it was doing before the failure. Since it maintained all of its state in recoverable resource managers, it was really up to the resource managers to reconstitute their states after failure. The resource managers recover to a state that includes all of the committed transactions and none of the aborted ones, up to the time of the failure. Now the application server can start processing requests again.

The application servers operating under a TP monitor are usually designed to be stateless servers so they do not need any recovery code. The only ambi-

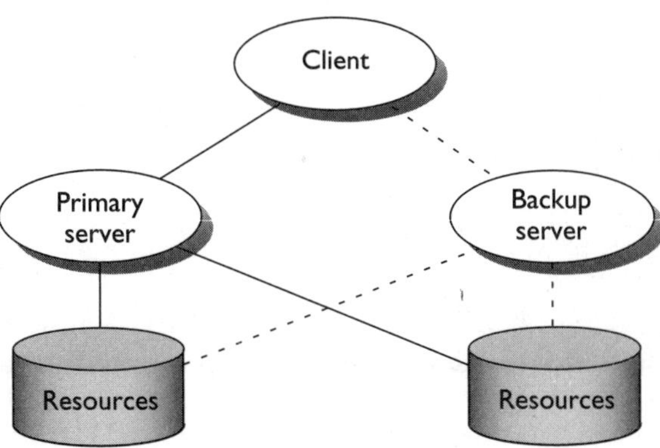

Figure 7.6 **Warm Backup Model** The primary server does the real work. The backup server is standing by, ready to take over after the primary fails.

guity is about the state of the last request that a client issued to the application server before the failure (e.g., that a presentation server issued to a workflow controller). This is where queued request processing comes in—to figure out the state of that last request and thereby determine whether it has to be rerun. For the application server that was actually executing the request, there's no ambiguity at all. It restarts in a clean state, as if it were being initialized for the first time.

7.4 Using Backups

Warm Backups

Even after we have worked as hard as we can to maximize a server's MTBF and minimize its MTTR, we can still expect periods of unavailability. To improve availability further requires that we introduce some redundant processing capability by configuring each server as two server processes: a primary server that is doing the real work and a backup server that is standing by, ready to take over immediately after the primary fails (see Figure 7.6). The goal is to reduce MTTR: If the primary server fails, then we need not wait for a new server to be created. As soon as the failure is detected, the backup server can immediately become the primary and start recovering to the state the former primary had after executing its last non-redoable operation. Since we are primarily interested in transactional servers, this means recovering to a state that includes the effects of all transactions that committed at the former primary and no other transactions.

This technique is applicable both to application servers and resource managers. When a server of either type fails, it needs to be recreated. Having a backup server avoids having to create the backup server at recovery time.

To further reduce MTTR, clients connected to the primary server should also have backup communications sessions with the backup server. This avoids recreating the sessions between the client and backup at recovery time. This is important, since the time to recreate sessions can be quite long, even longer than the time to recover resource managers.

As in the case of a server that has no backup, when the primary server fails, some external agent, such as a monitoring process, has to detect the failure and cause the backup server now to become the primary. The delay in detecting failure contributes to MTTR, so fast failure detection is important for high availability.

Once the backup server has been made the primary, it may be worthwhile to create another backup, for the new primary. An alternative is to wait until the former primary recovers, at which time it can become the backup. Then, if desired, the former backup (which is the new primary) could be told to fail, so that the original primary becomes primary again and the backup is restarted as the backup again. This restores the system to its original configuration, which was tuned to work well, at the cost of some unavailability while the original primary is recovering after the former backup was made to fail.

When telling a backup to become the primary, some care is needed to avoid ending up with two servers that both believe they're the primary. For example, if the monitor process gets no response from the primary, it may conclude that the primary is dead. But the primary may actually be operating. It may just be slow because its system is overloaded (e.g., a network storm is swamping its operating system), and it therefore hasn't sent an "I'm alive" message in a long time, which the monitor interprets as a failure of the primary. If the monitor then tells the backup to become the primary, then two processes will be operating as primary. Both primaries will perform operations against the same resource. They may conflict with each other and corrupt that resource—for example, by overwriting each other if the resource is a disk or by sending out conflicting messages if the resource is a communications line. Sometimes, the resource includes a hardware lock that only one process can hold (the primary), which ensures that only one process can operate as primary at a time.

Hot Backup

Using a backup server saves recovery time by avoiding the need to recreate the server. But it still requires that the backup, when it becomes the primary, recover to the correct state. For a stateless application server, there's no recovery to do. But a resource manager has to run a recovery procedure, which takes time. We can further reduce the recovery time by avoiding or speeding up this recovery step, by using a *hot backup* (sometimes called *process pairs*), as illustrated in Figure 7.7.

The goal of the hot backup model is to keep the backup in a state that is very close to that of the primary, so the backup has little recovery to do if the primary should fail. To meet this goal in a checkpoint-based server, when the primary checkpoints its state (before each non-redoable operation), it also sends that state to the backup. At that moment, the backup is in the same

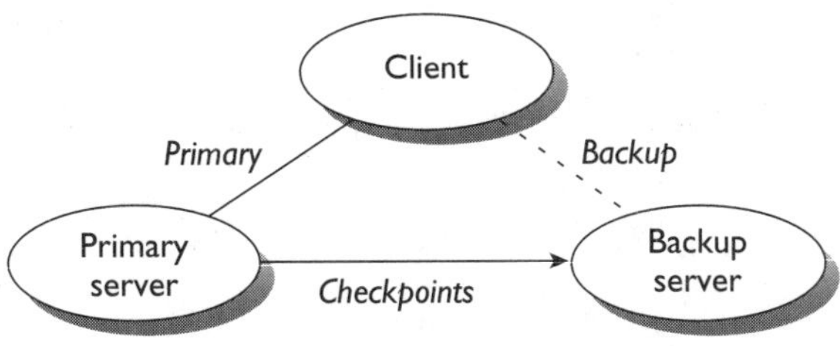

Figure 7.7 Hot Backup Model The primary checkpoints its state to the backup before each non-redoable operation, so the backup can recover more quickly, thereby reducing MTTR.

state as the primary, which is the state as of the primary's last non-redoable operation. If the primary were to fail shortly after sending the checkpoint to the backup, the backup would have very little recovery to do, since it already is in the state as of the last non-redoable operation.

Of course, the primary's memory state may be fairly large. To avoid sending all of that information to the backup, the server could send to the backup only a log of the changes that it made to its state since its last checkpoint. This is more efficient than sending the full checkpoint when the log of state changes is smaller than a copy of its entire state, as is often the case.

This technique of sending the log is usually used by servers that are resource managers, since most resource managers use a log to keep track of the operations of each transaction. Among the first general-purpose systems to do this were IBM's IMS/XRF and Tandem's Non-Stop SQL database systems. Now most database replication services work this way too (e.g., Oracle, Sybase, Informix, and Microsoft SQL Server). The primary sends the log both to the disk that contains the log and to the backup server, as shown in Figure 7.8. The backup server is constantly running recovery, using the log records coming from the primary, in much the same way that it would if it were an ordinary server recovering from a failure using a log it was reading from disk. Thus, if the primary fails, the backup is almost as up-to-date as the primary. It just has to process the last little bit of log that it did not receive from the primary before the failure. To get that piece of the log, the backup goes to the disk, reads it off the disk, and finishes its recovery procedure.

Another way to keep a hot backup up-to-date, without using checkpoints, is to have the primary and the backup perform the same work in parallel. Each request that's sent to the primary is also sent to the backup and is processed both by the primary and the backup. The primary and the backup have to be kept synchronized so that the backup processes the same input requests in the same order as the primary. Of course, only the primary should respond to the requests. The backup processes requests to keep its internal state up-to-date with the primary's, but it doesn't actually have any effect on the outside world until it becomes the primary. If the primary fails, then the backup can smoothly pick up from exactly the point at which the primary left off.

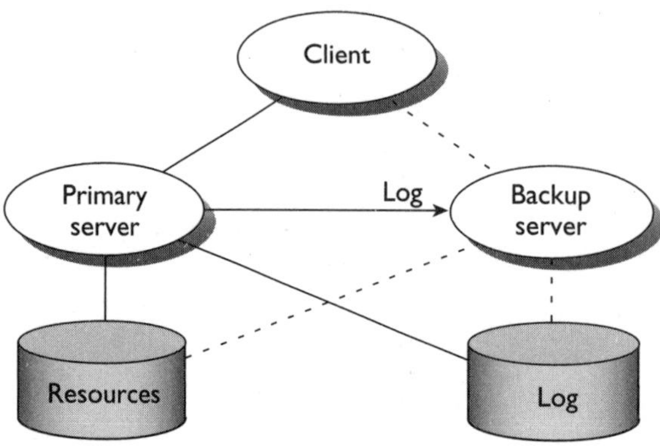

Figure 7.8 **Using a Log for Checkpointing** The backup server is a hot standby that constantly runs recovery using log records coming from the primary.

This is a relatively expensive way to improve availability because processing every request twice doubles the amount of resources needed. But some applications warrant that kind of expense to get high enough availability, such as stock market applications where even short failures are very costly. For example, some stock markets use Digital's Reliable Transaction Router (RTR) product, which implements hot backups that operate in this way.

7.5 Summary

TP systems often are expected to be available 24 hours per day, 7 days per week, to support around-the-clock business operations. Two factors affect availability: the mean time between failures (MTBF) and the mean time to repair (MTTR). Improving availability requires increasing MTBF and/or decreasing MTTR.

Computer failures occur because of

- environmental factors (power, air-conditioning, communication lines, acts of God, etc.)
- system management (operations staff errors, software upgrades, preventive maintenance, etc.)
- hardware (failure of any component, such as memory, disk, network controller, etc.)
- software (crash of operating system, database system, TP monitor, or application program)

If the operating system fails, then just reboot it. For other types of software failure, the TP monitor or database system must detect the failure of a process and recreate it. The recreated process must then run a recovery procedure to reconstruct its state.

When a client recovers, it needs to reconnect to its servers. It then should determine which calls were outstanding when it failed and what it needs to do to complete those calls. This is exactly the problem addressed in Chapter 4 on queuing.

When a server recovers, it needs to reconstruct a state that is consistent with the last calls that it processed before the failure. This requires taking checkpoints periodically during normal operation, so it can reload the checkpointed state at recovery time. Executing from that recovered state, the server must avoid redoing any non-redoable actions (such as printing a check).

Transactions simplify recovery by allowing a server to focus on restoring its state to contain only the results of committed transactions, rather than recovering to a state that is consistent with the last operations it ran. Transactional servers are often split into two types: resource managers that maintain state and stateless application servers. The latter store all of their state in the resource managers and therefore can recover simply by reinitializing.

To reduce MTTR and thereby improve availability, you can use a backup server that is ready to take over if the primary server fails. This avoids the delay of recreating a server after it fails, but it still requires reconstructing the server's state in the backup.

A *hot backup server* can further reduce MTTR by maintaining its state as close as possible to the primary's. The primary sends checkpoint information, such as log records, to the backup, which is constantly processing that information to keep up with the primary. When the primary fails, the backup processes the remaining checkpoint information to recover its state. Alternatively, the hot backup server can perform the work of the primary server in parallel, which doubles the required resources but ensures the backup can recover even faster when the primary fails.

CHAPTER 8

Database System Recovery

8.1 Introduction

A database system is a recoverable resource manager. To recover from a failure, its job is to quickly return to a state that includes the results of all transactions that committed before the failure and includes none of the transactions that aborted before the failure or were active at the time of failure. Most database systems do an excellent job of this type of recovery. The application programmer doesn't get involved at all.

The mechanisms used to recover from these failures can have a significant effect on performance. However, if a data manager uses a recovery approach that leads to mediocre transaction performance, there is not too much that the application programmer can do about it. This is rather different than locking, where program and database design can have a big effect. In view of the lack of control that an application programmer has over the situation, there is no strong requirement that he or she have a deep understanding of how a data manager does recovery.

There are a few things, though not many, that an application programmer or system manager can do that affect the performance of recovery. There are also things that a system manager can do to affect the degree of fault tolerance of a system, such as altering the configuration of logs, disk devices, and the like. To reason about performance and fault tolerance implications of application and system design, it helps a great deal to understand the main concepts behind database recovery algorithms. We describe these concepts and their implications for application programming in this chapter.

Types of Failure

Many failures are due to incorrectly programmed transactions and to data entry errors that produce incorrect parameters to transactions. Unfortunately, these failures undermine the assumption that a transaction's execution preserves the consistency of the database (the "C" in ACID). They can be dealt with by applying software engineering techniques to the programming and testing of transactions, by validating input before feeding it to a transaction, and by semantic integrity mechanisms built into the database system. However they're dealt with, they are intrinsically outside the range of problems that transaction recovery mechanisms can automatically handle. Since in this chapter we're interested only in problems that transaction recovery mechanisms can handle, we will assume that transactions do indeed preserve database consistency.

There are three types of failures that are most important to a centralized TP system: transaction failures, system failures, and media failures. A *transaction failure* occurs when a transaction aborts. A *system failure* refers to the loss or corruption of the contents of volatile storage, namely, main memory. For example, this can happen to semiconductor memory when the power fails. It also happens when the operating system fails. Although an operating system failure may not corrupt all of main memory, it is usually too difficult to determine which parts were actually corrupted by the failure. So one generally assumes the worst and reinitializes all of main memory. Because of system failures, the database itself must be kept on a stable storage medium, such as disk. (Of course, other considerations, such as size, may also force us to store the database on stable mass storage media.) By definition, *stable* (or *nonvolatile*) storage withstands system failures. A *media failure* occurs when any part of the stable storage is destroyed. For instance, this happens if some sectors of a disk become damaged.

Recovery Strategies

The techniques used to cope with media failures are conceptually similar to those used to cope with system failures. In each case, we consider a certain part of storage to be unreliable: volatile storage, in the case of system failures; a portion of stable storage, in the case of media failures. To safeguard against the loss of data in unreliable storage, we maintain another copy of the data, possibly in a different representation. This redundant copy is kept in another part of storage that we deem reliable: stable storage, in the case of system failures, or another piece of stable storage, such as a second disk or tape, in the case of media failures. Of course, the different physical characteristics of storage in the two cases may require the use of different strategies. But the principles are the same.

The main strategy for recovering from failures is quite simple:

- Transaction failure—If a transaction aborts, the data manager will restore the previous values of all data items that the transaction wrote.
- System failure—To recover from the failure, the data manager will abort any transactions that were active (but not committed) at the time of the failure, and it will ensure that each transaction that did commit before the failure actually installed its updates in the database.
- Media failure—The recovery strategy is pretty much the same as for system failures, since the goal is to return the database to a state where it contains the results of all committed transactions and no aborted transactions.

We concentrate on transaction and system failures for most of the chapter. Since media failures are so similar to system failures, we'll postpone discussing them until the end of the chapter, after we have a complete picture of system recovery mechanisms.

The most popular technique for recovering from system and media failures is logging. The log is that second, redundant copy of the data that is used to cope with failures. To understand how a log is used, why it works, and how it affects performance, we need to start with a simplified model of data manager internals, so we have a framework in which to discuss the issues.

8.2 The System Model

Locking Assumptions

From the viewpoint of transactions, the recovery system is part of the storage subsystem that processes read, write, commit, and abort operations. The recovery system makes few assumptions about the transactions that use its services. The main one is that the transaction is responsible for setting locks before issuing read and write operations to the storage system and that it holds onto its write locks until after the transaction commits or aborts.

Since a transaction holds a write lock on any data it updates until after it commits or aborts, no other transaction can read or write that data until then. This avoids two messy situations that nearly all database systems do not otherwise handle.

The first messy situation is cascading abort. If a transaction T_2 were allowed to read data updated by an active transaction T_1, and T_1 subsequently aborted, then T_2 would have to abort too, since its input would be invalid. This is called *cascading abort*, since the abort of one transaction (T_1) cascades to the abort of another transaction (T_2). This cannot happen if a transaction holds write locks until after it commits or aborts.

The second messy situation is being unable to abort a transaction simply by restoring the previous values of data it wrote. If a transaction T_1 does not hold its write locks until after it commits or aborts, then another transaction could overwrite data written by T_1. The effect is rather nasty, as illustrated by the following execution:

$$E = w_1[x]\ w_2[x]\ abort_1\ abort_2$$

In execution E, when transaction T_1 aborts, the system cannot simply restore the value x had before $w_1[x]$, since that would wipe out transaction T_2's write operation, $w_2[x]$. If T_2 later committed, its results would be lost. So, the right thing for the system to do when T_1 aborts is nothing. Now, when T_2 aborts, the system cannot restore the value x had before $w_2[x]$, since that would reinstall the value written by T_1, which just aborted. So, the right thing for the system to do when T_2 aborts is restore the value x had before $w_1[x]$. This is a pretty complicated analysis for the recovery mechanism to do, and this is just for two updates by two transactions. If multiple transactions were involved, the analysis that the system would have to do to figure out what to install would be very tricky indeed, and all systems we know of avoid it. They simply require that write locks are held till after the transaction commits or aborts.

Locking granularity is another aspect of locking that affects the complexity of recovery mechanisms. Recovery algorithms are a lot simpler when page granularity locking is used. Here's why.

The only truly reliable operation we have available is writing one page to the disk. Disk hardware is careful to make this an all-or-nothing operation; when it isn't all-or-nothing, we have a partially updated page, which is a type of media failure. Media failures aside, recovery algorithms for system failure

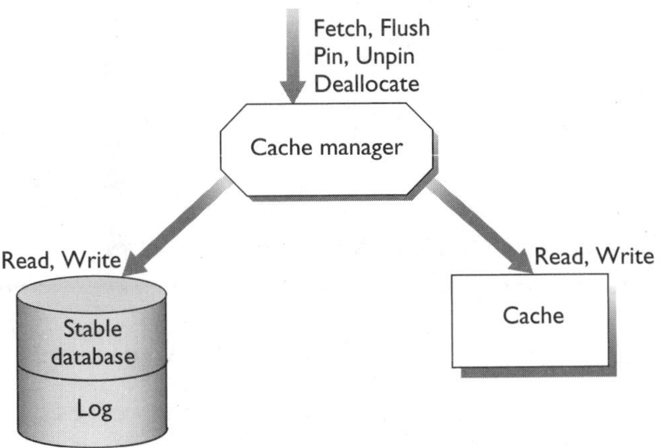

Figure 8.1 **The Storage Model** The cache manager controls the movement of pages between stable storage (the stable database and log) and volatile storage (the cache).

rely heavily on this property of disks, that page operations are all-or-nothing. So far, so good.

However, if multiple transactions can lock individual objects within a page, such as records, then they can update the page independently. Therefore, at recovery time, a page may have a mixture of new values and old values of objects updated by different transactions, and the bookkeeping to sort them out is quite challenging. This complexity is a problem that is worth solving, but for pedagogical reasons, it's one we'll postpone for awhile. So to keep things simple, we will start by using page granularity for everything:

- The database consists of a set of pages.
- Each update by a transaction applies to only one page.
- Each update by a transaction writes a whole page (not just part of the page).
- Locks are set on pages.

Page granularity simplifies the discussion, but it is too inefficient for high-performance systems. After we describe recovery using this assumption, we'll show what happens when we allow finer-grained updates and locks, for example, on records.

Storage Model

We model storage as two areas: stable storage (usually disk) and volatile storage (usually main memory). (See Figure 8.1.) Stable storage contains the *stable database*, which has one copy of each database page. It also contains the log, which we'll discuss in a moment.

Page	*Dirty Bit*	*Cache Address*	*Pin Count*
P_4	1	104	1
P_{16}	0	376	1
P_5	1	400	0

Figure 8.2 Cache Descriptor Table Each page in a cache slot is described by a row in this table.

Volatile storage contains the database *cache*. The cache contains copies of some of the database pages, usually ones that were recently accessed or updated by transactions. Using a cache is a big performance win because it helps transactions avoid the high cost of disk accesses for popular pages.

For recovery purposes, it really doesn't matter which pages are in cache, only that there are some. Pages in cache may contain updates that have not yet been written to the stable database. Such pages are called *dirty*. Correctly handling dirty pages is an important responsibility of the recovery system during normal operation.

The *cache manager* keeps track of what is in cache. It divides up the cache into *slots*, each of which can hold one database page. It uses a table to keep track of what is in each slot. Each row of the table contains a *cache descriptor*, which identifies the database page that is in the cache slot; the main memory address of the cache slot; a bit to indicate whether the page is dirty; and a pin count, which is explained below (see Figure 8.2). The cache manager supports five basic operations:

- Fetch(P)—P is the address of a database page. This operation reads P into a cache slot (if it isn't already there) and returns the address of the cache slot.
- Pin(P)—This makes page P's cache slot unavailable for flushing (it is "pinned down"). Usually, a caller pins P immediately after fetching it.
- Unpin(P)—Releases the caller's previous pin. The cache manager maintains a *pin count* for each page, which is incremented by each Pin operation and decremented by each Unpin. If the pin count is zero, the page is available for flushing.
- Flush(P)—If database page P is in a cache slot and is dirty, then this operation writes it to the disk. It does not return until after the disk acknowledges that the write operation is done. That is, a flush is a synchronous write.
- Deallocate(P)—Deallocates P so its cache slot can be reused by another page. Do not flush the page, even if the cache slot is dirty. (It is up to the cache manager's clients to flush a page before deallocating it, if that's what they want to do.)

Everything else that happens to pages is up to the transactions. If a transaction has fetched and pinned a page, it can do what it wants to that page, as far as the cache manager is concerned. Of course, we know the transaction will have an appropriate lock to read or write the page, but this is at a higher level than the cache manager, which doesn't know anything about these locks.

The cache manager is heavily used by database system components that read and write the database. This is usually the record management layer of the database system, which reads and writes records and provides indexed access to data. To read or write data on a page P, this component issues Fetch(P) followed by Pin(P). When it's done reading or updating the page, it calls Unpin(P). It does not call Flush(P).

It is up to two other database system components to call Flush(P). One is the cache manager's page replacement algorithm. Its job is to make the best use of cache by only keeping pages that transactions are likely to need in the near future. If a page P hasn't been referenced in awhile, it deallocates P from its page slot. If P is dirty, then it calls Flush(P) before Deallocate(P), so that recent updates to P aren't lost.

The other component that uses Flush(P) is the recovery manager, which is described in the next section.

The Log

The log is a sequential file, usually kept on disk. It contains a sequence of records that describe updates that were applied to the database. The record that describes an update includes

- the address of the page that was updated
- the identifier of the transaction that performed the update
- the value of the page that was written, called its *after-image*
- the value of the page before it was written, called its *before-image*

As described here, each log record is more than two pages long, which is much too inefficient. Like our other page granularity assumptions, we'll weaken it later on.

This log record is written by the same component that writes to the cache. That is, whenever it updates a cache page, and before it unpins that page, it writes a log record that describes the update. That way, the log is always consistent with the contents of the cache.

The log also contains records that report when a transaction commits or aborts. Such records just contain the identifier of the transaction and an indication whether the transaction committed or aborted.

It is crucial that the log accurately reflect the order in which conflicting operations really executed. That is, if one update precedes and conflicts with another update in the log, then the updates must really have executed in that order. The reason is that after a failure, the recovery system will replay some

```
Fetch(P)               /* read P into cache */
Pin(P)                 /* ensure P isn't flushed */
write lock P           /* for two-phase locking */
latch P                /* get exclusive access to P */
update P               /* update it in the cache */
log the update to P    /* append it to the log */
unlatch P              /* release exclusive access */
Unpin(P)               /* allow P to be flushed */
```

Figure 8.3 **Using Latches** Obtaining a latch on P ensures that the ordering of log records is consistent with the order of updates to each page.

of the work that happened before the failure. It will assume that the order of operations in the log is the order in which it should replay work. Note that it is not necessary that the log accurately reflect the ordering of *all* updates, only the conflicting ones, which are the only ones whose relative order makes a difference. Some systems exploit this distinction by logging nonconflicting updates in parallel in sublogs and merging those sublogs later, when conflicting updates occur.

Page-level locking ensures this ordering is enforced. If finer granularity locking is used, then two transactions can update a page concurrently. So the database system must ensure that it updates the page *and* writes the log record on behalf of one transaction before it performs these two actions on behalf of the other. This is done by setting a short-term exclusive lock on the page, called a *latch*, which can simply be a bit in the cache descriptor. The latch brackets the activities of updating the page and logging the update (see Figure 8.3). The latch ensures that if another transaction was concurrently attempting the same sequence, its update and log operations would either precede or follow those of T.

While most systems store before-images and after-images in the same log, some use separate logs. This is done because before-images are not needed after a transaction commits and usually are not needed for media recovery. They can therefore be deleted relatively quickly, unlike after-images, which are needed for very long periods. However, this can also lead to extra log writes, since there are now two logs to deal with.

8.3 The Recovery Manager

The recovery manager is the component that is responsible for processing commit and abort operations. It is also responsible for the restart operation, which initiates recovery from a system failure to bring the database back into a consistent state where it can process transactions again. In summary, the operations should have the following effects (see Figure 8.4):

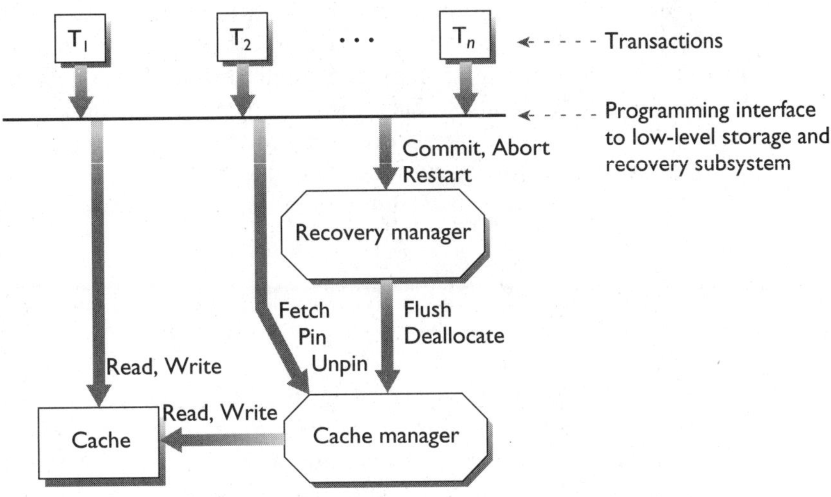

Figure 8.4 **Recovery Manager Model** The recovery manager calls the cache manager to help it implement the commit, abort, and restart operations.

- Commit(T_i)—Permanently installs T_i's updated pages into the stable database. Its effect must be atomic, that is, all-or-nothing, even in the event of a system failure. Also, its effect is irrevocable: once the transaction is committed, it cannot subsequently be aborted.
- Abort(T_i)—Restores all the data that T_i updated to the values it had before T_i executed. Like Commit, its effect is irrevocable: once the transaction is aborted, it cannot subsequently be committed.
- Restart—Aborts all transactions that were active at the time of the system failure. Also, any updates by committed transactions that were not installed in the stable database before the failure are installed now. (They may have only been written to the log and not have made it to the stable database before the failure.) The result should be that the database contains all committed updates and no aborted ones.

To implement these operations, the recovery manager must follow certain rules. The essence of these rules is in controlling when dirty data is flushed to disk.

Implementing Abort

Consider the operation Abort(T_i), and suppose only T_i wrote page P. If P was not transferred to stable storage, then the recovery manager can simply deallocate P. Otherwise, it has to write P's before-image to the stable database, that is, it must restore P's value to what it was before T_i executed. Ordinarily, this is straightforward, since T_i logged its update to P. However, what if the abort is being executed to help recover from a system failure? That is, T_i was executing at the time of the system failure and the restart procedure is executing Abort(T_i) to clean things up. It is conceivable that T_i's update to P was transferred to the stable database before the failure, but its update to the log was *not* transferred to the disk before the failure (see Figure 8.5). In this case, T_i's update to P cannot be undone, because the before-image has been lost. This is an unacceptable situation and must be prevented by enforcing the following rule:

The Write-Ahead Log Protocol Do not flush an uncommitted update to the stable database until the log record containing its before-image has been flushed to the log.

There is a simple way to avoid the bookkeeping required to enforce this rule, namely, never flush an uncommitted update to the stable database. Just flush it to the log. After the transaction has committed, then flush it to the stable database. That way, you never have to worry whether the before-image is in the log because it will never be necessary to undo an uncommitted update in the stable database. That is, undo will never be required.

Some systems avoid the bookkeeping by maintaining multiple versions of each page, as discussed in Section 6.6 on query-update problems. Instead of overwriting a page, they create a new version of the page. Periodically, old versions that are no longer needed are purged. By keeping old versions in the database itself, before-images need not be logged, so the write-ahead log protocol is automatically satisfied.

Implementing Commit

Now let's consider the operation Commit(T_i). Since Commit is a promise that all of a transaction's updates are durable, all of T_i's updates must be in stable storage before the Commit—in the log or in the stable database. This means that the recovery manager must enforce another rule:

The Force-at-Commit Rule Do not commit a transaction until the after-images of all of its updated pages are in stable storage (in the log or the stable database).

A simple way to implement the force-at-commit rule is to flush a transaction's updates to the stable database before it commits. This avoids any bookkeeping required to know which updates are not in the stable database and therefore have to be flushed to the log before commit. It also avoids any redo of committed updates because they are always in the database before they are committed.

As you can see, the simple ways of enforcing the write-ahead log protocol and force-at-commit rule are contradictory (see Figure 8.6). To avoid undo, the simple approach is never to flush an uncommitted update to the stable database. To avoid redo, the simple approach is always to flush all uncommitted

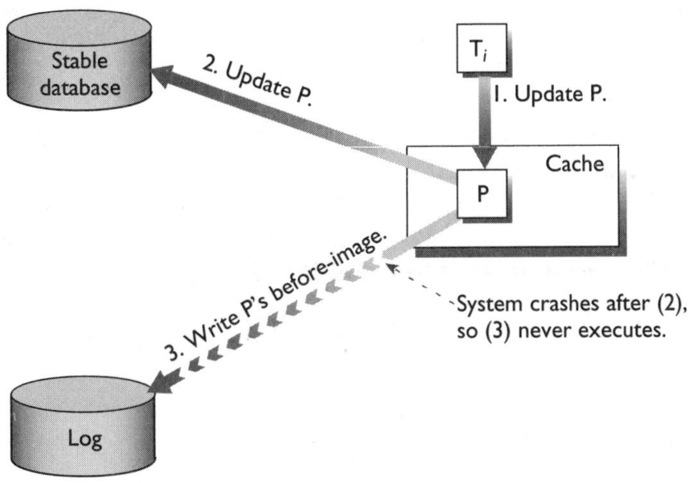

Figure 8.5 Why We Need the Write-Ahead Log Protocol If T_i is active when the system fails, then it can't be aborted after recovery because P's before-image was lost.

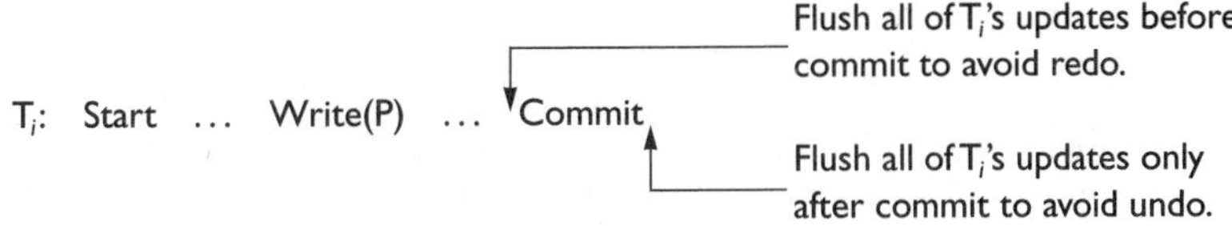

Figure 8.6 Avoiding Undo or Redo Depending on when a transaction's updates are flushed, undo or redo can be avoided.

updates to the stable database before the transaction commits. So whatever approach is taken, it would seem that *some* undo or redo will be required.[1]

The third operation of the recovery manager is restart. Restart requires a fair bit of bookkeeping. It needs to know which transactions were active at the time of the failure, so it can abort them, and which updates of committed transactions were not written to the stable database, so it can redo them. Moreover, restart must be fault-tolerant. That is, if the system fails when restart is running, it must be possible to reexecute restart. This means that

1 Undo or redo is required logging algorithms. However, there are techniques that avoid undo and redo. These techniques are called *shadow paging* or *careful replacement*. They are used in some object-oriented database systems, but since they do not perform well for transaction processing, they are not described in this book. Details can be found in Bernstein, Hadzilacos, and Goodman (1987), pp. 201–205.

restart must be careful that, at all times, the system is in a state from which restart can correctly execute (which is exactly the same requirement that normal executions have). This requires carefully ordering updates to stable storage.

Given all of these rules, we are ready to look at algorithms that implement a recovery manager. A good recovery manager algorithm should add little overhead to the normal processing of transactions. The principal ways it can contribute overhead is by flushing pages too often (creating excess disk traffic) and by logging too much data. A second goal is to recover quickly from a failure, so the system is only down for a short period. The shorter the downtime, the higher the availability. If the system could recover instantly from a failure, then it could fail very often and no one would care (as long at it can commit some transactions!).

8.4 Log-Based Recovery Algorithms

Logging is the most popular technique for implementing a recovery manager. As we described earlier, the log contains a record for each write, commit, and abort operation.

Implementing Commit

To process a commit operation, the recovery manager adds a commit record to the end of the log and flushes the log. The log manager is designed so that it doesn't acknowledge the flush operation until all of the log pages in memory, up to and including the one being flushed, have been written to disk and the disk has acknowledged that the disk writes completed successfully. At this point, the transaction has been committed and the recovery manager can acknowledge this fact to its caller.

Since all of the transaction's update records precede the commit record in the log, by writing the commit record and then flushing the log, the recovery manager ensures that all of the transaction's updates are on stable storage. That is, it ensures that the force-at-commit rule has been satisfied. It doesn't matter whether any of the updated pages have been flushed to the stable database. The updates are in the log, and the log is in stable storage, which is enough to satisfy the rule.

Flushing the log to commit a transaction is a bottleneck. If the disk that holds the log can do K disk-writes per second, then K is the maximum number of transactions per second for the whole system. This is too small a number, on the order of 25–100. This is especially annoying because the log page normally isn't full when the flush is invoked, so the full capacity of the disk channel isn't being used. This observation creates an opportunity to improve performance.

To relieve this bottleneck, the system uses an optimization called *group commit*. After adding a commit record to the log, the recovery manager introduces a small artificial delay before flushing the log page, something on the

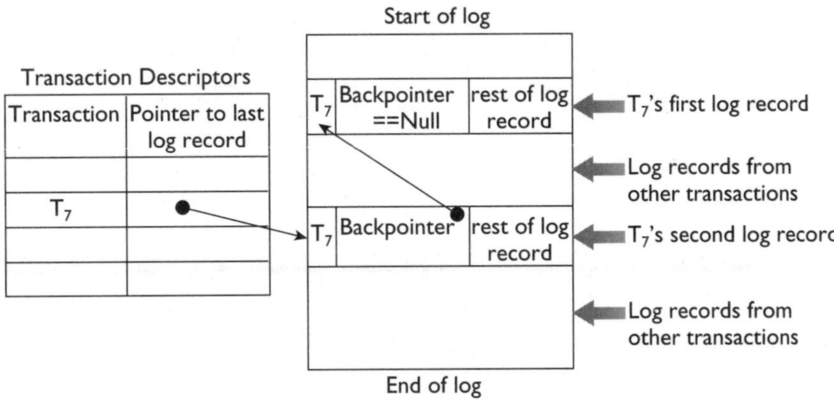

Figure 8.7 **Data Structure Supporting Abort Processing** Starting from the transaction descriptor, all of the transaction's update records can be scanned.

order of $^1/_K$, that is, a few tens of milliseconds. During that period, if there are other transactions running, they can add records to the end of the log—update records, commit records, and abort records. If the system is busy, then the chances are that the log page will fill up during this period, and when the recovery manager reaches the end of the delay period, it ends up flushing a full page. Thus, each flush operation on the log can commit many transactions, and the recovery manager is getting the full power of the disk channel. If the system is not busy, then it doesn't matter that a partially filled log page is flushed to disk, because not all of the disk capacity is needed to support the transaction load.

Implementing Abort

To process an abort operation, the recovery manager has to undo the updates of any stable database pages updated by the transaction. It does this by tracing through the transaction's log records, starting from the last one, and installing the before-image of each page that was updated by the transaction.

Sequentially searching the log for the transaction's update records is rather inefficient. To avoid this sequential scan, the recovery manager maintains a linked list of all of the transaction's update records in the log. The list header is a *transaction descriptor*, which is a data structure that describes each transaction that it knows about (see Figure 8.7). The descriptor includes a pointer to the last log record that was written by each transaction. Each update record in the log contains a pointer to the previous update record written by the same transaction. So, starting from the transaction descriptor, all of the transaction's update records can be scanned.

Maintaining the list is easy. When a transaction writes an update record to the log, it includes a backpointer to the previous log record for that transac-

Page	*Dirty Bit*	*Cache Address*	*Pin Count*	*Dependent Log Page Address*
P_4	1	104	1	1218
P_{16}	0	376	1	null
P_5	1	400	0	1332

Figure 8.8 Dependent Log Page Address Before flushing a page, the cache manager must check that the dependent log page is not in cache and dirty.

tion, and it updates the transaction descriptor to point to the new update record, which is now the last one for the transaction.

There is still the matter of the write-ahead log protocol to consider. The system needs to ensure that it doesn't flush a dirty page from the cache unless all the update records that describe updates to that page by uncommitted transactions have already been flushed to the log. To do this, it needs a little help from the cache manager.

We need to add a field to the cache descriptor of each cache slot. This field points to the log page that we need to worry about to enforce the write-ahead log protocol. That is, it contains the address of the log page that contains the update record describing the last update to this cache slot's page (see Figure 8.8). Let's call this the *dependent log page address* (there's no standard term for this). Every time a database page P is updated, the dependent log page address of P's cache slot is also updated to point to the page containing the update's log record. Before it flushes a cache slot, the cache manager must check that the dependent log page is not in cache and dirty. If it is, then the dependent log page must be flushed first, to ensure the write-ahead log protocol is satisfied.

Although the cache manager has to check the dependent log page address every time it flushes a page from cache, this rarely generates an extra cache flush of the log page. The reason is this: The log is a sequential file. As soon as a log page has been filled up, the log manager tells the cache manager to flush it. By the time the cache manager decides to flush a database page, the chances are that the database page has been sitting around in cache for awhile since it was last updated. For example, the cache replacement algorithm notices that the page hasn't been accessed recently and decides to replace it. Since the page hasn't been accessed recently, the chances are good that the dependent log page has already been flushed.

Of course, even hot pages must *eventually* be flushed. Since they're updated frequently, hot pages may have update records in the tail of the log. So flushing a hot page may cause an extra cache flush.

Implementing Restart

To implement restart, the recovery manager scans the log to figure out which transactions need to be aborted and which committed updates need to be redone. Many algorithms are known for this process. We'll just describe one of them here. We'll forego many optimizations to keep the explanation simple.

All restart algorithms depend on the recovery manager to perform checkpoint operations periodically, which synchronize the state of the log with the state of the stable database. The simplest checkpoint algorithm is as follows:

1. It stops accepting any new update, commit, and abort operations.
2. It makes a list of all the active transactions along with each transaction's pointer to its last log record.
3. It flushes all the dirty pages in cache.
4. It writes a *checkpoint record* to the log, which includes the list of active transactions and log pointers.
5. It starts accepting new update, commit, and abort operations again.

At this point, the stable database state is exactly consistent with the state of the log. We'll explain a more efficient checkpointing algorithm in a moment, but for now, let's assume we're using this one.

The restart algorithm scans the log forwards and fully processes each log record before proceeding to the next. Its goal is first to redo all updates that executed after the last checkpoint and then to undo the ones that did not commit. It starts at the last checkpoint record. There is no point in looking at log records before this point because their effects have been fully recorded in the stable database (see Figure 8.9). The restart algorithm maintains lists of committed and aborted transactions, which are initialized to be empty, and a list of active transactions, which is initialized to the value stored in the last checkpoint record. When the restart algorithm encounters a new log record, it does the following:

- If the log record is an update record, then it writes the after-image of the update to the cache, and it adds the transaction's identifier to the active list if it isn't already there. Notice that even if the update is already in the stable database, there is no harm in writing the after-image because the after-image contains an entire page image (remember our simplifying assumption that each update writes a whole page), so at worst, it's just redoing work needlessly.
- If the log record is a commit record, it adds the transaction to its commit list and removes it from the active list (if it was there).
- If the log record is an abort record, it undoes all of the transaction's updates in the same way as it normally processes an abort. Also, it adds the transaction to its abort list and removes it from the active list (if it was there).

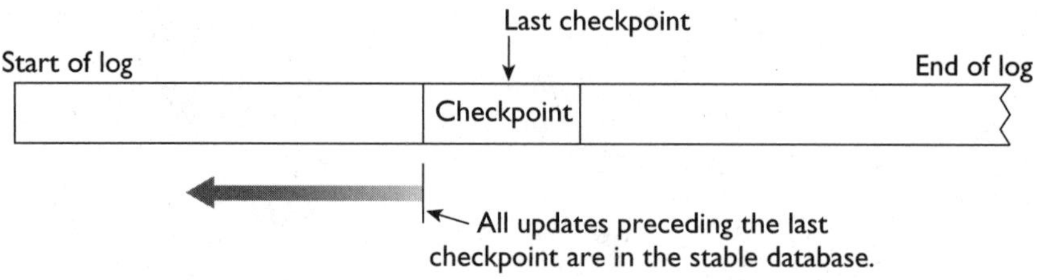

Figure 8.9 Basic Checkpointing All dirty pages are flushed before a checkpoint record is written.

When it reaches the end of the log, it has redone all of the updates of committed and active transactions and has wiped out the effects of any aborted transactions. At this point, the active list contains any transactions that started running before the failure but did not commit or abort before the failure. (Notice that since the active list was initialized from the last checkpoint record, this includes transactions that were active at the last checkpoint but had no later updates.) These transactions cannot continue running, since they lost their memory state during the system failure, so the restart algorithm aborts them too. Now the system is ready to process new transactions, since the combined state of the cache and stable database includes all committed updates and no aborted ones.

As long as the restart algorithm is running, users are unable to run transactions. Therefore, it's important to optimize it to minimize its running time and therefore maximize the system's availability. We will describe these optimizations in the next section.

8.5 Optimizing Restart in Log-Based Algorithms

Fuzzy Checkpointing

Checkpoints are an important way of speeding up the restart algorithm. The more frequently we run a checkpoint, the less log that the restart algorithm has to process, and therefore, the less time it takes to run restart. However, checkpointing isn't free. The checkpointing algorithm described earlier does quite a lot of work and causes the system to stop working for awhile, until it has finished flushing all of the dirty pages in cache. To speed up restart, we need a cheaper way to checkpoint, so we can afford to checkpoint often.

The solution is called *fuzzy checkpointing*. To do a fuzzy checkpoint, the recovery manager does the following:

1. It stops accepting any new update, commit, and abort operations.
2. It scans the cache to make a list of all the dirty pages in the cache.
3. It makes a list of all the active transactions along with each transaction's pointer to its last log record.

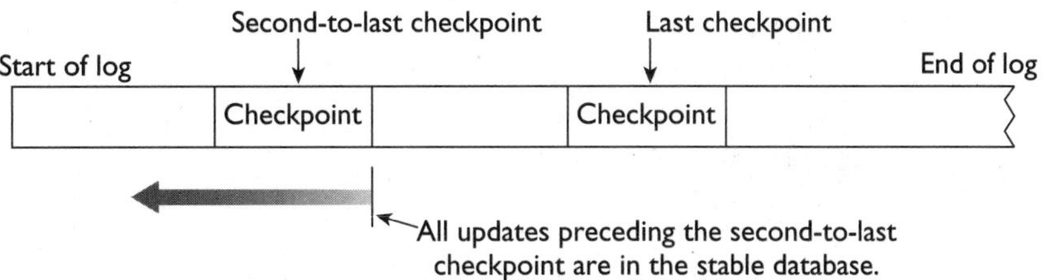

Figure 8.10 **Fuzzy Checkpointing** After a checkpoint record is written, all dirty cache pages are flushed. The flushes must be completed before the next checkpoint record is written.

4. It writes a checkpoint record to the log, which includes the list of active transactions and log pointers.
5. It starts accepting new update, commit, and abort operations again.
6. In parallel with running new update, commit, and abort operations, it issues flush operations to write all of the dirty pages on the list it gathered in step 2 to the stable database. These are low-priority operations that the cache manager should only do when it has spare capacity. It may take awhile.

The recovery manager is allowed to do another checkpoint operation only after step 6 completes, that is, only after those dirty old pages have been flushed. Thus, by the time the *next* checkpoint record is written, all of the updates that preceded the *previous* checkpoint record must be in the stable database.

Let's revisit the restart algorithm with this checkpointing in mind. Notice that it's the second-to-last (i.e., penultimate) checkpoint record that has the property we're looking for (see Figure 8.10). All of the updates in the log that precede the penultimate checkpoint record must be in the stable database. The checkpointing algorithm would not have written the last checkpoint record until it knew this was true. So, the restart algorithm should start with the penultimate checkpoint record. In the simple checkpointing algorithm of the previous section, all updates before the *last* checkpoint record were in the stable database, so it started with the last checkpoint record, not the penultimate one.

Notice that fuzzy checkpointing is a relatively fast activity. It needs to stop processing momentarily to examine the cache and then writes out dirty pages in parallel with normal operation, when the disk is otherwise idle. It therefore has very little impact on the performance of transactions that are executing and can be run frequently to minimize the amount of work that restart has to do.

The fuzzy checkpoint algorithm is so important to transaction performance and restart speed, it is worth optimizing it heavily. Commercial implementations use many optimizations of the algorithm described here.

Operation Logging

It is very inefficient to write the entire before-image and after-image of a page every time a transaction does an update. Worse yet, it does not work correctly if the database system does record-level locking. For example, suppose records *x* and *y* are on the same page P, and we have the following execution:

$$E = w_1[x]\ w_2[y]\ abort_1\ commit_2.$$

When transaction T_1 aborts, we cannot install its before-image of P, since this would wipe out T_2's update to *y*. This is essentially the same problem we ran into at the beginning of Section 8.2, on locking assumptions, where we argued for holding write locks until after the transaction commits.

A solution is to have each update record include only the before-image and after-image of the record that it actually updates on a page. This kills two birds with one stone. It greatly reduces the amount of logging, and it allows us to support record-level locking. It does have one unfortunate side effect, though. The restart algorithm has to read the page from disk before applying the update. This wasn't needed with page-level logging because the log contained a complete copy of the page. Since logging is a much more frequent operation than restart, this is a net win, but it does create another activity that needs to be optimized by the restart algorithm.

We can reduce the amount of logging even further by only recording a *description* of the change that was made. The description must have enough information that we can undo or redo it, but no more than that. That is, it doesn't necessarily have to include the entire before-image and after-image of the record. So, if the update only modified one field of a record, the update record only needs to contain the before-image and after-image of that field, plus the name of the operation being performed (e.g., "update-field"), so the restart algorithm will know how to interpret the log record later on. As another example, the update record might describe the insertion of a record, in which case it only needs to log the after-image of the record, since there is no before-image.

By reducing the amount of logging this way, we have complicated the restart algorithm. It can no longer simply start at the penultimate checkpoint record and redo update records because the redo operations might not be applicable to the stable database page in its current state. For example, it would be wrong to insert a record on a page if that record is already there because that would put two copies of the record on the page.

The restart algorithm has to know whether an update record is applicable to a page before redoing the update. To do this, each page is given a header that includes the log address of the last log record that was applied to the page (see Figure 8.11). This is called the *log sequence number* (LSN). After an update is performed on the page and the log record is written to the log, the LSN is written to the page header before releasing the latch on the page. This allows the restart algorithm to tell whether a page includes an update before redoing it: If

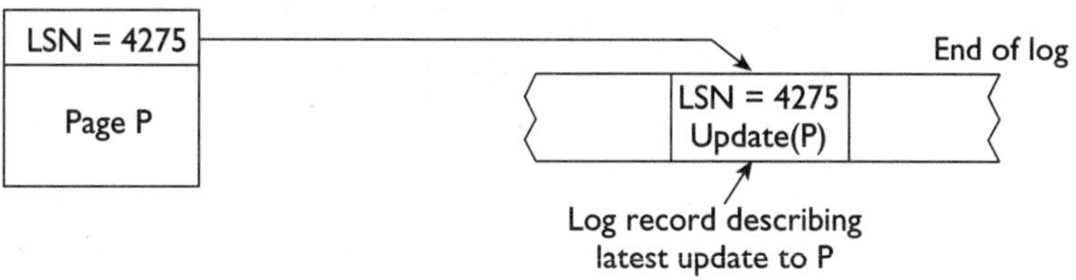

Figure 8.11 **Storing Log Sequence Numbers (LSNs) in Pages** When updating a page, include the LSN of the log record describing the update.

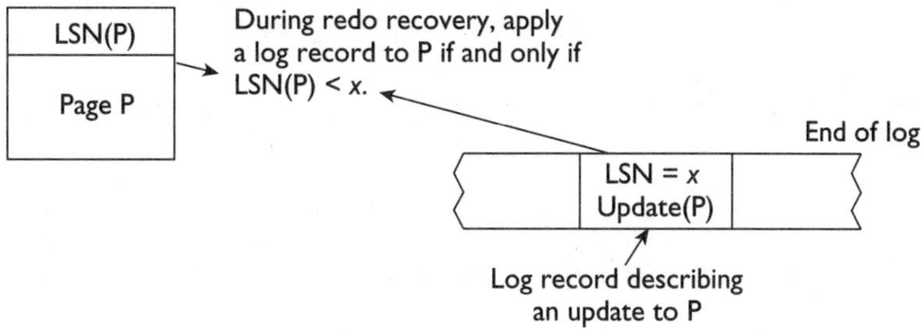

Figure 8.12 **Interpreting LSNs during Recovery** Redo an update if and only if the page's LSN indicates that the update isn't already there.

LSN(database page) ≥ LSN(log record), then the log record's update is already on the page and should not be redone (see Figure 8.12).

This LSN idea is useful, but it complicates undo operations. When the restart algorithm undoes an update to abort a transaction, T_1, there is no LSN that accurately describes the state of the page relative to the log. To visualize the problem, consider the example in Figure 8.13. Transactions T_1 and T_2 update different records R_1 and R_2, respectively, on the same page, P. T_2 writes to P after T_1, and then T_2 commits. When T_1 aborts, what LSN should it write in P? It cannot use the LSN of the previous update to P (219), since that would say that T_2's update did not execute, which is wrong. It cannot use the LSN of T_2's update either (221), since that says T_1's update was done but not undone.

A good solution to this problem is to log undo operations. That is, when T_1 aborts, each time it undoes an update operation, say, on page P, it writes a log record that describes that undo and it uses the LSN of that log record in P's page header. This is called an *undo record* or *compensation log record*. Now the LSN of the undo record accurately describes the state of the page relative to the log (see Figure 8.14).

Logging undo operations has an interesting side effect: Committed and aborted transactions look exactly the same in the log. They both have a sequence of update operations followed by an operation that says the transaction is done (committed or aborted). The restart algorithm processes both

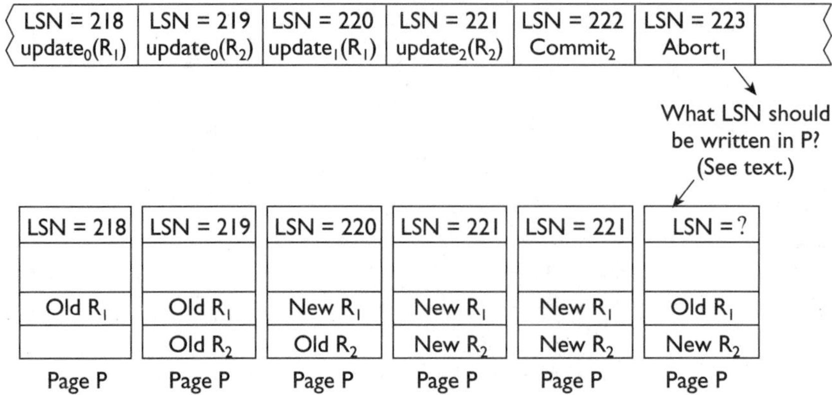

Figure 8.13 Installing an LSN during Undo The state of page P is shown after each log record is added. When aborting T_1, there is no LSN to store in P that accurately describes P's state.

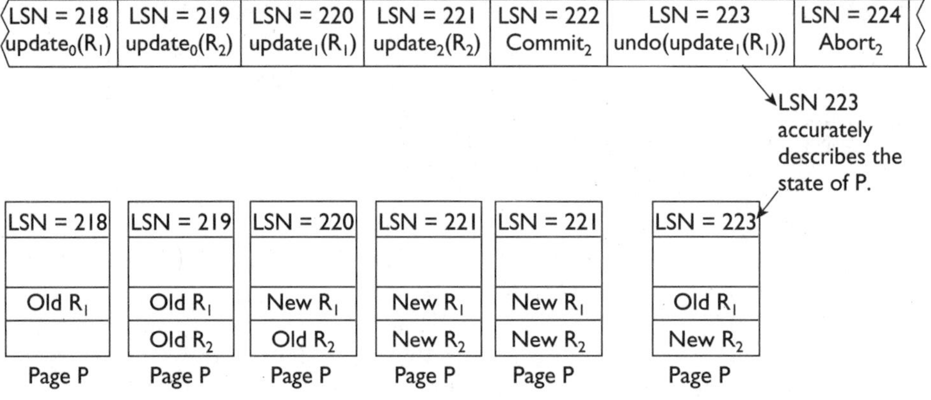

Figure 8.14 Using an Undo Log Record If the undo operation is logged, its LSN can be installed on page P to record the fact that the update was undone.

kinds of transactions in the same way: namely, it redoes their updates. The only transactions that the restart algorithm actually has to abort by scanning the log backwards are those that were active at the time of the failure.

There are many other optimizations that have been proposed for speeding up recovery and for reducing synchronization between recoverable operations to improve transaction concurrency. There are also many other tricky problems that arise in implementing recovery algorithms, such as redundantly storing pointers to the checkpoint record (so you can find it even if there is a media failure), finding the end of the log (it's too expensive to update a disk-resident pointer to end-of-log every time the log is updated), handling multipage update records (what if only one of the pages is written before a failure?), and so on. These details are of interest mainly to people building recovery algorithms and are therefore beyond the scope of this book. See the Bibliographic Notes for further readings.

User Techniques

Although most optimizations are only available to database system implementers, there are a few things that a user can do to speed up restart and thereby improve availability, such as the following:

- If the checkpointing frequency can be adjusted by the system administrator, then increasing it will reduce the amount of work needed at restart. Running a benchmark with different checkpointing frequencies will help determine the expense of using frequent checkpoints to improve recovery time. Depending on the overhead of the checkpointing algorithm used, this might require buying extra hardware to ensure satisfactory transaction performance while checkpointing is being done.
- Partition the database across more disks. The restart algorithm is often I/O-bound. Although it reads the log sequentially (which is fast), it accesses the database randomly. Spreading the database over more disks increases the effective disk bandwidth and can reduce restart time.
- Increase the system resources available to the restart program. After the operating system recovers from a failure, it runs recovery scripts that include calling the database restart algorithm. It may not allocate main memory resources optimally if left to its own defaults. The restart algorithm benefits from a huge cache to reduce its I/O. If memory allocation can be controlled, tuning it can help reduce restart time.

In general, you should benchmark the performance of restart to determine its sensitivity to a variety of conditions and thereby be able to tune it to balance restart running time against checkpointing overhead.

8.6 Media Failures

A media failure is the loss of a portion of stable storage. This is usually detected when an attempt is made to read a portion of the stable database, and the disk responds with an error condition. The solution is similar to recovering from a system failure. We load a usable state of the stable database from some backup device, such as tape, and then use the log to bring that state up-to-date.

Shadowed Disks

Media failures are a fairly serious problem, since as we will see, it can take a significant amount of time to recover from one. To avoid it, most TP systems use *shadowed* (or *mirrored*) *disks*. This means they use two physical disks for each logical disk that they need, so each disk has an up-to-date backup that can substitute for it if it fails. The disk hardware issues each write to both physical disks, so the disks are always identical. If one disk fails, the other disk is still there to continue running until a new disk can be brought in to replace the failed one. This greatly reduces the chances of a media failure.

A related technology is RAID—redundant arrays of inexpensive disks. In RAID, an array of disks is built to function like one high-bandwidth disk (see Figure 8.15). It is high bandwidth because the disks are read and written in parallel. Some RAID systems use extra disks in the array to store error correction bits, so they can tolerate the failure of one of the disks in the array without losing data. If a disk failure is detected, a replacement disk can be plugged in and recovered automatically, similar to the recovery of a failed disk shadow.

Even if it is judged to be uneconomical to use shadowed disks or a RAID for the stable database, one should at least use them for the log. Losing a portion of the log could be a disaster. *Disaster* is a technical term for an unrecoverable failure. There are two ways that a media failure of the log can be unrecoverable:

- After writing an uncommitted update to the stable database, the log may be the only place that has the before-image of that update, which is needed if the transaction aborts. If the tail of the log gets corrupted, it may be impossible to abort the transaction, ever.
- After committing a transaction, some of its after-images may only be in the log and not yet in the stable database. If the tail of the log gets corrupted and the system fails (losing the cache), then the committed after-image is lost forever.

In both cases, manual intervention and guesswork may be needed. Therefore, it's a good idea to put the log on a separate device and shadow it.

After one disk of a shadowed pair fails, another disk must be brought in to replace it. This new disk must be initialized while the good disk is still functioning. Often, this is done in the hardware controller, outside the control of users. The algorithm that accomplishes it usually works as follows: The algorithm scans the good disk and copies tracks, one by one, to the new disk. It has a temporary variable that identifies the track currently being copied. While it is copying that track, no updates are allowed to the track. Updates to tracks that have already been copied are written to both disks, since these tracks are already identical on both disks. Updates to tracks that have not yet been copied are only written to the good disk, since writing them to the new disk would be useless. This copying algorithm can run in the background while the good disk is handling normal processing load and thereby have a negligible impact on the performance of the good disk, as desired.

Even with shadowed disks, there is a chance that both disks will fail before the first failed disk is replaced. When configuring a system, there are some things you can do to reduce this chance. First, you can ensure there is as little shared hardware as possible between two shadowed disks. For example, if the

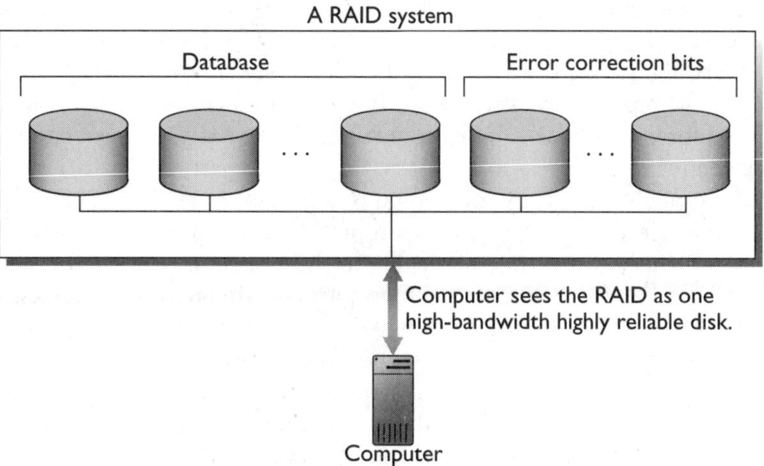

Figure 8.15 **Redundant Array of Inexpensive Disks (RAID)** An array of disks built to function as one high-bandwidth disk. Using extra disks for error correction bits increases reliability.

disks share a single controller, and that controller starts scribbling garbage, both disks will be destroyed. Second, you can keep the disks in separate rooms or buildings, so that physical damage, such as a fire, does not destroy both disks. How far to go down these design paths depends on the cost of downtime to the business if data becomes unavailable for awhile because of a media failure.

There is a general principle here. To protect against media failure requires redundancy. We need two copies of the log to ensure restart can run correctly if one log disk fails. We use shadowed disks or a RAID system that has built-in error correction to avoid requiring media recovery when a database disk fails. If the stable database is not shadowed and a disk fails, or if both shadows fail, then yet another copy of the stable database—an archive copy—is needed in order to run media recovery.

Archiving

Media recovery requires the system to have an archive (i.e., backup) copy of the stable database that it can use as a starting point. It also needs a copy of the log that includes all committed updates that executed after the archive copy was created. The media recovery algorithm can therefore load the latest archive copy and redo the corresponding log.

To create an archive copy, one can simply copy all of the stable database. If this is done when the system is not processing transactions, it will produce a consistent snapshot of the database. If archiving is done on-line—that is, if the system is processing transactions while the archive copy is being made—then different parts of the archive copy will include updates from different transactions. That is, pages copied later will have updates from more transactions than those copied earlier. It seems like this would be hard to sort out when it is time to recover from a media failure. However, essentially the same old restart algorithm that we described for system failures will work here too.

This approach requires that the system keep an archive copy of the log. Therefore, even after a checkpoint has made early parts of the log unnecessary for recovery from system failures, those early parts must still be saved for media recovery. Usually, they are copied to a separate *media recovery log* on tape.

To avoid disk head contention between on-line transactions writing to the end of the log and the media log archiver reading from the beginning of the log, it is worthwhile to have two pairs of shadowed log disks. One pair contains the tail of the log for active transactions. The other contains the early part of the log for archiving to the media recovery log. By the time the active transaction log is out of space, the media log archiver should have finished reading the other pair of log disks. So the latter can immediately be reused for the active transaction log and the media archiver can turn its attention to the other pair of log disks.

Suppose the recovery manager uses the optimization described in the operation logging subsection of Section 8.5, in which it stores on each page the log address of the last update applied to it (i.e., the LSN). This information will be in the archive copy too. So the media recovery manager knows the exact state of the page to recover in the same way as the restart algorithm.

As for system failures, recovery time for media failures affects availability, so checkpointing frequently is desirable for reducing recovery time. Making an archive copy of the entire stable database is slow. One can speed up archiving by only copying pages that have changed since the last time the archiving algorithm ran. A simple way to do this is to keep an *update bit* in each page header that indicates whether the page has been updated since it was last archived. This bit is set every time the page is updated. The archive algorithm clears the bit each time it copies the page to the archive. The archive algorithm still needs to read the entire stable database, to look at all the update bits, but it only needs to copy a fraction of those pages to the archive. We can speed things up even further by keeping the update bits in a separate location, so the archiving algorithm only needs to read pages that were recently updated, not all pages.

To recover from the media failure of a disk, one needs to load the most recent archive copy of the disk and process the log that includes all updates that were done since the archive copy was made. This means the archive algorithm should write a checkpoint record to the log, indicating when it started running, and another checkpoint record when it is done. When it is done, all database updates that preceded the first checkpoint record are definitely in the archive (and some later updates too, but we can't tell which ones by looking at the log). So the latter checkpoint record indicates that only updates occurring after the former checkpoint record need to be considered during media recovery.

A useful optimization to reduce the amount of log needed for media recovery is to avoid keeping undo information in the media recovery log, such as before-images. If the archiving procedure archives pages only when their entire contents is committed, then undo information is not needed at recovery time. Therefore, the archiving procedure should write-lock each page before it copies it to the archive, thereby ensuring there are no active transactions writing to the page at the time it does the copy operation. A postprocessing step on the log can strip out all undo information before setting it aside for future use during media recovery.

It is common that a media failure only corrupts a small portion of a disk, such as a few tracks. Depending on how the media recovery algorithm is organized, it may be necessary to recover the entire disk in this case. A distinguishing feature of database systems is whether they can recover from such failures efficiently. For example, a system could copy the readable portion of the damaged disk to a new one and then restore only the damaged portions from the latest archive copy. Moreover, it could have utilities to postprocess logs to partition them based on regions of the disk, so that the media recovery algorithm only needs to process a log containing records that are relevant to the damaged portion of the disk.

Not all media failures are permanent failures, where the damaged page is physically destroyed. Some failures are transient, where the contents of the page is wrong but it can be repaired simply by rewriting it. For example, a disk may not have written a page atomically (i.e., written out only part of its contents) because the disk arm strayed a bit during the write. In this case, it is worthwhile to reconstruct the page in place rather than replacing the disk or relocating the damaged page.

8.7 Summary

A database system must be able to recover from several kinds of failure. It recovers from a transaction failure (where a transaction aborts) by undoing all of the transaction's updates. It recovers from a system failure (where main memory is lost) or a media failure (where some stable storage is lost) by restoring the database to contain exactly the set of committed updates.

All of today's recovery mechanisms require every transaction to hold its write locks until it commits, to avoid cascading aborts and to ensure that undo can be implemented simply by restoring an update's before-image. For satisfactory performance, locks are usually held at record-level granularity, though recovery can be simplified considerably if page-level locking is used.

The recovery manager uses a cache manager to fetch pages from disk and later flush them. In addition to processing commit and abort operations, it implements a recovery algorithm to recover from system failures. The most popular recovery algorithms use a log, which contains a history of all updates, commits, and aborts.

The recovery manager must carefully control when updates are flushed to ensure the database is always recoverable. In particular, it must enforce two rules:

- The write-ahead log protocol: Do not flush an uncommitted update to the stable database until the log record containing its before-image has been flushed to the log.
- The force-at-commit rule: Do not commit a transaction until the after-images of all of its updated pages are in stable storage (in the log or the stable database).

The recovery manager tells the cache manager about dependencies between dirty database pages and log pages so the cache manager can enforce the write-ahead log protocol. To implement commit, the recovery manager appends a commit record to the log and flushes it. Since all updates are logged, this implements the force-at-commit rule. To implement abort, the recovery manager follows a linked list of the transaction's log records, undoing each update along the way.

To minimize the amount of log to process at recovery time, the recovery manager periodically does a checkpoint, which synchronizes the state of the log with the stable database. To recover from a system failure, it scans the log from the last or penultimate checkpoint record (depending on the checkpointing algorithm) and redoes updates as required. It can tell whether a log record should be redone by comparing the log sequence number (LSN) of the log record with the LSN stored in the corresponding database page, since each database page's LSN is updated whenever the page itself is updated. Using LSNs in this way allows the recovery manager to log operation descriptions, rather than before- and after-images, since it only redoes an operation if the page is in the same state as when the operation originally ran.

Recovery time should be short to maximize availability. Therefore, there are numerous optimizations to reduce checkpoint overhead so it can be done more frequently and thereby reduce recovery time. For the same reason, there are also many optimizations to speed up the recovery algorithm itself.

To cope with media failures, some redundant storage is required. Shadowed disks or RAID systems are commonly used for the database and for the log. Still, to cope with media failures of the stable database, it's important to periodically make an archive copy of the database plus an archive copy of the log that includes all committed updates that executed after creating the archive database copy. The recovery algorithm for media failures loads the archive copy and redoes committed updates in the log, just like the recovery algorithm for system failures. As for system failures, checkpointing should be frequent, and the recovery algorithm should be optimized to run fast to maximize availability.

CHAPTER 9

Two-Phase Commit

9.1 Introduction

The previous chapter showed how to use logging to ensure that a transaction is atomic with respect to failures, provided that the transaction only updates data in one resource manager. If two or more resource managers process updates for a transaction, then another technique is needed to ensure that the transaction commits at all resource managers or at none of them. This is called the *two-phase commit* protocol, briefly introduced in Chapter 1. This chapter will develop it in more detail.

The main goal of the protocol is to ensure that a transaction either commits at all of the resource managers that it accessed or aborts at all of them. The undesirable outcome that the protocol avoids is that the transaction commits at one resource manager and aborts at another.

Two-phase commit arises whenever a transaction is distributed, that is, whenever it accesses resource managers on different computer systems. It also arises if the transaction accesses two different resource managers on the same computer system, provided that the two resource managers can commit or abort transactions independently (as is usually the case).

At first, it may seem that committing at multiple resource managers is no more difficult than committing at one resource manager: Just send a message telling each resource manager to commit or abort. In the absence of failures, this would work. But failures can make it much harder to commit or abort everywhere. For example, what should be done while committing transaction T in each of the following situations?

- A resource manager that processed some of T's updates fails after T has committed at another resource manager.
- A resource manager that failed while T was committing has now recovered and wants to find out whether T committed or aborted. How does it know who to ask? What should it do if none of the other resource managers that processed T's operations are up and running?
- What if a resource manager R is not responding to messages? Should other resource managers assume R is down, and therefore its active transactions will abort, or that communications is down and R is still operational?

A complete solution must deal with these and all other failure situations that can arise.

In this chapter, we return to using the terms "resource manager" and "resource," instead of the terms "data manager" and "data item" that we used in Chapters 6 and 8. When discussing two-phase commit, it is common practice to talk about resource managers, rather than data managers or database systems. The reason is that when a transaction commits, all of the shared resources it accesses need to get involved in the commitment activity, not just databases. Nondatabase resources include recoverable scratch pad areas, queues, and other communications systems.

As in resource manager recovery, application programmers usually do not get involved in two-phase commit. Most database systems and TP monitors support it and make it transparent to the application. However, not all of them do. Some systems make some steps of the protocol visible to the application, and the application programmer needs to know what to do in these cases. Also, when configuring a system consisting of different resource managers, such as different database systems supplied by different vendors, you need to ensure that the two-phase commit implementations of the resource managers interoperate properly. This requires some understanding of how two-phase commit protocols are implemented. Moreover, such multidatabase configurations lead to additional communications overhead for two-phase commit, which can affect transaction performance. For all these reasons, a solid understanding of two-phase commit is needed to build robust TP applications.

9.2 The Two-Phase Commit Protocol

Assumptions

The protocol makes the following assumptions about each transaction T:

1. Transaction T accesses resources from time to time. If it experiences a serious error at any time, such as a deadlock or illegal operation, it issues an abort operation. If it terminates normally without any errors, it issues a commit. In response to the commit, the system runs the two-phase commit protocol.
2. Each resource manager can commit or abort its part of T, that is, permanently install or undo T's operations that involve this resource manager. This essentially says that each resource manager has a transactional recovery system, as described in the previous chapter.
3. One and only one program issues the commit operation on T. That is, one program decides when to start committing T by running the two-phase commit protocol, and no other program will later start running the protocol on T independently. In some cases, a second attempt to run two-phase commit while the first attempt is still running will cause the protocol to break, that is, will cause it to commit at one resource manager and abort at another. The protocol can be programmed to cope with concurrent attempts to run two-phase commit, but we do not investigate this type of error here. We just assume it does not happen.
4. Transaction T has terminated executing at all resource managers before issuing the commit operation. In general, this can be hard to arrange. If the transaction does all of its communications using RPC, then it can ensure T has finished processing at all resource managers by waiting for all of those calls to return, provided that each resource manager finishes all of the work it was asked to do before returning from the call. If T uses other communications paradigms, such as peer-to-peer, then it has to

ensure by some other means that T terminated. For example, the LU6.2 protocol, which was described in Chapter 3, carefully dovetails two-phase commit with the transaction termination protocol. This assumption allows us to avoid dealing with the complexity of transaction termination here.

5. Every system and resource manager fails by stopping. That is, the protocol does not make mistakes when its system or a resource manager malfunctions. It either does exactly what the protocol says it should do, or it stops running. It is possible for a failure to cause the protocol to do something that is inconsistent with its specification, such as sending bogus messages. These are called *Byzantine failures*. There are ways to cope with limited numbers of Byzantine failures, but they are quite expensive in terms of the number of messages exchanged and are not used in current TP systems, so they are not discussed here.

In the remainder of this section, we use the term *coordinator* as the name of the component that runs the two-phase commit protocol on behalf of one transaction. That is, the coordinator is the component that receives the commit or abort request and drives the execution of the protocol.

In our description of the protocol, the resource managers that did work on behalf of the transaction (by reading and updating resources) are called *participants*. The goal is to ensure that the coordinator and all participants commit the transaction, or the coordinator and all participants abort the transaction.

"Coordinator" and "participant" are abstract concepts that don't map exactly to a real component of a TP system. In Section 9.5, we will look at how the system is organized into components, including the transaction manager component that actually runs two-phase commit. We will explore how the transaction manager organizes its work, communicates with resource and transaction managers, and interacts with the communication system itself.

Being Prepared

A participant P is said to be *prepared* if all of transaction T's after-images at P are in stable storage. It is essential that T does not commit at *any* participant until *all* participants are prepared. The reason is the force-at-commit rule, which says not to commit a transaction until the after-images of all of its updates are in stable storage. To see what goes wrong if you break the rule, suppose one participant, P_1, commits T before another participant, P_2, is prepared. If P_2 subsequently fails, before it is prepared and after P_1 commits, then T will not be atomic. T has already committed at P_1, and it cannot commit at P_2 because P_2 may have lost some of T's updates when it failed. On the other hand, if P_2 is prepared *before* P_1 commits, then it is still possible for T to be atomic after P_2 fails. When P_2 recovers, it still has T's updates in stable storage (because it was prepared before it failed). After it recovers and finds out that T committed, it too can finish committing T.

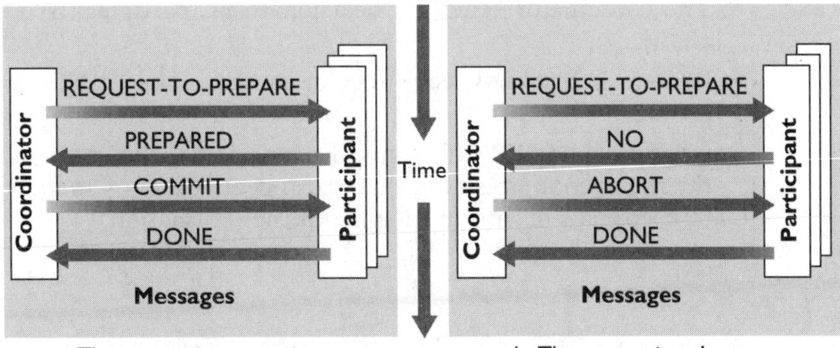

a. The transaction commits.

b. The transaction aborts.

Figure 9.1 **The Two-Phase Commit Protocol** Horizontal arrows indicate messages between the coordinator and participant. Time is moving down the page, so the first message in both cases is REQUEST-TO-PREPARE. The messages that are shown are exchanged between the coordinator and each participant.

Ensuring that all participants are prepared before any of them commits is the essence of two-phase commit. Phase 1 is when all participants become prepared. Phase 2 is when they commit. No participant enters phase 2 until all participants have completed phase 1, that is, until all participants are prepared.

The Protocol

The protocol proceeds as follows (see Figure 9.1):

1. Begin phase 1: To commit the transaction, the coordinator starts by sending a REQUEST-TO-PREPARE message to each participant.
2. The coordinator waits for all participants to "vote" on the request.
3. In response to receiving a REQUEST-TO-PREPARE message, each participant votes by sending a message back to the coordinator, as follows:
   a. It votes PREPARED if it is prepared to commit.
   b. It may vote NO for any reason, usually because it cannot prepare the transaction due to a local failure.
   c. It may delay voting indefinitely, usually because its system is overburdened with other work.
4. Begin phase 2: If the coordinator receives PREPARED messages from *all* participants, it decides to commit. The transaction is now officially committed. Otherwise, it either received a NO message or gave up waiting for some participant, so it decides to abort.

5. The coordinator sends its decision to all participants (i.e., commit or abort).
6. Participants acknowledge receipt of the commit or abort by replying DONE.
7. After receiving DONE from all participants, the coordinator can *forget* the transaction, meaning that it can deallocate any memory it was using to keep track of information about the transaction.

Analysis

Performance

The performance of two-phase commit is measured by counting the number of messages required to commit the transaction. There are four rounds of messages to or from all participants, as can easily be seen in Figure 9.1: REQUEST-TO-PREPARE, PREPARED or NO, COMMIT or ABORT, and DONE.

The transaction is actually committed before all of these messages are sent. After the second round, when the coordinator decides to commit, the transaction is committed and the coordinator can tell the user that this is true. Of course, there is still another round of messages, the commit messages, before the participants find out that the transaction is committed, at which point they can release their locks. The final round of messages, the DONE messages, is not performance sensitive, since this just tells the coordinator that it can clean up whatever control structures it has used for the transaction.

Blocking

Before a participant votes, it can abort unilaterally, any time it wants. Once it sends PREPARED, and until it receives a message containing the coordinator's decision, it is unable to commit or abort. If it did, it might make a decision opposite to the coordinator's, producing an inconsistent result. During this period, it is said to be *uncertain*[1] (see Figure 9.2).

The coordinator is never uncertain because it gets to decide. Until it decides, it can abort whenever it wants. And after it decides, it is obviously not uncertain. So, only participants are uncertain.

Uncertainty is a bad property of two-phase commit. If the coordinator fails while a participant is uncertain, the participant is *blocked*; it can neither commit nor abort. The coordinator could be down for a long time. This is a bad situation for the participant, since it is holding locks on data that the transaction accessed. Since the whole point of two-phase commit is to cope with failures (otherwise, one-phase commit would work fine), it is bad news that when a failure does happen, a participant could become blocked.

---

1 Called "in doubt" in Gray and Reuter (1992).

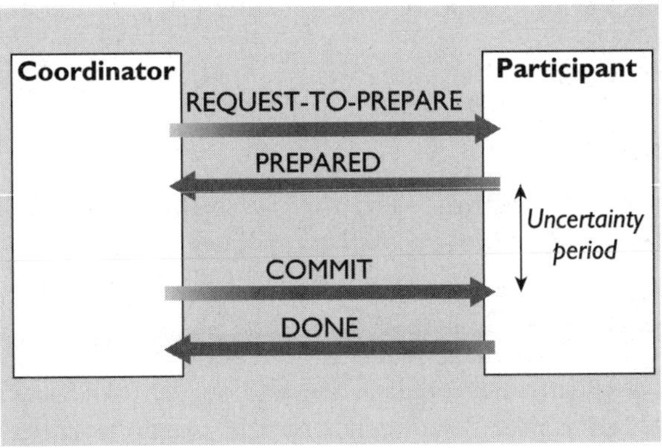

Figure 9.2 **The Uncertainty Period in Two-Phase Commit** From the time a participant replies PREPARED until it receives the decision from the coordinator, it is uncertain.

This leads one to wonder whether two-phase commit is a good protocol after all. Are there other protocols one could adopt that avoid blocking? Unfortunately, the answer is no, as stated in the following theorem:

Theorem 1 For every possible commit protocol (not just two-phase commit), a communications failure can cause a participant to become blocked.

There is a related problem, essentially the recovery time version of blocking. If a *participant* fails while it is uncertain, and subsequently recovers, it is possible that when it recovers the coordinator is down. In this case, it is still uncertain, and therefore cannot completely recover, since it doesn't know whether to commit or abort the transaction. That is, the participant cannot *independently recover*. Like blocking, this too is unavoidable.

Theorem 2 No commit protocol can guarantee independent recovery of failed participants.

We may be unhappy about the blocking problem in two-phase commit, but there is no avoiding it. Any other protocol that atomically commits a transaction that accesses multiple resource managers must have the same problem.

Nevertheless, there have been many attempts at circumventing the above theorems. One technique for handling blocking situations is to make a *heuristic decision*, which is simply to guess the outcome. The guess may be wrong, but at least the transaction can terminate and release locks. Another is to attempt to find out the decision from other participants, called the *cooperative termination protocol,* described in Section 9.4. Yet another technique is three-phase commit, which avoids blocking if the system has no communications failures. This protocol is much more complex than two-phase commit and still leads to blocking if a communications failure occurs (for details, see

Bernstein, Hadzilacos, and Goodman 1987, Section 7.5). Currently, it is not widely used in practice.

9.3 Failure Handling

The purpose of two-phase commit is to cope with the various failures that can arise. To complete the description of the protocol, we need to explain what happens in every possible failure situation.

We assume that all failures of messages and processes are detected by timeout. That is, a caller sets a timer when it sends a message to another process and assumes that a failure has occurred if the timer expires without having received the expected reply. The length of the timer is called the *timeout period*. The timeout period should be long enough to cover cases where the callee or the communications network is a little slow due to a backlog of work. But it should not be too long, since that will mean that failures are not detected promptly, which would be annoying to users. Notice that if a process detects a timeout, it cannot tell whether the process failed or the communications failed. All it knows is that something has gone wrong.

It is very realistic to assume that all failures are detected by timeout. In most distributed systems, messages are exchanged asynchronously (that is, whenever processes have something to say, rather than synchronously at fixed time intervals). So the only information that a process has about other processes is what it learns from messages it receives from them. If a failure occurs, the only hint it gets about the failure is that a message it was expecting has not arrived.

Sometimes the underlying communications system provides failure detection. A process can ask the communications system to establish a session. Later, if one of the processes or systems stops responding to messages, the communications system tells the other process that the session has failed. In this case, the failure was still detected by timeout, but by the underlying communications system rather than by the process itself.

The coordinator or a participant can fail in two ways. Either it stops running (assumption 5 in Section 9.2), or it times out waiting for a message it was expecting. The latter may happen either because the sender fails or because the communications system isn't functioning properly. The symptom is the same in both cases—the receiver does not get the message.

To analyze the failure cases, we walk through the protocol from both the coordinator's and participant's viewpoint and explain what happens in each case where a message was expected but does not arrive. Then we talk about what the coordinator and participant do if they stop running (i.e., fail) and subsequently recover.

The protocol from the coordinator's view is as follows:

1. Send REQUEST-TO-PREPARE messages to all the participants.

   Error handling: None, since it is not expecting any messages in this step.

2. Receive PREPARED messages from all participants, or receive a NO message from at least one participant.

   Error handling: It is waiting for PREPARED or NO messages. If it does not receive all of them within its timeout period, it can simply abort the transaction, just as if one of the participants had voted NO.

3. Depending on the messages received, decide to commit or abort.

   Error handling: None, since it is not expecting any messages in this step.

4. Send COMMIT or ABORT messages to all participants (depending on the decision).

   Error handling: None, since it is not expecting any messages in this step.

5. Receive DONE messages from all participants.

   Error handling: It is waiting for DONE messages. Nothing important depends on when these messages arrive, so it waits indefinitely for them. If its timeout period expires, it can send reminder messages to the participants to resolicit the DONE messages.

6. Forget the transaction.

   Error handling: None, since it is not expecting any messages in this step.

The participant's view of the protocol is as follows:

1. Receive a REQUEST-TO-PREPARE message from the coordinator.

   Error handling: After finishing its work for the transaction, if it does not receive a REQUEST-TO-PREPARE within its timeout period, it can unilaterally abort the transaction. If it later receives a REQUEST-TO-PREPARE from the coordinator, it votes NO (or ignores the message, since a nonvote has the same effect as NO).

2. Prepare the transaction.

   Error handling: None, since it is not expecting any messages in this step.

3. If step 2 succeeds, then send a PREPARED message to the coordinator; otherwise, send NO to the coordinator.

   Error handling: None, since it is not expecting any messages in this step.

4. Receive a decision message, COMMIT or ABORT.

   Error handling: If it does not receive a decision message within its timeout period, it is blocked. It is in its uncertainty period, so there is nothing it can do without risking a mistake.

5. Send a DONE message.

   Error handling: None, since it is not expecting any messages in this step.

If the coordinator or participant fails and subsequently recovers, then at recovery time it can only use information in stable storage to guide its recovery. This is the same assumption we used for recovering from system failures in the previous chapter. So to ensure that recovery is possible, we need to ensure that the coordinator and participant log information that they may need during the recovery activity.

We say that writing a log record is *eager* (sometimes called "forced" or "synchronous") if it must complete before the corresponding message is sent. Otherwise, it is *lazy* (or "asynchronous"). Eager log writes have a bigger performance impact than lazy ones because they must be completed before the protocol can continue, and they therefore add to the transaction's response time.

The coordinator needs to write three log records (see Figure 9.3):

- Before it sends a REQUEST-TO-PREPARE, it should log a start-two-phase-commit record, which includes a list of the participants. This writing is eager—that is, the coordinator must wait until this record is in the stable log before sending a REQUEST-TO-PREPARE to any participant. Otherwise, if it failed after sending the REQUEST-TO-PREPARE and before the log record was stable, it would not know which participants to notify about the decision.
- Before sending a commit decision, it should log a commit record. Indeed, writing the commit record to the log is what actually commits the transaction. This too is eager. Otherwise, if the coordinator failed after sending the COMMIT message and before flushing the commit record to the log, and it subsequently recovered, it would abort the transaction during its recovery procedure, producing an inconsistent outcome (since the participant that received the COMMIT message committed).
- After it receives the DONE messages, it writes a log record, which records the fact that the transaction is finished. This is lazy.

The participant writes two log records (see Figure 9.3):

- When it gets a REQUEST-TO-PREPARE from the coordinator, it writes a prepared record to the log. This is eager—that is, it waits until the prepared record is in the stable log before sending PREPARED to the coordinator. Otherwise, if it failed after sending PREPARED and before flushing the prepared record to the log, and it subsequently recovered, it would abort the transaction during its recovery procedure (since there is no prepared or commit record in the log). But since it sent PREPARED, it gave permission to the coordinator to commit the transaction, which would produce an inconsistent outcome.
- It writes a log record, a commit or abort record, after it receives the decision message. This too is eager, since once it sends DONE, it gives permission to the coordinator to forget the transaction. If it fails after

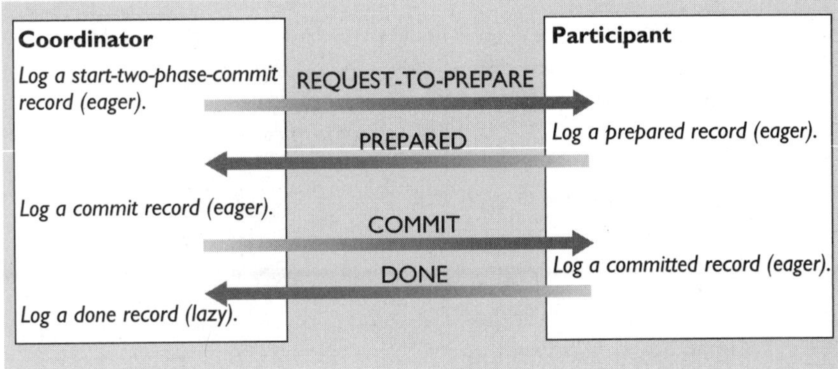

Figure 9.3 Log Operations in Two-Phase Commit (the Commit Case) Each eager log write must be completed before sending the next message, so the process can correctly handle failures that occur after the message is sent (see text).

sending DONE and before the decision message is stable, then at recovery time it might not be able to find out what the decision was. Moreover it holds locks for the transaction until after it commits or aborts, so the sooner it logs the decision, the sooner it can release locks.

We will see ways of turning some of the eager log writes into lazy ones in the next section, on optimizations.

Now that we know what information they log, we can look at how the coordinator and participant recover from failures. First, consider the coordinator. When it recovers it can be in one of four states (see numbered boxes on the left side of Figure 9.4):

1. It has no start-two-phase-commit log record for the transaction. It did not start two-phase commit before the failure. So no participant could have received a REQUEST-TO-PREPARE message and therefore all of them either aborted unilaterally while the coordinator was down, or they will abort on their own later (if the coordinator was down only briefly).
2. It has a start-two-phase-commit record only, so it did not reach a decision before the failure. It aborts the transaction. It is possible that participants are waiting for this decision, so it sends an abort decision message to all of them. Some of them may ignore the message, because they never got a REQUEST-TO-PREPARE message and therefore unilaterally aborted, but there is no harm in sending the abort decision message.
3. It has a commit or abort record in the log, but no done record. Again, it is possible that participants are waiting for this decision, so it sends a decision message to all of them.
4. It has a done record in the log. All participants acknowledged receiving the decision, so there is nothing to do.

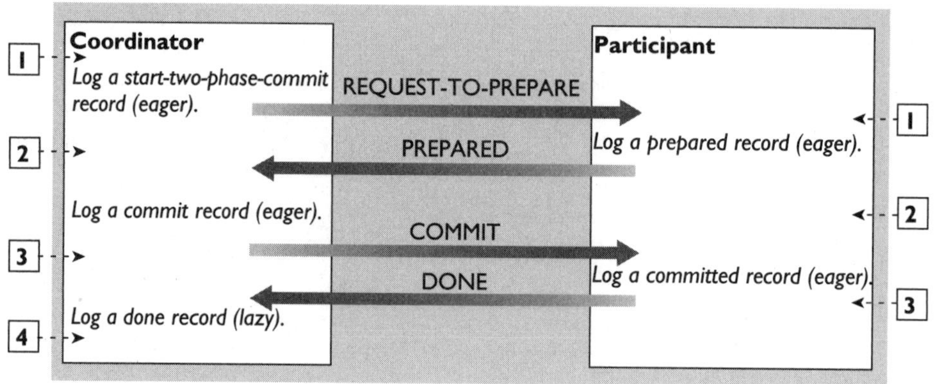

Figure 9.4 Possible States from which a Coordinator or Participant Must Recover See text for a description of recovery actions for the state labelled by each numbered box.

Now, consider a participant. When it recovers it can be in one of three states (see numbered boxes on the right side of Figure 9.4):

1. It did not log a prepared record. The transaction could not have committed, so the participant unilaterally aborts the transaction.
2. It logged a prepared record but did not log a committed or aborted record. This is the bad case, where the participant is blocked. It should run a *termination protocol,* which will be explained in a moment.
3. It logged the decision, commit or abort. It can either send another DONE message, or it can wait until the coordinator sends it a reminder message, reminding it of the decision, at which time it sends a DONE message.

A termination protocol is what a participant does to try to resolve a blocked transaction when the participant recovers from a failure. The simplest termination protocol is to wait until it reestablishes communication with the coordinator and to resend its vote. If the coordinator sees a redundant vote message, this must mean that the participant hasn't yet received the decision, so it resends the decision.

If communication cannot be reestablished in an acceptably short time, then a human operator may need to intervene and guess whether the transaction committed or aborted (perhaps making a telephone call to the operator of the other system to find out the decision). The protocol should log this *heuristic decision*, so that when communication between the two systems is reestablished, the systems can detect whether a consistent or inconsistent decision was made. In the latter case, the system can notify an operator that corrective action is needed.

Repairing an inconsistent decision can be difficult. The transaction that incorrectly committed or aborted left some incorrect data in the database. That incorrect data may have been read by later transactions that themselves wrote some data. In this way, the inconsistency may have spread beyond the data that was directly updated by the transaction that terminated inconsistently. Taking corrective action could therefore require some careful analysis of the database and transaction log.

This covers all the failure scenarios—timing out waiting for a message and recovering from a failure. So we now have a complete and correct two-phase commit protocol.

9.4 Optimizations

Many optimizations have been developed for two-phase commit, to save messages and reduce the number of eager log writes. The most obvious is to avoid two-phase commit altogether when there is only one resource manager in a transaction, and run one-phase commit instead. A few other popular optimizations are described below.

Presumed Abort

Ordinarily, the coordinator does an eager write of the start-two-phase-commit log record (see Figure 9.3). By a slight modification of the protocol, the coordinator can avoid logging this record at all—at recovery time, if there is no record of a transaction in the coordinator's log, then the coordinator assumes the transaction must have aborted. This assumption has several implications:

- If a participant asks the coordinator about a transaction, and the coordinator has no information, then the coordinator "presumes" the transaction aborted. (This is more than a presumption; according to this revised protocol, the transaction *must* have aborted.)
- If the transaction aborts, a participant can do a *lazy* log write of an abort decision and need not send DONE to the coordinator.
- If the transaction aborts, the coordinator need not log a done record.

To see why this works, suppose a participant is blocked at recovery time and sends a message to the coordinator (see Figure 9.5). If the transaction aborted, there are two cases to consider: (1) the coordinator has an abort record in the log (it aborted the transaction but failed before sending the ABORT messages), in which case it replies with an abort decision; (2) it has no record at all—it didn't abort the transaction (fully) before the failure—in which case it again replies with an abort decision (the "presumed abort" for the no-information case). If the transaction committed (see Figure 9.6), the

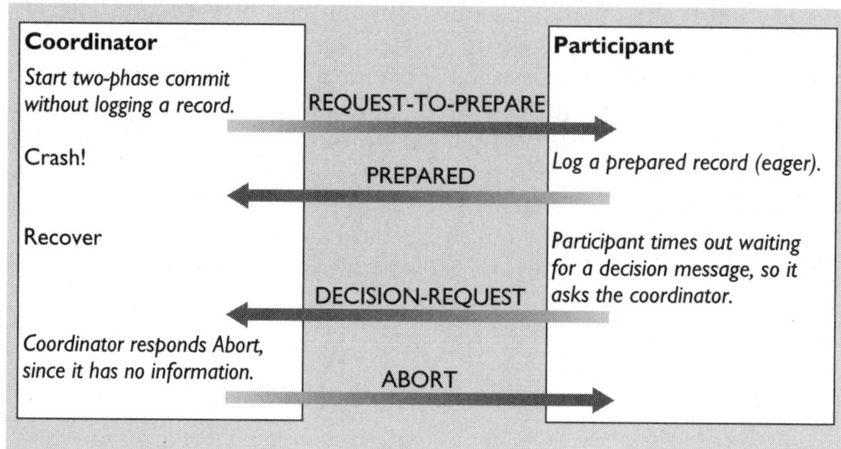

Figure 9.5 **Presumed Abort Optimization (the Abort Case)** The coordinator need not log a start-two-phase-commit record. If it fails before it commits, it has no information about the transaction. In this case, it responds Abort to requests for the decision.

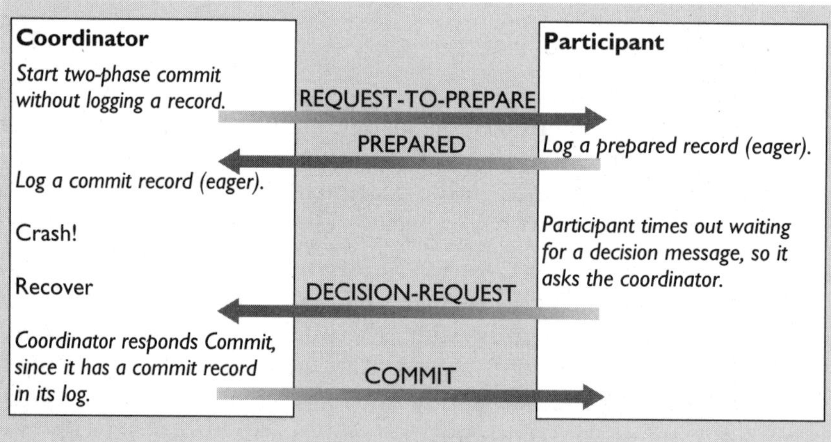

Figure 9.6 **Presumed Abort Optimization (the Commit Case)** The coordinator does not log a start-two-phase-commit record. Since it fails after it commits, it responds Commit to the request for the decision, exactly as if the optimization were not used.

coordinator must have a commit record in the log, since it is still obligated to remember commit decisions until all participants have replied DONE (i.e., the two-phase commit protocol is unchanged for the commit case, except that the coordinator doesn't log a start-two-phase-commit record).

Presumed abort is a popular optimization, used by most implementations of two-phase commit.

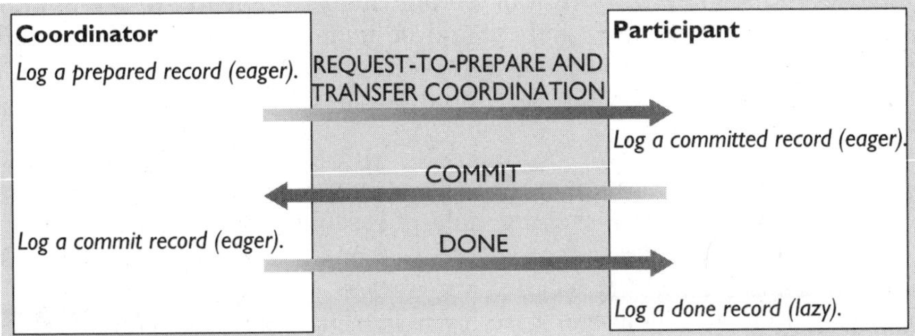

Figure 9.7 Transfer of Coordination Optimization The coordinator prepares and then tells the participant to prepare and commit, and thereby become the coordinator. This saves a message compared to standard two-phase commit.

Transfer of Coordination

If there is only one participant, then two-phase commit can be done with only three rounds of communication, instead of four. The trick is for the coordinator to transfer its "coordinator role" to the participant, which then becomes the coordinator. The optimized protocol works as follows (see Figure 9.7):

- The coordinator prepares and then sends a message to the participant that asks it to prepare *and* to become the coordinator.
- The participant (which is now the coordinator) prepares, commits, and sends a COMMIT message to the former coordinator.
- The coordinator commits and sends DONE to the participant.

Notice that the participant does not need a prepare phase in this case. However, since the participant is now performing the coordinator's role, it must remember the decision until it receives the DONE message from the former coordinator. This covers the case where the COMMIT message is lost, and the former coordinator must later ask the participant what the decision was.

Using this observation, we can run two-phase commit in a system that uses a resource manager that does not support a separate prepare phase and can only commit or abort, as long as there is only one such resource manager in any transaction. To do this, the coordinator goes through the usual first phase of two-phase commit with all participants but the one that doesn't support two-phase commit. After all the other participants have acknowledged that they're prepared, the coordinator prepares and transfers coordination to the resource manager that does not support two-phase commit. When it acknowledges that it committed, the coordinator can finish the job by sending COMMIT messages to the remaining participants.

This can only work with one resource manager that doesn't support the prepare phase. If there were two, then the coordinator would have to tell them both to commit without asking them to prepare. If one committed and the other didn't, the result would be inconsistent—the very situation that two-phase commit is designed to avoid.

Reinfection

If the coordinator starts two-phase commit before all of the participants have fully completed (thereby violating assumption 4 in Section 9.2), then it's possible that a participant will prepare and later be asked to do work for the same transaction. This is called *reinfection*.

This problem can arise if participants want to postpone certain work until after the transaction has completed its regular work, for example, with database triggers that should execute at the end of the transaction. Since the coordinator waits until the transaction completes its normal work before sending REQUEST-TO-PREPARE messages, participant P might use the arrival of a REQUEST-TO-PREPARE message to tell it to execute an end-of-transaction trigger. But the trigger could access data at another participant Q that has already prepared. So Q has to prepare again.

This is bad news. The coordinator may have already received Q's PREPARE. If the coordinator receives P's acknowledgment to its REQUEST-TO-PREPARE before Q prepares again, it could commit before Q is prepared. To avoid this bad outcome, if Q is reinfected by a call from P, it should not reply to P until it has processed P's request *and* has prepared again (see Figure 9.8). That way, when P sends PREPARED to the coordinator, it knows that Q is also prepared (again) and it's safe for the coordinator to commit.

Read-Only Transactions

If a participant only *reads* data on behalf of the transaction, then it does not care what the decision is. Whether the transaction commits or aborts, the participant does the same thing—namely, it releases the transaction's read locks. In fact, it need not wait to find out whether the transaction commits or aborts. It can release read locks as soon as it receives a REQUEST-TO-PREPARE, since that signals that the transaction has terminated, at which point it is safe to release read locks, as far as two-phase locking is concerned. Therefore, in response to a REQUEST-TO-PREPARE, it replies PREPARED-READ-ONLY, which tells the coordinator not to bother sending a decision message (see Figure 9.9).

While this optimization looks very appealing and intuitive, it often cannot be used in practice because some participants may have more work to do after they receive a REQUEST-TO-PREPARE (again violating assumption 4 in Section 9.2). For example, they may need to execute SQL triggers or integrity constraints, which can involve acquiring more locks. We saw this kind of situation in the last section, on reinfection. If a read-only participant releases a lock after receiving a REQUEST-TO-PREPARE, and another participant acquires a lock later on while evaluating a trigger, the transaction has broken the two-phase locking protocol and the result may not be serializable.

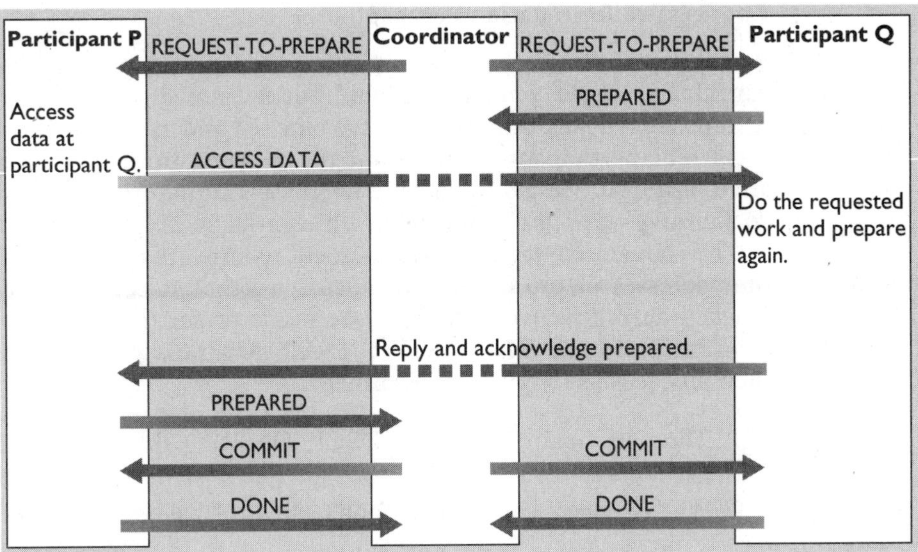

Figure 9.8 **Reinfection** Participant P reinfects participant Q after Q prepared. P waits for Q to prepare again and reply to P before P sends PREPARED to the coordinator, thereby ensuring Q is prepared before the coordinator commits.

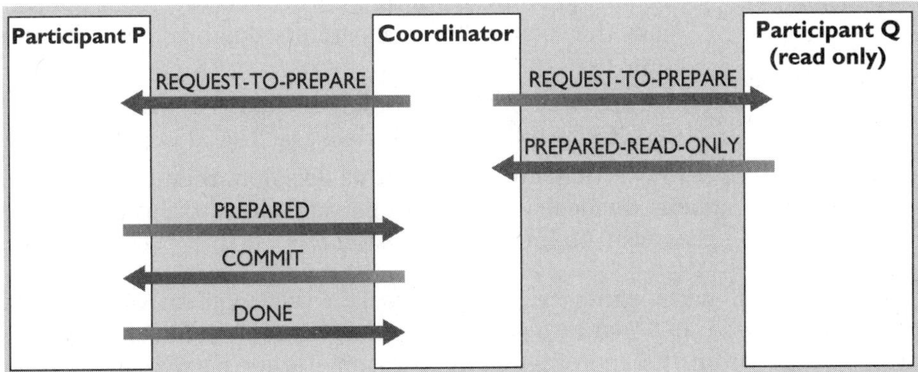

Figure 9.9 **Read-Only Optimization** Since participant Q is read only, it can release locks and finish the transaction when it receives a REQUEST-TO-PREPARE, and the coordinator does not have to send it a COMMIT.

Cooperative Termination Protocol

Recall that the bad case when a participant recovers from a failure is that the participant logged a prepared record but did not log a committed or aborted record. This means the participant is blocked and must run a termination protocol. The participant can find out the decision from the coordinator if it is alive. If not, it can avoid waiting for the coordinator to recover by using the *cooperative termination protocol,* which asks for help from other participants.

The cooperative termination protocol requires that each participant knows the addresses of the other participants, so that it can contact them if it is blocked during recovery. It therefore needs to get this information from the coordinator in the REQUEST-TO-PREPARE message. At recovery time, it then proceeds as follows (see Figure 9.10):

1. The participant P sends a DECISION-REQUEST message to the other participants.
2. When a participant receives a DECISION-REQUEST, it responds as follows:
   a. If it knows what the decision was (i.e., it got a COMMIT or ABORT from the coordinator), then it replies with the decision (COMMIT or ABORT).
   b. If it did not prepare the transaction, it replies ABORT. The transaction could not have committed, since this participant did not acknowledge PREPARED to the coordinator. Since another participant is blocked, there is no point in waiting for the decision from the coordinator, since the coordinator is apparently down or not communicating with some participants.
   c. If it prepared but does not know what the decision was, then it replies UNCERTAIN. This is the bad case that doesn't help participant P.
3. If any participant replies with a decision, then P acts on the decision and sends the decision to every participant that replied UNCERTAIN, since they want to know the decision too.

If participants are allowed to run the cooperative termination protocol, then it may not be a good idea to forget the decision shortly after they receive it from the coordinator because some other participant may later ask for it when it runs the cooperative termination protocol. Since a participant could fail and be down for a long time, there is no bound on how long participants should remember the decision. There are two ways to handle this problem. First, each participant can simply hold on to each decision for some fixed amount of time, such as five minutes, before discarding it. If asked later than that about the decision, it has to reply UNCERTAIN. Second, we could add a fifth round of messages from the coordinator to the participants, after the coordinator receives DONE from all the participants. This final message from the coordinator tells the participants that they can forget the decision, since all other participants know the decision and will not need to run the cooperative termination protocol after a failure.

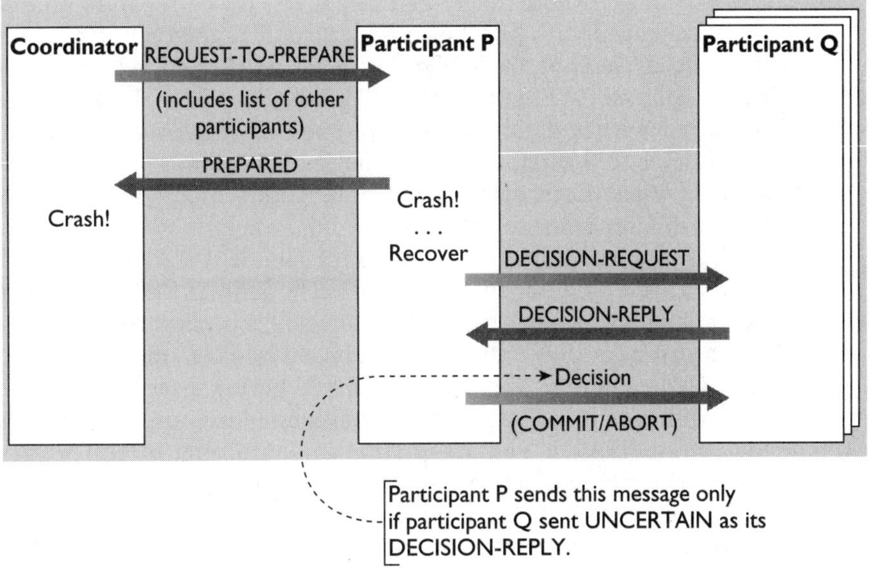

Figure 9.10 Cooperative Termination Protocol When participant P recovers, the coordinator is down. So participant P asks other participants what the decision was (via DECISION-REQUEST). Other participants, such as participant Q, reply with a DECISION-REPLY containing COMMIT, ABORT, or UNCERTAIN. If participant P learns the decision from some participant, then it sends a Decision message to each participant that replied UNCERTAIN in the previous round.

9.5 Process Structuring

Independent Transaction Managers

Now that we have studied two-phase commit from a single transaction's viewpoint, it is time to see how a system can manage two-phase commit on behalf of many transactions and resource managers. The usual approach is to have one module, the *transaction manager*, be responsible for running the two-phase commit protocol, performing *both* the coordinator and participant functions for a group of transactions.

One possibility is to have the transaction manager be part of the database system. This works fine for transactions that access multiple copies of one particular database system. But it generally does not work with other database systems because each database system uses its own two-phase commit protocol, with its own message formats and optimizations. A different approach is needed for transactions to interoperate across different database systems.

The standard solution to this problem is to have the transaction manager be an independent component. It runs two-phase commit for all transactions at its node of the network. To do this, it communicates with resource managers at the same node as the transaction manager and with transaction managers on other nodes.

The transaction manager can be packaged as a separate product but is more often packaged with another product, such as the operating system (as in Digital's OpenVMS) or the TP monitor (as in IBM's CICS, BEA Systems' TUXEDO, Transarc's Encina, and AT&T/NCR's TOP END). It might even be packaged with a database system, such as Microsoft's transaction manager, the Microsoft Distributed Transaction Coordinator (MS DTC), which first shipped with Microsoft SQL Server 6.5, but which will be independent of SQL Server in later releases.

This system model of having an independent transaction manager has been standardized by X/Open, which has also defined the interface between transaction managers and resource managers, so that transaction and resource managers from different vendors can be hooked up (see Figure 9.11). Notice that X/Open defines the transaction bracketing interface (TX or STDL) but not the interfaces to resource managers (which are covered by standards such as SQL and C-ISAM). The application programming interface may also include other operations, which are not shown in the model.

Although the X/Open model is widely supported, many transaction managers offer proprietary interfaces too. For example, the Microsoft DTC architecture follows the X/Open reference model—that is, it has the same types of components (see Figure 9.12). However, it has defined OLE transaction interfaces to substitute for X/Open XA and TX to fit within Microsoft's distributed computing architecture, which is object-oriented and OLE-based, and to support a wider variety of resource types. Microsoft's implementation supports XA too: an XA Mapper component allows resource managers that support the OLE transaction interfaces to work with XA-compliant transaction managers, and an XA transaction manager interface supports any XA-compliant resource manager on Windows NT.

Enlisting in a Transaction

In this architecture, each transaction manager can be the coordinator of a transaction; its participants are local resource managers accessed by the transaction and remote transaction managers at nodes where the transaction ran. Or, a transaction manager can be a participant, being coordinated by transaction managers at other nodes. (As we'll see, a transaction manager can be both, even for the same transaction.) Since each transaction accesses different resource managers at different nodes of the network, the transaction manager must dynamically figure out the coordinator-participant relationships for each transaction. To dynamically manage transactions in this way, each resource manager and transaction manager must *join* or *enlist in* a transaction, when it is first accessed on behalf of a transaction.

When the application calls a local resource manager, R, for the first time on behalf of a transaction T, R calls its local transaction manager with Enlist(T), which "enlists R in T." This tells the transaction manager that R needs to be notified about commit and abort operations later on (see Figure 9.13). When the transaction manager later receives a commit or abort operation for T, it runs two-phase commit with the local resource managers that enlisted in T.

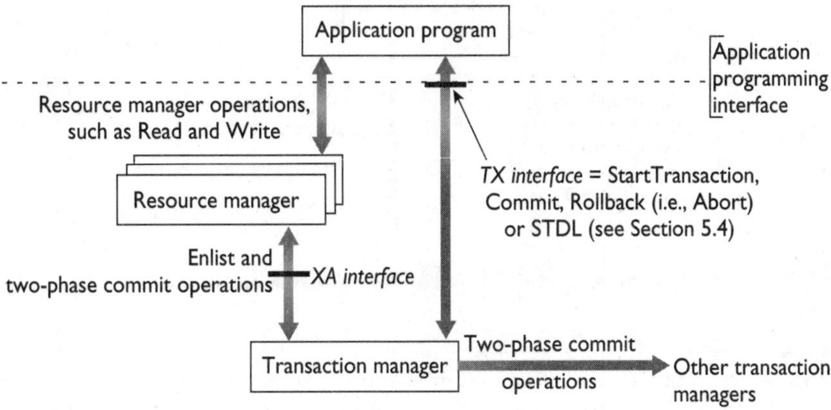

Figure 9.11 X/Open Transaction Model The transaction manager runs two-phase commit for all transactions at its node of the network and communicates with local resource managers and remote transaction managers.

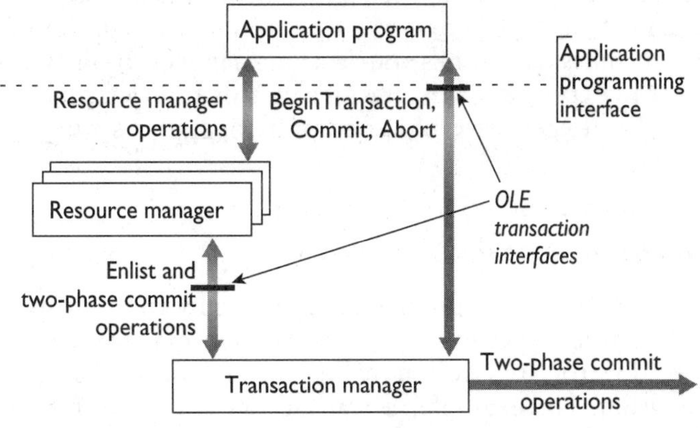

Figure 9.12 Microsoft Distributed Transaction Coordinator Architecture It has the same components as the X/Open transaction model (in Figure 9.11), but defines proprietary interfaces. Microsoft's implementation supports XA too.

Similarly, when the application calls an application or resource manager at a remote node N for the first time, the application's local transaction manager and node N's transaction manager must be notified that the transaction has moved, thereby starting a new *branch* of the transaction at N. This is done by the component that performs remote transactional communications, usually called the *communications manager.* Like the transaction manager, it may be part of the TP monitor, operating system, or resource manager (for remote resource manager calls).

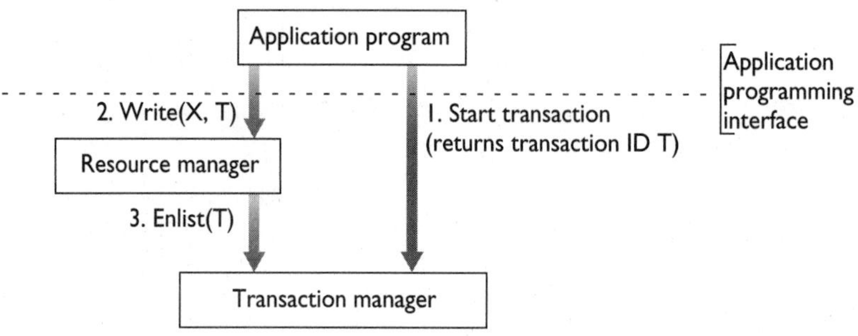

Figure 9.13 **A Resource Manager Enlists for a Transaction** When an application program executing a transaction first accesses a resource manager, the resource manager enlists with its local transaction manager. This tells the transaction manager to notify the resource manager about this transaction's commit or abort operation later on.

For example, in Figure 9.14, application AP_1 running transaction T at node M calls application AP_2 at node N. In addition to sending the message and calling the remote application, the communications manager creates a branch of T at N. This is needed so that M's transaction manager knows to send two-phase commit messages to N's transaction manager. It also tells N's transaction manager to expect Enlist operations on this transaction from N's resource managers and to expect two-phase commit operations from M's transaction manager.

The Tree-of-Processes Model

A transaction can migrate from node to node many times during its execution. This leads to a tree-structured set of transaction managers and resource managers involved in the transaction, called the *tree-of-processes model* of transaction execution. For example, a transaction could migrate as follows (see Figure 9.15):

- It started at node 1 and accessed resource manager RM_1.
- From node 1, it made a remote call to node 2, where it accessed resource managers RM_{2a} and RM_{2b}.
- From node 1, it made a remote call to node 3, where it accessed resource manager RM_3.
- From node 3, it made a remote call to node 4, where it accessed resource manager RM_4.

In the tree-of-processes model, the root transaction manager is the coordinator, and its children are participants. So in Figure 9.15, TM_1 is the overall coordinator, and TM_2, TM_3, and RM_1 are its participants. TM_2 is, in turn, the

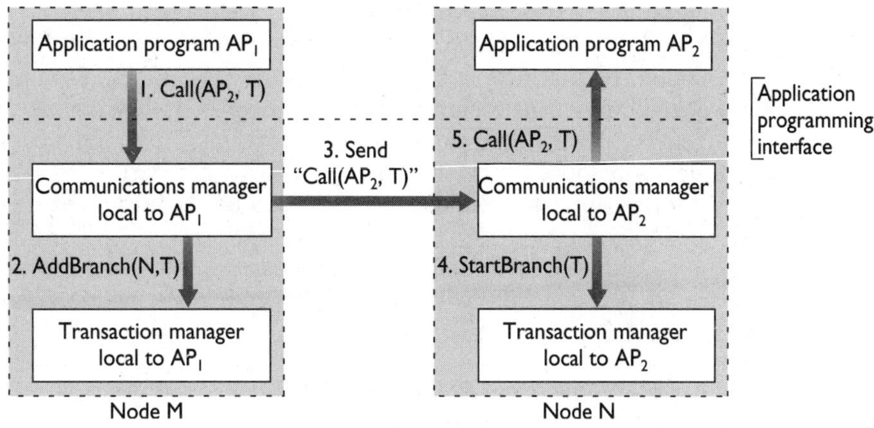

Figure 9.14 **A Remote Call That Starts a Branch Transaction** Application AP_1 calls application AP_2 at a remote node N, thereby creating a branch transaction at N. The communications manager tells the transaction managers at nodes M and N about the new branch by the AddBranch and StartBranch calls, respectively.

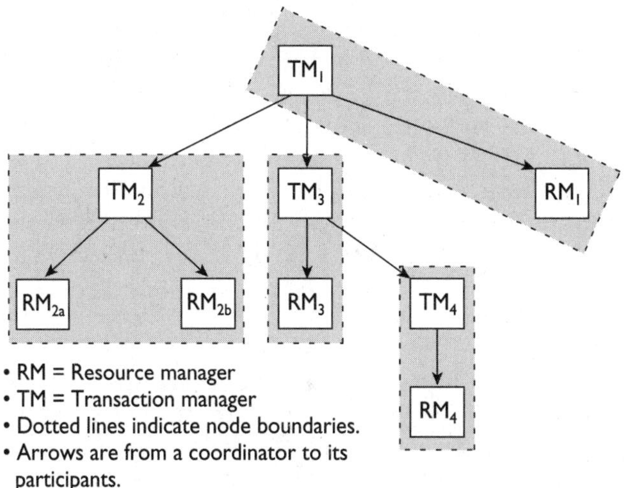

Figure 9.15 **Tree-of-Processes Model** By migrating from node to node and accessing resource managers, a transaction creates a tree of coordinators and participants that will run two-phase commit. A particular execution that leads to this tree is described in the text.

coordinator of RM_{2a} and RM_{2b}, and TM_3 is the coordinator of RM_3 and TM_4. So TM_2 and TM_3 play the role of both participant (with respect to TM_1) and coordinator (with respect to their children). Similarly, TM_4 is a participant (with respect to TM_3) and coordinator (with respect to RM_4).

In Figure 9.15, suppose the transaction executing at node 4 calls an application at node 1. This attempt to execute StartBranch at node 1 returns a warning that the transaction is already executing at node 1. This just means that TM_1 does not become a participant with respect to TM_4. This is not an error, so the call to the application at node 1 succeeds. That application's operations on node 1's resource managers, such as RM_1, are part of the transaction and are committed or aborted whenever TM_1 tells its local resource managers to commit or abort.

When a transaction manager is both a participant and a coordinator, it must prepare its subtree before it replies prepared to a REQUEST-TO-PREPARE message. For example, in Figure 9.15:

- After TM_3 receives REQUEST-TO-PREPARE from TM_1, it should send a REQUEST-TO-PREPARE to RM_3 and TM_4.
- TM_4 then sends a REQUEST-TO-PREPARE to RM_4.
- After RM_4 replies PREPARED, TM_4 can reply PREPARED to TM_3.
- After TM_4 and RM_3 reply PREPARED, TM_3 can reply PREPARED to TM_1.

A tree-of-processes can add delay to two-phase commit because of the daisy chain of communication, such as from TM_1 to TM_3 to TM_4 in the example. This delay can be reduced by flattening the tree, so that all transaction managers communicate with the root coordinator. For example, if TM_1 knew about TM_4, it could communicate with TM_4 directly and in parallel with its communication with TM_2 and TM_3. This short-circuiting of communications is called *flattening* the tree. It can be done by passing around knowledge of new branches back up the tree during normal execution. For example, when the transaction migrates from TM_3 to TM_4, TM_3 could tell TM_1 about the migration, so TM_1 can later communicate with TM_4 directly (see Figure 9.16).

9.6 User Checklist

There are several aspects of a two-phase commit implementation that are of direct interest to users of TP products. The most obvious is whether a given product supports two-phase commit at all. Today, most popular database systems and TP monitors support it. However, not all combinations of database systems and TP monitors work correctly together; that is, they don't all *interoperate*. Even if a database system supports the X/Open interfaces, there is still the question of whether it has been tested with a given TP monitor and whether it exploits any proprietary optimizations that a given transaction manager offers. Such optimizations can have a big effect on transaction performance.

Each transaction manager vendor generally uses their own two-phase commit protocol. For example, IBM systems running CICS use the two-phase commit protocol in SNA LU6.2, Digital Equipment Corporation systems running VMS use the DECdtm protocol, and those running BEA Systems' TUXEDO use TUXEDO's protocol. In a system that uses transaction managers from different vendors, a transaction might need to access applications or

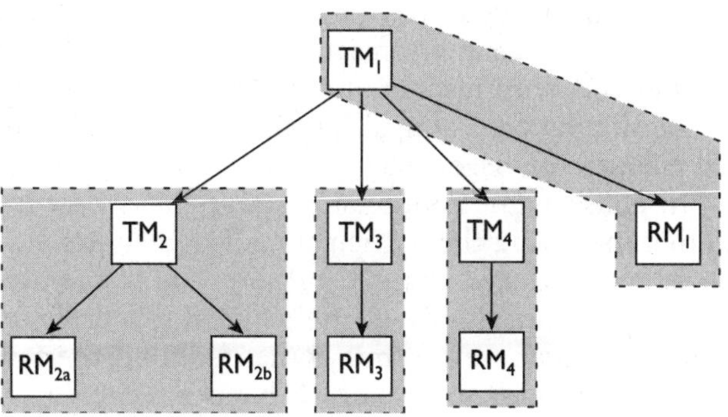

Figure 9.16 **Flattening the Tree-of-Processes** If TM_3 tells TM_1 about TM_4, then TM_1 can communicate with TM_4 directly. This flattens the tree of Figure 9.15, thereby reducing communication delay from TM_1 to TM_4.

resource managers that use these different transaction managers. To get all-or-nothing behavior, the transaction managers need to interoperate. That is, one of the transaction managers must be willing to communicate using the other transaction manager's two-phase commit protocol. A limited number of transaction manager products can do this today, usually using IBM's LU6.2 protocol for interoperability. The international open standard for interoperation is the OSI TP protocol, but it is not much used in practice.

For the most part, two-phase commit is transparent to system operators. However, when a transaction is blocked due to a failure, an operator may need to get involved. Although this event occurs rarely, when there is a failure, there is a good chance that *some* transaction will be blocked. Therefore, support for heuristic decisions is valuable, along with notification of inconsistent decisions when they are made.

Two-phase commit should be transparent to application programmers. If it isn't, then the vendor's implementation is incomplete. However, if a nonstandard or homegrown database system is used in an application, then it is unlikely to be supported by the TP system's built-in two-phase commit implementation. In this case, it is important that the resource manager interface to the transaction manager be exposed. This interface allows the user to integrate the nonstandard resource manager with the transaction manager, so the resource manager's operations can be included in distributed transactions.

9.7 Summary

The two-phase commit protocol ensures that a transaction either commits at all of the resource managers that it accessed or aborts at all of them. It avoids the undesirable outcome that the transaction commits at one resource manager and aborts at another. The protocol is driven by a coordinator that communicates with participants, which together include all of the resource managers accessed by the transaction.

Since failures are unavoidable, the protocol must ensure that if a failure occurs, the transaction can reach a consistent outcome after the failed component recovers. It therefore requires that, during phase 1, every resource manager prepares the transaction by recording all of the transaction's updates on stable storage. After all resource managers have acknowledged to the coordinator that they "prepared" in phase 1, the coordinator starts phase 2 by committing the transaction and then notifying the participants of this commit decision. If any participant fails to acknowledge phase 1, or votes "no," then the coordinator aborts the transaction and notifies the participants of this decision.

The complexity of two-phase commit comes from all the failure scenarios that can arise. The most annoying failure happens after a participant has acknowledged prepared and before it receives the decision, such as a failure of the coordinator or of participant-coordinator communications. This leaves the participant blocked. It can't commit or abort, since the coordinator may have decided the opposite and the participant can't find out the decision. This problem is inherent in any commit protocol when communications failures are possible and is not a special weakness of two-phase commit in particular.

The coordinator and participant must log certain changes in their state, so if either of them fails and subsequently recovers, it can tell what it was doing at the time of failure and take appropriate action. In particular, the coordinator must write a log record before beginning the protocol and before sending its decision, and each participant must log a prepared record before acknowledging prepared. Each participant should log the decision when it finds out what it was. Finally, the coordinator should write a log record when it gets all acknowledgments of its decision, so it knows it can forget the transaction. One then must go through a careful analysis to determine what the coordinator and each participant should do in every possible failure situation that can arise.

There are many optimizations of two-phase commit to reduce the number of log writes and messages. The most popular ones are presumed abort, which avoids requiring that the coordinator write a log record before beginning the protocol and before aborting a transaction, and transfer of coordination, which allows one participant to run one-phase commit by becoming the coordinator and thereby eliminating a round of messages.

Two-phase commit is implemented by the transaction manager component, which communicates with local resource managers and remote transaction managers. It plays the role of coordinator or participant, depending on whether the transaction started at its node or elsewhere. It needs to be notified when a transaction has first accessed a resource manager or moved to another node, so it will know with whom to communicate when it comes time to run two-phase commit. X/Open has standardized the transaction manager's interfaces with resource managers, called XA. This standard is widely supported, but most systems also have more efficient nonstandard interfaces too.

Most transaction managers support a unique proprietary protocol. The protocol that is most widely used to interoperate between transaction managers from different vendors is IBM's LU6.2.

CHAPTER 10

Replication

10.1 Introduction

Goals

Replication is the technique of using multiple copies of a server for better availability and performance. Each copy of the server is called a *replica*.

The main goal of replication is to improve availability, since a service is available even if some of its replicas are not. This helps mission-critical services, such as financial systems or reservation systems, where even a short outage can be very disruptive and expensive. It also helps when communications is not always available, such as a laptop computer that contains a database replica and is only intermittently connected to the network.

Replication can also be used to improve performance by creating copies of databases, such as data warehouses, which are snapshots of TP databases used for decision support. Queries on the data warehouses can be processed without interfering with updates to the primary database server. If applied to the primary server, such queries would degrade performance, as discussed in Section 6.6, on query-update problems in two-phase locking.

In each of these cases, replication can also improve response time. The overall capacity of a set of replicated servers can be much greater than the capacity of a single server. Moreover, replicas can be distributed over a wide area network, ensuring that some replica is near each user, thereby reducing communications delay.

Implementation Challenges

As we discussed in Chapter 7, a server usually depends on a resource, typically a database. One approach is to replicate the server without replicating the resource, so that all copies of the server share the same resource (see Figure 10.1a). This is useful in a configuration where processors share disks, such as in a cluster. If one processor fails, a server on another processor can continue to provide service by accessing the shared resource. This was discussed in Section 7.4 on using backups.

When the resource is a database, this approach improves availability but not performance. Since there is only one copy of the data, queries must be synchronized against updates, so query-update problems arise. Moreover, only one copy of the server can be processing requests at any one time. Other servers are only backups, ready to take over if the active server fails.

The more widely used approach to replication is to replicate the resource (i.e., the database), in addition to the server that manages it, thereby offering the many performance benefits of replication (see Figure 10.1b). The main technical challenge in implementing this approach to replication in a TP environment is in synchronizing updates with queries and each other when these operations execute on different replicas. This approach of replicating resources, and its associated technical challenges, are the main subject of this chapter.

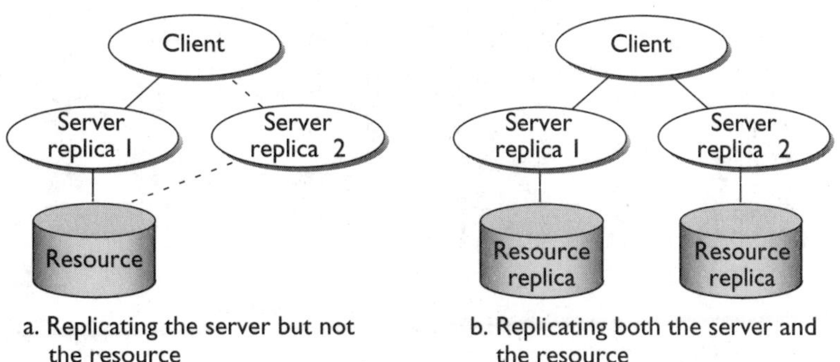

Figure 10.1 **Replicating Servers and Resources** In (a), the server is replicated but not the resource. Replica 2 is a backup that takes over if replica 1 fails. In (b), both the server and resource are replicated. Both server replicas can process requests.

Replicas should behave functionally like nonreplicated servers. Clearly, this would be true if replicas were kept instantaneously identical. One way to get this effect is for each transaction to update all of the replicas of each data item it updates. This is called *synchronous* replication, because all replicas are updated at the same time (see Figure 10.2a). While this is sometimes feasible, it often is not, because it produces a heavy distributed transaction load that can have poor performance.

Fortunately, looser synchronization can be used, which allows replicas to be updated independently. This is called *asynchronous* replication, where a transaction directly updates one replica and the update is propagated to other replicas later on (see Figure 10.2b). Asynchronous updates from different transactions can conflict. If they are applied to replicas in arbitrary orders, then the replicas will not be identical. The usual way to avoid this problem is to ensure that the updates are applied in the same order to all replicas. By executing updates in the same order, all replicas go through the same sequence of states. Thus, each query at any replica sees a state that could have been seen at any other replica. And if new updates were shut off and all in-flight updates were applied to all replicas, the replicas *would* be identical. So as far as each user is concerned, all replicas behave exactly the same way.

Applying updates in the same order to all replicas requires some synchronization. This synchronization can degrade performance because some operations are delayed until other operations have time to complete. Much of the complexity in replication comes from clever synchronization techniques that minimize this performance degradation.

Whether synchronous or asynchronous replication is used, applying updates to all replicas is sometimes impossible because some replicas are down. A possible approach to this problem is for the system to stop accepting updates when this happens, but this defeats the main goal of replication, to increase availability. If some replicas continue processing updates while other replicas are down, then when the down replicas recover, some additional work

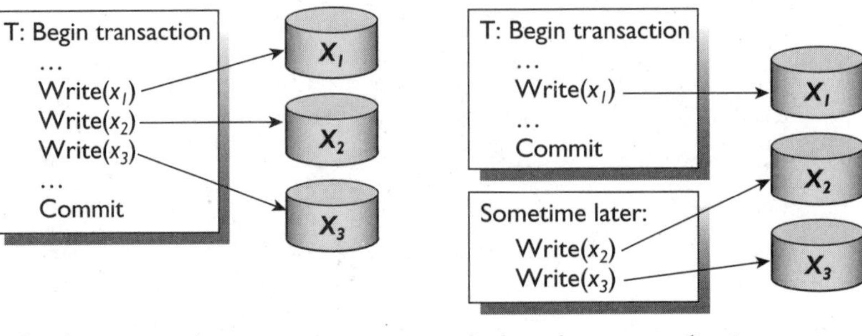

Figure 10.2 Synchronous vs. Asynchronous Replication In synchronous replication, each transaction updates all copies at the same time. In asynchronous replication, a transaction only updates one replica immediately. Its updates are propagated to the other replicas later on.

is needed to recover the failed replicas to a satisfactory state. Some of the complexity in replication comes from ways of coping with unavailable servers and handling their recovery.

Replicas can be down either because a system has failed or because communication has failed (see Figure 10.3). The latter is more dangerous because it may lead to two or more independently functioning partitions of the network, each of which allows updates to the replicas it knows about. If a resource has replicas in both partitions, those replicas can be independently updated. When the partitions are reunited, they may discover they have processed incompatible updates. For example, they might both have sold the last item from inventory. There are two solutions to this problem. One is to ensure that if a partition occurs, only one partition is allowed to process updates. The other is to allow multiple partitions to process updates and reconcile the inconsistencies after the partitions are reunited—something that often requires human intervention.

Circumventing these performance and availability problems usually involves compromises. To configure a system with replicated servers, one must understand the behavior of algorithms used for update propagation and synchronization. These algorithms are the main subject of this chapter.

10.2 Single-Master Primary-Copy Replication

Normal Operation

The most straightforward, and often pragmatic, approach to replication is to designate one replica as the primary copy and to allow update transactions to originate only at that replica. This is the primary-backup technique that was sketched in Section 7.4, on using backups for high availability. Updates on the primary are distributed to other replicas, called *secondaries*, in the order in which they executed at the primary, and are applied to secondaries in that order (see Figure 10.4). Thus, all replicas process the same stream of updates in

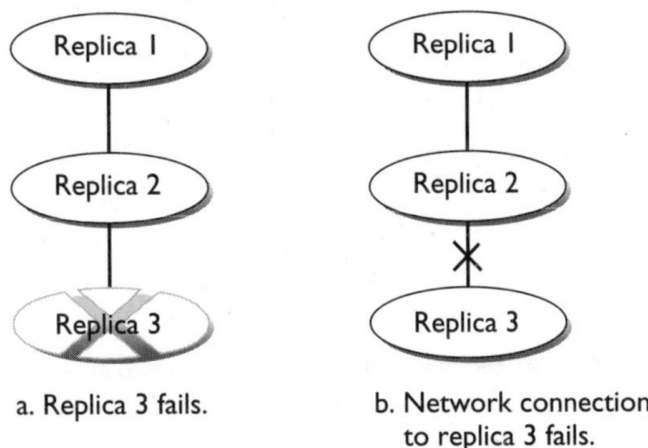

Figure 10.3 **Node and Communications Failures** Replicas 1–3 are connected by a network. In (a), replica 3 fails. In (b), the connection to replica 3 fails. Replicas 1 and 2 cannot distinguish between these two situations, yet the system's behavior is quite different.

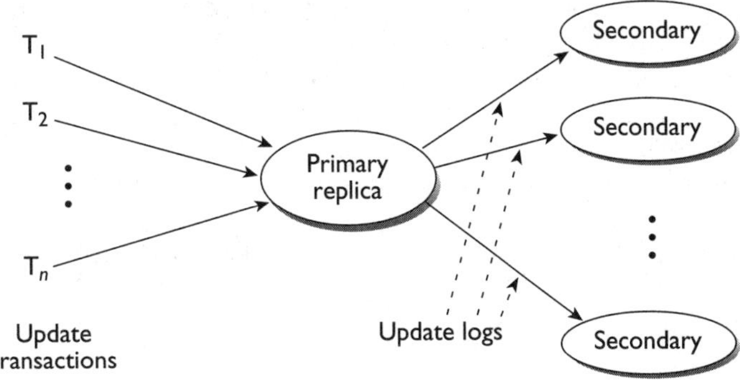

Figure 10.4 **Propagating Updates from Primary to Secondaries** Transactions only update data at the primary replica. The primary propagates updates to the secondary replicas. The secondaries can process local queries.

the same order. In between any two update transactions, a replica can process a local query.

Synchronous vs. Asynchronous Update Propagation

One way to propagate updates is by synchronous replication. For example, in a relational database system, one could define an SQL trigger on the primary table that remotely updates secondary copies of the table. This implies that updates are propagated right away, which may delay the completion of the transaction. It also means administrators cannot control when updates are applied to replicas. For example, in some decision support systems, it is desirable to apply updates at fixed times, so the database remains unchanged when certain analysis work is in progress.

Currently, the more popular approach is asynchronous replication, where updates to the primary generate a stream of updates to the secondaries, which is processed after transactions on the primary commit. For database systems, the stream of updates is often a log. The log reflects the exact order of the updates that were performed at the primary, so the updates can be applied directly to each secondary as they arrive.

Managing the Log

The log can be quite large, so it is worth minimizing its size. One technique is to filter out aborted transactions, since they do not need to be applied to replicas (see Figure 10.5a). This reduces the amount of data transmission and the cost of processing updates at the replica. However, it requires that the primary not send a log record until it knows that the transaction that wrote the record has committed. This introduces additional processing time at the primary and delay in updating the secondary, which are the main costs of reducing the data transmission. Another technique is to send only the finest granularity data that has changed, such as fields of records, rather than coarser-grain units of data, such as entire records.

Rather than using the database system's log, some relational database systems capture updates to each primary table in a log table that is colocated with the primary table (see Figure 10.5b). The system defines an SQL trigger on each primary table that translates each update into an insert on the log table. Periodically, the primary creates a new log table to capture updates and sends the previous log table to each secondary where it is applied to the replica. This approach to capturing updates can slow down normal processing of transactions, due to the extra work introduced by the trigger. If the database log is used instead, then creating the stream of updates to the replicas can be done as part of the normal processing of transactions.

The replication services of most database systems work in this way—by constructing a log stream or log table of updates and sending it to secondary servers. This approach was introduced in Tandem's Non-Stop SQL and in Digital's VAX Data Distributor in the 1980s. Similar approaches are now offered by IBM, Informix, Microsoft (SQL Server), Oracle, and Sybase. Within this general approach, products vary in the specific features they offer: the granularity of data that can be replicated (a database, a table, a portion of a table); the flexibility of selecting primaries and secondaries (can a server be a primary server for some data and a secondary for others); how dynamically the configuration of primaries and secondaries can be changed; and facilities to simplify managing a large set of replicas.

System Management

Most database systems offer considerable flexibility in configuring replication. Subsets of tables can be independently replicated, possibly at different locations. For example, a central office's Accounts table can be split by branch, and the accounts for each branch are replicated at the system at that branch.

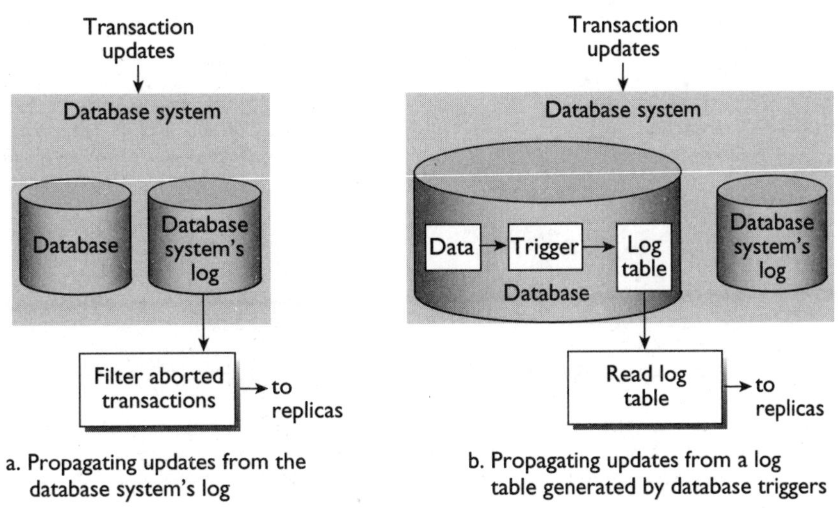

Figure 10.5 Generating Update Streams for Replicas An update stream for replicas can be produced from (a) the database system's log or (b) a log table produced by triggers.

As the number of replicated tables grows, it can be rather daunting to keep track of which pieces of which tables are replicated at which systems. To simplify management tasks, systems offer tools for displaying, querying, and editing the configuration of replicas.

Replicating Requests

An alternative to propagating updates is to send the *requests* to run the original transactions to all secondaries and ensure that the transactions execute in the same order at all secondaries and the primary (see Figure 10.6). Depending on the approach selected, this is either slow or tricky. A slow approach is to run the requests serially at each secondary, in the same order they ran at the primary. This ensures they run in the same order at all replicas, but it allows no concurrency at each replica and would therefore be an inefficient use of each replica's resources.

The trickier approach is to allow concurrency within each replica and use some fancy synchronization across replicas to ensure that timing differences at the different replicas don't lead to different execution orders at different replicas. For example, in Digital's Reliable Transaction Router (RTR), a replicated request executes at two or more replicas concurrently, as a single distributed transaction. Since it runs as a transaction, it is serialized with respect to other replicated requests (which also run as transactions). It therefore can execute concurrently with other requests. Transaction synchronization (e.g., locking) ensures that the requests are processed in the same order at all replicas. As usual, transaction termination is synchronized using two-phase commit. However, unlike ordinary two-phase commit, if one of the replicas fails while a transaction is being committed, the other continues running and

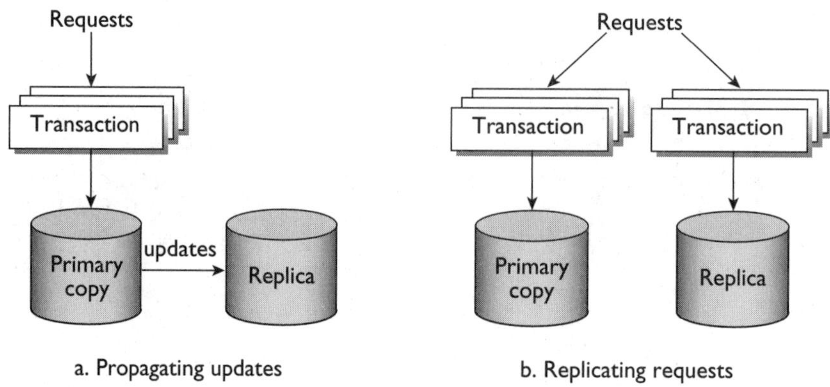

Figure 10.6 **Propagating Updates vs. Replicating Requests** In (a), each transaction executes once and its updates are propagated to replicas. In (b), each transaction runs independently against each replica. In both cases, conflicting updates must be applied in the same order against all replicas.

commits the transaction. This is useful in certain applications, such as securities trading (e.g., stock markets), where the legal definition of fairness dictates that transactions must execute in the order they were submitted, so it is undesirable to abort a transaction due to the failure of a replica.

Failures and Recoveries

This primary-copy approach works well as long as the primary and secondaries are alive. How do we handle failures? Let us work through the cases, assuming there is no communications failure that has led to independently functioning partitions.

Secondary Recovery

If a secondary replica fails, the rest of the system continues to run as before. When the replica recovers, it needs to catch up processing the log of updates from the primary. This is not much different than the processing it would have done if it had not failed; it's just processing the updates later. The main new problem is that it must determine what updates it processed before it failed, so it doesn't incorrectly reapply them. This is the same problem as log-based database recovery that we described in Chapter 8.

If a replica is down for too long, it may be more efficient to get a whole new copy of the database than process an update log. In this case, while it is copying the database, more log is generated at the primary, so to finish up, the secondary replica needs to process that last bit of log coming from the primary. This is similar to media recovery, as in Chapter 8.

Primary Recovery

If the primary fails, recovery is more challenging. First, to keep the system running, some secondary must take over as primary. All replicas must agree

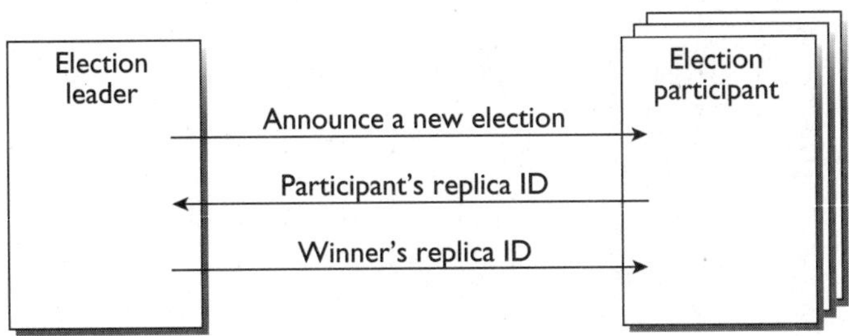

Figure 10.7 Election Protocol The election leader selects the replica with maximum replica ID among those with which it can communicate and tells it to become the new primary.

on this decision, since we cannot tolerate having two primaries—this would lead to total confusion and incorrect results. Second, the last few updates from the failed primary may not have reached all replicas. If a replica starts processing updates from the new primary before it received all updates from the failed primary, it will end up in a different state than other replicas that did receive all of the failed primary's updates.

The algorithm that decides who takes over as primary is called an *election algorithm*. Here is a simple one: Each replica is given a unique *replica identifier*. When a replica detects that the primary has failed, it sends a message to all other replicas announcing a new election. Each available replica replies with its replica identifier. The one with the highest identifier wins. The replica that called the election tells all the replicas who won (see Figure 10.7).

Synchronizing Replicas

Now that there's a new primary, all the replicas must ensure they have processed the same set of updates from the failed primary. One approach is to have the primary not commit a transaction's updates until it knows that all replicas have received those updates. Then, all replicas will have the same set of updates from the primary at the time the primary failed. Now we're back to synchronous replication, which involves running two-phase commit with all replicas. The performance degradation from this can be substantial. Two-phase commit is normally acceptable, in part, because most transactions are not distributed. If most of them are distributed, as is the case when data is replicated, the delay introduced by the protocol can be unacceptable. Moreover, the primary can fail during a transaction's uncertainty period, in which case the system is blocked and a heuristic decision must be made. An incorrect heuristic decision will cause some replicas to differ from the failed primary, but the whole point of running two-phase commit in the first place was to avoid such differences.

Therefore, most systems don't run two-phase commit with the replicas. (RTR, mentioned in the previous section, is an exception.) To avoid losing some of the updates, during the election algorithm each replica can report the log address of the last log record it received from the primary. So every replica

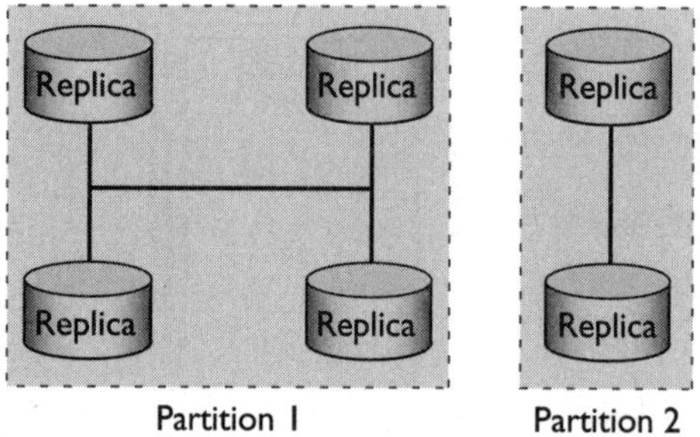

Figure 10.8 Majority Consensus Partition 1 has a majority of the replicas and is therefore allowed to process updates. Partition 2 may not process updates.

can become as up-to-date as the latest update received by any of them. It is still possible that the primary failed after committing an update transaction and before forwarding its results to any replica, thereby losing the update. This is the price of avoiding distributed two-phase commit.

Even without distributed two-phase commit, the cost of reconfiguring after a failure or recovery can be significant. An election must be held, replicas need to determine if they have the latest updates from the primary from before the reconfiguration, and communications sessions may need to be reestablished between nodes that were formerly not communicating. If failures and recoveries are too frequent, the system may end up spending much of its time recovering from these changes, thereby slowing down the processing of new requests.

Majority and Quorum Consensus

An apparent failure of a primary or secondary could be the result of a communications failure that partitions the network into independently functioning replicas. As explained in the first section, one approach is to allow only one partition to process updates.

To ensure this, we must ensure that only one primary can exist. One simple approach is to statically declare one replica to be the primary. If the network partitions, the partition that has the primary is the one that can process updates. This is a feasible approach, but it does have a major problem—namely, that no partition can process updates when the primary is down. Each partition has to assume the worst, which is that the primary is really running but not communicating with this partition.

A more flexible algorithm for determining which partition can have the primary is *majority consensus*: a set of replicas is allowed to have a primary if and only if the set includes a majority of the replicas (see Figure 10.8). Since a majority is more than half, only one set of replicas can have a majority. This is the critical property of majorities that makes the technique work.

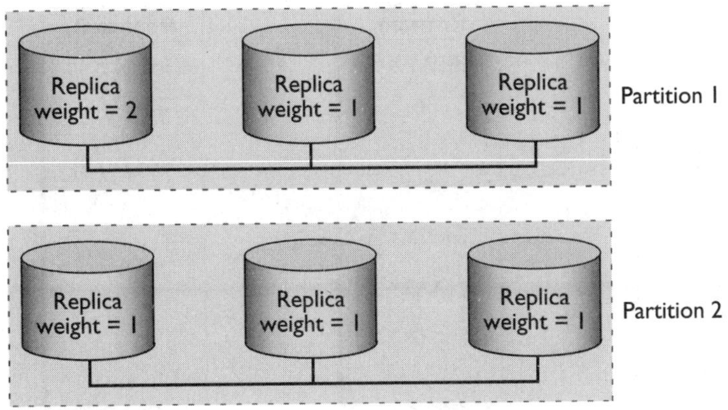

Figure 10.9 Quorum Consensus Since partition 1 has a total weight of 4, which is more than half of the total weight of 7, it therefore constitutes a quorum and is allowed to process updates.

A set of communicating replicas must determine whether or not they have a majority whenever a replica fails or recovers. Even if a set of communicating replicas includes a working primary, it still must check for a majority after it detects a replica failure, in case it no longer has a majority of the replicas. A set of replicas that does not have a majority must periodically check for recovered replicas because a recovery might give it enough replicas to have a majority, thereby giving it permission to elect a primary.

Majority consensus does have one annoying problem: it does not work well when there is an even number of copies. In particular, it is useless when there are just two replicas, since the only majority of two is two—that is, it can only operate when both replicas are available. When there are four replicas, a majority needs at least three, so if the network splits into two groups of two copies, neither group can have a primary.

The *quorum consensus* algorithm avoids these problems. It gives a weight to each replica and looks for a set of replicas with a majority of the weight, called a *quorum* (see Figure 10.9). For example, with two replicas, one could give a weight of two to the more reliable replica and a weight of one to the other. That way, the one with a weight of two can be primary even if the other one is unavailable. Giving a weight of two to the most reliable replica helps whenever there is an even number of replicas. If the network partitions into two groups with the same number of copies, the group with the replica of weight two still has a quorum.

When a replica joins a majority, it must get and process the updates that occurred since it failed before it processes any new updates. This is the same problem that we discussed in the nonpartition case. If a minority of replicas becomes a majority, and it doesn't include the primary from the previous majority, then the replicas must figure out which replica is most up-to-date, for example, by exchanging log addresses of the last update each replica saw.

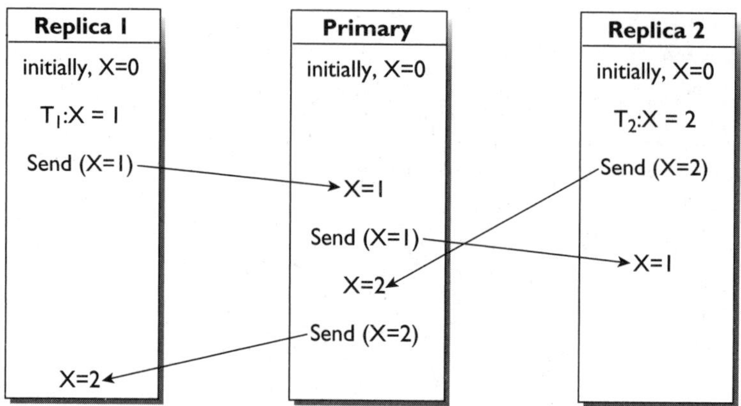

Figure 10.10 **Conflicting Updates Originating at Different Replicas** The updates to X are applied in different orders by replicas 1 and 2, so the resulting replicas are not identical.

All other replicas must apply updates from that most up-to-date replica that they are missing, as if they were joining an existing majority. However, as discussed at the end of the previous subsection on failures and recoveries, some updates may, in fact, be lost unless synchronous replication with two-phase commit is used.

10.3 Multimaster Replication

Partitioned Operation Can Be Useful

Rather than being the result of a communications failure, a partition is sometimes a planned event that happens frequently. For example, a laptop computer may only be connected to the network periodically. It could contain a replica of a database whose primary resides on a reliable server. When the laptop is disconnected, it might still be important that it process updates. For example, the laptop might be used by a salesperson. Its database might have a customer table (rarely updated), an orders table (insert mostly), and a customer log table (append only). Even when the laptop is disconnected from the network, the salesperson must be able to create an order and change basic customer information, such as address and phone number. In this case, it is not satisfactory to require that only the partition with a quorum of replicas be operative. Indeed, if there are many salespeople, there probably is no partition with a quorum of replicas, yet all salespeople need to be allowed to update their replicas.

Update Propagation with Multiple Masters

Despite the partition, we could try using the same primary-copy scheme as in the previous section, but allow there to be multiple primaries. So, suppose all

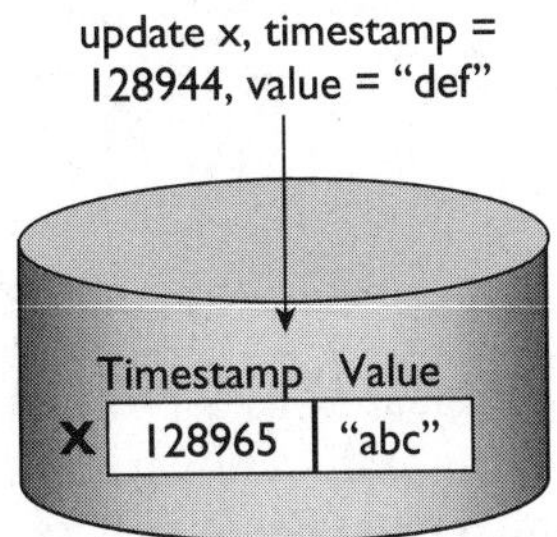

a. The update has a smaller timestamp than the database's timestamp of x, so it should not be applied.

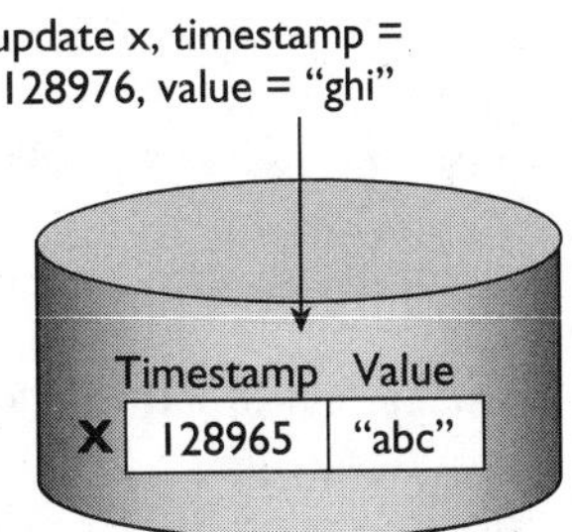

b. The update has a larger timestamp than the database's timestamp of x, so it *should* be applied.

Figure 10.11 Thomas's Write Rule An update to a data item *x* is applied only if its timestamp is larger than the one in the database.

disconnected replicas are allowed to process updates. Each replica logs its updates, as if it were a primary copy. When it reconnects to the network, it sends its log to the real primary that resides on a reliable server, which can process the log and forward it to other replicas. The one that just reconnected can ask the primary for the log of updates that occurred while it was disconnected.

The problem with this scheme is conflicting updates that originate at different replicas (see Figure 10.10). Each of these updates was applied first to the replica where it originated. Later, conflicting updates arrived, via the real primary, from other replicas. So the conflicting updates are applied in different orders by different replicas, and the resulting replicas are not identical.

One way to avoid this problem is to design the applications so that most updates do not conflict. Such updates can be applied in different orders by different replicas and still produce the same final state at all replicas. For example, in the sales database, a salesperson appends a row to the customer log table every time the salesperson interacts with a customer. This row is unique for each such interaction, so two rows generated by different salespeople cannot conflict; they may refer to the same customer, but they describe different interactions. The order table is also insert mostly. Each new order produces a new row in the order table.

Another approach is to tag each update with a unique timestamp. Unique timestamps can be constructed by concatenating the local clock time to a unique replica identifier, so timestamps generated at different replicas cannot be identical. Each data item at a replica is also tagged with a timestamp. Updates are applied using Thomas's Write Rule (Thomas 1979) (see Figure 10.11): If an update to data item *x* arrives at a replica, and the update's timestamp is larger than *x*'s timestamp at the replica, then the update is applied and *x*'s timestamp is replaced by the update's timestamp. Otherwise, the update is discarded, or it may be logged and examined later by a person who determines whether the discarded update needs to be reconsidered or merged into the primary somehow. Eventually, each data item *x* has the same value at all replicas because at every replica the update to *x* with the largest timestamp is the last one to be actually applied.

Multimaster Replication without a Primary

Variations of Thomas's Write Rule have appeared in a number of commercial products. One implementation is the Wingman replication system for relational tables in Microsoft's Access 7.0 and Visual Basic 4.0. Each row of a table has four special columns:

- A globally unique identifier (GUID), which distinguishes it from all other rows of all tables. When a transaction inserts a row, Wingman assigns the row a GUID.
- A generation number, which is used to tell which updates have already been sent to other replicas. Each replica R maintains a current generation number, which it stores in every row that it updates. For every other replica R′, R remembers the current generation number it had when it last exchanged updates with R′. Every time R exchanges updates with any other replica R′, R increments its current generation number.
- A version number, which is a count of the number of updates to this row.[1] The first time each transaction updates a row, it increments the version number.
- An array of [replica, version number] pairs, which identifies the largest version number it received from every other replica that updated the row and propagated that update to this replica.

When two replicas, R and R′, decide to exchange updates, R finds every local row whose generation number indicates that the row was updated since the last time R exchanged updates with R′ and therefore should be propagated to R′. R′ does the same, and then R and R′ exchange updated rows, each of which contains the new value of the row, its version number, and its array of [replica, version number] pairs (we'll explain the pairs in a moment). When R applies one of these updated rows, it compares the version number of the update with the version number of the row in its database. The one with the larger version number wins. If they're equal, an arbitrary but deterministic decision is made (e.g., the one with the larger node ID wins). That is, it uses Thomas's Write Rule, based on version numbers, extended by node ID (for example) to break ties.

The version number comparison produces a consistent result at both replicas, but it still may overwrite an update inappropriately. For example, suppose a row contains inventory information, with a version number of 1 (see Figure 10.12). Suppose R ran two transactions to decrement the row, which therefore

1 This version number is actually derived from the array of [replica, version number] pairs and is not physically stored.

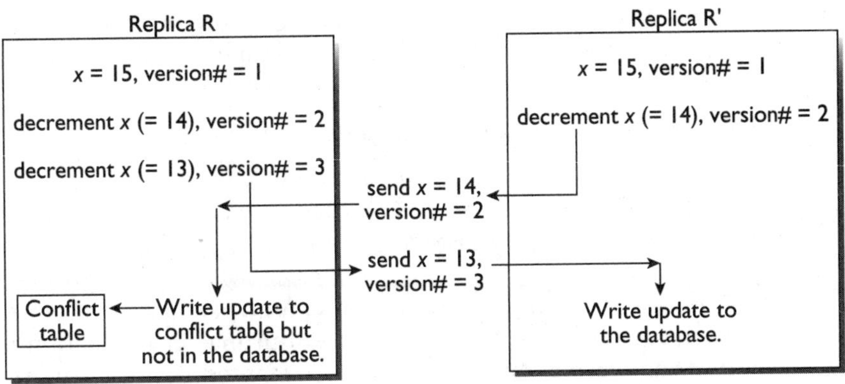

Figure 10.12 Applying Updates in Wingman The decrement operation at R′ is lost because its version number is smaller than the one at R and is therefore saved in R's conflict table.

had a version number of 3, and R′ started with the same initial value for the row and decremented it once, so the row had a version number of 2. R′'s update would be the loser, and its decrement transaction would be lost, which is incorrect. Such situations are inherent when disconnected replicas are allowed to do updates independently. To help reconcile this situation, if R does not apply an update from R′ because the update's version number (or version number plus node ID) was too small, then it saves the update in a *conflict table* that contains discarded updates, so it can later be reconciled by a software tool or human intervention.

Whenever an update is applied to a data item x at replica R, x's array of [replica, version number] pairs is replaced by the update's array, to reflect the latest updates to x that were seen by the replica that sent the update. This helps R to discard duplicate updates later on, which may arise because updates propagate in a daisy chain.

For example, replica R′ can send an update to replica Q, which later sends it to R; later still, R′ may send the same update directly to R. R will discard the update because it has a too-small version number. Moreover, by checking its array of [replica, version number] pairs for x, R can tell that it already saw this update and it therefore isn't worth saving in its conflict table.

Duplicate updates are detected as follows: For a given row, suppose [R′, V] is the entry describing R′ in R's array, and V′ is the version number sent by R′.

- If V ≥ V′, then R already saw R′'s updates.
- If V < V′, then R did not see R′'s updates, so R′'s update is stored in the conflict table and can be reconciled later.

There are many other complicated details like this in a complete implementation, such as database schema changes (which must be applied before updates that depend on them), integrity constraint violations (such as insertions of the same user-defined unique key in different rows at different replicas), and tools to reconcile discarded updates.

Behavior of Multimaster Replication

The reconciliation problem we just saw is inherent in multimaster replication. If conflicting updates are issued by transactions that execute on different replicas, then those updates will need to be reconciled when they arrive at each replica.

The way multimaster replication is used can greatly affect the probability of such conflicts. For example, when multimaster replication is used to support disconnected operation, such as laptops that are intermittently connected to the network, replicas can run for long periods without exchanging updates. The longer a replica executes transactions without exchanging its updates with other replicas, the greater the chance that reconciliation will be needed. That is, if updates are exchanged frequently, then the chances are better that an update will be propagated to all replicas before a transaction with a conflicting update executes, thereby avoiding the need for reconciliation.

Increasing the number of replicas increases the number of updates that need to be propagated because each update must be propagated to all replicas. This is true even if no update transactions originate at the newly added replicas. If each new replica also contributes new update transactions, then the load increases quadratically. That is, combining these two effects, if the number of replicas is n, then as n increases, the update load increases by n^2. In addition to having a direct effect on performance, this increased load can increase the time it takes to process updates, which further increases the chances that reconciliation is needed.

These problems are inherent in multimaster replication where conflicting updates are permitted. Therefore, when conflicting updates are likely, primary-copy approaches generally work better.

10.4 Other Techniques

Replication algorithms have been an active area of database research for over a decade. Many algorithms have been published beyond those described here, which are the ones that are primarily used in today's database systems. Some other interesting approaches include the following:

- Nontransactional replication, based on timestamped updates. That is, each original update executes as an atomic action outside the context of any transaction. These algorithms are often used for distributed system services, such as a directory service, where multimaster replication is needed but transactions are not.
- Quorum consensus applied to every transaction. Each transaction reads a quorum of copies of each data item it accesses and uses the most up-to-

date value among those copies as input. This approach avoids running elections and other reconfiguration algorithms, at the cost of more work for each transaction. It was also one of the first correct replication algorithms published.

- Read-one-write-all-available, where instead of using a primary copy, each transaction writes to all available copies of every data item it updates. One well-known algorithm, called Virtual Partitions, uses this approach along with quorum consensus, to ensure a data item is updatable only if the set of connected sites have a quorum of copies of that item.

Replication is an area where products are evolving rapidly. New approaches are likely to appear. And the performance and application design considerations of using replication will be better understood as the technology is more widely deployed.

See the Bibliographic Notes for further reading.

10.5 Summary

The main goal of replication is to improve availability, because a service is available even when some of its replicas are not. Replication can also improve response time, since the capacity of a set of replicated servers can be greater than the capacity of a single server.

The most widely used approach to replication is to replicate the resource (i.e., the database) in addition to the server that manages it. This requires synchronizing updates with queries and each other when these operations execute on different replicas, so that the effects are indistinguishable from a nonreplicated system. The synchronization mechanism must allow for replicas or communications between replicas to be down for long periods. Communications failures are especially troublesome because noncommunicating replicas may process conflicting updates that they are unable to synchronize until after they reconnect.

One popular approach to replication is to designate one replica as the primary copy and to allow update transactions to originate only at that replica. Updates on the primary are distributed and applied to other replicas, called *secondaries*, in the order in which they executed at the primary. Since all replicas process the same updates in the same order, the replicas converge toward the same state as the primary.

The stream of updates sent from the primary can be quite large, so it is worth minimizing its size by only including data items that are modified and by filtering out aborted transactions. The stream can be generated by processing the resource manager's log or by using triggers to generate the update stream directly from updates on the primary copy.

An alternative to propagating updates is to send the *requests* to run the original transactions to all secondaries and ensure that the transactions execute in the same order at all secondaries and the primary, either by physically running them in that order, which is slow, or by synchronizing their execution between primary and secondaries, which can be tricky.

In any case, when a secondary fails and subsequently recovers, it must catch up processing the updates produced by the primary while it was down. If the primary fails, the remaining secondaries must elect a new primary and ensure it has the most up-to-date view of the updates that executed before the primary failed.

When a primary or secondary fails, the remaining replicas must check that they have a majority or quorum of copies, to ensure that they are the only group of communicating replicas. If there were two partitions of replicas that could communicate within the partition but not between partitions, then the two partitions could process conflicting updates that would be hard to reconcile after the groups were reunited.

Sometimes partitioning is a planned and frequent event, as with laptop computers that contain replicas but are only periodically connected to the network. This requires that every partition be allowed to process updates, allowing for multiple masters, not just one primary. Some variation of Thomas's Write Rule is used for these multimaster situations: each data item is tagged by the timestamp of the latest update to it. An update is applied only if its timestamp is larger than the data item's tag in the database. That way, updates can arrive in different orders, sometimes with long delays, yet the replicas will all eventually have the same value, namely, the ones produced by updates with the largest timestamp. The problem with this approach is that an update can be lost if it's overwritten by another update with a larger timestamp that didn't see the output of the earlier update. There are several schemes for recognizing such occurrences, so they can be manually reconciled later on.

The primary-copy and multimaster algorithms described here are the ones used most widely in practice. However, since replication has been much studied by database researchers, there are many other published algorithms beyond the ones described here.

CHAPTER 11

Conclusion

11.1 Introduction

This book focuses on transaction processing technology that is widely available in today's products. Of course, this technology is not standing still. This chapter highlights a few of the changes we can expect to see in TP products in the next few years:

- Commoditization of the server market, greatly increasing the number of TP systems in the world
- Object-oriented programming, used for transaction programs
- Nested transactions and other advanced transaction models
- The Internet and World Wide Web as an infrastructure for distributed TP

11.2 Commoditization

Servers are becoming a commodity product. They are no longer just large mainframes bought by Fortune 1000 companies. They are also PC servers, bought both by small companies and by departments of large companies. This low-end server market was initially driven by file sharing and electronic mail applications. But, more and more, these servers are being used to run packaged applications. Some of these packaged applications use TP technology, such as order processing, inventory control, accounts receivable, and billing.

There are millions of places of business in the industrialized world. Given the low price of today's servers, and with prices continuing to fall, it is easy to imagine every place of business having at least one server running some TP applications. This will make TP servers a commodity product.

At the same time, today's trend toward downsizing will not diminish. As low-end servers become more capable, they will be used ever more frequently in place of high-end mainframes, especially for new applications that have only modest requirements for compatibility with existing systems. It will therefore continue to be important that low-end TP systems be scalable, so that a large TP system can be configured from a large number of small TP systems, to service the TP needs of large enterprises.

As TP servers become a commodity, they will increasingly run in environments where there is no computer system professional on hand to manage or customize them. Ease of use will therefore be increasingly important. TP technology has a very long way to go in this dimension, as today's TP systems can only be managed or customized by system professionals with special TP expertise.

The increased volume of TP systems is likely to increase the revenue stream for vendors of TP system software, such as database systems and TP monitors, which means increased investment in product development. This investment will be used by vendors to add new product features to compete more effectively. That is, commoditization will not only drive down prices, but it will also increase system capability.

The use of packaged applications for standard business functions will be of growing importance in minimizing overall system cost. Over time, customers will be less interested in which TP monitor is used than in which applications are available. Given the high cost of porting applications between TP monitors, TP monitors with the largest market share will attract more applications than others. This could lead to a consolidation of the TP monitor market, as has happened in other areas of base technology, such as operating systems and relational database systems.

Standard business processes are really not very standard. They vary significantly from one business to the next, so applications that support these business processes must be customizable. This will give an edge to applications that are well integrated with high-level programming tools, which in turn are integrated with TP monitors and database systems.

Customers will want to integrate packaged applications from different vendors into a single TP system. The most promising technology to simplify this kind of application integration is object-oriented programming. We therefore expect to see a growing importance of object-oriented methods for component-based application development in TP systems.

11.3 Object-Oriented Programming

In object-oriented application design, one starts by defining *business objects* that correspond to elementary functions of the business that change slowly, such as customer, account, product, order, and shipment. These objects are invoked by *business rules*, which are actions that the business performs in response to things that happen in the real world. For example, the business rule for placing an order might create a new order object, decrement the inventory for the products ordered, get the shipping address from the customer object, and increase the amount owed on the customer's account. Business rules change more frequently than business objects, in response to changes in the real world, such as changes in customer preferences, size of the business, or business processes.

As we discussed in Section 2.2, this application structure maps nicely onto the three-tier TP monitor architecture: business rules execute in workflow controllers, and objects execute in transaction servers. In this sense, TP monitors are already designed to cope with object-oriented applications. However, there are some new technical issues that need special attention, which we discuss here:

- Specifying composition rules when a program that may or may not run in a transaction calls an object that may or may not run in a transaction
- Optimizing operations on properties that would ordinarily require too many round-trips to the object
- Organizing operations as methods on objects rather than functions in modules

- Mapping objects onto processes and threads
- Negotiating interfaces when new versions of objects are introduced

Specifying Transaction Composition

A key goal of object-oriented programming is software reuse. Since elementary business functions change slowly, the objects that implement them can, in principle, be reused in many settings.

When reusing software, it is important that a module be reusable *without modification*. If even a single line of code needs to be changed, then the module's internals must be studied and changed by some software engineer, internal documentation must be updated, external documentation must be updated and distributed to users, new tests are needed, all tests must be run, and the revised module must be deployed in the operational system. Thus, even trivial changes can carry a high cost.

In object-oriented terminology, the program that implements an object is called a *class*. The operations supported by the class are called *methods*.

Some changes to classes are needed for purely technical reasons, unrelated to the business functionality of the object. Some of these technical reasons are related to transactions. A TP monitor can minimize the need for such changes by offering a way to specify the transaction requirements of a class and then ensuring that those requirements are always met.

To specify the transaction requirements of a class, one must decide when a method and its caller should be executed within a transaction. There are three cases:

1. The method should always execute within the caller's transaction. If the caller is not executing within a transaction, the call should be rejected. For example, if the method is updating two tables in an accounting database and is not bracketing the transaction itself, then it's important that the caller be executing within a transaction to ensure atomicity.
2. The method executes within the caller's transaction, if there is one. Otherwise, it starts its own transaction.
3. The method should never be executed within the caller's transaction. There are two subcases:
   a. The method always starts a new, independent transaction, whether or not the caller is executing within a transaction. For example, it might be recording a security violation that should be permanently installed whether or not the caller commits.
   b. The caller must not be executing within a transaction because this would force the method to run in the caller's transaction, which is not desired. For example, some TP monitors ignore a Start operation issued within a method that is already running within a transaction. So if the caller is running a transaction, the method would not start a new independent transaction, as desired.

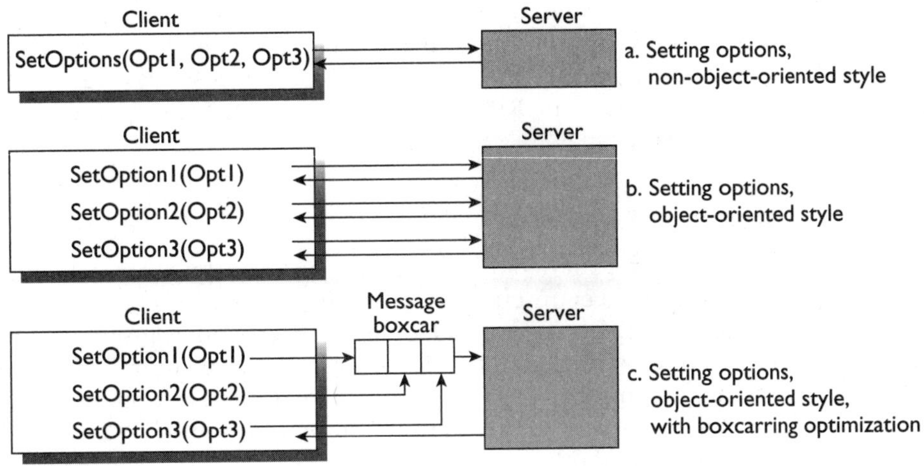

Figure 11.1 **Optimizing Set-Property Method** In an object-oriented style, properties are set one by one, as in (b), rather than in a single call, as in (a). If the SetProperty methods do not return values, then they can be boxcarred in a single message, to save round-trips to the server.

When implementing a reusable class, one should specify exactly which cases apply. This requires some discipline, since the class may initially be used in an application where some cases are irrelevant. For example, in its first deployment, a method may always be invoked by callers that are executing within a transaction, which makes case 2 irrelevant. Nevertheless, one should specify whether case 1 or 2 applies, to ensure the class can be reused later in an application that calls the method from outside a transaction.

Optimizing Property Updates

Another technical effect of object-oriented programming is inefficiency of certain interface styles. For example, it is common practice to use methods to expose public data members (i.e., variables that are accessible to callers of the class), often called *properties*. Each property is accessed using a Get or Set method. This style encapsulates the data member, so the caller can't tell whether the data is stored or computed. This allows a new implementation to be substituted later that computes a property that was formerly stored.

Options that are offered by a class may be exposed as properties. For example, options may specify what currency is used or whether backorders are allowed. A non–object-oriented application might offer a single function SetOptions, which sets all of the application's options (see Figure 11.1a). In an object-oriented application, one sets each property (option) separately, causing many more round-trips to the server that executes the class (as in Figure 11.1b). However, if the TP communications mechanism knows that the calls are just writing a value (and not returning a result, other than a success status), then several calls can be sent together in a single message (as in Figure 11.1c).

(If they did return a result, then they could not be sent together. For example, the second operation might use the result of the first.) This communications optimization, called *boxcarring* (i.e., shipping a set of calls in a boxcar), is not normally offered in RPC systems but may be quite valuable in an object-oriented setting.[1]

Organizing Functions

Object-oriented programs are organized slightly differently than their non–object-oriented counterparts. For the most part the differences are merely syntactic. For example, instead of passing around transaction identifiers, one passes around transaction objects, as in the Microsoft DTC transaction management architecture, where a call to BeginTransaction on a "transaction dispenser" returns a new transaction object, which supports the methods Commit and Abort.

Some differences do affect the mechanism used to solve a problem. For example, after a transaction commits, a non–object-oriented transaction manager deallocates the transaction descriptor, the data structure that it used to keep track of the state of the transaction. If a transaction is an object, then committing the transaction causes the transaction object to be garbage-collected using the garbage collection mechanism supported by the underlying object model, such as explicit reference counting or a mark-and-sweep garbage collection algorithm.

Objects as Units of Computation

In today's TP monitors, the unit of computation is a process or thread. When a program invokes a transaction server, the TP monitor maps that call into an RPC of a program in a process. If the caller needs to retain server context, then it gets a context handle for the called process and reuses it for the next call to that transaction server, usually within the same transaction. Eventually, it releases the context handle.

In an object-oriented system, the unit of computation is an object. To use an object, a caller creates the object, then makes some calls to it, and finally releases it. You could have objects be long-lived and create a process for each object. For example, you could create an Accounts object, which is a transaction server process that executes methods for different accounts (see Figure 11.2a). Different callers execute within different transactions. Since objects and processes are in one-to-one correspondence in this execution model, one of today's TP monitors could support it with little modification.

An alternative execution model is to have objects be short-lived. For example, one could create an Account(12365) object, which executes methods on account 12365 (see Figure 11.2b). This fine-grained object might only exist for

1 The group commit optimization in Section 8.4 is another example of boxcarring. It boxcars many log records in a single log page.

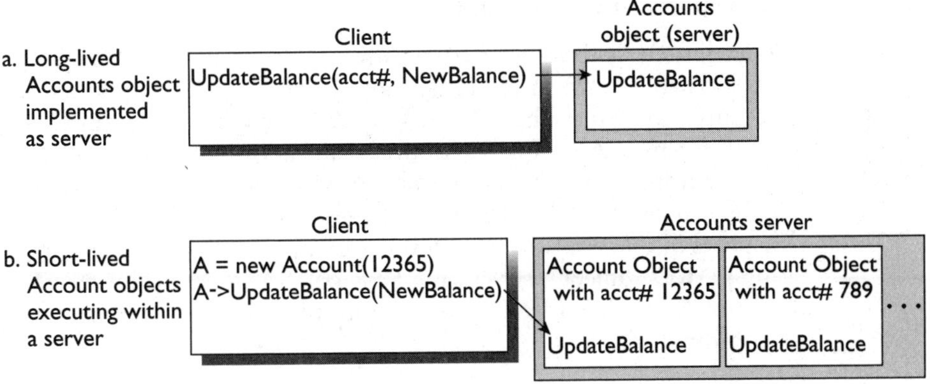

Figure 11.2 **Long- and Short-lived Objects** In (a), an Accounts object is a server supporting all accounts. In (b), each account is an object, which is created as needed.

the duration of the transaction that called it. It runs inside a process along with other Account objects, and it is assigned a thread every time a caller invokes one of its methods. When the transaction commits, it disappears, and all objects that it created should disappear as well.

In this short-lived object model, cleaning up some of these objects may be problematic, since they may have created context that needs cleaning up too. For example, a transaction may have created an object for branch B and called the method Audit-Branch("B"), which audits bank branch B. That object may, in turn, have created a database session. Within the session, it may have created a cursor on the accounts database, scanning accounts in branch B. When the branch B object is no longer needed, it is not enough just to dispose of the object's memory resources. In addition, either the object itself or some other agent has to recognize that the cursor can be dropped and the session reused for another object.

Negotiating Interfaces

To obtain the reuse benefits of object-oriented programming, it's important to be able to replace components with newer versions. Since programs depend on one another, when one component is replaced, other components must be able to cope with the change. And when a reusable component is added to an application environment, it needs to find out whether the right versions of the components that it needs are there.

We explained in Section 5.10 how Microsoft COM solves this problem, by requiring that interfaces be immutable and that all objects have a method that tells whether it supports any given interface. Other object models, such as OMG's CORBA, have been silent on this matter but need to address it if components are to be reusable in those environments.

Distributed Transactional Objects

Distributed objects have their own style of communication. Although the underlying communications mechanism is the same as for non–object-oriented systems, the API and terminology are different. This leads to the need for new APIs for distributed transactions in an object-oriented setting. For example, to start a transaction, instead of calling a Start operation, one calls a *new* operation to create a new transaction object. We described some aspects of distribution transactions in an object-oriented setting in Section 5.4 (on OMG's Object Transaction Service), Section 5.10 (on the Microsoft Transaction Server), and Section 9.5 (on the Microsoft Distributed Transaction Coordinator).

11.4 Nested Transactions

Programming Model

Like most programs, transaction programs are usually modularized. A top-level program consists of several subprograms. Many of these subprograms may be further decomposed. And so on.

For example, reconsider the program in Chapter 3 that pays a credit card bill by debiting a checking account. It has two subprograms: one to pay the credit card account and one to debit the checking account. Each of these subprograms can execute as an independent transaction. Or they can execute together within a larger transaction to pay a credit card bill from a checking account.

Nested transactions is a programming model that captures this program-subprogram structure within the transaction structure itself. In nested transactions, each transaction can have subtransactions. For example, the `Pay_Bill` transaction (which pays a credit card bill from a checking account) can have two subtransactions: `Pay_cc` (which pays a credit card bill) and `Debit_dda` (which debits a checking account).

Like ordinary "flat" (i.e., nonnested) transactions, subtransactions are bracketed by the Start, Commit, and Abort operations. However, these bracketing operations have different semantics than in the flat transaction model. They behave as follows (refer to Figure 11.3 for the examples):

1. If a program is already executing inside a transaction, then Start creates a *subtransaction* of its parent transaction, rather than creating a new, independent transaction. For example, when `Debit_dda` is called by `Pay_Bill`, which is already executing a transaction, the Start operation in `Debit_dda` starts a subtransaction.
2. If a program is not already executing inside a transaction, then Start creates a new, independent transaction, called a *top-level* transaction, which is not a subtransaction of another transaction. For example, if `Pay_Bill` is called from outside any transaction, then `Start` in `Pay_Bill` creates a top-level transaction.

3. The Commit and Abort operations executed by a top-level transaction have their usual semantics. That is, Commit permanently installs the transaction's updates and allows them to be read by other transactions. Abort undoes all of the transaction's updates. For example, the commit and abort operations in `Pay_Bill` have these effects.
4. If a subtransaction S aborts, then all of the operations of the subtransaction are undone. This includes all of the subtransactions of S. However, the abort does not cause the abort of the subtransaction's parent. The parent is simply notified that its child subtransaction aborted. For example, `abort(txn_dda)` in `Debit_dda` aborts the subtransaction.
5. While a subtransaction is executing, data items that it has updated are not visible to other transactions and subtransactions (just like the flat transaction model). For example, if `Pay_Bill` had subtransactions that executed concurrently with `Debit_dda` (which it doesn't), then they would not see `Debit_dda`'s updates until `Debit_dda` committed.
6. If a subtransaction commits, then the data items it has updated are made visible to other subtransactions. In a system that uses locking for concurrency control, this can be done by having the subtransaction's parent *inherit* (i.e., become the owner of) the subtransaction's locks. For example, after `Pay_cc` commits, any data it has updated is visible to `Debit_dda` and `Overdraw_dda`.

Rules 4 and 6 mean that a subtransaction is atomic (i.e., all-or-nothing) relative to other subtransactions of the same parent. Rules 5 and 6 mean that a subtransaction is isolated relative to other transactions and subtransactions. However, a subtransaction is not durable. Its results become permanent only when the top-level transaction that contains it commits.

The nested transaction model fits nicely with object-oriented programming. Each method on an object can be programmed as a transaction, bracketed by Start and Commit or Abort. It can therefore execute as an independent top-level transaction. In addition, the same method can be called from within another top-level transaction, in which case it executes as a subtransaction. For example, `Pay_cc` could be implemented as a method on the CreditCard class. It could be called as an independent top-level transaction or as a subtransaction of the method `Pay_Bill`.

Implementation

An implementation of nested transactions requires resource managers to implement functions beyond those of the flat transaction model. For example, each resource manager needs to implement

1. subtransaction abort, to undo updates of a given subtransaction
2. subtransaction commit, which allows the subtransaction's updated data items to be visible to and updatable by other subtransactions of the same parent

```
boolean Pay_Bill(dda_acct# int, cc_acct# int)
{ long int cc_amount;
  TRANSACTION_ID txn_pb;
  Boolean ok;
  txn_pb = start;
  cc_amount = Pay_cc(cc_acct#);
  ok = Debit_dda(dda_acct#, cc_amount);
  if (!ok)
  {if (customer has overdraft protection)
     { Overdraw_dda(dda_acct#, cc_amount);
       commit(txn_pb);
       return(TRUE);
     }
   else abort(txn_pb);
  };
  return(ok);
};

real Pay_cc(acct# int)
{ start; . . .; commit; };

boolean Debit_dda(acct# int, amount long int)
{TRANS_ID txn_dda;
 txn_dda = start;
 . . . // Subtract amount from Balance(acct#)
 if (Balance(acct#) < 0)
 { abort(txn_dda);
   return(FALSE);
 };
 commit(txn_dda);
 return(TRUE);
};

void Overdraw_dda(acct# int, amount real)
{start; . . .; commit;};
```

Figure 11.3 Nested Transaction Program `Pay_Bill` executes a top-level transaction. It calls `Pay_cc`, `Debit_dda`, and `Overdraw_dda`, which execute subtransactions.

3. start subtransaction, so it knows which updates are relevant to a subsequent subtransaction commit or abort

In addition, each operation on a data item must include the identifier of the subtransaction (not just the top-level transaction) that issued it.

If a nested transaction is a sequential program, then these resource manager functions can be implemented using the savepoint mechanism that was discussed in Section 2.4, as follows:

- When a subtransaction first accesses a resource manager, issue a savepoint operation.

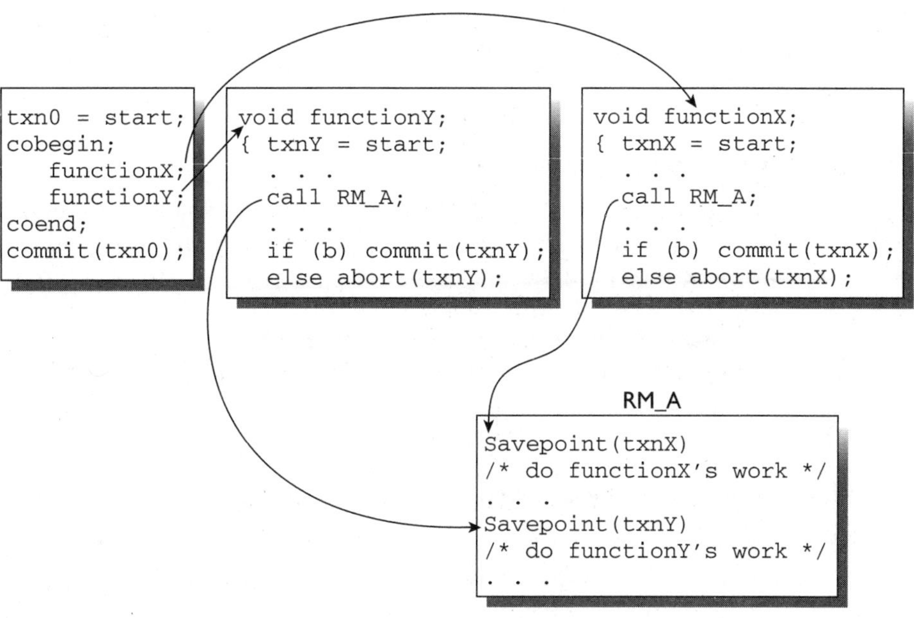

Figure 11.4 Savepoints Aren't Enough for Concurrent Subtransactions If `txnY` commits and `txnX` aborts, there is no savepoint in `RM_A` that produces the right state.

- When aborting a subtransaction, restore the savepoint that the subtransaction previously established at each resource manager that the subtransaction accessed.
- To commit a subtransaction, no special action is required by the resource managers. However, future accesses to resource managers are now done on behalf of the subtransaction's parent.

This implementation only works if the transaction program is sequential. If it has internal concurrency, then it can have concurrently executing subtransactions, each of which can independently commit or abort. Since a savepoint applies to the state of the top-level transaction, there will not always be a savepoint state that can selectively undo only those updates of one of the concurrently executing subtransactions. For example, in Figure 11.4, `txnX` issued its savepoint at `RM_A` before `txnY`. Therefore, if `txnX` commits and `txnY` aborts, then restoring `txnY`'s savepoint in `RM_A` produces the right state; that is, it includes `txnX`'s results but not `txnY`'s. However, if `txnY` commits and `txnX` aborts, then there is no savepoint that produces the right state.

Nested transactions are currently offered by Transarc in the Encina TP monitor, along with some resource managers that support nested transactions. They are also supported by some object-oriented database systems. However, none of the popular relational database systems support nested transactions. Neither do any of the interoperability standards for distributed transactions, such as X/Open XA. Therefore, while nested transactions are a desirable model that would enhance TP environments, the widespread availability of an interoperable solution that spans popular database products is not around the corner.

Other Exotic Transaction Models

The research literature abounds with novel transaction models. Most of them are motivated by workflow and design applications, where long-running activities need to be structured into semiindependent atomic steps. Many of them are related to queuing, such as the saga model described in Section 4.6, since the steps could be modeled as independent transactions within a multitransaction request. None of them are widely available in TP products, at least not yet.

11.5 The Internet and the World Wide Web

As we discussed in Section 2.8, the architecture of clients (browsers) and servers (web servers) in the World Wide Web is quickly evolving to resemble that of TP monitors. That is, URLs are effectively requests, which are processed by long-lived servers that access back-end databases.

In the forthcoming development of the WWW, we are likely to relive the evolution of TP monitors, from the early nonscalable solutions of the early 1970s to the large-scale TP systems that are supported today by airlines, financial institutions, telecommunications companies, and the like. For example, reviewing the sorts of problems we encountered in this book, we can expect the following problems to be addressed:

- The http protocol is connectionless, so all shared state must be sent by the client to the server on every call, such as authenticated client identity and request state (for multistep requests, such as pseudoconversations). Sessions are needed for secure efficient communication.
- The http protocol does not guarantee message delivery, so a persistent queued messaging service would be valuable for requests that have significant value, such as financial transactions.
- URLs are fixed addresses. If a server fails, a backup server must support the same URL to start receiving the traffic that was addressed to the failed server. If a server becomes overloaded, its workload must be spread across multiple servers. Dynamic parameter-based routing using a directory service is one way to approach this problem.

Whenever one relives a line of development from basic to more advanced technology, there is always the chance of a detour along the way, leading to a different outcome than the last time that line was followed. Today's TP monitor vendors are working hard to ensure that customers arrive at essentially the same TP architecture for WWW support that they have today in large enterprises. It will be interesting to see whether they succeed, or whether new products that are specially tuned to the needs of WWW TP servers steer us down a different path.

11.6 Summary

We discussed four trends in the computing field that are likely to affect the shape of TP technology in the next few years: commoditization of servers, object-oriented programming, nested transactions, and the Internet and World Wide Web.

Commoditization is being fueled by the declining cost of server systems and the growing popularity of packaged applications. The millions of business locations that could use such servers will drive up volume, thereby creating a low-cost high-volume market for TP systems.

This commoditization will have several effects. It will make ease of use more critical, since servers will be managed by less-skilled staff. It will generate higher software revenues, thereby funding increased product development efforts to improve system capabilities. And it will make tools for easy software customization more important, since customization must be low cost for a commodity system.

To keep costs down, application components must be reusable. This is the main goal of object-oriented programming. A TP environment places several new demands on object-oriented components:

- Certain modes of interaction with object-oriented components lead to too much communication traffic, which can be reduced by boxcarring messages.
- Objects must be mapped onto TP monitor processes and threads. This can be done with long-lived objects, such as Accounts, or short-lived objects, such as Account 12365, which lives only during the lifetime of the transaction that called it.
- To be able to replace components with newer versions, objects must be able to tell whether they're communicating with components that meet their interface requirements.
- Each component must identify its transaction requirements, such as whether it requires its caller to be within a transaction and, if not, whether it should start a new transaction if its caller is not in a transaction.

One way to address these transaction requirements is to use nested transactions, where the program-subprogram structure of objects (or other programs) is captured within the transaction structure itself. When a transactional program calls a subprogram, the subprogram starts a subtransaction. The subtransaction can abort, thereby undoing its work, without causing its parent transaction to abort. If the same subprogram is called from a nontransactional program, the subprogram starts a top-level transaction.

The final major trend is the growth of the Internet and World Wide Web as a network for accessing TP systems. To make a TP system available via the Web, a web server can be used as a gateway. This allows web browsers to access the TP system by communicating with the gateway.

As electronic commerce on the World Wide Web becomes a major business, TP systems will be an increasingly important part of the Web's infrastructure, to support scalable and reliable services on shared data.

Glossary of Acronyms

The following are acronyms used in this book. If an acronym is specific to a company or a product, the company or product name is appended.

2PC	two-phase commit
3270	block-mode terminal—IBM
3GL	third-generation language
4GL	fourth-generation language
ACC	ACMS Central Controller
ACID	atomicity, consistency, isolation, durability (properties of a transaction)
ACL	access control list
ACMS	Application Control and Management System—Digital
ACMSxp	Application Control and Managment System cross platform—Digital
AIX	IBM's version of UNIX
ANSI	American National Standards Institute
AP	application program
API	application programming interface
APPC	advanced program to program communications—IBM
ASN.1/BER	Abstract Syntax Notation One/Basic Encoding Rule—OSI
ATM	automated teller machine
ATMI	Application Transaction Manager Interface—TUXEDO
BMS	Basic Mapping Support—CICS
BQ	Batch Queue—TUXEDO
CGI	Common Gateway Interface—National Center for Supercomputing Applications, University of Illinois
CICS	Customer Information and Control System—IBM
C-ISAM	C Indexed Sequential Access Method—X/Open
COM	Component Object Model—Microsoft
CORBA	Common Object Request Broker Architecture—OMG

CPI-C	common programming interface for communications—X/Open
CRM	communications resource manager—X/Open
DBMS	database management system
DCE	Distributed Computing Environment—OSF
DCOM	Distributed Component Object Model—Microsoft
dda	demand deposit account
DES	Data Entry System—TUXEDO
DL/I	Data Language 1—IMS
DPL	Distributed Program Link—CICS
DRDA	Distributed Relational Database Access—IBM
DSOM	Distributed System Object Model—IBM
DTC	see MS DTC
DTP	Distributed Transaction Processing—X/Open Model
EBCDIC	Extended Binary Coded Decimal Interchange Code—IBM
ECI	external call interface—CICS
Encina	Enterprise Computing in a New Age—Transarc
EPI	external presentation interface—CICS
ESS	External Subsystem—IMS
FEPI	front-end programming interface—CICS
FML	Field Manipulation Language—TUXEDO
GB	gigabyte
GUI	graphical user interface
GUID	globally unique ID
HP-UX	Hewlett-Packard UNIX
HTML	HyperText Markup Language
http	HyperText Transfer Protocol
ID	identifier
IDL	interface definition language
IETF	Internet Engineering Task Force
IID	interface ID—Microsoft
IMS	Information Management System—IBM
IMS DB/DC	Information Management System Database/Data Communications—IBM
I/O	input/output
ISAM	Indexed Sequential Access Method
ISAPI	Internet Server API—Microsoft

ISC	Intersystem Communication—IBM
ISO	International Standards Organization
KB	kilobyte
LAN	local area network
LSN	log sequence number
LU6.2	Logical Unit 6.2 protocol—IBM
MB	megabyte
MFS	Message Format Service—IMS
MIA	Multivendor Integration Architecture—NTT
MIPS	million instructions per second
MQI	Message Queue Interface—IBM
MRO	Multi-Region Operation—CICS
MSC	Multiple System Coupling—IBM
MS DTC	Microsoft Distributed Transaction Coordinator—Microsoft
MTBF	mean time between failures
MTTR	mean time to repair
NDR	Numerical Data Representation—ISO
NMF	Network Management Forum
NSAPI	Netscape Server API—Netscape
NSK	NonStop Kernel—Tandem
NTT	Nippon Telegraph and Telephone
OLE	Object Linking and Embedding—Microsoft
OMG	Object Management Group
ORB	object request broker—OMG
OS/2	Operating System/2—IBM
OS/400	Operating System/400—IBM
OSF	Open Software Foundation—part of The Open Group
OSI	Open Systems Interconnect—ISO
OSI TP	Open Software Interconnect Transaction Processing—ISO
OSS	Open System Services—Tandem
OTMA	Open Transaction Manager Access—IBM
OTS	Object Transaction Service—OMG
PC	personal computer
PIN	personal identification number
PPC	Peer-to-Peer Communications—Transarc
PTP	Parallel Transaction Processing—Tandem
/Q	TUXEDO/Q, queuing service for TUXEDO

RAID	redundant arrays of inexpensive disks
RDF	Remote Duplicate Data Facility—Tandem
RM	resource manager
RPC	remote procedure call
RQS	Reliable Queue Service—Transarc
RSC	Remote Server Call—Tandem
RSR	Remote Site Recovery—IBM
RTI	Remote Task Invocation—X/Open TxRPC
RTQ	Recoverable Transaction Queuing—TOP END
RTR	Reliable Transaction Router—Digital
SAA	System Application Architecture—IBM
SABRE	Semi-Automated Business Research Environment—AMR Corporation
SCO	Santa Cruz Operations
SDF	Screen Definition Facility—IMS
SFS	Structured File System—Transarc
SMP	symmetric multiprocessor
SNA	System Network Architecture—IBM
SOM	System Object Model—IBM
SPIRIT	Service Providers' Integrated Requirements for Information Technology—NMF
SQL	Structured Query Language—ISO
SSA	segment search argument—IMS
STDL	Structured Transaction Definition Language—X/Open
/T	TUXEDO/T, the TUXEDO TP monitor
TCP	Terminal Control Process—Tandem
TCP/IP	Transmission Control Protocol/Internet Protocol—IETF
TDL	Task Definition Language—ACMS
TDS	Tabular Data Stream—Sybase
TIDL	Transactional IDL—Encina
TM	transaction manager
TMF	Transaction Management Facility—Tandem
TMIB	TUXEDO Management Information Base
TM/MP	Transaction Manager/Massively Parallel—Tandem
TOG	The Open Group, holding company for OSF and X/Open
TP	transaction processing
TPC	Transaction Processing Performance Council

TPC-A,-B,-C,-D	Transaction Processing Performance Council benchmarks -A, -B, -C, -D
tpmC	transactions per minute—TPC-C
tps	transactions per second—TPC-A
TRPC	Transactional Remote Procedure Call—Transarc
TS/MP	Transaction Services/Massively Parallel—Tandem
TX	Transaction Demarcation API—X/Open
TxRPC	Transactional Remote Procedure Call—X/Open
UPS	uninterruptible power source
URL	uniform resource locator
UUID	Universally Unique ID—DCE
VMS	Virtual Management System—Digital
VSAM	Virtual Sequential Access Method—IBM
WAN	wide area network
/WS	TUXEDO/WS, workstation gateway for TUXEDO TP
WWW	World Wide Web
WYSIWYG	what you see is what you get
XA	interface between TM and RM—X/Open
XA+	interface between CRM and TM—X/Open
XATMI	X/Open Application Transaction Manager Interface
XID	X/Open transaction ID
XRF	extended recovery facility—IBM

Bibliographic Notes

The definitive work on TP technology is *Transaction Processing: Concepts and Techniques*, by Jim Gray and Andreas Reuter (1992). Most of the topics in this book are covered there in more detail, often from a product development viewpoint. For the reader who wants to dig deeper into TP technology, this is the place to go.

CHAPTER 1 Introduction

The concepts of transactions and TP monitors appeared in the early 1970s. There is a rich literature on the theory of transactions, starting from the mid-1970s (see Bernstein, Hadzilacos, and Goodman [1987] for references), and on their implementation (first summarized in Gray [1978] and later in Gray and Reuter [1992]). However, very little has been written on TP systems and TP monitors, outside of product literature.

The two-phase commit protocol was first published in Lampson and Sturgis (1976).

TPC benchmark information can be found in Gray (1993), Burgess (1996), Levine et al. (1993), or directly from the Transaction Processing Performance Council in San Jose, CA (http://www.tpc.org).

Much of Section 1.6 on availability is from Gray (1986).

CHAPTER 2 Transaction Processing Monitors

Most of this chapter comes from Bernstein (1990); Bernstein, Emberton, and Trehan (1991); and from innumerable conversations with TP monitor developers over the years. See also Gray and Edwards (1995).

So far, not much has been written about transactions and the WWW. See Yeager and McGrath (1996) for a general treatment of web server technology. The Intergraph TPC benchmark is described in Intergraph (1996).

CHAPTER 3 Transaction Processing Communications

Most of the material on RPC is from Birrell and Nelson (1984), the classic research paper on this topic. Details of the DCE RPC in particular are from Rosenberry and Teague (1993).

The description of APPC and LU6.2 was mostly extracted from IBM documentation (IBM 1991a, 1991b, 1991c) and many helpful discussions with engineers who have implemented the protocol.

CHAPTER 4 Queued Transaction Processing

Most of this chapter evolved from Bernstein, Hsu, and Mann (1990), which in turn was influenced by many sources, such as Gray (1978) and Pausch (1988). Further information on MQSeries can be found in Blakely, Harris, and Lewis (1995); IBM (1995e, 1996c); and Mohan and Dievendorff (1994).

CHAPTER 5 Transaction Processing Monitor Examples

In addition to unpublished material and enormous help from engineers at each company, we used the following material to develop these system summaries:

- CICS (IBM 1995a, 1995b, 1996a; LeBert 1989; Malaika 1994)
- IMS (IBM 1995c, 1995d, 1996b)
- X/Open/MIA/SPIRIT/OMG (Bernstein, Gyllstrom, and Wimberg 1993; Conklin and Newcomer 1995; Network Management Forum 1995; Nippon Telegraph and Telephone 1991; Object Management Group 1995, 1996a, 1996b; Orfali and Harkey 1995; X/Open 1996a, 1996b)
- ACMS (Baafi et al. 1995; Digital Equipment Corp. 1995a-f; Newcomer 1994; Willis 1994)
- TUXEDO (Andrade et al. 1996; Andrade, Carges, and MacBlane 1994; BEA Systems 1996a, 1996b; UNIX International 1992)
- ENCINA (Transarc 1996a-d)
- TOP END (ATT/NCR 1994a-d)
- PATHWAY (Tandem 1994, 1995)
- Microsoft Transaction Server (unpublished material)

CHAPTER 6 Locking

Two-phase locking was introduced in Eswaran et al. (1976). The deadlock discussion is from Chapter 3 of Bernstein, Hadzilacos, and Goodman (1987). The discussion of lock managers is from Gray (1978). The view of locking performance is from Carey and Stonebraker (1984), Gray et al. (1981), Tay (1987), and Thomasian (1996); for further reading, see Shasha (1992). Most of the hot spot methods originated in IMS Fast Path (Gawlick and Kinkade 1985). Degrees of isolation originated in Gray et al. (1976); see Berenson et al. (1995) for an updated presentation. The multiversion technique is mainly from Rdb/VMS, described in Raghavan and Rengarajan (1991).

CHAPTER 7 High Availability

Section 7.2 on causes of failure is from Gray (1986). The explanation of recovery and checkpointing techniques was developed for this book but was much influenced by ideas in the early Tandem products.

CHAPTER 8 Database System Recovery

The model of recovery management is mostly from Bernstein, Hadzilacos, and Goodman (1987), which was in turn much influenced by Gray (1978). To learn more about logging, good places to start are Gray and Reuter (1992); Lomet (1992); Lomet and Tuttle (1995); and Mohan et al. (1992). There are also some interesting recovery algorithms that do not use logging, described in Bernstein, Hadzilacos, and Goodman (1987).

RAID was introduced in Patterson, Gibson, and Katz (1988).

CHAPTER 9 Two-Phase Commit

The two-phase commit protocol was first published in Lampson and Sturgis (1976) and explained further in Gray (1978) and Lampson (1981). This particular description borrows heavily from Chapter 7 of Bernstein, Hadzilacos, and Goodman (1987). The presumed abort optimization is from Mohan, Lindsay, and Obermarck (1986). Three-phase commit is described by Skeen (1982). OSI TP is described in ISO (1992). Digital's VMS-based implementation is described in Laing, Johnson, and Landau (1991). The Microsoft DTC description is from Microsoft (1996).

CHAPTER 10 Replication

The primary-copy approach was first published in Stonebraker (1979). Majority consensus comes from Thomas (1979), extended in Gifford (1979) to quorum consensus. Stacey (1995) describes replication in popular database products. Other approaches are presented in El Abbadi, Skeen, and Cristian (1985), El Abbadi and Toueg (1989), and Gray et al. (1996).

CHAPTER 11 Conclusion

The discussion of commoditization was heavily influenced by SIGMOD keynote lectures by David Vaskevitch of Microsoft and by Vaskevitch (1995).

Many of the ideas relating object-oriented programming to transactions come from the Microsoft Transaction Server team at Microsoft, especially Gagan Chopra and Pat Helland.

The nested transaction model described here is from Moss (1985); see also Lynch et al. (1993) for a mathematical treatment and Liskov (1988) for a language that embodies the model. Other advanced models are summarized in Chapter 4 of Gray and Reuter (1992).

Bibliography

Andrade, J. M., M. T. Carges, T. J. Dwyer, and S. D. Felts. 1996. *The TUXEDO System, Software for Constructing and Managing Distributed Business Applications.* Reading, MA: Addison-Wesley.

Andrade, J. M., M. T. Carges, and M. R. MacBlane. 1994. "The TUXEDO™ System: An Open On-line Transaction Processing Environment." *Bulletin of the Technical Committee on Data Engineering, IEEE Computer Society* 17(1): 34–39.

AT&T/NCR Corporation. 1994a. *TOP END Application Programmer's Guide.*

———. 1994b. *TOP END Product Overview.*

———. 1994c. *TOP END Programmer's Reference Manual.*

———. 1994d. *TOP END System Administration Guide.*

Baafi, R. K., J. I. Carrie, W. B. Drury, and O. L. Wiesler. 1995. "ACMSxp Open Distributed Transaction Processing." *Digital Technical Journal* 7(1).

BEA Systems. 1996a. *TUXEDO ETP System, Application Programming.*

———. 1996b. *TUXEDO ETP System, Transaction Monitor Client/Server Extensions.*

Berenson, H., P. A. Bernstein, J. N. Gray, J. Melton, E. O'Neil, and P. O'Neil. 1995. "Levels of Isolation." *Proceedings of the 1995 ACM SIGMOD Conference on Management of Data.* New York: ACM.

Bernstein, P. A. 1990. "Transaction Processing Monitors." *Communications of the ACM* 33(11): 75–86.

Bernstein, P. A., W. Emberton, and V. Trehan. 1991. "DECdta: Digital's Distributed Transaction Processing Architecture." *Digital Technical Journal* 3(1): 10–17.

Bernstein, P. A., P. Gyllstrom, and T. Wimberg. 1993. "STDL—A Portable Transaction Definition Language." *1993 International Conference on Very Large Data Bases.* Dublin, 218–229.

Bernstein, P. A., V. Hadzilacos, and N. Goodman. 1987. *Concurrency Control and Recovery in Database Systems.* Reading, MA: Addison-Wesley.

Bernstein, P. A., M. Hsu, and B. Mann. 1990. "Implementing Recoverable Requests Using Queues." *ACM SIGMOD Conference on Management of Data*. San Jose, CA, May, 112–122.

Birrell, A. D., and B. J. Nelson. 1984. "Implementing Remote Procedure Calls." *ACM Transactions on Computer Systems* 2(1): 39–59.

Blakely, B., H. Harris, and R. Lewis. 1995. *Messaging and Queuing Using the MQI: Concepts and Analysis, Design and Development*. New York: McGraw-Hill.

Burgess, G. 1996. *The Legacy of TPC-A and TPC-B*. TPC Quarterly Report, TP Performance Council (http://www.tpc.org). San Jose, CA, January.

Carey, M., and M. Stonebraker. 1984. "The Performance of Concurrency Control Algorithms for DBMSs." *Proceedings of the 10th VLDB Conference*. Singapore, 107–118.

Conklin, P. F., and E. Newcomer. 1995. "The Keys to the Highway." In D. Leebaert (ed.), *Future of Software*. Boston: MIT Press.

Digital Equipment Corp. 1995a. *ACMS for OpenVMS: ADU Reference Manual*.

———. 1995b. *ACMS for OpenVMS: Getting Started*.

———. 1995c. *ACMS for OpenVMS: Introduction*.

———. 1995d. *ACMSxp: Getting Started*.

———. 1995e. *ACMSxp: STDL Encyclopedia*.

———. 1995f. *ACMSxp: System Overview*.

El Abbadi, A., D. Skeen, and F. Cristian. 1985. "An Efficient Fault-Tolerant Protocol for Replicated Data Management." *Proceedings 4th ACM SIGACT-SIGMOD Symposium on Principles of Database Systems*. Portland, OR, March, 215–228.

El Abbadi, A., and S. Toueg. 1989. "Maintaining Availability in Partitioned Replicated Databases." *ACM Transactions on Database Systems* 14(2): 264–290.

Eswaran, K. P., J. N. Gray, R. A. Lorie, and I. L. Traiger. 1976. "The Notions of Consistency and Predicate Locks in a Database System." *Communications of the ACM* 19(11): 624–633.

Gawlick, D., and D. Kinkade. 1985. "Varieties of Concurrency Control in IMS/VS Fast Path." *IEEE Database Engineering* 8(2): 3–10.

Gifford, D. K. 1979. "Weighted Voting for Replicated Data." *Seventh SIGOPS Symposium on Operating System Principles*. New York: ACM, 150–159.

Gray, J. N. 1978. "Notes on Database Operating Systems." In *Operating Systems: An Advanced Course, Springer-Verlag Lecture Notes in Computer Science,* Vol. 60. New York: Springer-Verlag.

Gray, J. N. 1986. "Why Do Computers Stop and What Can We Do About It." *Fifth Symposium on Reliability in Distributed Software and Database Systems*, Los Angeles, 3–12.

Gray, J. N. (editor). 1993. *The Benchmark Handbook for Database and Transaction Processing Systems*, 2nd edition. San Francisco: Morgan Kaufmann.

Gray, J. N., and J. Edwards. 1995. "Scale up with TP Monitors." *Byte Magazine* (April).

Gray, J. N., P. Helland, P. O'Neil, and D. Shasha. 1996. "The Dangers of Replication and a Solution." *Proceedings of the 1996 ACM SIGMOD Conference on Management of Data*. New York: ACM, 173–182.

Gray, J. N., P. Homan, R. Obermarck, and H. Korth. 1981. *A Strawman Analysis of the Probability of Waiting and Deadlock in a Database System.* IBM San Jose Research Laboratory, Technical Report RJ3066, February.

Gray, J. N., R. A. Lorie, G. R. Putzolu, and I. L. Traiger. 1976. "Granularity of Locks and Degrees of Consistency in a Shared Database." In *Modeling in Data Base Management Systems.* Amsterdam: Elsevier.

Gray, J. N., and A. Reuter. 1992. *Transaction Processing: Concepts and Techniques*. San Francisco: Morgan Kaufmann.

Haerder, T., and A. Reuter. 1983. "Principles of Transaction-Oriented Database Recovery." *ACM Computing Surveys* 15(4): 287–317.

IBM Corporation. 1991a. *Application Development, Writing Transaction Programs for APPC/MVS, GC28-1112.*

———. 1991b. *Formats and Protocol Reference Manual for LU6.2, SC30-3269.*

———. 1991c. *Transaction Programmer's Reference Manual for LU6.2, GC30-3084.*

———. 1995a. *CICS Family: Client/Server Programming.*

———. 1995b. *CICS for Open Systems: Intercommunication.*

———. 1995c. *IMS/ESA Application Programming/Design Guide, Version 5, SC26-8016-00.*

———. 1995d. *IMS/ESA General Information Manual, Version 5, GC26-3467-00.*

———. 1995e. *Message Queue Interface Tech Reference, SC33-0850-02.* Technical publication.

———. 1996a. *CICS General Information Manual.*

———. 1996b. *Into the Future with IMS (white paper).*

———. 1996c. MQSeries home page, http://www.hursley.ibm.com/mqseries.

Intergraph Computer Systems. 1996. *TPC Benchmark C™ Full Disclosure Report, Intergraph InterServer MP-610 Using Microsoft SQL Server v.6.5 and Microsoft Windows NTS v.4.0.* May.

ISO (International Standards Organization). 1992. *Open Systems Interconnection—Distributed Transaction Processing (OSI-TP) Model, ISO IS 10026-1. Service Definition, ISO IS 10026-2. Protocol Specification, ISO IS 10026-3.* New York: ISO.

Laing, W. A., J. E. Johnson, and R. V. Landau. 1991. "Transaction Management Support in the VMS Operating System Kernel." *Digital Technical Journal* 3(1): 33–44.

Lampson, B. W. 1981. "Atomic Transactions." In G. Goos and J. Hartmanis (eds.), *Distributed Systems—Architecture and Implementation: An Advanced Course*. Berlin: Springer-Verlag, 246–265.

Lampson, B. W., and H. Sturgis. 1976. *Crash Recovery in a Distributed Data Storage System.* Technical Report, Computer Science Laboratory. Palo Alto, CA: Xerox Palo Alto Research Center.

LeBert, J. J. 1989. *CICS for Microcomputers.* New York: McGraw-Hill.

Levine, C., J. N. Gray, S. Kiss, and W. Kohler. 1993. *The Evolution of TPC Benchmarks: Why TPC-A and TPC-B Are Obsolete.* Tandem Technical Report 93.1. Cupertino, CA: Tandem Computers.

Liskov, B. 1988. "Distributed Programming in Argus." *Communications of the ACM* 31(3): 300–312.

Lomet, D. 1992. "MLR: A Recovery Method for Multi-Level Systems." *Proceedings of the 1992 ACM SIGMOD International Conference on Management of Data*. New York: ACM, 185–194.

Lomet, D., and M. R. Tuttle. 1995. "Redo Recovery after System Crashes." *Proceedings of the 21st VLDB Conference*. San Francisco: Morgan Kaufmann, 457–468.

Lynch, N., M. Merritt, W. E. Weihl, and A. Fekete. 1993. *Atomic Transactions in Concurrent and Distributed Systems*. San Francisco: Morgan Kaufmann.

Malaika, S. 1994. "A Tale of a Transaction Monitor." *Bulletin of the Technical Committee on Data Engineering, IEEE Computer Society* 17(1): 3–9.

Microsoft. 1996. *Guide to Microsoft Distributed Transaction Coordinator*. In Microsoft SQL Server 6.5 documentation set. Redmond, WA: Microsoft Corp.

Mohan, C., and D. Dievendorff. 1994. "Recent Work on Distributed Commit Protocols, and Recoverable Messaging and Queuing." *Data Engineering* 17(1): 22–28.

Mohan, C., D. Haderle, B. Lindsay, H. Pirahesh, and P. Schwarz. 1992. "ARIES: A Transaction Recovery Method Supporting Fine-Granularity Locking and Partial Rollback Using Write-Ahead Logging." *ACM Transactions on Database Systems* 17(1): 94–162.

Mohan, C., B. Lindsay, and R. Obermarck. 1986. "Transaction Management in the R* Distributed Database Management System." *ACM Transactions on Database Systems* 11(4): 378–396.

Moss, E. 1985. *Nested Transactions: An Approach to Reliable Distributed Computing.* Boston: MIT Press.

Network Management Forum. 1995. *NMF SPIRIT Issue 3, SPIRIT Platform Blueprint.*

Newcomer, E. 1994. "Pioneering Distributed Transaction Management." *Bulletin of the Technical Committee on Data Engineering, IEEE Computer Society* 17(1): 10–15.

Nippon Telegraph and Telephone. 1991. *Technical Requirements, Multivendor Integration Architecture, Division 1: Overview.*

Object Management Group. 1995. CORBA IDL interface, 1995/95-12-15.

———. 1996a. CORBA services IDL interface, tc/96-02-01.

———. 1996b. CORBA 2.0 specification, ptc/96-03-04.

Orfali, R., and D. Harkey. 1995. "CORBA's Object Transaction Service." Special Report Client/Server Computing. *Byte Magazine* (April).

Patterson, D. A., G. Gibson, and R. H. Katz. 1988. "A Case for Redundant Arrays of Inexpensive Disks (RAID)." *Proceedings 1988 ACM SIGMOD Conference on Management of Data.* New York: ACM, 109–116.

Pausch, R. 1988. *Adding Input and Output to the Transaction Model.* Ph.D. Thesis, Computer Science Dept., Carnegie Mellon University, August (CMU-CS-88-171).

Raghavan, A., and T. K. Rengarajan. 1991. "Database Availability for Transaction Processing." *Digital Technical Journal* 3(1).

Rosenberry, W., and J. Teague. 1993. *Distributed Applications Across DCE and Windows NT.* Sebastopol, CA: O'Reilly & Associates.

Shasha, D. 1992. *Database Tuning—A Principled Approach.* Englewood Cliffs, NJ: Prentice-Hall.

Skeen, D. 1982. *Crash Recovery in a Distributed Database System.* Technical Report, Memorandum No. UCB/ERL M82/45, Electronics Research Laboratory, University of California at Berkeley.

Stacey, D. 1995. "Replication: DB2, Oracle, or Sybase." *Database Programming and Design* 7(2). Reprinted in *SIGMOD Record* 24(4): 95–101.

Stonebraker, M. 1979. "Concurrency Control and Consistency of Multiple Copies of Data in Distributed INGRES." *IEEE Transactions on Software Engineering* 3(3): 188–194.

Tandem Computers, Inc. 1994. *Introduction to NonStop Transaction Manager/MP (TM/MP).* December.

———. 1995. *Introduction to NonStop Transaction Processing.* December.

Tay, Y. C. 1987. *Locking Performance in Centralized Databases.* Orlando, FL: Academic Press.

Thomas, R. 1979. "A Majority Consensus Approach to Concurrency Control for Multiple Copy Databases." *ACM Transactions on Database Systems* 4(2): 180–209.

Thomasian, A. 1996. *Database Concurrency Control: Methods, Performance, and Analysis.* Boston: Kluwer Academic Publishers.

Transarc Corporation. 1996a. *Encina Monitor Programmer's Guide and Reference* [ENC-D5008-06].

———. 1996b. *Encina Toolkit Server Core Programmer's Reference* [ENC-D5002-07].

———. 1996c. *Encina Transactional-C Programmer's Guide and Reference* [ENC-D5003-07].

———. 1996d. *Writing Encina Applications* [ENC-D5012-00].

Ullman, J. 1982. *Principles of Database Systems.* Rockville, MD: Computer Science Press.

UNIX International. 1992. *Open Enterprise Transaction Processing: Integrating the TUXEDO System with Mainframe CICS.*

Vaskevitch, D. 1995. "Is Any of This Relevant?" In D. Leebaert (ed.), *Future of Software.* Boston: MIT Press.

Willis, J. M. 1994. *TP Software Development for OpenVMS.* Horsham, PA: CBM Books.

X/Open Ltd. 1996a. *X/Open CAE Specification Structured Transaction Definition Language (STDL).*

———. 1996b. *X/Open Guide Distributed Transaction Processing: Reference Model. Version 3.*

Yeager, N. J., and R. E. McGrath. 1996. *Web Server Technology: The Advanced Guide for World Wide Web Information Providers.* San Francisco: Morgan Kaufmann.

Index

D

E

F

N

O

P

Q

X,Y, Z

About the Authors

Philip Bernstein is lead architect for the repository group at Microsoft Corporation, which develops Microsoft repository products. He was previously the lead architect for Digital Equipment Corporation's transaction processing products group and wrote Digital's distributed transaction architecture. In addition, he has been technical director for Digital's systems integration tools support group and, before that, for the NAS group, a large engineering group responsible for Digital's middleware. Phil has published over 70 articles on implementation aspects of database and transaction processing systems. He is coauthor of *Concurrency Control and Recovery in Database Systems,* 1987 (Addison-Wesley) and was recipient of ACM's SIGMOD Innovations Award in 1994.

Eric Newcomer is a TP consultant and program manager in the systems engineering group at Digital Equipment Corporation. He is editor and coauthor of the X/Open Structured Transaction Definition Language (STDL) specification and manager of Digital's STDL licensing program. He represents Digital at the Service Providers' Integrated Requirements for Information Technology Consortium and previously represented Digital at the Multivendor Integration Architecture Consortium, where he has worked with large TP customers and other TP vendors on the practical application of TP standards. STDL and the X/Open TxRPC resulted from this work. Eric joined Digital in 1984 and prior to the consortium work held various positions within database and TP software engineering. Before joining Digital, Eric designed and developed TP applications in the public and private sectors.